DIRTY LITTLE SECRETS OF THE
VIETNAM WAR

Also by James F. Dunnigan and Albert A. Nofi

Dirty Little Secrets: Military Information You're Not Supposed to Know

Dirty Little Secrets of World War II: Military Information
No One Told You About the Greatest, Most Terrible War in History

Victory at Sea: World War II in the Pacific

The Pacific War Encyclopedia

DIRTY LITTLE SECRETS OF THE
VIETNAM WAR

James F. Dunnigan

AND

Albert A. Nofi

THOMAS DUNNE BOOKS
ST. MARTIN'S GRIFFIN
NEW YORK

THOMAS DUNNE BOOKS
An imprint of St. Martin's Press

Library of Congress Cataloging-in-Publication Data

Dunnigan, James F.
    Dirty little secrets of the Vietnam War / James F. Dunnigan
and Albert A. Nofi.
        p.   cm.
    Includes bibliographical references.
    ISBN 0-312-19857-4 (hc)
    ISBN 0-312-25282-X (pbk)
    1. Vietnamese Conflict, 1961–1975—Miscellanea.   I. Nofi, Albert A.
II. Title.
DS557.7.D85   1999
959.704'3—dc21   98-40892
                                                                  CIP

First St. Martin's Griffin Edition: April 2000

10 9 8 7 6 5 4 3 2

For John S. Mohr

RA 12-694-984

Wherever you are.

CONTENTS

ACKNOWLEDGMENTS

Thanks are in order for Bill Howell, Jr., Doug McCaskill, Richard Korn, Leonid Kondratiuck and the other fine people at Office of Historical Services of the National Guard Bureau, Kimball D. Parker, Scott Whitting, Donald Levesque, Richard M. Kirka, Vincent A. Katinas, and Mary S. Nofi, who has to put up with one of us.

The impact of the Vietnam War is incalculable. For the United States it shattered a sense of mission and invincibility that had endured for nearly two centuries and exacerbated domestic political, cultural, and social rifts, with effects that are not yet clear. Given that studies of the war, or aspects of it, are numerous, adding yet another requires some explanation.

A war is an extraordinarily complex phenomenon, and one as politically charged as that in Vietnam was even more so. Even in the most thoughtful and profound studies of the war much has to be omitted. And when one gets to some of the more politically motivated writings—whether from a "hawkish" or a "dovish" perspective—what gets included can often be false, one-sided, or misleading. *Dirty Little Secrets of the Vietnam War* tries to deal with things usually left out. Such as "deep" background items that influenced actions and developments many years later, things often falsified, such as the state of Vietnam veterans; the purely commonplace, which it is presumed "everyone knows," such as what the troops were actually doing; and a lot of other things besides. Of course, we can't include everything either. Our focus is on the American war, and even then we cannot tell the whole story, as it is a tale that can never be told in the compass of a single work. So veterans of the war must forgive us for omitting things like how they went about forming little spontaneous enlisted men's clubs on isolated outposts, or the dangers of taking a pedicab ride in Saigon, and 33 beer. While those more interested in the political side must forgive us our failure to attempt to delve into the minds of the respective leaders, LBJ, Ho, and the rest.

This book also takes into account that for a great many Americans the Vietnam War is ancient history. So we included a lot of basic stuff so those who were not yet born in 1975 can make sense out of it all. At times this may seem a bit elementary, and occasionally there will be some repetition, but it seemed necessary. The veterans will know what's there for them.

This is the third of our *Dirty Little Secrets* books to be published since 1990. All have used the same format and approach. All have been quite successful. So if you've read the other two, you'll know what to expect here. For those who haven't seen the earlier two books, just enjoy and illuminate yourself. These books stress an easy-to-read format (each item is self-contained and rarely over a page in length) and easy access (all the items are grouped in chapters and indexed).

The authors have tried hard to make an accurate, evenhanded presentation. We welcome legitimate comments, corrections, suggestions, and the like, which may be sent to us via the publisher or directly, via E mail, to:

jfdunugan@aol.com
anofi@aol.com

There are a number of ways of rendering the names of various places and peoples in Southeast Asia. For example, the capital of the Democratic Republic of Vietnam is variously "Hanoi" and "Ha Noi," while the tough upland people of Laos are the "Hmong" or the "H'mong." There are various "officially approved" ways of spelling many of these names, but the authors have not always adhered to these guidelines, particularly if they are at variance with the spelling in common use during the war, which is likely to be more familiar.

Military units of the United States, the Republic of Vietnam, and their Allies have been rendered in normal type, while those of the People's Army of Vietnam (the North Vietnamese Army) and the People's Liberation Armed Forces (the Viet Cong) are in *italics*. Thus, the *304th Division* is a PAVN unit, while the 18th Division is an ARVN formation.

The notation "3/503rd Parachute" indicates the 3rd Battalion of the 503rd Parachute Infantry Regiment. In fact, with the exception of a handful of armored cavalry regiments, the army had no regiments except on paper, as a means of preserving the historic lineage of units that in some cases stretch back into the seventeenth and eighteenth centuries.

In some instances the statistics we use may not tally with those we have used in another place. This is due to the varying nature of statistics. In fact, there are often differences in official figures for the same thing, such as the number of American dead in Vietnam. This is due not to a "cover up" or similar criminal conspiracy (indeed, the differences are usually too small to warrant tampering), but rather to figures that have been issued at different times, which are often done on differing bases of calculation. For example, the number of persons officially listed as having been killed in action or died of wounds has been slowly rising by small increments since the end of the war, as veterans occasionally succumb to the lingering effects of wartime injuries.

The form "Xuan Loc (Long Khanh)" indicates a location in Long Khanh Province.

ABBREVIATIONS

ARVN. Army of the Republic of Vietnam

BG. Brigadier general (one star)

CDR. Commander, in the navy

COL. Colonel

CPT. Captain (army or air force only; navy captains are written out)

GEN. General (four stars)

LG. Lieutenant general (three stars)

LT. Lieutenant in the navy; 1LT first lieutenant, 2LT second lieutenant, in the other services

LTC. Lieutenant colonel

MAAG. Military Assistance Advisory Group

MAJ. Major

MG. Major general (two stars)

NVA. North Vietnamese Army, properly, the People's Army of Vietnam

PAVN. The NVA

ROK. Republic of Korea

SSG. Staff sergeant

VC. Viet Cong, the South Vietnamese Communists

DIRTY LITTLE SECRETS OF THE
VIETNAM WAR

CHAPTER 1

The Enduring Myths
of the Vietnam War

All wars attain a certain mythic character as time passes, but the myth rarely invades historical treatments. Not in the case of Vietnam. Much of the writing on the war has been tainted by the political outlook of the authors, and so much "common knowledge" about it is so flatly wrong that we decided to group the myths together.

AMERICA SUFFERED A MILITARY DEFEAT

American troops were not defeated in combat, but the American people refused to pay the price of victory. That's an important distinction. Several presidents got sucked into Vietnam because, first, they didn't want to offend France, and, later, no one wanted to risk appearing reluctant to confront Communist aggression. Once President Johnson realized he could not generate enough popular opinion to get the forces he knew he needed to win the war, he simply quit politics and retired. The next president, Nixon, got elected on the promise to "get America out of Vietnam," and he did just that, though it took a long time. This was not without precedent. As early as the War of 1812, the American people showed a marked reluctance to support what it would take to win the war. In 1812, it was the conquest of Canada (or at least some parts of it). In 1952, Eisenhower got elected on the promise of "getting America out of Korea." It takes a lot to get Americans into a war big time, always has, and probably always will. As the casualties build up, and especially if there is no dramatic progress, public support quickly wanes. In our long wars, such as the Revolutionary War, the Civil War, and World War II, it became very difficult to keep things going on the home front toward the end. We still commemorate the harsh Winter of 1777–78, when General Washington pulled off a seeming miracle by keeping his army together during that season of discontent. Had Washington not been able to hold things together that winter, the British would have likely won the war the following spring and summer. During the American Civil War, the number of Union voters eager for a negotiated settlement grew as the 1864 elections approached. President Lincoln had to jump through a lot of political hoops to head off the peace movement. Even World War II, seen as the "good war," found the American people quite war weary by 1945. Despite what many feel we should have thought then, the use of two atomic bombs was enthusiastically received by Americans quite tired of war and its sacrifices. There's little doubt we could have defeated the Vietnam Communists, but it would have meant risking war with China and/or the Soviet Union and the application of a lot more airpower and infantry. There might have been twice as many Americans dead, and a lot more Vietnamese dead. Still, it was certainly possible. But too many of the people were not behind it. That's how a democracy works. Sometimes you can't win. Or don't want to win. That doesn't mean you were defeated, but simply that you changed your goals. In 1964, America wanted to keep the Communists out of South Vietnam. By 1968, we were well on the road to accomplishing this, but by then most Americans just wanted to keep *Americans* out of South Vietnam. The American people got what they wanted.

THE AMERICAN SOLDIER WAS "DIFFERENT" IN VIETNAM

An oft-repeated myth of the Vietnam War is that the American soldier was somehow "different" in that conflict than in previous ones. Some of the biggest myths about the American soldier in Vietnam are that in contrast to his predecessors in previous wars, and most notably World War II, he was:

- Young. The commonly cited figure is that the average soldier in Vietnam was only nineteen, in contrast to twenty-six during World War II.
- Poorly Educated. The conventional wisdom is that the war was fought by "high school dropouts."
- Drafted. After all, who would join the army during a war?
- Black. Some commentators have placed the proportion of black troops "in the front lines" as high as 80 percent, "most of whom didn't come back."

In fact, although frequently encountered, and indeed a part of the popular culture of the war, none of these assertions are correct, as can be seen in the opposite table.

It's worth looking at these myths in some depth.

1. **The "Young Soldier" Myth.** The origins of the notion that the average age of the troops in Vietnam was nineteen are difficult to determine. It may derive from the fact that the average age of *recruits* during the war was slightly less than twenty. The draft normally took twenty-year-olds, so those younger than that were volunteers. In any case, most recruits had several months of training before shipping out. As a result, although there were some soldiers in combat as young as seventeen (indeed, a handful were even younger), men

America's "Average Soldier" in Three Wars

	Civil War	WWII	Vietnam
Age	26	26	22
Induction			
Drafted	c. 0.4%	c. 65%	c. 35%
Volunteered	c. 99.6%	c. 35%	c. 65%
Race			
Black	c. 8%	c. 8%	12.5%
White	c. 92%	c. 91%	86.3%
Other	> 0.5%	c. 1%	1.2%

Key: All figures are for infantrymen, who do most of the fighting. For the Civil War, figures are for the U.S. Army only, Confederate statistics differing markedly (e.g., virtually all Confederate manpower was conscripted). *Race* omits "Hispanic" as the term is a cultural designation, and persons of Hispanic heritage can be white, black, Native American, or East Asian.

under twenty never constituted a majority of the troops in a particular unit. Looking at the average age of American military personnel who died in the war (see page 4) gives a pretty good picture of the age of the average soldier.

Even excluding warrant officers and officers, who were on average older than enlisted personnel, the average soldier in Vietnam was rather more than twenty-two years old. If that isn't enough evidence, consider the figures for men with the Military Occupational Specialty (MOS) 11B. "Eleven Bravo" is the MOS for infantry rifleman (there are also MOSs for other infantry specialties, such as mortarman or machine gunner). The ultimate "grunt," 18,465 "Eleven Bravos" died in Vietnam, accounting for 31.76 percent of American deaths in the war. Their average age at death was 22.55, actually slightly higher than the average for all enlisted personnel.

It is true, of course, that the average member of the armed forces during the Vietnam War was younger than the average in the Civil War or World War II. But those were total wars, and enormous efforts were made to mobilize the maximum manpower. In World War II this was done by conscription, while during the Civil War it was accomplished by offering generous cash bonuses to those who enlisted, up to $1,100 in some jurisdictions, more than three years' pay for the common workingman.

Footnote: Underage Soldiers in Vietnam. One of the true secrets of the Vietnam War—indeed of most wars—is the number of underage boys who enlisted using false identification, sometimes with the knowing consent of their parents. The number of underage soldiers who died in Vietnam is also unknown. At least five of the men killed in Vietnam are known to have been under seventeen years of age. One, a Marine, seems to have been only thirteen.

Average Age of American Military Personnel Who Died in Vietnam

Grades	Deaths	Percent	Age
E-1 to E-9	50,274	86.46%	22.37
W-1 to W-4	1,276	2.19%	24.73
O-1 to O-8	6,598	11.35%	28.43
Total	58,148	100.00%	23.11

Key: Grades are standard military pay grades for enlisted personnel (E-1 through E-9), warrant officers, and officers up to major general (no higher-ranking officers died in the war). *Deaths* include all those from combat, accidents, disease, and other causes (e.g., murders, suicides, and so forth), occurring in the "war zone." The figures omit some twenty personnel for whom both a birth date and death date—or presumed death date—cannot be determined. *Age* is at time of death, rendered decimally.

2. The "Poorly Educated Soldier" Myth. The origins of this myth are rather mystifying. The troops during the Vietnam era were, on average, the best educated in American history to that time. Fully 79 percent of them had completed high school. This was a proportion that actually declined for a while after the war, with the introduction of the "All Volunteer Army" in the early 1970s, before rising to the point where today you must have a high school diploma to enlist (no GEDs need apply). In all earlier wars the educational standards had been lower. Only 24 percent of the enlisted personnel in World War II were high school graduates, a figure almost matched by the 20 percent of Vietnam-era enlisted personnel who had some college. In fact, the academic preparation of the average recruit in World War II was so bad the army found itself having to institute special literacy programs for draftees, about 20 percent of whom were more or less functionally illiterate. One probable source for the notion that the average Vietnam-era soldier was poorly educated may have been the approximately 354,000 men who entered the service through Project 100,000. Instituted in 1966, partially in response to criticism that the armed forces "weren't doing enough" to promote social change in America, this program involved the recruiting of up to 100,000 men a year who fell into Mental Category IV. This was the second lowest of five groupings based on test scores, personnel whom the armed forces had been reluctant to accept in the past. In essence, Project 100,000 was a large-scale remedial education program. Over the life of the project, about 157,000 "New Standards" men were drafted and nearly 200,000 more voluntarily enlisted, the total comprising about 10 percent of all recruits in the period from October of 1966 to December of 1971. About 37 percent of the "New Standards" men were members of various racial and ethnic minority groups. Like nearly everything about the Vietnam War, Project 100,000 is controversial. Left-wingers (who originally supported the program) tend to argue that it was merely a way for the Pentagon to lay its hands on more cannon fodder. Right-wingers (who opposed it) argued that it was a fuzzy-minded "do-gooder" program that ruined the armed forces by bringing in all sorts of mentally deficient men. Claims have simultaneously been made that these men suffered disproportionately from their experience, to the assertion that most of them benefited greatly from it. In fact, the actual effects of the program cannot be determined, as the army was never able to establish a reliable system for monitoring the success of "New Standards" men. It is known that about 2,100 "New Standards" men were killed in action, a proportion *lower* than their percentage of those in the service.

3. The "Reluctant Draftee" Myth. This one is easy to nail down. It is based on the fact that during the Vietnam era a lot of recruits entered the army through the Selective Service System (SSS). Seeing this, a good many people have assumed that all of those who served were drafted. To some extent this was correct, at least for the army, but in fact this conclusion ignores the common practice of "volunteering for the draft." During the fifties and sixties it was by no means unusual for a young man fresh out of high school, with no immediate plans, to request to be drafted. It may sound a bit crazy, volunteering to be drafted in the middle of a war, an increasingly unpopular war at that, but as the proverb has it, these men were being "crazy like a fox." There were a lot of benefits to volunteering to be drafted. For one thing, it got your service out of the way with only a two-year liability rather than the three (for the army) or four (for the other services) you would incur if you enlisted. Local draft boards liked the practice because it was a relatively painless way of filling their manpower quotas. The army— and the Marines, when they began taking draftees—liked it because they were getting men who were better motivated than those who waited around for their numbers to come up. As a result, a lot of guys who "pushed up their number" ended up in special training programs to emerge as "Shake 'n Bake" NCOs, helicopter crew chiefs, and the like, a fact not lost on those waiting around to get the famous letter that began "Greetings . . ."

A lot of men also genuinely volunteered to enlist, signing up for three years in the army or four in the Marines, navy, Coast Guard, or air force. The navy and air force never accepted draftees during the war, and the Marines only took about 20,000 a year, combing through each batch for men who were willing to opt for the corps. If you volunteered for the army, your chances of being sent to Vietnam were actually rather lower than if you waited to be drafted. While the war was going on in Vietnam, the armed forces still had to maintain troops in Germany and Korea, and a strategic reserve at home as well. A tour of duty in Germany was eighteen to twenty-four months, one in Korea was twelve or thirteen, depending on the service, just as for Vietnam. A draftee was only in the service for twenty-four months, which meant he had just enough time in uniform to complete basic training and some advanced training in order to be sent to Vietnam for a thirteen-month tour of duty. As a result, it was not unusual for draftees to be discharged some weeks before their enlistments expired. After several months in training, a few more with a unit stateside, and then twelve or thirteen in Vietnam, the armed forces didn't have much they could do with these troops for the last few weeks. So volunteering was a good way to "beat the draft."

Incidentally, during the Vietnam era (1960 through 1975, which was two years after draft calls ended) some 26.8 million men were legally liable for compulsory military service. About 8.7 million voluntarily entered the service and 2.2 million were drafted, some of whom later volunteered for additional hitches (and thus may have been double counted). Of the balance, 15.4 million were either disqualified or deferred. So approximately 500,000 men were technically draft dodgers, but of these only about 210,000 were charged and only 8,700 actually convicted.

4. The "Black Army" Myth. This is strongly felt among African Americans and generally believed by most liberals and leftists. In fact, there is some substance to the idea that the armed forces were "blacker" during the Vietnam War than in earlier wars, but not in the sense that is usually assumed. In fact, the notion that the war was fought by a "Black Army" is a myth created out of whole cloth for political purposes. Since the outbreak of the Revolutionary War, African Americans have numbered between 10 percent and 12 percent of the population. There were times when no black men were permitted to serve. And even when blacks were recruited for military service, their numbers were kept small, never more than about 8 percent of the total force, figures attained during the Civil War and the World Wars. In these three wars few African-American troops were permitted to enter combat, so that black combatants usually numbered no more than about 3 percent of total manpower committed to action. This began to change in 1947, when Pres. Harry S. Truman issued his famous order ending segregation in the armed forces. The full effects of this measure were not felt until the late 1950s, by which time the armed forces, and particularly the army, had become relatively the most integrated institution in America. With opportunities far more equal in the service than in society as a whole, a military career held distinct advantages for black Americans. As a result, by the early 1960s the percentage of career military personnel who were black had risen to more than the proportion of African Americans in the overall population. This was particularly the case among career enlisted personnel in the army, and notably so in volunteer specialties such as the airborne, which received higher pay for "hazardous duty," which resulted in reports of airborne platoons composed "mostly of blacks." Perhaps a fifth of the NCOs in the army

Black Personnel in Service, 1972

Branch	Percent
Air Force	4.4
Army	17.0
Marines	8.2
Navy	6.0
Overall	11.1

were of African descent, though the number of black officers lagged in all services. This had serious consequences when American troops became engaged in the war on a large scale. During the first two years of serious American involvement (1964–66), black Americans do seem to have comprised about a fifth or a quarter of those killed in action. Casualties were particularly heavy among career NCOs, the guys leading the troops. Thereafter, as the armed forces expanded, the percentage of troops who were black fell markedly, as the draft brought in proportionately *more* whites.

As a result, the percentage of black casualties fell, so that overall about 12.5 percent of those killed in action were black (see table on page 8). This was still somewhat higher than the proportion of blacks in society, but was about the average percentage of blacks in the army over the course of the war, and did reflect the proportion of blacks among men of military age in the population as a whole. Of course the notion that the frontline troops were mostly black had by then become pervasive, spread for political reasons by pacifists, black radicals, and the merely misinformed.

So black Americans were not disproportionately represented in the ranks in Vietnam.

There was, however, one group that was very overrepresented in Vietnam, though this is often overlooked. About 30 percent of the Americans who died in Vietnam were Roman Catholics, who constituted only about 24 percent of the population, most of whom were of Irish, Mexican, Puerto Rican, Italian, or Polish background. Like African Americans, these groups were more likely to come from lower socioeconomic levels. A young man from the lower half of the American economic spectrum seems to have been about 300 percent more likely to die in Vietnam than one from the upper half.

After Vietnam, the pattern of ethnic participation in the armed forces slowly changed. By the Gulf War, whites were a substantial majority in combat units, while nonwhite troops tended to be in jobs requiring more technical training. This switch was caused by the increasing tendency of white soldiers to stay for only one enlistment and to choose combat arms jobs for the greater, well, "adventure and excitement" would be the best way to explain it. Black and Hispanic troops wanted professional and technical training, either because they wanted to make a career of the military or wanted

Racial Distribution of Combat Dead in Three Major Wars

Percentage of Battle Deaths by Race

Conflict	Whites	Blacks	Others
Civil War	c. 97.0%	c. 2.7%	c. 0.3%
World War II	c. 96.0%	c. 3.0%	c. 1.0%
Vietnam	c. 86.0%	c. 12.5%	c. 1.2%

a leg up in the civilian job market when they got out. In the 1980s, the military raised the educational qualifications for enlistment. There were not a lot of poorly educated recruits of any ethnic persuasion, thus making just about everyone eligible for some kind of technical training and an interesting career. Many recruits who would have never gotten beyond high school took the opportunities, thus making a repeat of the Vietnam "dying for the white man" controversy remote. Or so it seemed until the Gulf War. As American troops poured into Saudi Arabia, the media picked up on the (woefully ill-informed) laments of some prominent African Americans that "black soldiers would suffer disproportionate losses." The Pentagon was quick to point out that the situation had changed, but the damage was done. Bad news travels farther and faster than good news, and for over a year it became much more difficult to recruit African Americans. Some recruiters saw drops of over 50 percent.

Old myths die hard.

VIETNAM WAS A WAR OF COMMUNIST AGGRESSION

Well, partially, but mainly it was a civil war, the latest such conflict in the area that had seen such wars for many centuries. The peoples of North and South Vietnam are different in many ways, always have been, and still are. Although many of the language and cultural differences have been eroding over the centuries, there is still a strong feeling of "us" and "them" between the northerners and southerners. This was exacerbated after 1945 by religious and political differences. The unification of Vietnam was much like that of Italy in the mid-nineteenth century. The North thought it was a swell idea and imposed it on the South, which wasn't so sure. Note that in the last ten years there has been a growing movement in the north of Italy to cut the southern part loose again. Similar North-South tensions are manifest in Vietnam, even among dedicated Communists.

Among the many French imports to Vietnam over the previous century were a number of new political philosophies to compete with the ancient royalist and Buddhist ones. Communism and socialism were the most popular among the young, educated Vietnamese. But the main motivation of politically active Vietnamese was self-rule. While the various parts of Vietnam were often at odds with each other over who would rule the entire country, there was little disagreement that a unified Vietnam, ruled by Vietnamese, was a fine idea. For some sixty years up to the start of World War II, the French had been running Vietnam as a colony. There were still old-timers who remembered what it was like "before the French." And many younger Vietnamese were eager to experience life "after the French." The French had managed, often with considerable brutality, to prevent a unified opposition to their rule and had created a local bureaucracy to help them control the country. But in 1940 and 1941, the Japanese took over first North Vietnam, then the South. The French administrators were left in place until just before the end of the war. In early 1945, the Japanese established a Vietnamese government. It was a political ploy, but it didn't fool the Vietnamese rebels. Japanese rule had not been gentle. So much rice was exported that some two million Vietnamese died of starvation.

The French returned in late 1945 with reinforcements, but they now had a full-scale uprising on their hands. By 1953, the French had lost. All they could salvage was a division of Vietnam so that the groups (religious, political, and ethnic) that did not get along with the Communist-led rebels could set up shop in South Vietnam. The Communist North Vietnamese went along with this because they had also taken a beating in the war and, more important, felt they could easily subvert and take over the "puppet [of the French and various special interests] government" in the south and unite the country. This led to the American stage of the war. Vietnam was a "war of Communist aggression" in the same way that the American Civil War is described by some southerners as "the War of Northern Aggression."

But did this make the 1960–75 phase of the fighting a true civil war? Well, yes, sort of. It's rather more complicated than that. North and South Vietnam have, over the centuries, been separate countries more often than not. The two Vietnams were one country because the French came in during the previous century and put an end to yet another period of violent disunity. Had Vietnam been united then, the French would not have been able to take over. The 1954 treaty creating two Vietnams did so for plenty of reasons beyond the long-standing differences between North and South Vietnam. Many Vietnamese wanted nothing to do with communism. Either for political or religious reasons, about 5 percent of North Vietnam's population fled south in 1954 to escape the Communist government. The North Vietnamese kept escalating their effort in the South, even before American combat units entered, because they found the anti-Communist attitudes in South Vietnam were quite strong. Many South Vietnamese were willing to resist communism, both at the local level and by joining the South Vietnamese armed forces. Although the southern armed forces had a 20-percent-a-year desertion rate, this wasn't a lot different from the rate the Viet Cong and North Vietnamese troops suffered from. No one really wanted to get involved in an all-out war. But, alas, this was yet another ancient Vietnamese tradition. Many times in past centuries, one faction or another had called in foreign assistance to help win a civil war. Chinese, Cambodian, Thai, French, and now American and Russian outsiders were being called in. What made this particular Vietnamese civil war so extraordinary was that both major factions were able to call in heavy hitters. The Chinese and Russians not only supplied most of the weapons, supplies, and technical assistance, but they used the fear of their nuclear weapons to keep the United States from invading North Vietnam. Lacking the option of invading North Vietnam, the United States tried to kill so many North Vietnamese troops in the South that the Communists would give up. It didn't work, and the North Vietnamese publicly said it wouldn't. All that firepower just got a lot of South Vietnamese killed, along with those North Vietnamese soldiers.

If the United States had backed out of Vietnam in the early 1960s, there might have been problems with Communist insurgents in Thailand. This was the Thai's big fear. There were also ancient hostilities between the Vietnamese and China, which briefly flared into a war in 1979. Had the North Vietnamese Communists taken over South Vietnam earlier, and the Russians had more time to establish military and economic ties to Vietnam, the Chinese might have gotten even more agitated. We'll never know. One thing that is certain, within twenty years the Communist government in Vietnam would be an economic basket case. Unless, of course, the United States treated Vietnam like an Asian Yugoslavia. This could have happened, and there was much less chance you'd have the kind of mess Yugoslavia produced after the Communist government collapsed.

We'll never know. . . .

IT WAS JUST ANOTHER WAR

Vietnam was a very different war from America's previous ones. Consider some of the specific differences from most of our other wars.

• America lacked the will to win, to see it out to the end. This had never happened before and there was a reluctance on the part of the government to admit this was where it was all going. American politicians allowed more and more U.S. troops into Vietnam because it was easier to do that than to draw the line and demand that prowar partisans consider the implications of increased involvement. No one wanted to risk a small failure in the short term because, as politicians see it, long-term problems will be someone else's responsibility. The troops and the voters slowly came to realize the mess they had gotten into and there were bad feelings all around as a result.

• Angry and frustrated troops attacked their leaders on a large scale. This was commonly called "fragging." That term came from "fragmentation grenade," the weapon often used for such attacks, as it could be rolled into a tent or bunker silently. All wars have had some "fragging" against particularly unpopular officers or NCOs. But by 1969, the morale in American units was so low that fragging became relatively common. And was noticed by the media. Over the next three years, a number of officers and NCOs were killed in these attacks. Almost all of these incidents were in the army, which was the only branch (except the marines) where a large number of troops had easy access to weapons, especially hand grenades. The fraggings were a direct result of the breakdown in leadership and discipline. This, coupled with the rising antiwar sentiment back home, left the ground troops in a very foul mood. The officers often could not control their troops, and the threat of fragging was an attempt by the troops to control their officers. It often worked. Indeed, all the soldiers had to do was leave a safety pin for a hand grenade in an officer's quarters, or anyplace he was sure to see it, and the officer usually got the message.

• Drugs became widely used by the troops, leading to discipline problems unique in American military history. The drug dealing became a big business and brought with it the usual corruption, murder, and criminal activity not normally seen in a military organization.

• For many, it was considered more honorable not to serve. This had been unheard of before, and was a major indicator of the degree to which the war was unwanted and unsupported among the American people.

• For the first time in American history, the sons of the well off had a way to legally avoid military service, and they took it. While the American Civil War saw the use of "buying substitutes for the draft," this was so discredited that it was never used again. And even with this way out, most eligible men who could afford it refused to take it. Not so in the Vietnam War, where millions sought college (and other deferments) to avoid military service. This had a divisive effect on the nation and was a major reason for the elimination of the draft in 1975.

• Media reporting of the war was faster than in any other war, and it was the first war where the folks back home saw TV images of what was going on, often only a day or two later. Vietnam has been called the first television war. This turned out to be a major advantage for the North Vietnamese. The Communist leadership knew from the beginning that when dealing with Western democracies, whether it be France or the United States, images in the media (words or pictures) could be more useful than more troops and weapons. Although the Communists were more ruthless and murderous in their use of terror, they also controlled media access to their operations. Moreover, the Communists knew that the vast firepower used by their opponents would hit a lot of innocent civilians, and that the numerous journalists wandering around (except in Communist-controlled areas) would have splendid opportunities to get pictures, images that would turn the American voter against the American war effort. Since there was no voting, and no independent media, in Communist-controlled areas, this media advantage was pretty much one-sided. The North Vietnamese did use videos, mainly in newsreels shown throughout the country, depicting the war as one of virtuous Davids battling evil, foreign, high-tech Goliaths. It worked. Playing on nationalism usually does.

• Race became a major issue. U.S. ground forces had largely used segregated units up until the Korean War (1950–53.) The armed forces were in the midst of integrating when that war broke out, a time when civilian life was still very segregated in many parts of the country. Racial problems were minor during Korea, and this pattern continued into the first few years of the Vietnam War. But then the racial reforms back home caught up with the troops. The Vietnam War was unpopular and many racial reformers took the generals to task for real or imagined indignities suffered by black soldiers. The troops, especially the younger ones, took these accusations to heart, and race relations in the ranks took a nose dive. It got pretty ugly, right into the early 1980s.

• Territory was commonly taken, lost, and retaken repeatedly, a particularly disheartening experience for the troops who got shot up doing it. This was not unknown in any war, but became particularly common in Vietnam where U.S. units went out on "search and destroy" missions. Often, much blood was shed to take a hill or valley, only to abandon it so the troops could move off to pacify another area. While this practice made sense given the large area being contested and the lack of enemy bases to go after, it was bad for morale and hard to explain to the folks back home.

• The American Civil War caused a division in public opinion over the wisdom of the war, as did several other wars (Mexican, Civil, Spanish, the Philippine Insurrection, and Korea), leading to social unrest and violence. But nothing like what was seen during the Vietnam years. The nation was truly divided, and when it was clear that unified support of the war would never be achieved, the practical result was no support at all. One president refused to run for reelection because of the lack of popular support for the war, and another was elected on the promise of getting the United States out of Vietnam.

• The average age of a combat soldier in Vietnam was twenty-two, while during World War II the average age was twenty-six. In all of America's earlier wars, the troops had been older. But in the Vietnam era, you were eligible for the draft at eighteen, and the potential older troops avoided service. Many potential draftees avoided service by staying in college or finding other deferments (parenthood, certain occupations, joining another military service like the navy or air force, or leaving the country).

• The system for giving out decorations, in recognition of battlefield performance, was corrupted. From Purple Hearts and Combat Infantry Badges, up to the highest awards, the standards fell as increased use of decorations was used to prop up falling morale and to enhance the careers of ambitious officers. This was another aspect of the breakdown in military leadership during the war.

• There was no front line. Since many of the Communist troops were guerrillas, attacks were made on American troops wherever they were. Allied combat units did tend to duke it out with Communist regular units and take most of the casualties. But all the other units that would normally be relatively safe "in the rear" got shot at too. While the rear-area troops did not take a lot of casualties, they were certainly uneasy about this war without a front line.

• There was no hero's welcome for the returning soldiers. Many people did not realize how important it was to the troops to get a little respect and appreciation for their overseas service. Many people went out of their way to castigate the returning soldiers. Such was the mood of the nation that there was no public outcry over this shabby treatment, and the faithful servicemen (and women) carried the physic wounds for the rest of their lives.

• Ticket punching. This was a form of careerism unheard of in wartime. What it meant was that officers sought to get the minimum amount of time with the troops so that it would look good on their résumés. The more different positions an officer could spend a few months in, the more promotable he was. The U.S. military encouraged this sort of thing, especially the army. This was made possible by the Korean War practice of keeping soldiers overseas in the war zone for only thirteen months. This was called a "tour of duty," and it was originally implemented because many World War II reservists had been mobilized for Korean War service. These troops, their families and neighbors, voters all, did not consider it fair that they should be stuck in Korea "for the duration" (the "normal" tour of duty) in a limited war that was not mobilizing America's full strength. So the more politically acceptable thirteen-month tour was introduced. That spread the pain a bit, as more people had to go, and the combat troops knew they had a much better chance of surviving thirteen months, rather than several years, at the front. Initially, the Vietnam War was about as unpopular as the Korean one ("What, more Communist aggression?"). So the thirteen-month tour of duty was immediately used in Vietnam. Big mistake, for the U.S. armed forces had changed a lot in the previous ten years. There were a lot more careerists among the officers. The custom had developed of rating an officer's suitability for promotion on the basis of how many different jobs he had held. It was particularly important to command troops at several levels, and especially useful if you commanded them in a combat zone. The armed forces had also grown top-heavy with officers. There were far more potential commanders than there were units for them to command. So the custom arose of letting a combat unit commander spend only a few months leading his unit, then moving on to give another officer an opportunity to "get his ticket punched." This rapid turnover in leadership had a negative effect on unit performance and got a lot more of the troops killed and injured.

• Troop leadership got worse as the war went on. This was unheard of, for in past wars everyone was in until the war was over or they were killed or mutilated. Thus the officers who survived got more experienced and effective. But because of the thirteen-month tour of duty, and the practice of putting an officer through several different jobs while he was in the war zone, you didn't have any officers with several years of combat experience. Rather, you had a much larger number of officers with a few months' experience. Increasing morale problems and casualties caused many of the World War II and Korea-era officers and NCOs to retire (which they could do after twenty years). Some just quit, lacking twenty years' service but not willing to risk getting killed in another tour of duty with amateurs. Thus the combat-experienced NCOs and officers available early in the Vietnam conflict became increasingly scarce as time went on, and they were not replaced. Hence the amazing decline in leadership quality.

• Vietnam was the first war the United States lost. Well, that was not exactly the case. U.S. forces had never been beaten on the battlefield; they were withdrawn. It was actually the first war the United States refused to win. The price of victory was considered higher than it was worth. Nevertheless, it was a first, and a dubious one at that.

• We didn't keep sending more and more troops to the front until victory was won, and then send everyone home to victory parades and civilian life. In Vietnam troops were constantly being transferred in and out of Vietnam just like it was another peacetime assignment. Even when we decided to end our participation in the war, the troops came home gradually. And there weren't many parades.

THE VIETNAM WAR WAS NOT AS INTENSE AS WORLD WAR II

This myth seems to have developed because Americans had been fed a steady diet of World War II films, documentaries, histories, and memoirs. These depicted epic events, great clashes of arms that had clear, readily understandable results. In contrast, what we got from Vietnam was endless accounts of little actions, most hardly more than skirmishes by the standards of World War II. World War II was certainly one of the most intense wars in history. But Vietnam could get pretty intense too, in different ways, and for longer periods. In Vietnam the American frontline soldier saw much more combat than the troops had in "the Big One" or, indeed, in any previous war. This despite the fact that troops in the rear were more exposed to hostile action than in earlier wars. And yes, there most certainly was a "frontline soldier" in Vietnam.

During the Civil War (1861–65), most troops were infantrymen, and most of them saw combat. A soldier in the Army of the Potomac may have seen

Average Daily Combat Deaths in the Nation's Major Wars

Conflict	Daily Losses
Revolutionary War (1775–83)	1.8
War of 1812 (1812–15)	2.5
Mexican War (1846–48)	2.9
Civil War (1861–65)	
Union	76.4
Confederate	51.1
Combined	128.2
Spanish-American War (1898)	6.4
World War I (1917–18)	198.2
World War II (1941–45)	221.3
Korean War (1950–53)	30.3
Vietnam War (1959–75)	17.5
Gulf War (1991)	4.9

Key: In several instances the daily combat death rate has been calculated, not on the overall duration of the war, but on the actual period of combat. The Spanish-American War, for example, lasted about four months, but there were virtually no combat deaths until the final seven weeks. Likewise, for the United States World War I lasted eighteen months, but virtually all U.S. casualties occurred in the final eight months. For Vietnam, the daily loss rate has been calculated on the period from the introduction of major U.S. forces in mid-1965 to the withdrawal of U.S. forces in early 1973, though there were some American combat deaths before and after those dates. Note that in most pre-twentieth-century wars there were few combat deaths during the winter months, when armies found it very difficult to sustain themselves, to maneuver, and to fight. So figures for those wars could easily be recalculated to reflect this.

100 to 150 days of combat over the four years of the war. By World War II (1939–45), infantrymen were less than 25 percent of the army, and a lot of tankers, artillerymen, and other troops got into action too. During that war the average number of days in combat for an infantryman in the Pacific was only about forty. The 1st Marine Division, which saw more action than any other American division in the Pacific, spent about 275 days in combat, spread over nearly three years, from August 1942 through June 1945. Needless to say, most individual marines had less than 275 days of combat. Of course the Pacific Campaign was mostly a matter of numerous offensive leaps by amphibious forces, with the resulting battles, though often incredibly violent and costly, usually short. Several American divisions in the ETO (European theater of operations) spent more days in combat, the record being held by the 2nd Infantry Division, perhaps 400 days of combat between 8 November 1942 and 8 May 1945, in North Africa and Europe, where the war was a matter of ongoing campaigning. Infantry comprised about the same percentage of the army in Vietnam as it had during World War II. However, the nature of combat in Southeast Asia put a proportionally much

heavier burden on the infantry than on the other arms. The average infantryman in Vietnam saw about 240 days of combat in a single year.

There were relatively few major battles in Vietnam compared with the Civil War or the world wars. Nevertheless, there were times when the intensity of combat could match that in the world wars, as during the 1968 Tet Offensive, for example. The single bloodiest day in the war for the United States was 17 November 1966, when the 2/7th Cavalry lost 155 dead and 124 wounded in an ambush by two NVA battalions, the *8/66th* and *1/33rd*. Moreover, there were many actions in Vietnam that were bigger than many of the most famous battles in the nation's history, such as those in the Revolution, the War of 1812, or those with Mexico and Spain. Yet no one would argue that combat in those wars was not intense.

Vietnam was a matter of endless days of dangerous patrolling or of manning isolated outposts under constant harassment, punctuated by occasional clashes on a larger scale, such as the battles of the Ia Drang Valley and Khe Sahn, or during the Tet offensive. But that seemingly interminable routine was just as deadly, and at least as emotionally taxing as such great hammer blow clashes as Antietam, Gettysburg, D-Day, the Bulge, or Iwo Jima. The comparison of marine casualties in the two wars is instructive.

Marine Casualties Compared

Conflict	Combat Deaths	Injured	Total	Ratio
World War II	19,733	67,207	86,940	3.4
Vietnam War	13,067	88,633	101,700	6.8

Key: *Combat Deaths* includes killed in action, mortally wounded, and missing in action. *Injured* includes wounded in action not mortally. *Total* is the sum of these. *Ratio* is the number of injured to each combat death. More marines became casualties in Vietnam than in World War II, which gives some idea of the degree of intensity of the conflict. The fact that more of those who became casualties in Vietnam survived the experience is due to improved medical care and, mostly, to the introduction of helicopters: by World War II casualties who made it to a medical facility survived in almost the same proportion as those in Vietnam.

So the war, to use a currently fashionable phrase, was differently intense. In some ways it was much more intense. For example, American aircraft dropped about six times more bombs than they had in World War II; that's a lot of explosives. To be sure, there may not have been any battles on the scale of Iwo Jima, Anzio, or the Bulge, but there were an awful lot of smaller clashes that were just as hard on the infantry as the bigger ones had been.

A comparison with World War II is interesting. Although the military participation ratio (the proportion of the population on active duty) during Vietnam was something like 4.3 percent, while that for World War II was

12.2 percent, about half as many people served in uniform during the Vietnam War as during World War II. Roughly 8.7 million in Vietnam compared with about 16.3 million, though the Vietnam War did last twice as long, ninety months as opposed to forty-four months. During World War II somewhat over 1.8 percent of the 16.3 million men and women who served were killed in action (291,557). Some 0.7 percent died from other causes, such as accidents and disease (113,842), and 4.1 percent were wounded in combat but survived (679,846), not to mention that about half of the people in the service were injured by accident or suffered from disease during their time in uniform. In contrast, of approximately 8.7 million men and women under arms during the Vietnam War, about 0.5 percent (47,369) were killed in action, 0.1 percent (10,799) died from other causes, and 1.8 percent (153,303) were wounded in combat but survived. However, those figures are on a service-wide basis. Even during World War II only about a third of U.S. military personnel saw combat, and, indeed, about a third never left the Americas. During the Vietnam War about 40 percent of all military personnel served in Southeast Asia (including personnel in Thailand, with the fleet in the South China Sea, and on B-52 missions out of Guam), for a total of some 3.5 million men and women. Nearly a third of the personnel in the armed forces actually served in Vietnam, all of which was at least sometimes a combat zone. Of the 2.6–2.8 million Americans who served in Vietnam, there was a 1.8-percent chance of being killed in action (c. 47,400), a 5.6-percent chance of being seriously wounded but surviving the experience (c. 153,300), and about the same chance of being lightly wounded; an estimated 150,000 troops suffered wounds that did not require a hospital stay. It's worth noting that combat casualties amounted to only about 60 percent of American casualties in Vietnam, with disease accounting for another 25 percent, and misadventure—accidents, suicides, murders, drug overdoses, and the like—for another 15 percent. Casualties from all causes, both combat and noncombat, amounted to somewhat over 58,000 dead and about 362,000 wounded, sick, or injured, for a total of about 418,000. Statistically this means that just about one in every six Americans in the war zone became a casualty of some sort. Actually, since there were some troops who were injured or ill several times, the actual figure was somewhat lower.

What was different about Vietnam was that those who did get into combat got a lot more of it than their fathers and uncles did in World War II. But unlike World War II, a lot fewer people got to go fight the enemy. Vietnam saw a much higher proportion of the troops away from the intense fighting, providing support for the guys who were getting shot at every day. While the support troops could say they were in a "combat zone," the amount of danger (as illustrated by how many casualties your unit takes) was a bit higher than their World War II counterparts, but still a small fraction of what the infantry boys in the bush confronted.

WHO SERVED AND WHO GOT HURT?

During the Vietnam War period, about 8.7 million Americans served in the armed forces. Only some 2.6–2.8 million of them were sent to Vietnam and fewer than 300,000 served in the bush under fire. So if you went into the armed forces during the Vietnam era, your chances of being shot at regularly in Vietnam were about one in thirty. Depending on how you dealt with military service, the chances could vary a lot, a whole lot.

Only about 2.2 million men were drafted during the Vietnam War, and about 90 percent of them went into the army. Prior to 1966 only about 65 percent of those eligible had been called, but many men who were classified as ineligible, or given lower priority classifications, were in later years reclassified (one was liable for the draft until age twenty-six).

Draft Calls by Fiscal Year

1965–68

FY	Draftees
1965	130,000
1966	320,000
1967	300,000
1968	334,000

But less than 10 percent of these draftees ended up in a frontline unit. Most of the troops in Vietnam were volunteers, as were over 80 percent of those who served during the Vietnam War. Many soldiers quickly realized, often before they became soldiers, that there were quite legal ways to avoid getting anywhere near Vietnam or, failing that, avoiding the actual fighting and dying.

The Vietnam War saw an unprecedented amount of public opposition to serving in the armed forces while a war was going on. Part of this was due to the presence of a peacetime draft. This was a side effect of the Cold War and the equally unprecedented demand for large peacetime armed forces. Until 1975, all eighteen-year-old U.S. males were liable for two years of involuntary military service. There were exceptions. College students could put off their service until they graduated. The military went along with that because they got the use of better educated and more mature troops that way. There were plentiful deferments for hardship (father of children) and occupation (police, teachers, etc.). The deferments and exemptions were possible because there were far more young men eligible for the draft than the military needed. There were over a million new eighteen-year-old young men considered physically, mentally, and morally (no police record) fit for military service each year. Even during the Vietnam War, less than a third of those eligible were drafted. The 4,200 local draft boards could afford to be generous. But each of these draft boards got quotas periodically, and they had to "produce the live bodies."

Young men quickly learned that those who waited for the draft got the worst jobs. The military knew that this aspect of the draft encouraged many potential draftees to volunteer for three or more years. By agreeing to go in for a longer time, the military could justify spending more on training these troops. The military was getting a lot more technical. Some specialties required a year or more of training. The military wasn't going to spend more than four or five months on training a draftee. It only took four months to train an infantryman and half of that was the basic training that everyone got.

One reason so many Vietnam-era veterans were so mad at Bill Clinton's draft dodging is that they knew Clinton wasn't trying to avoid Vietnam service, he was trying to avoid any service at all. And this from a guy who now preaches "national service." Any Vietnam vet would tell you that someone with young Bill Clinton's education would likely end up in a cushy staff job somewhere stateside or, at worst, in an air-conditioned bunker in Saigon. The latter situation would have paid off big time later on, as Clinton could have justifiably claimed he "served in Vietnam." People like Bill Clinton rarely became infantry, unless they volunteered for it.

During the Vietnam years, a draftee with a college degree only had a 42-percent chance of going to Vietnam, while high school grads had a 64-percent chance and high school dropouts a 70-percent chance. If you volunteered for three or four years in any service, you had less than a 20-percent chance of going to Vietnam. Remember, only 25–30 percent of all those in uniform during the Vietnam era went to Vietnam.

The better educated and generally brighter young men became aware of the many ways of avoiding exposure to death on the battlefield. The surest way to avoid infantry combat was to join the air force or navy. In both of these services, the only people in real danger were the crews of fighters and bombers, who were all volunteers and officers. While a navy enlistee had a very small chance of being assigned as a medic ("corpsman") in a marine unit, you were generally safe as a sailor. Even those joining the army could expect to avoid the infantry if they were highly educated or already had skills the army needed (like the ability to type or speak a foreign language, like Russian). But there were always volunteers for combat, even in the late 1960s when a glance at the nightly TV news demonstrated how dangerous that could be. Going into the marines was asking for it, but the marines made sure recruits knew what they were getting into. The marines only had to take a few draftees in the late 1960s. People joining the marines were likely to find themselves under fire within three or four months. Anyone drafted into the army, and without much education, was about as likely to end up in the infantry. You could also enlist in the reserves or National Guard, and over two-thirds of these troops admitted they had done so to avoid Vietnam service. About one million men took this route, although about 15,000 were called up for active service anyway, though only a few specifically for Vietnam. Not bad odds.

Once the war really got going, 'round about 1966, the general public, and potential draftees, became aware of who was getting hurt over there. Some 83 percent of all Vietnam casualties were a result of infantry operations. Since fewer than 10 percent of the troops in Vietnam were involved in infantry duty, you can do the math and see that the other 90 percent had about a 17-percent chance of being injured or killed in Vietnam. In an infantry unit, you had a nearly 50-percent chance. The infantryman was much more likely to get seriously injured, for the support troops were largely exposed to rocket and mortar attacks, and when, under fire, did not have to fight back but only seek shelter. The infantry had to fight back, usually without access to the prepared shelters the support troops had available.

Although there were still a lot of volunteers for the infantry (including the later movie director Oliver Stone), a lot of potential grunts began to see this war as a losing proposition and not necessarily in the best interests of the United States. So the army, more and more, had to fill up the infantry units with draftees. These were less-educated draftees, since the better prepared fellows were still needed for the more technical jobs. There was a lot of truth in the old GI saying, "If you can type, you'll never have to carry a rifle."

But there was a more tragic side to this growing reluctance of the better educated to step forward for combat duty. It was known since World War II that the best infantry were men with above average intelligence and good mechanical skills. These lads used to be farmer's or storekeepers sons, but now they were the sons of men who had gone to college on the GI Bill after World War II. In 1964 and 1965, they agreed with their fathers' attitude that Vietnam was a just war and it was one's duty to do what had to be done. But after two years of fighting, the public mood changed (as it tends to do in any war America has ever been involved in). The way the draft was set up, the middle- and upper-class lads had a legal way out. No need to run off to Canada or go to court over it. The infantry units began to fill up with the less capable young men, who would, in times past, have been sent into jobs requiring less skill (and more muscle). The better-educated draftees had also provided a lot of the low-level unit leadership and depth for when casualties were heavy. They weren't there now. As a result, the quality of leadership declined and morale suffered. Indiscipline increased, drug use became more common, effectiveness declined. The rotten attitudes in the combat units spread to the more numerous support units. It took the army some fifteen years to clear up this problem.

Since 1975, the U.S. armed forces has been filled with volunteers. No more draftees. In the 1980s, recruitment standards were raised considerably. The troops are now a bit older and more educated than in the draft days. Although the armed forces get a lot fewer of those recent college graduates in the ranks, they do get people for at least three years and keep more of them beyond the first enlistment. The draft law is still on the books, and eighteen-year-olds still have to register. If there were another major war, the draft would be used again. But like World War II, and unlike Vietnam, nearly everyone would go. That makes a big difference.

THOSE TRAUMATIZED VIETNAM VETS

One of the most persistent myths of the Vietnam War is that most Vietnam veterans, deeply ashamed of their service, often drug abusers, haunted by memories of the atrocities they have committed, and suffering from "post-traumatic stress" have proven to be failures in life. It is alleged that tens of thousands of them have committed suicide, while many others are time bombs waiting to explode, as demonstrated by numerous instances of headlines reading "Viet Vet Goes Berserk." For more than twenty years now we've seen this in movies, television programs, novels, journalistic articles, and even songs. In fact, of course, Vietnam veterans sometimes do have problems. It's called "post-traumatic stress." Post-traumatic stress commonly has the following symptoms: fatigue, shortness of breath, palpitations, headache, muscle or joint pain, dizziness, disturbed sleep, forgetfulness, difficulty concentrating.

But the veterans of every war usually suffer from stress.

After the American Civil War much was made of veterans suffering from "irritable heart" or "nostalgia." Symptoms were fatigue, shortness of breath, palpitations, headache, excessive sweating, dizziness, disturbed sleep, fainting. This led to a general fixation on "nervousness" for the rest of the nineteenth century, and at the beginning of the twentieth century the medical community recognized the syndrome as a catchall diagnosis for a host of conditions that were later found to be something else. Women, back then, were thought to be particularly prone to attacks of "agitated nerves."

World War I veterans sometimes suffered from "shell shock." Symptoms were fatigue, shortness of breath, palpitations, headache, excessive sweating, dizziness, disturbed sleep, and difficulty concentrating.

After World War II and Korea we had "combat stress reaction." Symptoms were fatigue, shortness of breath, palpitations, headache, excessive sweating, dizziness, disturbed sleep, and forgetfulness.

And two decades after Vietnam we had another generation of combat veterans, who came down with "Gulf War syndrome." Common symptoms of this are fatigue, shortness of breath, headache, muscle or joint pain, disturbed sleep, forgetfulness, difficulty concentrating. And the Gulf War was a lot shorter and a lot less intense than Vietnam or any of these other conflicts.

There seems to be a pattern at work here. In fact, "post-traumatic stress" (PTS) is a common problem afflicting soldiers—and other people who have spent some time under great pressure—when they return to "normal" life.

As General Sherman said, "War is hell," and anyone caught up in it is marked forever. Vietnam was a more stressful war than World War II and Korea. American combat troops saw more combat, over all, than their fathers had a generation earlier. Some people can handle PTS better than others. After a short time "in the world," most veterans adjust to normal life. It helps if the public makes the veteran feel that his service and sacrifice were praiseworthy. Unfortunately, in the aftermath of the Vietnam War, there was a certain lack of respect shown for the veterans by many civilians. Unlike World War II, where the nation was behind the troops, Vietnam saw a very vocal and prominent 13 percent of the American people energetically disapproving of the troops. Vietnam vets had to fight two campaigns, one in Vietnam and another back home. The image of the Vietnam veteran was not helped by the occasional instance in which one did "go berserk," which received widespread play in the press. One estimate has it that about 500,000 to 700,000 Vietnam veterans were afflicted by PTS, some 20 percent to 25 percent of those who served. About 10 percent of the men in this group suffered from the more extreme "post-traumatic stress disorder" (PTSD). They have had great difficulties reintegrating, and are prone to antisocial behavior, substance abuse, unemployment, and other serious problems. This is nothing new. In fact, there was a lot of veteran violence in the period immediately following World War II. So much, in fact, that in the late forties cartoonist Bill Mauldin had one of his now-veteran pair "Willie and Joe" reading to the other from a newspaper, saying, "Here's one . . . 'Ax Murder, No Veteran Involvement.' " If you were around in the late 1940s and early fifties (as the authors were), you may remember the news stories featuring World War II combat vets "going berserk." No one thought much of it, largely because there were over 15 million World War II vets in the population and they could sympathize with the poor fellow, knowing where he was coming from.

In fact, Vietnam veterans seem no less well-adjusted than were those of the nation's earlier wars, though perhaps public awareness and tolerance of problems among them has been more acute. There have been a few genuinely objective surveys of Vietnam veterans. These suggest a considerably different picture from the common one. Some 91 percent of Vietnam veterans are proud to have served, and 74 percent believe their service was necessary. The overwhelming majority (91 percent) of Vietnam veterans received discharges that were honorable, the same percentage that had prevailed in the decade before the war. Nor have most of them found adjustment to civilian life unusually difficult. About 88 percent of them made the transition without difficulty, and the average income of Vietnam veterans is about 18 percent higher, and their unemployment rate rather lower, than that for their non-veteran contemporaries. Drug abuse patterns among Vietnam veterans and nonveterans of the same era are not particularly different; remember that it was the era of "Turn on, tune in, and drop out." Fewer than 0.5 percent of them have been in jail, in contrast to a national incarceration rate of about 1.5 percent.

Perhaps the most persistent myth is that Vietnam veterans have committed suicide in extraordinary numbers, figures ranging from 50,000 to 150,000 being casually tossed about, rates six to sixteen times higher than the norm for Americans. Extraordinary indeed. If true, it would mean that more Americans who fought in Vietnam had killed themselves than been killed by the enemy, as many as 300 percent more! So prevalent was this assumption that the Centers for Disease Control (CDC) undertook "The Vietnam Experience Mortality Assessment," part of a series of studies intended to identify patterns of dysfunction among Vietnam vets. The CDC determined that by 1987 there had been some 9,000 suicides among Vietnam veterans. Vietnam veterans *were* about 1.7 times more likely than the "average" American to commit suicide within five years of their discharges. However, after that initial five-year post-discharge period, deaths from suicide fell below that for society as a whole. In the dozen years since the study the figure has probably risen to about 11,500, still within the "normal" range for Americans.

Another assumption about Vietnam veterans is that they are homeless in disproportionate numbers. It is true that veterans are more likely to be homeless than nonveterans. About 34 percent of the adult male population of the United States are veterans, but veterans constitute about 40 percent of the homeless. But that's all veterans, including the 25,000 World War I vets still among us, the eight million World War II vets, and the millions of veterans who have served since World War II.

In a detailed study completed in 1996, it turned out that the veterans who had served in combat were *less* likely to be homeless than those who had not seen action. And Vietnam vets are less likely to be homeless than men (only 1.6 percent of homeless veterans are women) who served post-Vietnam. This may seem surprising, but for about a dozen years after the abolition of the draft the quality of the manpower in the armed forces was pretty abysmal.

One factor complicating the study of problems among Vietnam veterans is that a lot of people lie about being veterans. This is so common that it has been satirized in film. In a minor scene in the 1993 picture *Falling Down* Michael Douglas, the protagonist, is approached by a panhandler who asks for a handout, saying, "I'm a Vietnam vet," to which, after eyeing the guy for a moment, Douglas replies, "What were you, a drummer boy?" Unfortunately, a number of "studies" of the problems of veterans have relied on anecdotal information, rather than a rigorous pursuit of evidence.

So, yes, Vietnam vets were traumatized by their experience. But no more so than veterans of any other war. The major difference was the lack of respect shown for the veterans by many civilians. Even civilians who supported the war effort in Vietnam usually treated the veterans badly. And despite denials from antiwar activists, returning veterans *were* sometimes called "baby killers" and worse. As marine veteran Donald Levesque said, "That's the beauty of America, that's what we fought for, the right to speak our minds." But the veterans will never forget the shabby treatment they got from some Americans.

CHAPTER 2

The Forty-Year War

The Vietnam War was long in coming. It began long before the average American had ever heard of Vietnam. A lot of history led up to the war, which actually began in the 1930s and went on into the 1970s against French, Japanese, and American troops, as well as a civil war between the Vietnamese.

WHAT IS VIETNAM?

Vietnam has been, until the last few centuries, more of a region than a country. It is also a crossroads, where several different cultures have blended to create what we now know as the Vietnamese people. Three principal ethnic groups met in Vietnam, beginning some 2,500 years ago. From the north came the Han (Chinese) people. Originally from north China, where they cultivated wheat and barley, the Chinese figured out how to cultivate rice. This was a complex process, but it produced far more food per acre, and more reliably. Slowly, the ever-increasing Chinese population moved into southern China. Their superior food-producing technology gave the Chinese greater numbers, and this allowed them to overcome, absorb, or drive away other peoples they encountered. When several of the Chinese tribes moved past Hong Kong and into the Red River area of North Vietnam 2,500–3,000 years ago, all they found were smaller numbers of Malay and Polynesian hunter gatherers and primitive farmers. At this point, a distinctive Vietnamese culture began to form.

Until six hundred years ago, Vietnamese attempts to push into what is now southern Vietnam were thwarted by organized resistance from local Malay and Khmer (Cambodian) groups. Even though these peoples had not adopted rice cultivation, the Vietnamese used greater numbers and Chinese technology to eventually prevail. One of the consistent advantages of the Vietnamese was their better organization and leadership. Both of these qualities came from China, where rice farming was developed largely because of the ability to organize people to perform the numerous and complex tasks required to grow rice. China also had a long literary history, which provided past experience and solutions in written form. The rice farming was advantageous in more ways than superior food production. The Chinese rice-farming techniques required exacting teamwork and coordination of effort at the village level and above. The Chinese, and Vietnamese, learned early on that these organizational skills were useful for war as well as farming.

Five hundred years ago, the Khmer Empire collapsed. The Khmer had controlled everything from parts of Thailand to most of South Vietnam. Central Vietnam was controlled by another Indian/Malay culture, the Champa. But the math was against the Khmer, who at this point had a population of 1–2 million. The Thai also had 2 million and the Vietnamese 4 million (including nearly a million under Khmer control). Caught between their more numerous Thai and Vietnamese enemies, the Khmer saw their empire evaporate and Vietnamese take control of southern Vietnam. The Malay/Indian Champa kingdom in central Vietnam held out a bit longer, but eventually it was also absorbed by the greater Vietnamese population, a bit of cultural genocide not unfamiliar in history

In this process, the Vietnamese ceased to be Chinese. The Chinese-speaking Han gradually absorbed more Malayan words and grammar into their language (as did many people in southern China) until there was a distinctive Vietnamese language. Centuries of marrying into non-Chinese families, and adopting bits and pieces of non-Chinese languages, created a distinct Vietnamese people and language.

But the Vietnamese still considered themselves Chinese, even as they maintained a national independence from the Chinese government. Although the Vietnamese language diverged from Chinese over a thousand years ago, Chinese writing was used into the nineteenth century. Vietnam has been politically independent from China for about a thousand years, although, again into the nineteenth century, they still recognized China as their "elder brother." In turn, the Vietnamese considered themselves the top dogs in Indochina, something the Cambodians, Thais, Lao, and various tribal groups (Montagnards) disputed. When the French took over in the late nineteenth century, it was because Vietnam had lapsed into a civil war as a result of its expansion. By the nineteenth century, Vietnam had grown to its current size and this included a lot of Vietnamese who had absorbed local ethnic groups to the extent that there was a significant difference between northern and southern Vietnamese.

The 1945–75 war against the French, the United States, and each other united the Vietnamese, as had previous wars against foreigners. But as before, the Vietnamese absorbed much from the foreigners, to the extent that the Vietnamese are now a much different people than they were before the war began.

WHERE THE FRENCH CAME IN

France got involved in Vietnam during the "Age of Exploration" from the sixteenth through the eighteenth centuries. Nearly every European nation with a merchant fleet got involved in searching out new trading partners and colonies during that period. Columbus reaching the Americas was one of the early examples of this trend that took Europeans all over the globe. First there was trade, then missionaries converted local peoples to Christianity. Warships sometimes were used to settle commercial disputes and later to coerce local authorities to stop persecuting the missionaries and their converts. France and England fought several wars in India, the richest of the overseas colonies. England won, and France was left to scramble for other opportunities. One area France showed interest in was Indochina. The area was so named because the cultures of India and China collided here. It was something of a buffer zone. Because of the intermingling of so many cultures, it was an unsettled area. Civil wars and conflicts between kingdoms were common. This created opportunities for France to gain another colony. One faction or another, with their backs to the wall, would call on the French for aid. French warships and troops became more active when, in the 1850s, Tu Duc, the emperor of Vietnam, began persecuting Christian missionaries and their local converts.

The French and Spanish invaded North Vietnam in 1858, in response to the murder of the Spanish bishop of Tonkin, in northern Vietnam. Resistance was too much to handle, so the Franco-Spanish force went south and occupied Saigon. France was also distracted by its participation, with Britain, in the second phase of the Opium War against China. A Treaty of Tientsin ended that conflict, and the French reinforced their besieged garrison in Saigon. By 1862, France had a treaty with the Vietnamese emperor and control over much of South Vietnam.

Meanwhile, Emperor Tu Duc had yet another civil war to contend with. The French got involved, and extracted still more territorial and trading concessions from the Vietnamese. In the early 1880s, the French proceeded to take over all of Vietnam and, in 1893, Laos and all of Cambodia. By 1887, the major rebellions had been put down and a colonial government established in their new Indochina colony. But armed resistance went on until 1895, and never really went away completely.

In 1914, World War I plunged France into a military and industrial crisis. With so many French men in the army, or dead, more workers were needed to keep the war industries going. One solution was to bring in hundreds of thousands of workers and soldiers from the colonies. Although France had already been introducing some young Vietnamese to education in France (and back in Vietnam), the use of colonial laborers in France during World War I exposed many more Vietnamese to European culture and politics. Thus was laid the groundwork for the forty-year war that would lead to

Vietnamese independence. Most of the key twentieth-century Vietnamese revolutionaries trace their beginnings back to time spent in France. Socialism and communism were the popular movements in post–World War I France, and the young Vietnamese visitors eagerly absorbed it all. Many Vietnamese lingered on in Europe after World War I and became active in the most popular radical political movement of the day, communism. One of the eager new Communists was Ho Chi Minh, who went on to found the Vietnamese Communist Party in 1930.

What the French had taken over was a Vietnamese empire that had been plagued by generations of civil wars among several feudal clans. Vietnam did not lack brilliant military commanders nor the means to buy the more advanced Western weapons. But the French were better organized and more adroit politically. Also, the Vietnamese nobility had discredited itself with all its infighting, which reduced resistance to the French. What was needed was something that could unite enough Vietnamese to eject the French. That something turned out to be communism. But the French had the Vietnamese Communists under control throughout the 1930s. What seriously weakened French control was Japan, which, unofficially, if quite effectively, took control of Vietnam in 1940–41. This made the Vietnamese realize that the French were not invincible.

The French were now on their way out.

UNCLE HO, GENERAL GIAP, THE RED MENACE, AND POWER POLITICS

Ho Chi Minh (born 1890) was of that generation of Vietnamese who came of age as France was changing the face and culture of Vietnam with industrialization and exposure to Western thought. The massive construction projects (railroads, plantations, factories, etc.) also upset the traditional economy, leaving many Vietnamese destitute, or just upset. The Western education given to many young Vietnamese, like Ho Chi Minh, produced a generation of revolutionaries dedicated to throwing the French out while, at the same time, further modernizing Vietnam. The Vietnamese could see, from their own experience and that of China in the 1800s, that France, and Europeans in general, were more powerful than Asians. The Europeans had better technology, organization, and policies. As Ho Chi Minh was growing up, the French were seen as unassailable. But Ho, and most other Vietnamese, knew that the French would eventually be thrown out. Expelling foreign invaders was an ancient Vietnamese custom. All Vietnamese grew up hearing the stories of heroic rebels of the past. Ho would be the latest in a long line of such Vietnamese rebel leaders.

What will probably be less well remembered is the odd ideology Ho used to achieve his ends. In his twenties, Ho came across socialism and communism, European inventions of the nineteenth century. Ho was attracted to communism because it seemed to combine the traditional Vietnamese methods of organizing themselves into highly structured groups to accomplish a common goal, with modern technology. Ho was determined and persistent, a good organizer, able to select the best subordinates, who continually made useful contacts, and was generally in the right place at the right time. Ho also knew that he had to play up the folk hero aspect of what he was trying to do. During Ho's time in France during World War I, he became a founding member of the French Communist Party. The Russian Communists noted his abilities, and by 1923, Ho found himself in Moscow to receive training. An able student, by 1930, Ho had founded the Vietnamese Communist Party. Shortly thereafter, on orders from Moscow, this was changed to the Indochinese Communist Party (ICP). Ho was not in Vietnam during the 1930s. First, he was held in a Hong Kong prison by the British for two years; then he went back to Moscow and stayed out of the way as Stalin's purges killed many other Communist revolutionaries. In 1940, the paranoia level in Moscow had abated, World War II had begun, and Japan was moving into Vietnam. Suddenly, Ho saw enormous opportunities opening up. The Japanese officially regarded the Vichy (pro-German) colonial government in Vietnam as allies; in practice, the Japanese did little to hide their disdain for the French. The Vietnamese noted this and all at once the French no longer appeared invincible. This changed everything, for as the Japanese defeated the British, Dutch, and Americans in early 1942, Asians realized they could do it too. Ho remained in Vietnam for the rest of World War II, keeping a resistance movement going. There wasn't much resistance, for the French had been ordered by the Japanese to be quiet, and the Japanese themselves had more pressing things to attend to than restless natives in Vietnam. The Vietnamese Communists were more interested in building up their strength for that day when the Japanese were defeated and the French had to be confronted. Those days came in August 1945. Ho and his Communist guerrillas moved into Hanoi and seized control. This was also the first public appearance of Ho Chi Minh as Ho Chi Minh. The name means "the enlightener." The man born Nguyen That Thanh had gone through several pseudonyms in his life, but now, at age fifty-five, he adopted a name he would take to his grave, and the history books.

Ho was a charismatic Nationalist who, like many other bright young folks in the first half of this century, thought communism was the future. Well it was, for some decades, but then just as quickly it became the past. Ho didn't know this at the time and since communism, especially the Russian strain, employs so many government techniques East Asians are already familiar with, Ho, and many other Vietnamese, felt comfortable with it. Communism, after all, was about science and progress. It was also about a police state and dictatorship. But these negative aspects got swept under the Nationalist rug, for the appeal of "driving the foreigners out of the motherland" made many blind to all the trouble they were getting themselves into.

Ho took credit for defeating the French, although he shared it with other key players. In particular, Vo Nguyen Giap was recognized for his military skill in winning the final 1954 battle at Dien Bien Phu. Born in 1911 (and thus nineteen years younger than Ho), Giap did not travel widely as Ho did, but grew up and was well-educated in Vietnam. A teenage Communist, Giap early on began to move up in the party. An aspiring high school history teacher with an interest in military history (Napoleon was his boyhood hero), in 1939, Giap was identified as a key Communist leader and had to flee Vietnam. He joined Ho in China and both returned after French power was curtailed by the Japanese in 1940. Although lacking much military training or experience, Giap was widely read in military history and had considerable organizational talents that more than made up for his lack of formal training. He put together the Viet Minh forces and turned them into a guerrilla army capable of defeating the French. After that, he reorganized the Viet Minh into a regular army. But here, in the late 1950s, Giap came into conflict with his mentor and boyhood hero, Ho.

In the late 1950s there was a debate among the leadership of North Vietnam about how to proceed with the "liberation" (conquest) of the South. Giap led a faction that proposed letting guerrillas and political activists take care of it, while North Vietnam rebuilt its economy and infrastructure. For some fifteen years, not much had been built and a lot had been destroyed in the fighting. The people were worse off than they were before World War II, and Giap saw turning that around as a key goal. But the other faction in the leadership, containing many who had been born in South Vietnam, argued for a faster (military) solution, to liberate the South as soon as possible. The "fast" faction won the debate, and Ho ordered Giap to implement the decision. Ho had several reasons for going with the "win it fast" faction. Many of the "fast" group were pro-Chinese and quite enthusiastic Communists. Moreover, Ho himself was unhappy with the situation in South Vietnam. He had gone out on a limb with his senior comrades in order to get the 1954 peace agreement that divided Vietnam. There were supposed to be elections throughout Vietnam in 1956 to decide if the division would remain or the country would unite under a Communist (North Vietnam) or Democratic (South Vietnam) government. Ho had used his popularity, and the propaganda tools he had picked up from the Chinese and Russian Communists, to turn himself into a genuine hero to most Vietnamese. It became obvious to all that if the 1956 election were held, Ho would win. When the South Vietnamese government refused to hold the elections on the grounds that it had not signed the 1954 Geneva Accords, the United States backed it. This disturbed Ho and his leadership team, and made Ho's decision to allow the 1954 partition appear mistaken. This gave the North

Vietnamese hard-liners an opening against him. As a result, Ho adopted the more radical option, to unite the country quickly and at whatever cost.

Giap was a team player and began sending men and weapons to South Vietnam in order to obtain a quick victory. The strategy was working until 1963, when the Communists' success alarmed the United States and by 1964 U.S. aircraft were regularly bombing North Vietnam and more U.S. troops were entering South Vietnam. By 1965, North Vietnamese combat units were getting chewed up by American soldiers and marines. Giap had been right, the Americans would prevail in a conventional fight. The Communist defeats in 1965–66, plus the death of one of the loudest "fast victory" North Vietnamese leaders, allowed Giap to pull back and try to do things his way. This meant no more big battles with the Americans (and their massive air and artillery support). But the die had been cast and Ho could not allow a complete reversion of guerrilla warfare and political work.

By 1967, it was obvious to all that the Communists would win if they could keep substantial forces in South Vietnam, but American firepower was making that increasingly difficult. At that point the Communists figured it would take five or ten years, tops, to get their way. This was too slow for the more radical Communists, who feared a defeat by the Americans. Under considerable political pressure Giap undertook the Tet Offensive in early 1968. The massive series of attacks was intended to liberate many towns and parts of cities long enough for the locals to join the Communists in a general uprising. It was felt that the situation was ripe for an "all or nothing" offensive and a call for the people of the South to "rise up" and throw off their capitalist leaders.

Things didn't work out that way. Militarily, the Tet Offensive was a disaster for the Communists. The people did not rise up, in fact many ferociously fought the Communist troops. But at the same time reports of these military defeats were coming in, Ho, Giap, and company noted that the Western media had declared the Communists the winners. More accurately, the Americans had been declared losers. Why? Because the American leadership had been assuring the American public (and the rest of the world) for the previous year that the Communists in South Vietnam were finished, that the end was near. Actually, Tet did put the Communists even further in the hole. Several years of determined and heavy effort could have ended the Communist resistance in South Vietnam. But it was not to be. The American people felt deceived and wanted no more of Vietnam. Ho and Giap took their good fortune and ran with it.

By the end of 1968, Richard Nixon had been elected U.S. president by promising to "get the U.S. out of Vietnam." Giap could taste victory, but that was all he got for a while. Nixon was determined to get some North Vietnamese guarantees, or at least recognition of, South Vietnam's independence. Peace talks, which got under way in May of 1968, took five years to get anywhere. From the start, the United States wanted to get out, but South Vietnam didn't want that and North Vietnam was determined to unite Vietnam under its own terms as quickly as possible.

Ho died in September 1969, at a time when reunification was still in doubt. For a year or more before Ho's death he had been unable to fully exercise his control over North Vietnam's war effort, which passed to the younger generation. This included Giap, who was taking the heat for the faltering Communist war effort. But the younger generation of North Vietnamese leaders was still split on how to deal with the situation. Many of Giap's peers were more radical and impatient. In particular, Van Tien Dung, Giap's long-time chief of staff. Dung ended up replacing Giap in 1974 and commanded the final offensive in 1975. Giap's reputation had suffered from the military failures of Tet in 1968 and the Easter offensive in 1972, both of which he actually appears to have opposed. Although Giap was much honored for his victory over the French, he was eventually seen as less capable when it came to dealing with the Americans. While the 1972 defeat involved few American ground troops, the Communist troops were on the receiving end of massive U.S. airpower. The 1975 offensive was another story. No American aid was available to the South Vietnamese and either Dung or Giap could have won that one.

On the American side, the politics were a bit different. In 1945, having just finished winning World War II, a war America had to be forced into, the United States again tried to retreat into its customary isolationism. But communism changed that. This revolutionary doctrine preached worldwide revolution and the overthrow of non-Communist governments. Communism was a clever combination of beliefs that demanded religious faith and ruthless dedication from its followers. Throughout the twentieth century, communism appealed to many people seeking a change for the better. Instead they got a change for the worse. By the end of the twentieth century, it became known that communism had killed over a hundred million people outright and ruined the economies of a third of the world's population. But in 1945, communism was flying high and America found itself surrounded by Communist revolutions and insurgencies, and there were a lot of intellectuals who thought communism was the wave of the future. The Russian Communists had taken over the nations of Eastern Europe, while China was taken over by local Communists. Communist revolutionaries were popping up everywhere and Americans were scared. The Red Menace *was* very real.

The industrialized nations (North America and Western Europe) formed NATO (North Atlantic Treaty Organization) to defend themselves against the Communist menace. But in 1950, Communist North Korea invaded non-Communist South Korea. It was suspected at the time, and proven many years later, that Russia and China were behind this. American public opinion supported a major military effort to stop the North Koreans. This was not a popular war, but fear of communism made it tolerable for a while. However, after the war settled down to trench fighting in its second year, popular support began to erode. The Communists agreed to a cease-fire in 1953. Back in America, anxious eyes turned toward other countries suffering from Communist insurgencies. One obvious one was Vietnam, where in 1954, the French had been defeated in their war against Communist rebels.

From the late 1940s until the 1980s, a common political trick in America was to accuse your opponent of being "soft on communism." There were also accusations against some in government that they were responsible for losing China (and other nations) to the Communists. It was all very nasty and opportunistic. But it played well to the voters. Richard Nixon, who was elected president in 1968 on his promise to "get America out of Vietnam," had his first political success in the late 1940s by tagging his opponent with the "soft on communism" label. Former General of the Army Dwight D. Eisenhower was elected president in 1952 on a promise to "end the war in Korea," but even he had to agree to provide military support to other nations fighting native Communists. What it all came down to was that in the early 1960s no politician could afford to be seen (correctly or otherwise) as "soft on communism."

When, in the early 1960s, the South Vietnamese government appeared closer and closer to defeat by the Viet Cong, American politicians fell all over each other to provide aid. This led to 1964, when Pres. Lyndon Johnson found himself with crisis on his hands. If he sent more aid to South Vietnam, he risked "another Korea." If he let South Vietnam fall to the Communists, he would get tagged for "losing Vietnam." In the political arithmetic of the day, it was generally considered better to risk "another Korea" than to be called "soft on communism."

Getting involved in "another Korea" meant that you had to do at least as well as we did in Korea. There, nearly 40,000 Americans died, but South Korea had remained non-Communist. This was the measuring stick no one spoke about out loud but was always implied. By 1968, it looked like the Communists in South Vietnam were being beaten to the ground. Actually, this was the case. But with the Communists' ability to move more troops and supplies into South Vietnam, the fighting could be kept going a much longer time. Tet revealed this fact and Americans decided, while communism was bad, fighting Communists in Vietnam was worse.

The change in attitude got Richard Nixon elected president. But Nixon was still looking over his shoulder lest he be nailed as "soft on communism." Thus, instead of just pulling U.S. troops out of Vietnam and telling the South Vietnamese that we were terribly sorry, he insisted on "peace with honor." But the American people had spoken and they wanted U.S. troops out of Vietnam. Chances are that the Communists would have taken over South Vietnamese by 1970 if Nixon had ordered an immediate pullout. But there were still many in the United States who were not keen on just leaving South Vietnam in the lurch. So Nixon did what any politician would do and tried to please as many voters as possible. While promptly beginning to withdraw U.S. units, Nixon insisted that the North Vietnamese back off and at least publicly agree to leave South Vietnam alone. Everyone knew any such agreement would be worthless and the North Vietnamese were still determined to control all of Vietnam. The North Vietnamese resisted Nixon's demands, and the response was increased bombing of North Vietnam. In addition, the North Vietnamese bases in Cambodia were bombed and then overrun by American troops.

With Ho's passing in 1969, the rifts in the North Vietnamese leadership became more factious than usual. While the "win quickly at any cost" faction still called most of the shots, Nixon's ever more energetic bombing campaigns began to give the "take it more slowly" faction more adherents. By 1973, the North Vietnamese were willing to agree to American terms, even though the North Vietnamese had no intention of abiding by most of them.

A major factor in the Vietnam War was the instability of the South Vietnamese government versus the discipline of the one in North Vietnam. Essentially, South Vietnam was founded by a lot of anti-Communist people who, much more so than those in the north, collaborated with the French. Moreover, millions of South Vietnamese were quite nontraditional by Vietnamese standards. There were nearly two million Catholics, plus an equal number of others belonging to new religious movements. To further mix things up, the South Vietnamese had always been more fractious and disorganized than their kinsmen in the North. North Vietnam was, culturally and ethnically, much closer to China. But the northerners were also the keepers of an ancient tradition of Vietnamese resistance to Chinese, and other, invaders. The southerners were more accommodating and ethnically and culturally closer to Malaya, India, and Cambodia. The most successful South Vietnamese politician in the 1950s was Ngo Dinh Diem. His first act after partition was to hold an election that enabled him to replace the traditional Vietnamese emperor (Bao Dai, who wasn't interested in the job anyway). Diem then spent the next nine years fighting various factions in South Vietnam and paying little attention to the Communists. A Catholic, his favoritism toward those of his faith, at the expense of the majority of the Buddhists, caused no end of problems (and often open rebellion). Finally, the United States, more concerned with the growing Communist insurgency, stood aside as a military coup took place and the Diem clan members were either killed, arrested, or driven into exile. The new government wasn't much better than Diem's. GEN Duong Van Minh led a council of officers to run the country at first. This first military government was less stable than Diem's and soon was even less popular. In 1965, another coup took place, led by Nguyen Cao Ky and Nguyen Van Thieu. These two imposed some order on the South Vietnamese and thus gained the active support of the United States. But American politicians still needed some democracy in South Vietnam in order to justify the war. Ky and Thieu complied and in 1966 a new legislature was elected and in 1967 a new constitution was drawn up. Later that year, presidential elections were held and Thieu became president and Ky vice president in a new government similar in form to the American one. Thieu proved a pretty able ruler, and won reelection in 1971. But a decade of bad government, the flood of American troops and money, the hordes of refugees generated by the war, and the war itself left the South Vietnamese unable to hold the country together.

Under the terms of the 1973 Paris agreement, the United States and North Vietnam were supposed to withdraw their troops from the South. The United States complied, but the North Vietnamese didn't, leaving some 300,000 men behind. Two years after the peace agreement, the North Vietnamese launched yet another conventional invasion of South Vietnam. This time there was no American airpower to help out. Once all American troops were out of Vietnam, the U.S. voter wanted nothing more to do with Southeast Asia. The war was over, the politicians were worn out, and the people had spoken.

THE FRENCH CAMPAIGNS

There was some armed resistance to the French in the 1930s, and a guerrilla movement against the Japanese appeared during World War II, but no serious fighting got done until the late 1940s. The reason was simple: the rebels had a hard time obtaining weapons until the Russian, and especially the Chinese, Communists agreed to support them. But the rebels were aided by some events that made it a lot easier to recruit troops. The massive famine in 1945 (caused mainly by the Japanese exporting most of the rice crop) killed two million people and created a tremendous resentment toward foreigners. The Japanese occupation of Indochina from 1940 to 1945 had not been gentle, and the French were still around, although the Japanese had finally disarmed or killed the French colonial troops in early 1945. Shortly after Japan surrendered, the British arrived and began to reassert foreign control and facilitate the return of the French colonial government. But the Viet Minh, a Communist-led coalition of Vietnamese patriots, had already proclaimed the independence of Vietnam and seized control of the major cities. For about a year, the Viet Minh negotiated with the French, but money (French commercial interests in Vietnam) and pride (France had been beaten by Germany in 1940 and was not about to give up its colonies) caused the French to renege on earlier promises of independence. Actually, the French demonstrated bad faith from the beginning. When the British arrived in September of 1945, they released and rearmed the French soldiers held captive by the Japanese. These French soldiers and officials promptly tried (with some success) to block the Viet Minh attempt to govern Vietnam. In early

1947, the French forced the Viet Minh out of Hue, the last city the Communists held. Thereafter the Viet Minh went back to guerrilla warfare.

At first, the French exercised their usual advantage in military skill and superior weapons. But the French could no longer depend on most of the population being passive. The upheavals of World War II and the effective political techniques of the Communists had turned that passive population to one that was willing to fight for change. The people, at least many of them in North Vietnam, were behind the Viet Minh. By 1950, the Chinese Communists were supplying the Viet Minh with massive amounts of American weapons and ammunition they had captured from the Nationalist Chinese in the civil war that had only ended in 1949.

From early 1947 (when the Viet Minh left the cities and began their grass roots campaign) until 1950 (and the Chinese aid), the Viet Minh did not look unbeatable. In that period the French sought out other Vietnamese willing to take as much "independence" as France was willing to grant (some, but not all). The French found many takers. The Viet Minh wanted complete independence, and in northern Vietnam, the traditional source of Vietnamese patriots for over a thousand years, that theme played well. But the French proceeded to reestablish the traditional Vietnamese emperor, ruling the country as an "associated" part of "the French Union." This played better in southern Vietnam than in the north, and that was to be the basis of the eventual partition of Vietnam in 1954 and the subsequent involvement of American troops in the war.

The French underestimated what a difference all that Chinese aid could make. China allowed the Viet Minh to set up training bases in southern China and provided the Vietnamese guerrillas with supplies and technical assistance. By 1950, the Viet Minh had also organized thousands of villages and city neighborhoods to provide assistance for the revolution. It wasn't just the armed Viet Minh guerrillas that were keeping the French pinned down, it was the millions of Vietnamese people who actively supported the Viet Minh in so many ways. These people provided the Viet Minh with information, places to hide, couriers, food, labor, and, of course, recruits for the fighting units. In 1947, the French had only 15,000 troops in Vietnam, and the Viet Minh had 60,000. Granted, many of the Viet Minh fighters didn't have rifles, but these men (and some women) were willing to fight, even if only armed with knives or farm implements.

By 1949, the Viet Minh had thirty battalions of regular troops (about 12,000 soldiers), who could fight it out with the French. This wasn't enough for the Viet Minh to win. Total Viet Minh troop strength was only about 100,000. While the French concentrated on controlling the large population centers in Vietnam, the Viet Minh had a hard time building their combat strength up to 200,000 troops. However, because of the Chinese assistance, most of the Communist troops were now regulars, not guerrillas. By late 1950, this assistance had enabled the Viet Minh to field 117 combat battalions, plus artillery units. The French would build up to a peak force, in 1954, of 100,000 French troops and over 200,000 Indochinese troops (some of the latter becoming the core of the later South Vietnamese army). In that year, the Viet Minh attained a strength of 300,000.

French Casualties in Indochina, 1945–54

	KIA/MW/MIA	WIA	Total
French Troops	75,867	65,125	140,992
Indochinese Troops	18,714	13,002	31,716
Totals	94,581	78,127	172,708

Key: KIA/MW/MIA indicates troops killed in action, mortally wounded, or missing in action (only c. 25 percent of prisoners taken by the Viet Minh were ever liberated). WIA indicates wounded in action not mortally. The KIA/MW/MIA figure for French Troops includes 11,710 Algerian, Moroccan, and other colonial forces as well as the Foreign Legion, and c. 720 air force and naval air personnel. Excluding Indochinese personnel, the total force France committed to Indochina over the nine years of the war was only about 175,000 men, an astonishing 80 percent of whom became casualties, over half of them dead or missing in action. Nearly 14 percent of the approximately 225,000 Indochinese troops who served in the French army or the various locally raised "national armies," became casualties, more than half of whom were killed or missing in action, an equally astonishing rate of loss.

The French could not muster enough military and political strength to crush the Viet Minh, nor could the Communists do the same to the French. It had become a test of wills, who would get tired of the fighting first and drop out. Part of the French problem was having a commander who could cope with this situation. The circumstances were unique, for Indochina (Vietnam, Laos, and Cambodia) was a vast area of jungles, swamps, and mountains. The French had a largely motorized army that was unable to move into areas without roads. The Viet Minh had also learned the value of ambushes and how vulnerable motorized troops were when they were traveling from one place to another along roads.

In late 1950, the French sent one of their better generals, Jean de Lattre de Tassigny, to Vietnam and he made a difference. But he was ill and only lasted about a year before he had to go back to France, where he died shortly thereafter. Before he went back, de Lattre de Tassigny defeated the Viet Minh's first major offensive. The Viet Minh then backed off and went back to guerrilla warfare. The next two French generals were less able than de Lattre de Tassigny and their increasingly desperate attempts to crush the Viet Minh led to the battle of Dien Bien Phu in late 1953. By early 1954, the

French had lost that siege, as the Viet Minh cut off French reinforcements and brought up their artillery to finish off the affair.

But the French still had a lot of support in Vietnam, and the Viet Minh were willing to accept a compromise. Vietnam was divided, with the Communists getting complete independence in North Vietnam, while the many anti-Communist Vietnamese set up a separate country in the South. Laos and Cambodia became independent under their former royal families. The Viet Minh rested and planned the eventual unification of Vietnam under Communist rule. Meanwhile, the North Vietnamese supported Communist movements in Laos and Cambodia. With China, North Korea, Eastern Europe, and Cuba run by Communists, it seemed that the worldwide "socialist revolution" was at hand.

The political and military ground was laid for the American phase of the Indochina war.

THE VIET MINH–JAPANESE ALLIANCE

Although "alliance" is perhaps too strong a word for it, for a short period in early 1945, the Viet Minh more or less laid off fighting the Japanese because the Japanese began fighting the French. Having muscled in on the French in 1940–41, the Japanese were soon more or less in complete control of Indochina. But there were still French officials and French troops in the country, going through the motions of preserving French sovereignty. With the liberation of France from the Nazis in mid-1944, relations between the Japanese and the local Vichy (Pro-German) French became increasingly tense, particularly since the French Committee of National Liberation had declared war on Japan. In early 1945, the Japanese decided to get rid of the French. The Viet Minh appear to have gotten wind of what was to come. Recognizing that it was in their best interests to sit on the sidelines, they ceased making attacks on Japanese forces. In a well-executed coup on 9 March the Japanese managed to capture virtually all important French civil and military personnel, only about a thousand Foreign Legionnaires managing to escape from the disaster by a long and arduous march into China. Perhaps 4,500 French personnel were massacred, and the rest imprisoned. This effectively broke the remnants of French power in Indochina, and thus greatly benefited the Viet Minh, who shortly resumed their attacks on the Japanese.

THE VIET MINH'S FOREIGN LEGION

One of the genuine "dirty little secrets" of the First Indochina War was the fact that the Viet Minh had serving in its ranks some former Imperial Japanese troops and even Nazi German personnel.

When Japan surrendered to the Allies, between 1,500 and 4,000 Japanese troops joined the Viet Minh. Led by a Lieutenant Colonel Mukayama, who was later killed in action fighting the French, these troops included some members of the dread *Kempetai*, or military secret police. Many of the Japanese troops served as technicians and trainers with the Viet Minh, and some also served in combat. The Japanese 51st Mountain Artillery Regiment, some nine hundred strong, seems to have provided the core about which the Viet Minh built their first artillery units.

Joining these Japanese troops were some former Nazi officials and even German troops recruited in Asia by the Nazi *Auslander* organization who had been serving in Indochina (a forgotten footnote to World War II), preferring to take their chances with the Communists than with an Allied war crimes tribunal.

The Viet Minh also acquired some erstwhile Nazi troops through capturing members of the French Foreign Legion, which was heavily German in the post–World War II period. In fact, Ho Chi Minh went so far as to "adopt" one, who took the name Ho Chi Long, an obvious ploy to entice more defections from the ranks of the French.

This co-option of former enemy troops was by no means an unusual occurrence in the post–World War II period. Both sides in the post–1945 Chinese Civil War made use of former Japanese personnel who, for various reasons, preferred not to return home. Despite "denazification" in Germany and other parts of Europe, a lot of former Nazis managed to turn up in positions of authority on both sides of the Iron Curtain. The infamous Nazi commando Otto Skorzeny reportedly served as a technical advisor to the South Vietnamese Army for a time in the 1950s.

LESSONS FORGOTTEN: THE AMERICAN MILITARY AND INSURGENCY

Prior to the Vietnam War the U.S. armed forces had amassed considerable experience in the conduct of insurgency and counterinsurgency warfare. A lot of lessons were learned; but when the Vietnam War came along, they were either forgotten or misapplied.

The Philippine Insurrection, 1899–1902. A Filipino insurrection against Spanish rule that had begun in 1896 was quickly crushed through a combination of effective counterinsurgency operations, the judicious use of bribes, and internal rifts among the rebels. With American help, the insurgents made a comeback during the Spanish-American War (1898). It soon became clear to Emilio Aguinaldo and the other leaders of the "Republic of the Philippines," that the United States was not leaving the islands. Open war began in February 1899. The Filipinos initially tried to wage a conventional war. This proved unwise, and they were soundly beaten in a series of battles. In November 1899, they switched to guerrilla warfare. U.S. troops adopted a sophisticated counterinsurgency policy. While some forces held critical posts, others relentlessly pursued insurgent bands. A lot of political and civic action projects were undertaken, and a "carrot and stick" policy was adopted toward the insurgents, with generous terms for anyone declaring his loyalty to the United States (one erstwhile guerrilla general became a provincial governor). Serious guerrilla resistance continued into 1901, when Aguinaldo was captured (he took the oath and was soon active in insular politics). The last insurgent bands surrendered in 1902. Although there would later be problems with Moslem "Moro" tribesmen in the far south of the archipelago, these were unrelated to the attempt to establish a Filipino Republic. The war had cost over four thousand American lives (only a quarter in battle), as well as thousands more Filipino lives, though far fewer than the hundreds of thousands usually charged by self-proclaimed anti-imperialists. Although short, it had been a hard, brutal war (though hardly as brutal as has usually been suggested, considering the degree of loyalty most Filipinos soon developed for the United States). Victory ultimately had been the result of a judicious mixture of force and political measures, as well as the failure of the insurgents to effectively broaden their political base beyond the Tagalog-speaking regions.

Most senior American officers in the first half of the century had seen service during the Philippine Insurrection. Surprisingly, the army never published an official history of the war, nor did it issue any manuals or guidelines on lessons learned.

The "Banana Wars," 1912–34. For most of the first third of the twentieth century U.S. Marines repeatedly found themselves engaged in counterinsurgency operations in several Caribbean and Central American countries. Indeed, "the Banana Wars" were the primary mission of the Marine Corps in the period, with nearly a score of operations, the most notable of which were Nicaragua, 1912–13; Haiti, 1915–34; the Dominican Republic 1916–22; and Nicaragua again, 1927–33. Usually American intervention was prompted by a self-proclaimed leftish insurgency against an ostensibly conservative, pro-U.S. government (actually, in most cases the war was less about ideology than about conflicts among the local elites over which aristocratic clan held power). However, the marines also occasionally helped fight rightist rebels against liberal regimes, as occurred for a time during the late 1920s in Nicaragua, when—much to their astonishment—the liberals won a marine-supervised election, with the result that the conservatives took to the hills.

Success in "the Banana Wars" was accomplished by the judicious use of force and the delivery of services. In the end, most of the populace preferred stability to insurgency, and once provided with some measure of security cooperated willingly with the marines.

In 1935, two majors, Samuel M. Harrington and Harold H. Utley, distilled the Marine Corps' experience in counterinsurgency warfare into a useful handbook, the *Small Wars Manual*. Unfortunately, the lessons embodied in this work received little attention outside of the Marine Corps. Worse, in the post–World War II period the Marine Corps rewrote its standard manual on counterinsurgency, lifting some bits from *Small Wars Manual* and taking a lot from the army's contemporary thoughts on the matter. Nevertheless, in Vietnam some marines remembered *Small Wars Manual*, and a few of the ideas embodied in it were tried, such as in the Civic Action Platoons, with some success. Surprisingly, this meant that marine "body counts" were often lower than some "bean counters" at MACV (Military Assistance Command, Vietnam) liked, which led to some criticism from senior army officers. The army, in effect, forced the marines to abandon their more effective tactics.

Philippine-American Guerrilla Operations in World War II. One of the most successful guerrilla campaigns in World War II was conducted in the Philippines during the Japanese occupation (1941–45). In fact, guerrilla operations by Filipino and American forces actually began before the formal surrender of regular troops in April and May 1942. In late December 1941, some troops on Luzon who had been unable to join the retreat to Bataan began operating as guerrillas, and in one case killed a Japanese general in an ambush. At first there was little more the guerrillas could do but survive. Some of them did this badly, preying on local villagers, who often turned them in to the Japanese. Others, with better leaders, formed more effective ties to local villagers. The numerous small guerrilla bands eventually merged into increasingly larger ones (not always peacefully, since some guerrilla leaders—both American and Filipino—were more interested in their prestige than developing a better organization). Bolstered by popular support, the guerrillas, initially mostly soldiers who had refused to surrender, began to recruit more fighters. The Japanese made strenuous attempts to eradicate them, but with relatively little success. By late 1942, Douglas MacArthur began to become aware of the character and vigor of the guerrilla movement in the Philippines, a movement for which no preparations had been made in the prewar period or during the early months of the war. He formalized the status of the guerrilla leaders (some of whom had spontaneously promoted themselves as high as brigadier general), organized them into ten regional commands, and instituted a system by which submarines and aircraft carried supplies, equipment, and even personnel into the Philippines in support of the guerrillas. The clumsy and brutal Japanese antiguerrilla tactics only increased support for the guerrillas. By late 1944, the guerrillas had become a substantial force. When MacArthur returned, there were perhaps 150,000 reasonably trained and equipped guerrillas ready to lend a hand. The Filipino guerrillas conducted preinvasion intelligence, undertook sabotage and harassment raids, made diversionary attacks, served as scouts, helped rescue downed pilots, performed security duties to prevent Japanese infiltration, and undertook mopping up operations, among many other missions. Amazingly, almost as soon as World War II was over, it became fashionable in military circles to dismiss the importance of the Filipino guerrillas, based largely on their one major failing, their inability to confront Japanese troops in regular combat. There was no formal study of the guerrilla campaign, and it was barely mentioned in the army's official accounts of the liberation of the Philippines.

Toss in peripheral American participation in several other guerrilla wars (e.g., Greece, Malaya, etc.), and it can be seen that the United States had a lot of experience in insurgency and counterinsurgency warfare. Of course there were significant differences between the war in Vietnam and American's earlier guerrilla experiences. In the Philippine Insurrection and in the Caribbean interventions the numbers of the guerrillas were generally small and their organization, motivation, and discipline fairly poor, and there were severe ethnic tensions among the populace. Moreover, they had no "brothers" right next door sustaining them with propaganda, arms, supplies, and even troops, as was the case with the Viet Cong. In its guerrilla war in the Philippines against the Japanese, the United States benefited from a largely loyal local populace. Loyal, that is, to the notion of an independent Philippines, as had been promised by the United States long before the Japanese invasion. Japanese ineptitude in coping with unrest and America's own increasingly growing military power also encouraged resistance.

However, there were many lessons for fighting guerrillas that were overlooked. They can be readily summarized:

Travel Light. Experience showed that the best antiguerrilla troops were those who operated with a minimum of equipment. In Vietnam helicopters made this possible, although U.S. troops still had to carry twenty to thirty pounds more gear than the Communist troops they were stalking through the jungle. But the main thing with "traveling light" was a mind-set of mobility. Helicopters could get troops and equipment to remote areas, but you still had to have fast-moving troops on the ground to go after the elusive guerrillas. Aside from LRRPs (Long Range Reconnaisance Patrol) and some similar forces, this was where most American troops were found lacking.

Keep to the Jungle. Relentless pursuit of the enemy was an important ingredient in successful counterguerrilla operations; never let him rest. When this was done in Vietnam, the Communists were put on the defensive and were often forced to flee to their sanctuaries outside of South Vietnam. U.S. troops did this often, but not often enough, since their senior commanders were much more interested in trying to set the enemy up for some smashing battles.

Offer Generous Terms. In effect, bribe the guerrillas and the peasants into coming over to your side. During the Philippine Insurrection one rebel commander was turned into a provincial governor, a fine example of the benefits of collaboration. Some of this was done in Vietnam, such as the *Chieu Hoi* program, but not enough. Defecting guerrillas needed to be given high visibility, not merely used as scouts.

Offer a Viable Alternative Political Solution. Give the common people something different from their present situation and from what the rebels were offering. In Vietnam the Communists were making pie-in-the-sky offers of "land reform" and "democracy," offers that were, of course, merely a subterfuge to secure peasant support. A solid program of distributing land and some genuine democratic reforms might have turned the Vietnamese peasants from supporting the possibility of reform to defending very real reforms. Indeed, there were many areas of South Vietnam where substantial reforms were made and the locals subsequently turned hostile to the Communists. Unfortunately, the political leadership of South Vietnam preferred strong man rule to any form of participation by the people and was reluctant to institute genuine land reform. Americans proposed democracy, but few Vietnamese leaders were interested.

Protect the People. In most insurgencies the average person really wants to be left alone. Whichever side offered the most in services and protection usually received the passive support of the common people. The United States tried to do this in Vietnam, but ran across several obstacles. One was terrorism, which frightened the peasantry into supporting the Communists or, at the very least, not supporting the South Vietnamese government. In addition, the United States brought a lot of firepower to the war to protect its troops. A lot of Vietnamese civilians found themselves caught in the middle, with often fatal results. With a major war being waged in populated areas, there's not much protection you can offer. The USMC had the right idea, but the army refused to follow their lead. That said, most South Vietnamese only wanted to be left alone so they could live their lives. When these conditions were created, and they often were, the people were willing to support whoever was providing the peace and quiet.

Negotiate. Having contacts with the rebels could sometimes bring them to a compromise. This was not really possible in Vietnam, because the North Vietnamese Communists were a totalitarian power who wanted it all. In all other insurgencies America was involved in, there was a possibility for compromise. Not so in Vietnam, and this put America in a situation where it had to fight to win in the conventional way (conquering North Vietnam) or not fight at all. Eventually, America chose the latter option.

Perhaps because of the declining interest in history manifested by the armed forces in the decade prior to the Vietnam War, none of this wealth of experience in guerrilla warfare was brought along when American troops began arriving in Southeast Asia in large numbers.

COMMUNIST INSURGENCIES, 1945–65

The idea that a Communist insurgency was unbeatable was rather firmly established by the Vietnam War, particularly in leftist circles. This is hardly the case. Indeed, in the two decades prior to the insertion of massive American forces into Vietnam, Communist guerrillas had not done very well overall.

The belief in the early sixties that the Viet Cong could be beaten was not a fantasy. But to defeat them certain realities had to be addressed. Of course the important thing was not that the guerrillas could be beaten, but rather that each war was a unique case. There was no formula that the insurgents could apply to ensure success, nor one that their opponents could apply to ensure *their* success. The conduct of unconventional warfare depended upon such things as objectives, leadership, organization, discipline, culture, foreign support, and a myriad of other factors, any or all of which could be different depending upon the country. To win as a guerrilla or to beat the guerrilla one had to tailor one's activities to the particular situation.

Just as the United States had failed to study the lessons of its own experiences with insurgency, so too it failed to do more than take superficial cognizance of the details of those occasions on which guerrillas had been defeated. American political and military strategists failed to take notice of the differences among the many insurgencies that had been defeated and Vietnam, and therein lay their most grievous failing.

THE OFFICIAL AMERICAN ARMY CAMPAIGNS IN VIETNAM, AND THE UNOFFICIAL ONES AT HOME

The armed forces divided the Vietnam War into sixteen campaigns. Historically a campaign is a connected series of military operations (maneuvers, marches, battles, etc.) that form a coherent whole, such as the Normandy Campaign in World War II. In Vietnam the term "campaign" was used differently. It referred to a distinct period in the war, which did not always have a coherent character. In fact, there were actually "campaigns" in the traditional sense during the "campaigns" in the new sense. But there was more going on off the battlefield. North Vietnam won its war to conquer South Vietnam by using propaganda and media manipulation to encourage an isolationist American public to abandon their South Vietnamese ally. The Gulf of Tonkin was no Pearl Harbor when it came to keeping the American people mad enough to stay with the war until the American side was victorious. So we include the political and diplomatic battles as well.

Communist Insurgencies, 1942–65

Conflict	Period	Victor
Greek Civil War	1944–49	Government
Spanish Republican Insurgency	1944–52	Government
Chinese Civil War	1945–49	Insurgents
Indochina War	1945–54	Insurgents
Iranian Communist Uprising	1945–46	Government
Philippine Huk War	1946–54	Government
Madagascan Nationalist Revolt	1947–49	Government
Korean Partisan War	1948–53	Government
Malayan Emergency	1948–60	Government
Kenyan Mau-Mau Rebellion	1952–55	Government
Cuban Revolution	1956–58	Insurgents
Sarawak/Sabah "Confrontation"	1960–66	Government

Key: The table lists Communist—or apparent Communist—insurgencies only. In the same period there were also several clearly non-Communist or even anti-Communist insurgencies (e.g., the Ukrainian National Army insurgency of 1942–53). It omits the Communist-supported partisan campaigns in Russia, Yugoslavia, and Italy during World War II and insurgencies that were still in progress as of 1965 (e.g., in Portugal's African colonies, which began in 1960–62 and ended with their independence in the mid-1970s.

Advisory (March 1962–March 1965). Year by year during this period, the United States increased the number of advisory troops in Vietnam. In addition, there was a growing number of support troops for the officers and NCOs providing training and technical assistance to the South Vietnamese armed forces. In 1962, U.S. pilots began operating helicopters in Vietnam, and later that year they were allowed to open fire first (instead of waiting until attacked). In 1963, United States' efforts to help the South Vietnamese fight against the Communists were sidetracked by a virtual civil war in South Vietnam between the Roman Catholic leadership and Buddhist groups. This led to the overthrow of the South Vietnamese leader Diem (with the United States' assent). Taking advantage of this, the Viet Cong increased their attacks and the North Vietnamese sent many more guns and troops south. By August of 1964, the U.S. Congress passed the Gulf of Tonkin resolution, which gave the president all the power he needed to send an American army to South Vietnam.

The United States also got many of its Asian allies to contribute to this effort. By the end of 1964, there were 23,310 American, 200 Australian, 200 Korean, 30 New Zealand, and 20 Filipino advisers in South Vietnam.

But it wasn't working out as expected. The North Vietnamese were sending more and more troops, political "cadres," and weapons south, and the Viet Cong were taking control of larger chunks of South Vietnam each month. The South Vietnamese armed forces were not able to cope. Beginning in the summer of 1964, American military force was used against North Vietnamese aggression in South Vietnam. Until 1965, the bulk of the fighting had been done by the South Vietnamese army and they were losing. Initially, the American contribution was air strikes and gunfire from ships offshore. Ground combat for Americans would come later in 1965. Meanwhile, in early 1965, the situation in South Vietnam became more critical. Viet Cong attacks against Americans increased, including a bombing of the U.S. Embassy. The massive U.S. air raids against North Vietnam were not having the desired effect and it was obvious that either many American ground troops would have to get involved or South Vietnam would fall to the Communists.

Defense (April to December 1965). In April, a Logistical Command Headquarters was set up to control the coming flood of men and equipment needed to fight a major war in South Vietnam. At the same time, America continued to try diplomacy. North Vietnam was offered a billion dollars in economic aid if they would cease their military operations in the South. The Communists refused the offer, and any others that would halt their campaign to take over the South. About the same time, the first major antiwar demonstration took place in Washington, D.C.

American combat units began to show up in Vietnam. In March, the 173rd Airborne Brigade and 9th Marine Amphibious Brigade arrived. That same month, the U.S. Navy began to shut down the North Vietnamese coastal shipping operation that had been going on for some ten years. The South Vietnamese had done some damage to this Communist shipping, but with the larger U.S. naval resources, the Communist shipping was reduced to a trickle. In June, an Australian infantry battalion arrived, as did the first South Korean units. The U.S. Air Force began using B-52s for bombing targets in South Vietnam. Throughout the summer, more U.S. troops began to arrive, including the 1st Cavalry Division and its hundreds of helicopters.

But there were only twenty-two U.S. infantry battalions in the country by the end of 1965, and the Viet Cong and North Vietnamese were ready to fight it out. Two campaigns were fought that year. The marines up north conducted Operation Starlight for four days in August. The marines killed over seven hundred Communist troops and earned a little respect from their opponents. Later that year, the 1st Cavalry Division, an airmobile unit, assisted South Vietnamese units in Pleiku Province to defeat more than a division of Communist troops. This resulted in nearly two thousand dead North Vietnamese and a particularly bloody battle in the Ia Drang valley. This campaign lasted twenty-nine days and also made the Communists aware that the Americans did not fight like the French or the South Vietnamese. While this was considered a defensive phase of the war, these two campaigns demonstrated to the Communists that American troops would fight and fight aggressively. In an ominous sign to the young men of America, by the end of 1965, twice as many of them were being drafted as at the beginning of the year. This had something to do with the increase in antiwar activity by the end of the year. By Christmas, the United States halted the bombing campaign against North Vietnam, but this was not reciprocated

Attempts to get peace talks going went nowhere, with North Vietnam insisting that any such talks be on their terms or not at all. The year ended with 185,000 American troops in Vietnam and the fighting increasing.

Counteroffensive (January to June 1966). In January, the 1st Marine Division arrived. More troops arrived throughout the year, many to fill out divisions that had begun arriving piecemeal in 1965. The ground fighting increased throughout the year, as U.S. and South Vietnamese forces went after areas that had become Viet Cong strongholds.

During this period, the largest operation was Masher, where the 1st Cavalry Division, plus Korean and South Vietnamese units, spent forty-two days fighting Communist troops in Binh Dinh Province. Toward the end, there was a link up with U.S. Marines nearby. The enemy suffered over six thousand casualties. This campaign convinced the Communists that there was nothing to be gained by fighting head-to-head battles with the Americans.

President Johnson was being dragged into a war he did not want. Fearful of losing support for his domestic programs by appearing "soft on Communist aggression," he went to the United Nations seeking either UN support (as was the case in Korea) or UN pressure to get the North Vietnamese to negotiate. Neither ploy worked. The North Vietnamese blocked every effort to start negotiations and mustered enough support from its Communist allies to prevent any UN involvement. Johnson was warned that a major war in Vietnam would take money away from domestic programs. At this point, Americans were behind the war effort and attempts to repeal the Gulf of Tonkin resolution were defeated. A new GI Bill for Vietnam veterans was passed. But the antiwar movement was getting stronger and Johnson could see that he had only a year or two to resolve the Vietnam situation before public support turned against the war. To this end, Johnson ordered more use of bombing, especially in North Vietnam.

South Vietnam went through a civil war of its own in 1966, with a non-Communist insurrection in Danang put down by South Vietnamese troops. The largely Catholic leadership of South Vietnam was locked in a struggle with many politically active Buddhists. Most Vietnamese were Buddhists. Throughout 1966, the United States put pressure on South Vietnam to clean up the corruption in their government.

Counteroffensive Phase II (July 1966 to May 1967). The tempo of American offensive operations picked up. U.S. divisions were now often in constant action. The Communists were less and less willing to stand and fight. By avoiding contact, the Communist troops had to give up ground. It appeared that American tactics were winning.

In September 1966, the United States began using defoliants (Agent Orange and the like). In October, President Johnson visited South Vietnam and offered to withdraw U.S. troops in six months if North Vietnam stopped fighting. The Communists declined the offer.

By the end of 1966, the United States had 385,000 troops in South Vietnam.

In early 1967, Johnson ended many draft deferments and introduced a lottery for the draft to make it more equitable. But the antiwar sentiment grew, and the U.S. commander in Vietnam claimed that the antiwar activity was hurting the U.S. war effort.

The bombing of North Vietnam became more intense, and U.S. troops moved into the DMZ (demilitarized zone) between North and South Vietnam.

Counteroffensive Phase III (June 1967 to January 1968). By the end of 1967, there were nearly half a million U.S. troops in Vietnam. There were seventy-two infantry battalions, eleven armor battalions, and fifty-nine artillery battalions. The Viet Cong were steadily losing control of more and more of the population, while North Vietnamese combat units, under heavy pressure from American troops, were often forced to retreat into Laos or Cambodia to rebuild.

But back in the United States, antiwar sentiment grew, with surveys showing (by the end of 1967) that a majority of Americans did not approve of the way the war was being conducted. Some Americans were wholly opposed to the war, but most thought the United States should either make an all-out effort to win, or just go home. This showed in Congress during the summer of 1967 when Johnson proposed a 10-percent tax surcharge to pay for the war and ran into much resistance. By the end of the year, Johnson offered to stop the bombing of North Vietnam if the Communists would join peace negotiations. The Communists declined the offer.

By the end of 1967, Cambodia gave the United States permission to enter Cambodia and attack Communist bases there.

In January 1968, the Communist siege of Khe Shan began. Four months earlier the base had been established as part of an effort to cut the Ho Chi Minh Trail. U.S. commanders saw this attack as a desperate Communist attempt to achieve a decisive victory. American government spokesmen proclaimed that the end was in sight and that the Communists were just about beaten. Sen. Eugene McCarthy declared he would run for U.S. president and if elected would get Americans out of Vietnam.

South Vietnam elected a new president, who promised an end to corruption and many reforms.

Tet Counteroffensive (February to April 1968). The Communists read the situation differently. Although they were taking a beating out in the bush, all this fighting was sending hundreds of thousands of refugees fleeing for the cities. It wasn't safe out in the countryside with all those "search and destroy" operations. And the Americans provided free food in the cities. But the Viet Cong provided political cadres who preached armed resistance against the Americans and their South Vietnamese "puppets." The Communists thought all this strife and preaching was having the desired effect and that a major attack on South Vietnam's cities would enable the people to join the Viet Cong fighters and win the war in one dramatic uprising (a bit of Marxist "popular uprising" romanticism there). It didn't work out that way. The offensive began at the end of January 1968, during a truce for the Lunar New Year. The people didn't join in and the Americans and South Vietnamese troops were a lot more effective fighting inside the cities than the Communists expected. The Viet Cong suffered a major defeat, losing most of their more experienced combat leaders. The North Vietnamese units that joined in the fighting in northern South Vietnam fared no better. However, the offensive became a major propaganda "victory" for the Communists, because American political leaders had been pronouncing the Communists "on the run" and the "war almost over." Actually the Tet Offensive was a desperate attempt by the Communists to reverse their sinking fortunes, and it failed. For the next two years the Communists laid low and rebuilt their combat capability.

Meanwhile, the American people were demanding that the United States get out of Vietnam. In February of 1968, Richard Nixon announced he was running for president. The next month, Johnson had Robert McNamara replaced as secretary of defense and a few weeks later announced he was not running for reelection. In April, North Vietnam agreed to begin peace talks in Paris. About the same time, the siege of Khe Shan ended (with a thousand American dead, two thousand South Vietnamese dead, and nearly forty thousand North Vietnamese dead). At the end of April, VP Hubert Humphrey announced he would run for president.

Although the North Vietnamese had lost the Tet and Khe Shan campaigns in a military sense, they had won on the diplomatic front and had shaken American domestic politics up in ways that still reverberate today.

Counteroffensive Phase IV (May to June 1968). After Tet, U.S. military forces rushed to take advantage of the enormous Communist losses. This was largely unnoticed back home, where Richard Nixon was pledging that as president he would get America out of the war. The North Vietnamese

Casualties in the Tet Offensive

	Killed	Wounded	Miss/PW	Total
RVN	4,954	15,097	926	20,977
US & Allies	4,124	19,285	604	24,013
NVA & VC	58,000	80,000	9,461	144,461
Civilian	14,300	24,000	0	38,300
Total	81,378	138,382	10,991	230,751

Key: Figures do not include refugees. In the Hue area alone c. 90,000 people became refugees.

noticed how enthusiastically this pledge was received by Americans and also ignored their continuing losses in South Vietnam.

On May 12, the Paris Peace Talks began. On June 6, Robert Kennedy, also a candidate for president, was assassinated. This made it all the more likely that Nixon would be elected.

Counteroffensive Phase V (July to November 1968). In this period most of the fireworks occurred in the American presidential campaign. In August, the Democratic Convention was in chaos as antiwar demonstrations turned into riots. Humphrey was nominated as the party candidate for president, but he was off to a bad start. The Paris Peace Talks were also off to a bad start, with the North Vietnamese demanding that the Viet Cong be included in the talks. In October, President Johnson halted the bombing of North Vietnam in order to move the Paris Peace Talks along. It didn't help much, as the North Vietnamese saw this as a sign of American weakness. South Vietnam refused to get involved in the Paris Peace Talks, for they could see that the talks were mainly a face-saving way for the Americans to get out of Vietnam. In November, Richard Nixon was elected president on the issue of getting America out of Vietnam.

Counteroffensive Phase VI (December 1968 to February 1969). During the summer, Creighton Abrams had taken over as U.S. commander in South Vietnam, and he had a different approach to defeating the Communists. Abrams believed the Communists in South Vietnam were now weak enough that their political organization could be attacked. Abrams was right, and for the rest of the war, North Vietnam relied more and more on its regular armed forces to keep the fight going. By the end of 1969, there were 536,000 U.S. troops in Vietnam.

But the knowledge that the new president had given up on winning in Vietnam had had a demoralizing effect on U.S. troops. Morale and discipline, hitherto good, began to decline and, for American troops, the ugliest period of the war commenced. Fueling this malaise was the word from Paris, where it was agreed that South Vietnam and the Viet Cong would both join the talks.

Tet 69 Counteroffensive (March to June 1969). The North Vietnamese tried yet another Tet (Vietnamese New Year) Offensive, and this one was crushed more handily than the previous one. As a consequence of that, and the continued bombing of North Vietnam, on 20 May 1969, the Paris Peace Talks officially began. Meanwhile, in March, President Nixon ordered a se-cret bombing of North Vietnamese bases in Cambodia. The North Vietnam-ese weren't supposed to be there, so they could not publicly protest. These bases, via Russian ships and Cambodian ports, supported several divisions of North Vietnamese troops operating in the vicinity of Saigon. Cambodia was officially neutral, but looked the other way in return for bribes and help in keeping the local Communists under control. At the same time, the United States began to use the term "Vietnamization" to describe how U.S. troops would leave and have their work taken over by South Vietnamese forces. Few in Vietnam expected this to work, but it was the official U.S. policy and popular with American troops and voters. Nixon felt that by more vigorously attacking North Vietnamese supply lines in Laos and Cambodia, plus beefing up the South Vietnamese armed forces, America could get out of Vietnam without the Communists taking over the entire country. It was a long shot, but given the mood of the American public it was the best that could be done for the South Vietnamese.

Summer–Fall 1969 (July to October 1969). The name (Summer–Fall 1969) given to this "campaign" says it all. Offensive action by U.S. troops was being scaled back in preparation for the departure of all American troops over the next three years. In July, President Nixon announced the first troop withdrawals (25,000 men) from South Vietnam. In August, discussions be-gan between the United States and North Vietnam on the subject of secret peace negotiations in Paris. The public negotiations were going nowhere, partly because South Vietnam saw itself being sold out for the benefit of domestic politics in the United States, and partly because the talks had be-come a major media event more than anything else. On September 3, Ho Chi Minh died.

Winter–Spring 1970 (November 1969 to April 1970). In November, a quarter million antiwar protestors went to Washington, D.C. On the day after this, the word got out about the My Lai Massacre (which took place the year before). An even larger demonstration was held in April. By the end of 1969, American troop strength in Vietnam had been reduced by 60,000. In February 1970, the secret Paris peace talks got going on a regular basis. In March, the marines sent home one regiment. In April, the army sent home its 1st Infantry Division. At the end of April, South Vietnamese and American troops invaded Cambodia in order to finish off North Vietnamese bases there.

Sanctuary Counteroffensive (May to June 1970). The major operation in this period was the fighting in Cambodia, which went on until the end of June. In May, there was another large antiwar demonstration in Washington, and this time President Nixon wandered out into the crowd and talked to some of the protesters. Also in May, an antiwar demonstration at Kent State University in Ohio saw four students shot dead by National Guard troops. Later that month, Nixon found Congress up in arms over his Cambodia operation and voting against it. In June, the Senate repealed the Gulf of Tonkin Resolution of 1964, which had given the president the go-ahead to move troops to Vietnam. At the end of June, Congress passed a resolution forbidding any more operations in Cambodia.

Counteroffensive Phase VII (July 1970 to June 1971). While there was still quite a bit of fighting during this period, the main emphasis was on getting U.S. troops out of Vietnam. By the end of 1970, the army's 4th Infantry Division went home. In early 1971, the 5th Special Forces Group left, as did the 11th Armored Cavalry Regiment, the 1st Marine Division, and the 1st Cavalry Division. By the end of 1970, there were only 334,000 U.S. troops left in South Vietnam.

Congress continued to push through laws limiting presidential war-making powers. Public opinion was pretty clear: the people wanted U.S. troops out of Vietnam and as soon as possible.

But Nixon still wanted to do something to hurt North Vietnamese military power in the South. So in February 1971, ARVN forces invaded Laos to get at the North Vietnamese supply bases there. This attack was not as successful as the one into Cambodia. The lack of U.S. troops and stiffer Communist resistance turned it into a defeat for the South Vietnamese. In May, there was another major antiwar rally in Washington; and in June, the Pentagon Papers (secret U.S. government reports about the Vietnam War) were released. The government tried to stop the publication of these documents; but in July, the Supreme Court allowed publication to proceed.

Consolidation I (July to November 1971). This was the period when major portions of the U.S. war effort in Vietnam were turned over to the South Vietnamese. In July, the DMZ area, the scene of about half the fighting by U.S. forces, was turned over to the South Vietnamese. In August, the

United States allowed Communist China to be admitted to the United Nations. By opening a diplomatic dialogue with the Communist Chinese, the United States was gaining some leverage in the Paris Peace Talks. In November, U.S. forces went on the defensive, leaving all offensive operations up to the South Vietnam.

Consolidation II (December 1971 to March 1972). In December, the bombing of North Vietnam was resumed as a way to move the Paris Peace Talks along. By the end of 1971, most U.S. troops had departed. In January 1972, the secret peace talks in Paris were revealed. In February, Nixon went to Peking, establishing formal diplomatic relations with Communist China, and putting more pressure on the North Vietnamese. Despite this, in March the Paris Peace Talks stalled, and the United States resolved to use more muscle. But the North Vietnamese moved first, launching an invasion of South Vietnam.

Cease-Fire (April 1972 to January 1973). The North Vietnamese invasion of South Vietnam (the "Easter Offensive") was turned back with the aid of massive U.S. airpower and, to everyone's surprise, robust fighting by South Vietnamese forces. In April, B-52 bombing missions into North Vietnam increased, and this forced the North Vietnamese back to the Paris Peace Talks within eleven days. In May, an even more intensive bombing campaign of North Vietnam began, including the mining of North Vietnamese ports. In early May, the Paris Peace Talks stopped again. By July 13, they resumed. Henry Kissinger, Nixon's key diplomatic adviser in dealings with Vietnam and Communist China, announced in October that peace was at hand in Vietnam. The following month, Nixon was reelected president. In December, it appeared that the Paris Peace Talks were not going all that well, and Nixon ordered a resumption of bombing in North Vietnam. By the end of 1972, there were only 24,200 U.S. troops in South Vietnam.

In January, there was some last-minute arm-twisting with the South Vietnamese. At one Point Nixon stopped all U.S. air support in South Vietnam and threatened to cut aid as well. On January 23, an agreement was reached, and on January 27 the cease-fire began. Thus ended the U.S. Army campaigns in Vietnam.

But the story does not end there. On February 21, a peace agreement was signed in Laos.

In March, U.S. prisoners of war were released. By the end of 1973, the U.S. Congress ordered a halt to bombing in South Vietnam and forbade spending any more money on Vietnam, which severely limited the military capability of the South Vietnamese armed forces. Congress also passed the War Powers Act, which limits the president's ability to engage in military activities without congressional approval.

In early 1974, the fighting resumed in South Vietnam. In August, President Nixon was forced to resign because of illegal political campaign activities and attempts to cover up same. The vice president, Gerald Ford, became president, and in September offered clemency to Vietnam War draft dodgers and deserters. Congress cut economic aid to South Vietnam.

In January 1975, the North Vietnamese launched another invasion of South Vietnam. This time there was no American air support and much less United States support of any kind. By March, the South Vietnamese had abandoned the central highlands and shortly thereafter the North Vietnamese took Hue and Danang. In April, the U.S. Congress rejected a presidential request for more aid to South Vietnam. By the end of April, sixteen North Vietnamese divisions were approaching Saigon, and on May 1 the city fell.

The forty-year Vietnam War was finally over.

A STRATEGY OF UNCERTAINTY

American military strategists never figured out what was the "best" way to fight the war in Vietnam. This was a logical consequence of the fact that the political leadership never quite explained what the nation's strategic objectives were. Ostensibly, U.S. troops were in Vietnam to "help" the "freedom-loving" South Vietnamese defeat a foreign-sponsored Communist insurgency. This was supposed to save all of Southeast Asia from becoming Communist.

In pursuit of this ill-defined objective, senior American commanders considered a number of different approaches to fighting the war and actually adopted several, none of which worked very well.

Advisory. This was the initial approach, adopted long before the large-scale commitment of U.S. ground forces, and it continued despite whatever other strategies were adopted. The idea was that U.S. personnel would help the Vietnamese learn to do better militarily. This meant going out in the field with South Vietnamese units. The flaw was that South Vietnamese commanders didn't have to listen to their advisers. And there wasn't much the adviser could do about it. It's worth recalling that even after more than a decade of guidance some Vietnamese units never quite got it together. Part of this was due to cultural differences that American advisers never bridged. A larger problem was the culture of corruption in the South Vietnamese government, and apparently endemic in Vietnamese culture as a whole, since there seems to have been considerable—if less obvious—corruption in North Vietnam as well. Even though there was a war going on, many South Vietnamese officers saw their job as an opportunity to steal. And many were too busy stealing to bother with military matters. The tragedy of this is that many, if not the majority, of South Vietnamese officers did know what was at stake, were honest (at least by Vietnamese standards), and strove to do their best. Many were exceptional military leaders, but these officers never took over the senior command.

Graduated Response. Perhaps the most ill-conceived strategy of the war, this one was based on the assumption that if you hurt the North Vietnamese a little at a time they would eventually come around and negotiate. It didn't the work that way. The North Vietnamese took the incremental use of force as a sign of timidity. To make matters worse, the frequent American use of bombing halts and cease-fires was seen by the Communists as a sign of weakness to be exploited. The graduated response strategy was more than some intellectual exercise that got made into policy; it was also an attempt to coax a reluctant American public into supporting the war. That didn't work either.

Attrition. This was the strategy that senior American military commanders believed would win the war: delivering repeated blows against the enemy until he quit from exhaustion. All else was to be subordinated to this. The primary objective was to kill the enemy, and by 1967, more than 80 percent of U.S. forces were being employed offensively. Unfortunately, the strategy was flawed on several levels. To kill the enemy one had to find him; and after their initial experience with American firepower, the VC and the NVA both proved quite elusive. This led to things like "search and destroy" missions and "free-fire zones," not to mention the infamous "body counts." Of course the enemy did bleed, suffering enormous losses, disproportionate to those of the United States and South Vietnam. But they were much more willing to lose lives, and measured victory not in terms of bodies but in terms of political support. Ultimately, a strategy of attrition was the worst policy the United States could have adopted.

Counterinsurgency. This was also an ongoing strategy. The idea was to undertake political, economic, and social initiatives in order to "win the minds and hearts of the people." An enormous amount of effort was put into counterinsurgency. Thousands of U.S. technical specialists (physicians and other medical personnel, agronomists, engineers, public officials, and so forth) went to South Vietnam and spread out over the country to open clinics, undertake development projects, and so forth. As part of this effort, the CIA and other agencies undertook psychological warfare operations to sway the opinions of the local people, and special warfare experts tried to develop local defense units, such as the Popular Forces, to protect the rural populace from the enemy. And, on the darker side, programs such as Phoenix took a more direct approach at rooting out enemy cadres, with tens of thousands of casualties as Phoenix assassination teams went after Communist officials.

There were several flaws in the strategy of counterinsurgency. Perhaps the principal one was that in most cases the "minds and hearts of the people" were too firmly committed to the Viet Cong to be shaken, even by the Phoenix Program, which was never as ruthless as the Communist terror it was designed to counter. In addition, the senior commanders who were supposed to oversee the program were much more interested in a battlefield victory than in a political one. They even neglected the protection of the rural populace, despite the fact that the Popular Forces were taking most of ARVN's casualties and inflicting more than their share of casualties on the enemy. As a result, although a great deal of money was spent on rural development, pacification, and all the other facets of a counterinsurgency strategy, the amount spent never approached outlays for conventional operations. In fact, Congress frequently turned down relatively modest appropriations for development funds for Vietnam, such as a proposal made in 1970 to spend $100 million. This was in marked contrast to spending patterns during several earlier successful counterinsurgency operations against Communist insurgents. In Greece, the Philippines, and Malaya, for example, outlays for economic and political development exceeded military expenditures. Nevertheless, Americans are only now discovering that their wartime economic aid built a large amount of good will in South Vietnam. Current American visitors to Vietnam find the people in the North eager to do business with Americans, while those in the South are also nostalgic for the "good old days" of American aid.

Enclave. When large numbers of U.S. ground forces were first committed to South Vietnam this was the strategy that they were sent to implement. The idea was that the Americans would establish base areas along the coast from which they could support the South Vietnamese, who would do most of the work in the field. Unfortunately, although endorsed by such distinguished senior officers as Maxwell Taylor, then serving as the ambassador to South Vietnam, James Gavin, and Harold K. Johnson, chief of staff of the army, the strategy ran up against the institutional culture in the armed forces. The "enclave strategy" was too passive. GEN William Westmoreland, commander in Vietnam, and GEN Earle Wheeler, chairman of the Joint Chiefs, both objected that "no one ever won a battle sitting on his ass." As a result, the enclave strategy was soon abandoned. Nevertheless, it did have its champions, who continued to argue its merits, finally more or less winning the argument with the adoption of Vietnamization, which essentially returned the United States to an enclave strategy.

Ink Blot. This was advocated by several marines and some army officers, who had studied the history of counterinsurgency warfare. The "ink blot" strategy is essentially a variant of the enclave strategy. Begin by establishing firmly controlled and secure base areas. Then extend the perimeters of these areas. As the perimeter advances, you clear the enemy out, conduct rural development programs and intensive political indoctrination projects, and build up your base. A slow but, to some minds, surer way of gaining control of a territory than trying to take it all at once. This was a classic technique employed in colonial warfare by the French and others in the nineteenth century, and it had certainly worked. Whether it would have worked in Vietnam is moot because the American people had little patience in these matters.

Take the War North. This was one proposal made early and often by senior U.S. commanders, an invasion of North Vietnam, to "bring the war" home to Ho and the other Communist leaders. It would be a conventional war, one in which America's enormous firepower would tell. The enemy would be smashed quickly, and the insurgency in the South would collapse for want of support from the North. However, they could never convince the nation's political leadership to adopt this policy, which still finds support among some commentators on the war.

In fact, an invasion of the North was a seriously flawed concept. The assumption that an American victory was a foregone conclusion ignores the ferocity and tenacity which North Vietnamese troops had already displayed in the South. Even if the regular North Vietnamese forces collapsed early under a storm of American firepower, the enemy would have fled back into the jungles and swamps and the United States would have been left with an enormous occupation problem. Moreover, such an undertaking would have required full mobilization of the National Guard and reserves. And despite tensions within the Communist community, it would almost certainly have provoked a Chinese response and, possibly, a Soviet one as well. And then there is the historical angle. The Vietnamese, especially those in the North, had long been known as ferocious fighters. It was North Vietnamese soldiers who had defeated the Chinese in many wars, and the Vietnamese were one of the few peoples to defeat the Mongols when those formidable warriors were at the peak of their power.

Cut the Ho Chi Minh Trail. GEN William Westmoreland wanted to do this very early in the war. He proposed a massive invasion of Laos, from South Vietnam and Thailand (using Thai and American troops.) The troops would remain to prevent easy access to South Vietnam by Communist troops and supplies from the north. This might have worked, given the enormous effectiveness of American troops in conventional warfare. But the operation would have required an enormous number of troops. Moreover, as Laos was officially "neutral," by a 1962 U.N. agreement brokered by the U.S. and U.S.S.R., the political fallout would have been considerable.

In the Bush (Ground Combat)

The most riveting images of Vietnam are those of U.S. troops—whether army or marine—in the rural areas of the country, searching for and fighting an elusive foe. While only a small percentage of Americans in Vietnam operated in the bush, it was the ground combat that provided the most vivid images of the war for the folks back home and the troops involved.

FIRST IMPRESSIONS

Most soldiers first saw Vietnam as they got off a jet airliner in one of the large airports that buzzed with military and commercial aircraft round the clock. Heat was the first thing soldiers arriving in South Vietnam felt, a lot of heat, and a lot of humidity too. North Vietnam is the same latitude as southern Florida; South Vietnam is closer to the equator. Coming off an air-conditioned commercial passenger plane, the most common form of travel, you climbed down the stairs from the plane into a well of heat.

When entire units were shipped over to Vietnam, the equipment went by ship, and sometimes the troops did too. While a three-week cruise across the Pacific on a troopship might not seem like an ideal way to spend your time, it did allow young men not accustomed to the tropics to ease their way into it—at least the heat and humidity part.

Right after the heat came the smells. American noses had never been assailed by the kind of olfactory assault Vietnam presented. First of all, it was a tropical country, so a lot more things were growing, and rotting. But Vietnam was a preindustrial intensive farming culture that used human and animal excrement to fertilize the fields. There were a lot of farm animals about, none of whom used a deodorant. Vietnamese food was spicy and used many ingredients pungent to the nose, as well as the tongue.

Then came the sounds. Fewer machines and more people, and the people were often louder than folks back home, and they spoke an alien tongue. Vietnamese was different than Chinese, and much different from English.

The people, the architecture, and the landscape were different. Many American soldiers had been to big city "Chinatowns" and occasionally walked down streets where whites were the minority. But except in a few neighborhoods, the majority of people you saw on the streets were Vietnamese, and Americans new to Vietnam quickly realized, with their eyes if not their ears, that the Vietnamese were different than the Chinese or any other Asian ethnic group. After a few weeks, an observant GI in Saigon could walk down the street and tell who was Vietnamese, Chinese, Cambodian, Montagnard, Thai, and so on. Special Forces troopers out in the bush quickly discovered the differences between the many Montagnard tribes and other ethnic groups.

But the newly arrived American soldiers were not in Vietnam as tourists, but for the more somber business of killing and avoiding same. Some 80 percent of the American soldiers went off to jobs that offered more exotic experiences, but not much exposure to death or mutilation. The other 20 percent went off to the bush to join a combat unit, usually an infantry unit, and confront some rather more frightening first impressions.

The combat soldier got a second set of vivid impressions when he arrived, by truck or helicopter, at his unit. Combat units were usually out in the bush, living part of the time in scruffy base camps, the rest in the bush, playing grab ass with Mister Charlie (the Viet Cong or North Vietnamese). Getting to their base camp, within a few days of arriving in Vietnam, brought more shocks, this time from Americans, Americans living and fighting in the bush. You could instantly tell who had been "out there" mixing it up with the enemy. The bush soldiers had a tan, and a look. Not just the "thousand-yard stare" that many twentieth-century warriors developed, but a wary glance. Always looking for a hidden enemy, or a booby trap.

Everything seemed so different. And it was. Soon, the new arrival would be different too. Or dead.

THE NATURE OF COMBAT

One of the more interesting studies undertaken by the army's "bean counters" during the Vietnam War was an analysis of the ways in which combat occurred. As early as 1966, they began to notice that most engagements were being initiated by the enemy.

As can be seen in the table on page 61, American forces were on the offensive (attacking) in only about a third of their engagements, while more than half the time they were at the receiving end of the enemy's attentions. So much for seeking out and destroying the enemy.

An ambush is a surprise attack on someone who is moving at the time. Ambushes accounted for nearly a third of all American engagements in Vietnam, a much higher proportion than in previous wars. And the enemy did most of the ambushing, nearly three times as many as American forces were able to execute, a tribute to the VC/NVA skill at moving around in the bush. In contrast, the more traditional assault on a fixed position, the most com-

The Pattern and Character of American Engagements in Vietnam

Type of Action	Frequency	U.S. Troops Reaction
Ambush by Enemy Forces	23.3%	Defensive
Ambush of Enemy Forces	8.7%	Offensive
Attack on Enemy Position	17.9%	Offensive
Deliberate	(5.4%)	
Spontaneous	(12.5%)	
Defense of Position	30.4%	Defensive
"Hot" Landing Zone	12.5%	Defensive/Offensive
Meeting Engagement	7.1%	Mutually Offensive

mon form of combat in previous wars, accounted for less than half of all engagements; yet here again the enemy was more active than American forces, nearly twice as much. A "deliberate" attack on an enemy position is one where you know in advance the location of the enemy, while a "spontaneous" attack was the sort that occurred when troops out patrolling detected an enemy position and engaged it. A "hot" landing zone was a peculiar development of the Vietnam War. It occurred when troops being landed by helicopter were suddenly taken under enemy fire. Thus it was both offensive and defensive: getting the troops on the ground was offensive, protecting them while doing so was defensive. A "Meeting Engagement" is an action that results when two opposing forces on the move run into each other.

Almost all of the American casualties took place in a small portion of Vietnam. Two locations actually. One was up north near the DMZ. The other was way down south around Saigon and in the nearby Mekong River Delta. The rest of Vietnam was the scene of action from time to time, but was generally peaceful compared to the two major battlefronts.

AIR ASSAULT

Vietnam saw the first use of air assault forces in war. Air assault was a new idea, filling a niche between airborne (parachuting out of aircraft) and airmobile (being transported to a combat zone by aircraft) forces.

Airborne forces were first used in combat by the Germans in 1940. The use of parachutes to insert troops into combat proved very successful. It was also very expensive in money and manpower. In fact, the cost of capturing Crete by airborne forces in 1941 was so high the Germans virtually abandoned the concept. But the Allies picked it up and used it with mixed effectiveness on several occasions. Only twice were they of decisive value, at Salerno in 1943 (when several battalions of airborne troops were dropped onto the beleaguered beaches to prevent the Germans from overrunning them) and particularly at Normandy in 1944 (when three airborne divisions facilitated the forcible entry of Allied troops into Europe). But the cost had remained high.

Airmobile forces are somewhat different. They are troops organized, equipped, and trained to be transported by air, to land under fire, and to immediately go into combat. The Germans had also pioneered this technique and used an airmobile division along with airborne forces in the invasion of Crete in 1941. But it proved so expensive in men and equipment, especially transport aircraft shot down while landing under fire, that the technique was discredited. Air assault revived the concept of airmobile forces, but substituted helicopters for fixed-wing airplanes. Helicopters allowed for a much greater number of potential landing sites and could also be used to scout LZs (landing zones) selected. As a result, only about 10 percent of the LZs used turned out to be "hot" (occupied by well-hidden enemy troops who could fire at the helicopters). Even a hot LZ was not a disaster, because helicopters were mobile enough to quickly back off from such enemy fire.

In the late 1950s, the American army received its first UH-1 (Huey) transport helicopters. The UH-1 was the first really effective combat helicopter, having sufficient capacity (ten troops) and range (over a hundred miles) to be useful on the battlefield. Over the next few years, many experiments were conducted on how to best use the UH-1 on the battlefield. The Marine Corps was quite enthusiastic about this idea. In fact, they had experimentally used the technique in Korea with some success, with older and less efficient helicopters. The marines saw air assault as a way to add additional effectiveness to their amphibious capabilities. Some army officers came up with this idea too. In the early 1960s, they managed to get the ear of Secretary of Defense Robert S. McNamara. Over the protests of the brass, who thought air assault would be too expensive and not very effective, McNamara authorized extensive testing of the concept (one of his better decisions). In 1963, the 11th Air Assault Division (actually a brigade) was created to continue these tests on a larger and more realistic scale. The tests proved successful, and even before the president decided to send combat troops to Southeast Asia, air assault forces seemed a natural for such duty, given that Vietnam was to be a rugged country, not suitable for America's many mechanized combat units. Helicopters would give U.S. troops a major, perhaps decisive, advantage.

Air assault did prove to be frightfully expensive. But primarily in terms of money, rather than lives. It also proved to be highly effective. Contrary to what one might think of the term "air assault," the helicopters were not usually used to carry troops right into battle. Helicopters provided quick transportation for infantry and artillery around the battlefield, especially over mountains and jungles. This came as a rude shock to the Communist troops, who had used their ability to tramp through the jungle to defeat the road-bound French in the 1946–53 phase of the war. But helicopters flew over the mountains and landed American troops in the middle of the jungle.

Communist bases deep in the back country were no longer safe. No matter how well hidden, the constant patrolling of helicopters all too often found signs of these bases and before long helicopters full of American or South Vietnamese troops landed nearby. Other helicopters provided machine-gun and rocket firepower, plus still more helicopters flying in artillery some miles off. Many troops joked about their "flying trucks" (helicopters) and they weren't far wrong. Just as motor vehicles had made it possible to move troops at unheard of speeds (twenty to thirty miles an hour) over roads earlier in the twentieth century, by the 1960s, helicopters were moving troops over anything at a hundred miles an hour. But the flying truck cost about ten times as much as the one with wheels and cost even more to maintain. One reason there were so many support troops in Vietnam, compared to guys carrying rifles, was because of the need for maintaining and repairing thousands of helicopters and other aircraft. Air mobility came at a high price.

TRASHING THE BATTLEFIELD

Even when encamped in fairly remote firebases or while patrolling in the bush, American troops maintained a rather high standard of living. And they generated a lot of trash. Of course, one man's trash is another man's treasure. What passed for garbage among Americans was often immensely valuable to some poverty-stricken Asians. Some things were obvious, like picking through leftover food for dinner or recovering metals for recycling. But there was more.

In Vietnam the enemy often made use of American trash. Things like broken boxes, old pallets, empty ration tins, and so forth, could be turned into raw materials. Lots of reparable items were often found, such as broken radios, damaged tools, worn clothing, and so forth, and the enemy seems to have had workshops devoted to repairing damaged items of this sort. American troops were often careless about policing up spent ammunition cases, which provided a useful supply of brass for the enemy. And sometimes "dud" ammunition was left behind, rather than being destroyed, to be recovered and repaired by the enemy. Worst of all, perhaps, was that Americans were often careless of paper.

It takes a lot of paper to run a modern army. Officially all paperwork likely to be of use to the enemy is supposed to be destroyed. But this was not always done efficiently. Things like preliminary drafts of reports or other official papers were sometimes not treated with the respect the final versions received.

So whenever they had the chance, the enemy pawed through American garbage.

This should have been something senior American commanders were aware of. After all, during the 1960s it was not unusual for U.S. warships making port calls in Hong Kong, Thailand, or some other Asian country, to trade the "rights" to their garbage to someone who agreed to paint the ship. In Vietnam some lower- and mid-level officers tried to convince their subordinates and their superiors of the importance of more efficient trash management, but they were not very successful. The troops were mostly worried about getting through the war alive, and the senior officers were perhaps looking at "the big picture" too much.

Only among the LRRPs did "garbage control" become a major issue. The LRRPs never left anything behind that could give the enemy a clue that American troops had been in the area. They took very careful pains to clean up all signs of their presence, calling it "sterilizing" an area.

ALLIED FORCES IN VIETNAM

Americans were not the only allies South Vietnam had during the war. Several other Asian and Pacific countries sent troops as well, some in quite substantial numbers. Since some of the Allied contingents—South Korean, Filipino, and Thai—were armed and subsidized by the United States, a cynical view might suggest that America was buying troops with which to fight the war, rather than use its own manpower. But all of these countries did have a very real concern about the possibility of a Communist victory in South Vietnam. South Korea had suffered an invasion from the Communist North in 1950, which led to three years of war, causing enormous casualties and material damage. For South Koreans, a Communist victory in Vietnam would strengthen the North Koreans. The Philippines had actually begun a military assistance program in Indochina in 1953, when the French were still in power, largely because they had themselves just broken the back of a major Communist insurgency, the "Huk" movement, that had begun in 1948. Thailand had a common frontier with Laos, which was certain to go Communist if South Vietnam succumbed.

Both New Zealand and Australia also provided troops, at their own expense, considering the threat to their security a serious one.

Considering their populations, the manpower contributions from Australia, Korea, and Thailand were quite substantial. In 1968, for example, Australia's contingent amounted to nearly 0.1 percent of the country's population, South Korea's to about 0.2 percent, and Thailand's to about 0.1 percent, at a time when the comparable figure for the United States was about 0.2 percent.

In addition to these contingents, small delegations of soldiers from a number of countries, particularly those having problems with Communists (e.g., Argentina, Nationalist China, and Spain), seem to have seen some service in Vietnam as observers and occasionally became involved in more than just observing.

There might have been other allies. With the gradual ebbing of the empire, in the mid-1960s Britain seriously considered disbanding its famed Gurkhas,

Allied Military Manpower in Vietnam

Country	1964	1965	1966	1967	1968	1969	1970	1971	1972
Australia	200	1,557	4,525	6,818	7,661	7,672	6,763	2,000	130
Korea	200	20,620	45,566	47,829	50,003	48,869	48,537	45,700	36,790
Thailand	0	16	244	2,205	6,005	11,568	11,586	5,700	200
New Zealand	30	119	155	534	516	552	441	100	50
Philippines	17	72	2,061	2,020	1,576	189	74	50	50
	447	22,352	52,531	59,406	65,761	68,850	67,401	53,550	37,220

Key: Only military personnel are included. These countries, and thirteen others (including Argentina, Britain, the Republic of China, Spain, West Germany, and Canada) also sent military or civilian technical advisers, medical personnel, and relief workers as well, and several countries permitted South Vietnamese military personnel to train with their own forces.

who constituted a substantial brigade of all arms. In October 1966, Westmoreland asked that a study be made of the possibility of hiring the entire Brigade of Gurkhas for service in Vietnam. The principal objection to the project was the traditional American aversion to mercenaries, so the proposal went little further than Westy's musings. And in any case, Britain decided to keep the Gurkhas around for a while longer. In addition, there might easily have been more Nationalist Chinese troops in Vietnam than the handful (c. twenty to thirty per year) who did serve as advisers. In 1964, the CIA proposed securing two or three Nationalist Chinese divisions for service in Vietnam. As this would have been politically disastrous (almost certainly provoking Communist Chinese intervention), the idea did not get very far.

Footnote: Canada, the Unknown Ally. One of the less well-known aspects of the Vietnam War is the large number of Canadians who served. Although precise figures are uncertain, apparently about 40,000 Canadians voluntarily enlisted in the U.S. armed forces during the Vietnam War. This was far more men than the number of deserters and draft dodgers who fled to Canada. An estimated 30,000 Canadians saw service in Vietnam, and some suffered the same problems postwar as did their American comrades. Not for many years was the service of Canadians in the war recognized, on either side of the border.

A PLAGUE OF RADIOS AND THE "FLYING CP"

Two developments, each separately important and useful innovations, had, in combination, a pernicious effect on the conduct of the war, leading to what became known as "micromanagement," the overcontrol, and occasionally remote control, of operations by senior personnel.

By the mid-1960s, the introduction of transistors and later semiconduc-

Communications Standards. 1945–70

Conflict	Level	Channels
World War II	Division	4
Korea	Division	8
Vietnam	Brigade	32

tors had so greatly reduced both the cost and the weight of radios that it led to a dramatic increase in communications capabilities at all levels.

There was a similar increase in communications links among lower formations. Every infantry platoon had a couple of radios, as did even LRRP patrols, with less than a dozen men. Unlike the experience in previous wars, patrols were never undertaken without radios, usually two. This explosion in communications capabilities at even the lowest levels was an important factor in the effectiveness of American troops. Within minutes of coming into contact with the enemy, the airwaves would begin to heat up as calls went out for air and artillery fire support, reinforcements, and medevac, while information was passed back and forth between the troops in the field and higher headquarters. This was all to the good. On more than one occasion radios proved the lifeline that saved beleaguered patrols, firebases, and downed pilots. But there was a down side to this facility with communications.

With so many radio links, senior officers began taking a greater role in small unit operations. This trend was worsened by the increasing use of helicopters as flying command posts. As the war went on, it became more and more common for commanders to take to the air in order to oversee operations. Sometimes this was to the good, as when a company or battalion commander overhead helped the men on the ground by coordinating the delivery of air and artillery support and the movement of relief forces and reinforcements. But this was not always the case. Often the man in the air understood the situation less well than the one on the ground, from whom he more or less wrested control. Moreover, the number of guys overhead sometimes multiplied, so that a lieutenant or platoon sergeant in a desperate fight found not only his company commander issuing instructions from on high but also his battalion commander, possibly even his brigade and perhaps his division commanders as well. In some extreme instances, it was even worse, with the links reaching even further upward, through the corps commander, on up to Westmoreland, and even into the White House itself. In short, there was sometimes too much communication, so that the man on the ground lost control of the fight as higher echelons got their two cents in. So while all those radios and helicopters were usually good for the troops, sometimes they also created some unique problems.

INFANTRY WEAPONS

The Vietnam War was an infantryman's war. Although the primary weapons of the infantry are the rifle and the machine gun, there are a number of others of considerable importance as well.

AntiTank Weapons. The use of antitank weapons in infantry combat was one of the more interesting tactical developments of the Vietnam War. There were very few tanks in Vietnam, and the introduction of A/T weapons was something of an accident. American forces were dispatched to Indochina on such short notice that there was no time to leave these seemingly useless devices behind. Since the troops had to lug them along, they began using them in ways for which they had not been intended. They soon proved extremely useful for "bunker busting" and house-to-house combat. Pretty soon everyone was doing it.

Mines and Booby Traps. Mines and booby traps were used extensively in Vietnam, by both sides. Some 7 percent—perhaps 11 percent, of U.S. casualties in the war were from mines (*not* 65 percent, as has been alleged by some antiland-mine activists), as were about 75 percent of tank and other armored vehicle losses. This was a much higher percentage than in previous American experience, since the introduction of mines in the Civil War. The United States, South Vietnamese, and Allied forces used

Infantry Rifles of the Vietnam War

Maker	*Model*	*Year*	*Caliber*	*Weight*	*Length*	*RPM*	*Magazine*	*Notes*
U.S.	M-1	1940	7.62 mm	9.55 lb.	41.0"	50	8	A
	M-14	1960	7.62 mm	8.55 lb.	44.0"	750	20	B
	M-16A1	1966	5.56 mm	7.71 lb.	39.0"	800	20–30	C
USSR	AK-47	1947	7.62 mm	9.48 lb.	34.6"	600	30	D

Key: The table includes only weapons in standard issue. Many specialized infantry rifles were also issued in limited numbers, such as sniper rifles, including the Winchester M-70 .30–06-cal. rifle originally introduced in the 1930s, and the new Remington M-40 7.62 mm. *Model* is the standard designation. As many of these weapons had a number of modifications, these could often get very complex (e.g., the M-14A1, which was a bipod-mounted, light machine-gun version of the standard M-14 rifle). *Year* is that of introduction. *Caliber,* the diameter of the bullet, given in millimeters. *Weight* is loaded, but without bayonet, which usually added a pound or so. *Length* is without bayonet; The M-7 bayonet for the M-16 had a 6.75-in. blade. *RPM,* or "rounds per minute," is the "cyclic rate of fire," which is actually rather theoretical (one does have to reload occasionally); the practical rate for the M-1 was about thirty to thirty-five rounds per minute, and the other weapons from a third to about half that shown. *Magazine* is the standard reloading "package"; some weapons had specially designed magazines that could greatly increase capacity. *Range* has not been given, as all of these weapons were lethal at a kilometer or two, and normally aimed fire could not be employed beyond about five hundred meters and rarely more than a hundred meters. *Notes* refer to the lettered comments below.

A. The standard American infantry weapon from 1942 to the early 1960s, the M-1 was the first semiautomatic (i.e., self-loading, but you still had to squeeze the trigger to fire) weapon to be generally issued by any armed force in the world. But it was heavy, and by the Korean War it was becoming obsolete. ARVN was issued many M-1s, which were even clumsier for the lighter built Vietnamese than for Americans.

B. Designed as a replacement for the M-1, the M-14 was a notable improvement in many ways. It had a selector switch to permit single shot as well as automatic fire. However, if was still rather heavy and had a tendency to overheat when firing on automatic. The United States procured c. 1.5 million of them by the end of 1964, at which point production was terminated. The first U.S. combat units in Vietnam were equipped with it. By 1967, it had been replaced by the M-16 in Vietnam, though it equipped units in Europe for a few years more.

C. The second version of the M-16 is shown. The original version was foisted on the armed forces by the Defense Department before it had been thoroughly field tested. The only way to tell if a piece of military equipment really works is to use it for years, unless you want to try it out in combat, which was done with the M-16. The initial model (1963) proved prone to fouling (dirt building up in the mechanism, making it likely to jam) and was difficult to clean. It also lacked a bolt-assist plunger (making it difficult to free a frozen bolt), and had a number of other problems, which caused many difficulties—and probably some casualties—in Vietnam. Most of these problems arose when army ordnance "experts" attempted to improve the original field-tested AR-15 design. The improvements were a disaster and when they were in turn fixed, the weapon's performance was excellent, making it one of the premier infantry rifles of the world. In addition to equipping U.S. troops, nearly one million M-16s were supplied to the South Vietnamese from 1967 onward.

D. The famous Kalishnikov rifle, produced in greater numbers than any infantry firearm ever (by the mid-1980s there were an estimated forty million in existence and it was still being manufactured). It was simple ("soldier proof") and effective. U.S. special warfare personnel often used the AK-47, and the United States even manufactured ammunition for it, a special type, without identifying markings.

Machine Guns of the Vietnam War

Maker	Model	Caliber	Weight	RPM	Feed	Notes
U.S.	M-60	7.62	24.2 lb.	200	100 belt	A
Soviet	PD	7.62	18.4	200	250 belt/pan	B

Key: Data is as on the preceding table. Not shown are various older machine guns that saw extensive use, such as the United States .50-cal. heavy machine gun, mounted on tanks, armored personnel carriers, and river and coastal craft, or the old .30-cal. Browning machine gun found on some riverine craft.

A. The standard U.S. machine gun since the early 1960s, the M-60, was used not only by the infantry but also on helicopters. It was easy to use, barrel change was quick, and it had few failings, though in the field troops did modify it by welding a piece of ration tin to allow easier entry of the ammo belt into the weapon.

B. Used extensively by the NVA and VC, the DP or RDP was a modification of a German World War II design (as, indeed, was the American M-60).

Principal AntiTank Weapons of the Vietnam War

Maker	Weapon	Weights			Speed	Range		Accuracy at		Notes
		Missile	Launcher			Min	Max	300m	500m	
U.S.	M-72 LAW	5.5 lbs	0	lbs	3.8 mph	5m	75m	50%	0%	A
U.S.	106 mm RR	37.0	460		11.3	10	1100	90	80	B
Soviet	RPG-7	5.0	15.4		7.5	5	500	80	30	C
Soviet	AT-3 Sagger	25.0	0		5.6	300	2000	0	80	D

Key: Most entries are self-evident. Under *Range, Min* is for minimum, *Max,* for maximum effective range. *Accuracy* is the percent probability of a hit at the indicated range. *Notes* refers to the lettered comments below.

A. The M-72 LAW (light antitank weapon) was a man portable device that eventually became standard issue for every grunt who had to go into the bush. It was not so hot as an A/T weapon, but was ideal for close infantry combat: light, very effective at short ranges, although it did have a back blast, so it could not be fired with friendly troops behind it.

B. The 106 mm was a recoilless rifle, a sort of bobtailed artillery piece. It had a powerful back blast and required a vehicle to move it (the Ontos fighting vehicle mounted six of them); its accuracy fell off markedly beyond a thousand meters. For close combat it was provided with a "beehive"-type round as well as armor-piercing types.

C. Termed the B-40 by U.S. forces, the RGP-2 and RPG-7 were essentially knock-offs of the old German *Panzerfaust* of World War II. Used widely by the VC and NVA for harassing attacks on firebases and other installations, and often in combat as well

D. The Sagger was a man portable A/T weapon, which was not particularly suited to infantry combat, having much too great a range. It began turning up in VC and NVA arsenals late in the war and saw considerable use against ARVN armor in the final two years.

mines primarily as a defensive weapon, to strengthen firebases, protect patrols on overnight bivouacs, and so forth. Use of booby traps by these forces was severely restricted. The NVA, and particularly the VC, used mines and booby traps both defensively and offensively (randomly planting mines or booby traps where anyone might walk on them constitutes offensive use).

Many types of mines were used by both sides, including both antitank and antipersonnel ones. Communist forces were adept at improvising mines from dud ammunition and at recovering Allied mines that were either duds or had not been detonated. U.S. forces often scattered antivehicular mines by air in an effort to stem the movement of supplies down the Ho Chi Minh Trail.

The most commonly employed U.S. mine was the M-18A1 claymore, which is not a traditional "in the ground" device. A smallish, curved box, the claymore is erected on a small stand and can be detonated either by trip wire, by someone pulling a cord, or by a timer. When detonated, it throws out hundreds of steel balls in a conical pattern that will instantly shred anyone within about fifty to fifty-five yards. Although the outward face of the curve is clearly marked "This side toward enemy," to insure no mistakes are made, it is a good idea not to stand behind a claymore either, as some material is ejected backwards as well. Communist sappers sometimes infiltrated Allied positions and turned around the claymores, so that they would explode toward the defenders.

The most famous booby trap used in Vietnam was the *punji* stake, which numbered among its victims the later chairman of the Joint Chiefs of Staff GEN Colin Powell. Although considered quite inhumane, a *punji* stake is actually one of the most elementary forms of "mine" known, merely a sharpened stick planted firmly in a hole that is then lightly covered up, a device old even before Caesar used it at Alesia 2,000 years ago. Although much was made of the alleged fact that the VC and NVA dipped their *punji* stakes in excrement in order to induce infection, in fact a wound resulting from a wooden stake being driven through the foot that does not become infected would be quite surprising. And despite much being made about them, *punji* stakes caused only about 2 percent of American casualties and virtually no deaths. Other forms of booby traps included explosive devices, death falls, and the like.

THE BIG GUNS

While some six million tons of bombs were dropped in Vietnam, several million tons of artillery shells were also used. The artillery was not lumped into the same category with bombs because there were important differences. An artillery shell was only about 10-percent explosive (the rest was the metal case), while most bombs are 50-or-more-percent explosive. Then again, a shell was more dangerous in its own way because it threw off more metal fragments. But the bomb had more blast effect, which could kill or injure a soldier who was hunkered down in a foxhole or shallow bunker.

Artillery was also more controllable. The army troops didn't have to make arrangements with another service (the navy or air force) to get bombers to help them out. The big guns belonged to the army, and individual infantry battalions would often be given the exclusive use of one or more artillery battalions for some operations.

Through most of the 1960s, U.S. and South Vietnamese forces had about a thousand artillery pieces available (105 mm, 155 mm, 175 mm, and 203 mm). Most of these were 105 mm and 155 mm and they fired a lot of ammunition. A ton of 155 mm ammo meant about twenty shells. A single gun could fire over a hundred shells a day, and many did when there was major combat going on.

Most of the shells missed the Communist troops, who quickly developed tactics to minimize the deadly effects of artillery. Nothing new in this, it's happened in every war where artillery was the dominant weapon. Nevertheless, the heavy use of American artillery defined the way the war was fought. The basic situation was this. U.S. troops almost always operated within range of their artillery, and every unit had a guy with a radio who knew how to "call in" artillery fire. This fellow, the "forward observer," was usually an artillery officer himself, although infantry officers, and many sergeants, could also call in artillery fire in a pinch. All that artillery fire saved American lives, but it limited how American infantry could operate. When they ran into trouble, the troops got used to having enormous firepower (hundreds of rounds) within five or ten minutes of calling for help, depending on how desperate the situation was. Especially in 1965–66, when the Communists met U.S. infantry battalions with equally large units, the prompt and abundant use of artillery created massive Communist losses versus much fewer on the American side.

The Communists quickly developed new tactics in 1966–67 to take advantage of the American dependence on artillery and airpower.

• When they came in contact with an American unit, they got as close as possible to it. The fear of hitting their own troops made American forward observers more cautious in the use of artillery. With some Communist troops shooting it out less than a hundred meters from the Americans, the rest of the Communist troops could withdraw.

• As soon as it got dark, the surviving Communist troops could sneak away. The Communists knew that most U.S. infantry (but not marines nor elite units like Rangers and Special Forces) were reluctant to get in close. So a few snipers could pin down a lot of American troops.

• Aim for anyone using a radio. Each American infantry platoon had one or two twenty-five pound radios, complete with distinctive tall antenna. Each was carried by an RTO (radio telephone operator) and next to the RTO there was usually a unit commander or forward observer. Either officer was capable of calling in artillery fire. Shoot the RTO and those officers, or the radio itself, and the damn artillery fire would stop.

• When you know American units are in the area, but they have not spotted you yet, remember that U.S. infantry will not normally advance beyond the range of their supporting artillery. If you know where the American artillery units are (and the Communists were good at patrolling and gathering information) then you knew what direction to go in, and how far, to get away from the U.S. ground troops.

ARMOR IN VIETNAM

Although guerrilla warfare is essentially infantry work, a surprising amount of armor turned up in Vietnam. Tanks and other armored fighting vehicles

Tanks and Other Armored Fighting Vehicles in Vietnam

Tanks

Model	Country	Weight	Spd	Rng	Crew	Gun	MGs	Armor	Notes
Centurion Mk5/1	Australia	52.0	22	123	4	105 (64)	1	229	A
M-4A3	U.S.	31.0	25	130	5	75 (97)	2	183	B
M-41	U.S.	25.2	45	100	4	76 (57)	2	38	C
M-48A3	U.S.	48.0	32	160	4	90 (51)	2	238	D
M-551 Sheridan	U.S.	17.5	45	375	4	152 (20)	2	40	E
PT-76	USSR	16.1	27	210	3	76.2 (40)	1	14	F
T-34/85	USSR	35.0	31	186	4	85 (56)	2	192	G
T-54	USSR	39.7	31	320	4	100 (34)	3	203	H
Type 59	China	39.7	30	275	4	100 (34)	3	100	I
Type 69	China	40.0	30	275	4	100 (34)	3	1000	J

Other Armored Fighting Vehicles

Model	Country	Weight	Spd	Rng	Crew	Gun	MGs	Armor	Notes
BTR-50P APC	USSR	15.7	26	155	3	–	1	10	K
M-113A1 APC	U.S.	12.3	35	300	2	–	1	44	L
Ontos M-501A1	U.S.	9.1	30	115	3	6×106 (18)	1	16	M

Key: Tanks are armored combat vehicles with a full tread and a heavy cannon (75 mm or better since the 1940s) mounted in a rotating turret. *Other Armored Fighting Vehicles* includes armored personnel carriers (APC), armored cavalry assault vehicles (ACAV), APCs equipped for light offensive combat, armored cars (AC), wheeled armored vehicles, usually for reconnaissance, and the unique Ontos anti-tank system: it omits armored self-propelled artillery. *Model* is the common designation of the principal variant used in Vietnam. *Country*, the manufacturers. *Weight*, in tons. *Spd*, is speed in miles-per-hour cross-country for all but armored cars—road speed was often up to forty to fifty miles per hour. *Rng* is range in miles on one tank of gas. *Crew*, the normal number of soldiers required to operate the vehicle. *Gun*, the main gun carried, if any, in millimeters, with the normal number of rounds of ammunition carried indicated in parentheses. *MGs*, total of machine guns carried. *Armor*, the thickest carried, in millimeters, usually covering the sides. *Notes* refer to the lettered comments below. Because of numerous minor variations even among vehicles of the same mark (e.g. "M4") and model e.g. ("M4A3"), all figures should be taken as somewhat approximate.

A. The Centurion Mk 5/1 was an Australian manufactured version of the British Centurion, introduced in 1957.

B. The M-4A3 was the famous "Sherman" of World War II, which had seen some use by the French during the First Indochina War, some of which were owned by the ARVN.

C. The M-41 "Walker Bulldog" light tank served with both American and South Vietnamese forces.

D. The M-48A3 "Patton" entered service in the late 1950s.

E. Introduced in 1966, the Sheridan, an air portable light tank, saw limited service in Vietnam. As designed, the 152 mm gun could also fire A/T missiles, of which ten were carried.

F. An amphibious light tank used with some effect for reconnaissance.

G. First introduced in late 1941, the T-34 was a highly effective vehicle that is still found in some poorer armies today.

H. The T-54 series began entering service in the late 1940s. Production ended in the late fifties, but it remained the backbone of Soviet tank forces into the 1960s. It was "crude but uncomplicated."

I. The Type 59 Tank was a Chinese version of the Soviet T-54A.

J. The Type 63 Tank was a Chinese knockoff of the Soviet PT-76 light tank.

K. The BTR-50P, introduced in 1955, could carry twelve to twenty troops in addition to its crew.

L. The M-113A1, introduced in 1959, could carry eleven soldiers. There were many, many variants.

M. Ontos entered service with the Marine Corps in 1955, and 297 were procured before production ended in 1957. It did not prove very effective in Vietnam. The back blast from the 106 mm recoilless rifles made life miserable for troops following behind, and to reload the six tubes one had to exit the vehicle. They were withdrawn after Tet, during which they had actually proven rather useful in urban fighting. They were dropped from the marine inventory in 1970.

(armored personnel carriers, armored cars, cavalry combat vehicles, and so forth) were of great value in supporting the infantry.

Tanks could provide useful support in situations where the infantry had difficulty closing with the enemy, were useful in mounting quick blows against enemy forces in suitable terrain, could be really handy in helping to defend a fixed position, and proved excellent escorts for road convoys.

Armored personnel carriers (APCs) are essentially armored buses that could carry an infantry squad into action, providing not only some protection but also some firepower support from their organic machine guns. Armored cavalry assault vehicles (ACAVs) were essentially all-terrain reconnaissance versions of APCs, provided with more machine guns and sometimes light antitank weapons.

Armored cars are just that, largely road-bound vehicles provided armor protection and some weapons—often quite heavy weapons—for reconnaissance, patrolling, and convoy escort. The United States used the V-100 armored car in Vietnam. It proved handy for escorting road convoys and useful in urban fighting, which occurred only rarely.

If any AFV (armored fighting vehicle) can be said to have been *the* AFV of the Vietnam War it was the American M-113 APC. Entering service shortly before Vietnam began to heat up in the early 1960s, during the war this boxy American-built vehicle seemed ubiquitous, and it can often be seen in pictures and news footage, rolling down roads, trundling across rice paddies, serving as a temporary bunker, and so forth.

Although well protected, the M-113 had some vulnerabilities, particularly from antitank mines, which prompted the troops to put sandbags on the floor to help absorb the blast of such. There were numerous versions, such as the M-577, which was taller than the standard model and could be used as a command post, a communications center, or a mobile medical aid station. There was also the M-132A1 flamethrower version, the ACAV (armored cavalry assault vehicle), which had some more armor, a shield for the .50 caliber machine gun, and mounts for two M-60 light machine guns, and so forth. Some 75,000 were eventually built, and many are still serving with some armies and are likely to be around well into the twenty-first century.

Despite its reputation as a guerrilla army, the NVA had armor, quite a lot of it. However, NVA use of armor, particularly of tanks, was poor. The NVA practiced poor dispersal (i.e., they failed to keep safe intervals between vehicles), which made their armor quite vulnerable to air attacks, whether during road marches or in the field. NVA tactical use of tanks was also quite poor. It was not uncommon for them to use tanks in attacks unsupported by friendly infantry or artillery, and to use too few tanks when making attacks. However, NVA tank tactics—if their use of armor can be so dignified—worked fine in Laos against Royalist and Hmong forces since the latter lacked antitank weapons.

There were a surprising number of tank-to-tank fights in Vietnam, most of them small and most of them between the NVA and the ARVN, particularly during the Lom Son (1970 ARVN invasion of Laos) operation and the NVA 1972 Easter Offensive. The biggest tank battle of the war was probably during the Easter Offensive.

On 2 April, the NVA sent about one hundred tanks—a mixed bag of T-54s and PT-76s—across the DMZ against elements of the ARVN 3rd Division. The division, only recently formed, broke. But the ARVN 20th Tank Regiment, which was itself only a few weeks old, counterattacked at An Loc, more or less restoring the front, in the process destroying eleven of the attacking tanks, while friendly aircraft took out a dozen more as the enemy withdrew. The NVA attack had been very poorly conducted, with the infantry-carrying tanks deployed much too close together, in more or less straight lines. This was fine against brittle troops, who could be expected to panic, but didn't work against the well-trained ARVN tankers, equipped with M-48A3s. There were several more tank-vs-tank clashes in the area over the next few weeks, with the ARVN tankers usually coming away the winners. Their success prompted the NVA to look for a better antitank weapon, and they shortly introduced the Sagger AT-3 wire-guided, vehicle-mounted A/T missile, which had a devastating effect on tanks. Nevertheless, the ARVN tank force, only formed in 1970, grew to four armored brigades, including three M-48A3 regiments by the end of the war.

Apparently American tanks encountered NVA tanks on only three occasions.

In mid-1968, a marine M-48A3 from the 3rd Tank Battalion, destroyed a PT-76 at very long range by cannon fire, with the help of a very good forward observer.

On 3 March 1969, M-48A3 Pattons of the 1/69th Armor took out two PT-76s and a BTR-50 before the enemy gave up trying to overrun the Special Forces camp at Ben Hat in the central highlands.

On 19 February 1971, during Operation Lom Son, nine M-41A3s of the 1/11th Armored Cavalry destroyed six T-54s and sixteen PT-76s in defense of firebase LZ-31. About a week later, a second NVA tank assault on LZ-31 succeeded in overrunning it, U.S. armor having been pulled out.

BODY COUNTS

In a war where capturing territory was not as important as eliminating enemy troops, the success or failure of an operation was often difficult to determine. The army initially would merely report that "enemy casualties were heavy" or "medium" or "light" as seemed appropriate and left it at that. But folks back home, namely politicians, and journalists, demanded something more. So the army came to evaluate operations on the basis of something called the "kill ratio," that is, the number of enemy troops killed for each friendly soldier lost in action. Thus was born the notorious "body count." As the

Unit Body-Count Ratio Effectiveness Evaluation Scale

Ratio	U.S. Unit	ARVN Unit
1:50	Excellent	Excellent
1:25	Good in close terrain Fair in open terrain	Excellent
1:15	Acceptable	Good
1:10	Average	
1:6	Poor	Average

Key: Ratio is the number of enemy dead to each friendly soldier killed in action. Close terrain includes things like jungle or urban areas, open terrain is relatively free of obstacles, such as rice paddies or grassland.

war went on, the Americans back home became more and more sensitive to battlefield losses. Thus there was not only pressure to end the war, either by killing the Communist troops or negotiating, but also to minimize American casualties. In addition, the "kill ratio" was seen as an excellent way to evaluate combat unit commanders.

There actually was a scale to determine how good a unit was in the body-count department.

The body count was quickly corrupted. Since an impressive body count was clearly a career-enhancing event, and the bodies were counted out in the bush by low-ranking troops who might be dead the next day, there was ample opportunity to adjust the numbers as they passed from the infantry platoon level to the White House. Even with all the padding, it was still publicly acknowledged that Communist troops were not being "killed fast enough," and could not be without the addition of many more American troops and an invasion of North Vietnam. The troops in the field were not very enthusiastic about the body-count process, as they were sometimes ordered to go counting while the enemy was still shooting. This situation did not do much for accuracy in the count. But, then, accuracy was never a major factor in the body-count department.

THUNDER RUN

The Vietnam landscape was not suitable for mechanized warfare using tanks and armored personnel carriers (APCs). The lowlands tended to be rice paddies and forests, while the mountains didn't have many roads and did have a lot of trees. But armored units were brought over, and because of some modifications to the standard U.S. APC (the M-113), mechanized operations became viable. By putting armored shields in front of one 12.7mm and two 7.62mm machine guns, these boxy armored vehicles could be used to attack. This modified M-113 was called the ACAV (armored cavalry assault vehicle). Normally, the M-113 was just used to get the troops close to the fighting, the armor being there to protect passengers from shell fragments and stray bullets. Since the Viet Cong had few antitank weapons, it was thought that these modified M-113s could go after Viet Cong troops ambushing American truck convoys.

The U.S. 11th Armored Cavalry Regiment, arriving in Vietnam during 1966, developed the ACAV and began using it in these attacks. With the noise the revved-up engines and machine guns of M-113s made as they took off after the enemy, these assaults were called "Thunder Runs" and proved very successful. Although the Viet Cong soon got some antitank weapons (RPG rocket launchers), the speed and firepower of the Thunder Runs usually made it difficult for the defenders to get a good shot at the advancing armored vehicles. The U.S. Armored Cavalry Regiment had forty-eight tanks, as well as 290 M-113s, and the presence of a tank among the three machine gun M-113s made ambushing U.S. truck convoys a decidedly risky proposition. The use of Agent Orange to clear the underbrush from the sides of roads made it even more difficult for the Viet Cong to ambush or harass road traffic, and took nothing away from the fast moving M-113s. Over two thousand M-113s were used in Vietnam, and many were officially, or unofficially, converted to ACAV standard.

FNGs, GETTING SHORT, AND STAYING ALIVE

Every new American soldier arriving in Vietnam knew that if he could survive the next thirteen months he was home free. The new soldier lived for the day, a month or two before he was to leave, when he would display his short timer's calendar (a calendar with the days until departure written in countdown fashion). This told the world that he was "short" and not only determined to get out of Vietnam alive, but reasonably sure he could pull it off.

But first the new arrival had to survive the first three months. The trouble was, especially for combat soldiers, there weren't a lot of people willing or eager to show the FNG (fucking new guy) the ropes. With the exception of that few percent of returning troops who had been in combat before, the guys who had been in the bush for six months or so, and survived the process, were leery of getting to close to an FNG. New troops did not know how to move, they made mistakes, and often those mistakes got the FNG killed, as well as anyone standing close to him. Walking into booby traps, minefields, and ambushes were common FNG mistakes. What was the effect of all this? Let us look at the numbers.

Pick out, at random, a hundred infantrymen who got killed in Vietnam. Take a look at how long they had been in Vietnam when they were killed. About 40 percent were there three months or less, many still considered

FNGs. Only about 6 percent of the deaths were in the last three months of the one year tour.

Although strenuous efforts were made to train recruits back in the states specifically for Vietnam, it didn't always work. Vietnam itself was different. It was hotter, smelled differently, and had people, places, plants, and animals not found in the United States (a few valiant efforts were made to redress this in some army training bases). Although many of the sergeants handling the training were, as the years went by, Vietnam vets, they only had three to four months to turn a civilian into an infantryman able to stand up against the more experienced Viet Cong and North Vietnamese veterans. The Communists didn't have thirteen-month tours. Their troops stayed in action until killed, maimed, or victory was won.

Perhaps the worst handicap the U.S. soldier had to work with was the individual replacement system. Created during World War II (it didn't work then, either) and carried over to the Korean War (another failed attempt to make it work), this system regarded a combat unit as a machine and the troops in it as parts of a machine. If a part became broken (i.e., killed or wounded) you just ordered up a new part (an individual replacement soldier) and the machine would keep chugging along. It worked, after a fashion, but with the following negative side effects:

• New soldiers, the replacements, were not trusted by the more experienced soldiers. As replacements were often added to units while they were in the field, or about to go out and look for some action, none of the experienced soldiers was about to trust his life to this unknown fellow. Actually, what the experienced troops did know for sure was that most of these replacements were as green as can be and likely candidates for a body bag or emergency surgery once they got into action. Better to ignore the FNGs and wait for them to prove they could survive out there and become reliable enough to work with safely.

• Except when new units were sent to Vietnam, you never had squads and platoons full of people who had worked together with each other for very long. Every American infantry battalion originally came over to Vietnam with a full complement of people who had trained and worked together for a while. True, the two-year obligation of draftees had the same effect as the thirteen-month tour, but you benefitted greatly by having experienced troops for a few more months. And these stateside units had had their NCOs, and even some of their officers, around for years. That made a big difference. Now you would think that in a dicey business like infantry combat, you would want people who had worked with each other for a while. The historical record shows that units training and working together for years are clearly superior to those that have not. But such units are rare in history. It's expensive to keep all those professional soldiers together doing the same thing for years. Only elite units (like a lot of the royal bodyguards) or unique organizations (like the Roman legions) were full of well-trained troops. In the twentieth century, the problem has been the ability to mobilize a nation's manpower and industry on short notice and to arm and put millions of civilians in uniform. Those few units you could afford to keep together in peacetime had to be broken up during the mobilization to provide instructors for all those drafted civilians. In Korea and Vietnam there was the added problem of the thirteen-month tour of duty.

• As soon as a soldier became experienced enough to be effective, his tour of duty was over and he was sent home, to be replaced by another FNG.

• Units were never as effective as they could be, with 1 or 2 percent of their most experienced troops leaving every week, plus a similar additional attrition rate because of combat losses. During World War II, when everyone was in for the duration, units were better able to deal with the individual replacements because of the larger number of experienced troops available. But in Vietnam, your best people went bye-bye after a year.

The thirteen-month rotation system was first invented so that an unpopular and undeclared war (first Korea, then Vietnam) would not see a handful of infantry (and combat support) troops doing most of the dangerous work for the entire war. It was a noble idea, to spread the pain around. But it also spread the pain further. Based on the casualty statistics, it was obvious that the longer a soldier stayed in the field, the better he became. The Communists recognized this, thus their units most always had the experience advantage. American units suffered higher losses if they had more new troops, lower losses if they had a higher proportion of experienced troops. As random and chaotic as the battlefield might appear, skill and experience still make a difference, and that difference is most often seen in more enemy dead and fewer of the more experienced troops hit.

LRRPs AND RANGERS

LRRP, or long-range reconnaissance patrols (pronounced "lurps"), were one of the more successful innovations of the Vietnam War. Or perhaps "revivals" might be a better term. Inspired by the example of the British Commandos in the early years of World War II, even before the United States became involved in that war, the notion of creating commando forces had begun to circulate in the army. When the decision was made to create such special operations forces in 1942, they were given the name "Rangers" to commemorate the special warfare forces raised in colonial times to fight the Indians and the French. The Rangers did well in their intended role, undertaking unusually arduous or important specialized missions. But the army made several mistakes. For one thing, it raised too many Ranger units. It also tended to overburden the Rangers with too much heavy equipment. Worse, it let theater commanders commit Ranger units to conventional operations, for which they were highly unsuited. As a result, by the end of the war the army decided that the Rangers had been a mistake and disbanded them. Briefly revived during the Korean War, the Rangers once again performed well, but were once more disbanded at the war's end. Going into the 1960s, at a time when the armed forces were supposedly devoting unusual attention to unconventional warfare, there were no Ranger units in the army, though a Ranger school continued to exist.

Then came Vietnam. The first LRRP detachments were organized in the early 1960s by U.S. Special Forces troops operating along South Vietnam's borders, in some cases taking over earlier CIA espionage operations. The Special Forces were in Vietnam in 1961, running LRRP operations into Laos. The Special Forces considered LRRP work as part of their job. These cross border LRRP operations continued throughout the war and LRRP operations were conducted under fire as recently as the 1991 Gulf War.

But the Special Forces were not the only LRRPs, nor were they the most numerous folks doing long-range recon. LRRP detachments were informally organized in the 173rd Airborne Brigade, the first major unit in Vietnam shortly after it arrived in country in May of 1965, in response to the need for "deep reconnaissance." The call went out for volunteers, and the response was good, as there were a lot of soldiers with Ranger qualifications and a lot of others who wanted more than just the normal "thrill of combat."

Additional provisional LRRP teams—with a plethora of different titles—were formed by every other major unit arriving in Vietnam. All this was officially unofficial. Not until mid-1966 did MACV (Military Assistance Command, Vietnam) deign to recognize the existence of and need for LRRPs, and issue some guidelines for their organization, training, and deployment. Soon afterward a "Recondo" school was established to train men for LRRPs (also sometimes abbreviated as LRPs). Yet even then the existence of LRRP teams was no more than provisional, partially because to make them formal parts of the army's organization would automatically increase manpower. Not for another year would the army approve the existence of LRRPs, formally authorizing their existence as independent companies within the army structure. By then LRRPs had conducted literally thousands of missions with stunning success, at little cost in American lives.

LRRP missions were numerous and varied. Recon teams normally numbered only six men. A team might be assigned to locate a downed pilot, identify enemy units deep in the rear, select drop zones for upcoming operations, identify targets for air or artillery attack, support indigenous Allies (e.g., the Hmong and the Montagnards), conduct demolitions, and so forth. Combat was not a primary objective, and in about a third of all LRRP missions no direct contact with the enemy occurred. Altogether there were about

23,000 LRRP missions, of which some 14,300 involved contact with the enemy, who suffered nearly 10,000 dead as a direct result of the operations of LRRP teams. The number of enemy dead caused by conventional infantry, air, and artillery forces operating under information derived from LRRP operations cannot be determined. But, for example, Operation Junction City, February–May 1967, which resulted in the killing of over 2,000 NVA troops, was a direct consequence of the identification of a large NVA concentration by an LRRP team.

Despite engaging in extremely high-risk operations, there were always more than enough volunteers for assignment to LRRP detachments. One reason was that both seasoned veterans and smart recruits realized that soldiers assigned to LRRPs received a lot more training than ordinary troops, and that the more training one had, the better were one's chances. In fact, despite the very high-risk nature of their trade, LRRP casualties were surprisingly low. Of about 5,000 men who served in LRRPs during the war (many of whom voluntarily extended their tours of duty several times), fewer than 450 were killed in the course of operations. Despite this relatively low overall loss rate, three of these men earned the Medal of Honor in Vietnam. This was a ratio of about 1 award to every 150 killed, testifying to the fact that although LRRP teams may not have seen combat as often as conventional troops, when they did it was often extremely intense. There were never more than about 1,600 men assigned to LRRPs in Vietnam at any one time. Peak strength was probably attained in February 1969, when there were fifteen LRRP companies in Vietnam, including one from the Indiana National Guard. At the same time, all LRRP companies were redesignated as Rangers, and numbered sequentially as companies of the newly revived 75th Infantry Regiment, itself deriving from several World War II–era special operations forces such as "Merrill's Marauders" and the original Rangers. This made LRRPs a permanent part of the army organization. Since Vietnam, Rangers have served in Grenada, Panama, the Gulf, Somalia, and Haiti, with commendable effectiveness, and there are currently three battalions of Rangers active in the army.

The overall value of LRRPs to the war effort was not automatically accepted by everyone in the army. LRRPs were slovenly by Regular Army standards, often running around in the "boonies" dressed in black pajamas and grease paint, toting all sorts of outlandish weapons, including captured enemy arms, rather than going into action properly armed and equipped like "real soldiers." The nature of LRRP operations often found more senior personnel taking orders from their juniors, hardly proper military procedure. LRRPs were not team players, were not always bureaucratically efficient, and tended to be know-it-alls about operating in the bush. These criticisms may be taken as "sour grapes." A more important criticism is that the LRRPs, like all elite units, absorb manpower that might be more usefully employed in stiffening conventional forces: in effect, LRRPs used a lot of very high-quality troops, men who might have been better assigned to leadership positions in the regular forces. On balance, while there is some truth to this, it's important to realize that (1) so few men were employed in LRRPs that spreading them out among the regular units would probably not have had much impact (and, by the way, make this same argument about the far more numerous airborne forces or the Marine Corps and see how far you get); (2) your typical LRRP tended to be a loner, effective enough working with his small team, but perhaps less efficient if forced to become part of a larger organization; and (3) the LRRPs provided a training ground for NCOs and officers. No one spent all of his career in the LRRPs. After a while they usually went back to regular units. So successful was the LRRP experience in training excellent combat leaders that the army began providing LRRP ("ranger") training as a regular part of NCO and officer preparation. Not every combat soldier went through this training, but those who did were seen as above average, and it usually paid off.

LRRP RULES

Long-range reconnaissance patrols (LRRPs) were the elite of the infantry profession. They survived days, sometimes weeks, deep in enemy territory. At any moment they could be discovered by the thousands of enemy troops around them. The LRRPs were out there to observe the enemy. Sometimes they just watched what the enemy was doing and reported back. At other times the LRRPs would call in air strikes or artillery when they found something particularly worthy of immediate destruction. To do their job, the six to ten LRRP troopers in each patrol used a number of proven techniques in order to survive this decidedly risky business.

• Careful planning: A week or more of work might go into some of these patrols. At the very least, the patrol leader would go over maps of the area to be covered. If possible, aerial photos of the area were examined. For SOG (studies and observation group) LRRPs going into Laos, Cambodia, or North Vietnam, the team leaders often flew over the patrol area, took more photos, and could call upon U.S. intelligence resources not available to other LRRPs. The planning was essentially a dry run of the mission, figuring out the best landing zones, march routes, and areas where the patrol could be taken out by helicopter in an emergency. Other details like radio call signs and new codes had to be agreed on and taught to the troops.

• Practice: The LRRPs were supposed to be the best of the best, but often the volunteers were a bit green and needed practice. Even the LRRPs who were accomplished infantrymen had to practice constantly to keep their edge. The least little mistake on an LRRP mission could get everyone killed, so not only were the LRRPs very selective about whom they let in, but they insisted on keeping everyone up to the job. The training never stopped, for shooting, patrolling, and skill with much infantry gear is lost without practice. LRRPs were out on patrol less than half the time, and when back at a base they practiced nearly every day. There were special drills the LRRPs used, like the "break contact drill" used when LRRPs were discovered by the enemy. This thirty-second wall of fire was triggered by a shot from their point man or the enemy (especially in the case of an ambush). The six to ten LRRPs would quickly step to the right or left, depending on whether they were odd- or even-numbered men in line. The man closest to the fire emptied his magazine in three round bursts and then moved away from the fire (inserting a new magazine as he went). The next man in line did the same until all men had fired their weapons. Some men had 40 mm grenade launchers on their rifles and these were fired also. Some of the 40 mm shells were high explosive, but sometimes a tear gas shell was used. It was common for the first magazine to have all tracer rounds, to make it look like there were more bullets heading toward the enemy than was actually the case (machine guns usually had one tracer round in ten or twenty). One of the troops carried a claymore mine, which he would point in the direction of the oncoming enemy and then set off a timer. All the troops would have fired their weapons and gotten away in thirty seconds. The oncoming enemy would have thought they had run into an ambush or a much larger force. This drill had to be practiced, using live ammunition, for it was only effective if done quickly, efficiently, automatically, and without hitting any of your own people. Each soldier also had to be able immediately and accurately to read hand signals from the team leader or the situation, if the team leader was out of sight, and make the right moves quickly and in the right direction. There were dozens of other procedures only LRRPs used. Like how to set up a quick defensive position. Or how to arrange themselves (everyone sleeping heads out in a circle) and their equipment (wearing everything) so team members could catch some sleep but respond quickly and effectively if the enemy caught up with them in the middle of the night.

• After the helicopter leaves you, disappear as quickly as possible. The usual way of getting into enemy country was by helicopter. Sometimes an LRRP would walk in, but this meant making your way past more Communist troops to get where you were going. Even helicoptering in was risky because if any enemy troops saw your chopper dropping you off, the alarm would be given and first hundreds, then thousands of enemy troops would be out looking for you. Chopper pilots had their own bag of tricks to help out here. Two or more phony landings could be done, each one, if spotted, likely to send the enemy off in pursuit of a nonexistent patrol.

• When an LRRP entered bandit country, he was decked out in a precise fashion, with all his weapons and equipment placed where they would do the most good. Additional M-16 magazines were kept on the left side, making it possible to change magazines, even while moving, in three seconds. The drill here was: cradle the M-16 under one arm, extract the empty magazine with one hand, grab and load the fresh magazine with the other hand, hit the bolt release with the left hand, and resume firing. Grenades were on the right side, with their pins straightened and wrapped with a piece of tape. That way, even if wounded or really busy, the LRRP could pull the pin with his teeth (to try this without a straightened pin is, unlike what you see in the movies, impossible). Compass was always on the left wrist, so you could move it away from the metal rifle, to get an accurate reading, without letting go of the rifle. Other gear was packed in the rucksack with similar care and forethought. The LRRPs may have appeared to be casually dressed, but they were anything but.

• LRRPs were silent when they moved through the bush, really silent. That was no accident. Tape and rubber bands were used to silence every piece of equipment carried. Before starting out, LRRPs walked and jumped around, listening for anything that would jangle or clank, and silencing it. This made a big difference in the field, where one out-of-place sound could alert the enemy to your presence.

• Travel light, except when it comes to arms and ammunition. Here is one real situation that did look like the movies. An LRRP would go to work carrying twenty to thirty M-16 magazines, a dozen or more grenades (of various types), plus one or two claymore mines, a dozen or so "toe-popper" mines (M-14s), and some C-4 plastic explosive. Some men carried pistols or a shotgun. One or more men would carry AK-47s, for the sound of that in a firefight would confuse the North Vietnamese and an LRRP team could make something of that confusion to make their getaway. Lightweight food was carried, enough to last for a few days. The current MRE ("Meals, Ready to Eat") field rations used by U.S. forces were first developed for LRRPs. Some LRRPs, however, went native, carrying rice balls and similar local munchies. There were some medical supplies, radios (each patrol carried at least two), and maps. There were no flak jackets or steel helmets. Even so, each LRRP was carrying over fifty pounds.

• Dealing with pursuit: LRRPs were often discovered while prowling around in enemy-held territory. At that point, survival depended on how effectively the LRRP team could elude its pursuers. The initial tool was the break contact drill. This involved firing a lot of bullets at the enemy and having one AK-47-armed LRRP then cover the rest of the team. The enemy, finding itself shot at with one of their own weapons, assumed they had a friendly fire situation on their hands and the several minutes it took them to sort things out gave the LRRPs more time to get lost. The next move was to run in the direction of previously selected spots where helicopters could lift the team out. But this would only work if the team could get there without enemy troops near enough to shoot down the choppers. While the rescue choppers would come with a gunship or two, these could only handle so many enemy soldiers. So the team had to evade and delay. They evaded by trying to cover their trail. If they came across a shallow stream, they would travel through it for a few hundred yards. Otherwise, they had to look for rocky ground that would be more difficult to track over or just delay the pursuers as much as possible. The M-14 mine was the favorite tool for slowing pursuers down. Sort of like a hockey puck, but only two inches in diameter and two inches thick, it contained two ounces of plastic explosive. This mine was not designed to kill, but to disable. There was a perverse logic to this. If you kill one of the pursuing soldiers, his comrades will just leave his body there (for later burial). But if an M-14 blows off a pursuer's foot, the wounded man will make a lot of noise, plead for some first aid from at least one of his comrades, and generally disrupt the pursuit more than a corpse would.

The LRRP program was one of the more successful in the war, and it was all because the men who served as LRRPs developed useful rules and used them.

CREATING ARVN

The Army of the Republic of Vietnam (ARVN) grew out of the Vietnamese units serving in the French army during the First Indochina War. As the French never really trusted the Vietnamese and, despite the demonstrable abilities of the Viet Minh, discounted their martial qualities, virtually all of the officers for their Vietnamese troops were French. In 1949, the French took about 25,000 of their 40,000 or so Vietnamese colonial troops and formed the Vietnamese National Army, as the army of the "independent" Vietnam within the so-called French Union. This grew rapidly, reaching 125,000 by 1952 and a surprising 240,000 by 1954. With the 1954 Geneva Accords, more than half the men in the Vietnamese National Army were sent home. A year later, what was left became the ARVN. However, the army was still essentially a collection of miscellaneous units left over from the French, ill-trained, ill-equipped, and badly officered.

An American officer, LG John W. "Iron Mike" O'Daniel, had a critical role in the creation of the ARVN and also for a number of its shortcomings. O'Daniel was a veteran of both world wars and Korea. In Korea he had helped create the ROK Army, among the toughest and most effective ground forces in the world. He had already served in Indochina in 1953, when Eisenhower had sent him to assess French military prospects and needs. In 1954, O'Daniel was appointed the first chief of the American Military Assistance Advisory Group (MAAG) in Vietnam. In assessing the possible threats to the security of South Vietnam, O'Daniel concluded that guerrillas were not a serious problem. Although they had beleaguered the French in Indochina, the real victory had belonged to the Viet Minh regulars, who had

The O'Daniel Plan for the RVN Armed Forces

Component	Number and Strength	Total
Army		
Field Divisions	4 at 8,500	34,000
Light Divisions	6 at 5,225	31,350
Airborne Brigade	1 at 4,000	4,000
Territorial Regiments	13 at 1,625	21,125
Regional Forces		9,000
Infrastructure		42,225
Air Force		4,000
Navy		4,000
Total		**150,000**

Key: *Infrastructure* includes headquarters, staffs, army and corps troops (i.e., some heavy artillery, armor, engineers, and the like), logistical tail, and training establishments.

overrun Dien Bien Phu. Moreover, Communist guerrillas had themselves been defeated in Iran, Greece, and Korea, and were clearly in the process of being defeated in the Philippines and Malaya. As a result, like most senior officers, O'Daniel, and his successor as head of the MAAG, LG Samuel T. "Hanging Sam" Williams, believed guerrillas would primarily be used to distract the ARVN while a conventional assault was mounted across the DMZ or the Laotian border. This had appeared to be the case in Korea in 1950, when an important part of the ROK Army had been involved in counterguerrilla operations well below the thirty-eighth parallel. So O'Daniel recommended an army of 142,000 men trained and equipped for conventional fighting in a jungle environment, plus a small air force and navy, for a total regular force of about 150,000 men.

The light divisions were designed for combat in areas where motor vehicles and heavy equipment would constitute a handicap, such as jungles, mountains, and swamps. Compared to the contemporary U.S. infantry division, which had 300 percent more men, the Vietnamese light divisions would have 30 percent more machine guns, 10 percent more BARs, and about the same number of 60 mm and 81 mm mortars, with no artillery and only rudimentary combat service and support contingents. The field divisions were intended to be the heavyweight conventional combat units. Not only did they have more motor vehicles than the light divisions, but, with about half the strength of an American infantry division, they would have about 30 percent more machine guns, 50 percent more BARs (automatic rifles), and 30 percent more mortars, plus a battalion of twelve 105 mm howitzers and one of twelve 4.2-in. mortars, as well as small combat support contingents, including medical, transportation, ordnance, quartermaster, and engineer companies. These forces might seem rather light by conventional standards, but the NVA was not expected to be much more heavily armed and the terrain favored lighter forces. In fact, O'Daniel later observed that "some people had the idea that armor and other heavy stuff would be needed in Vietnam," a proposal that would have made the ARVN even less suitable for a guerrilla war than was the case.

The basic war plan assumed that guerrilla activity in the South would presage a conventional assault by the NVA. The territorial regiments, regional forces, and the Civil Guard would cope with this, while the regular forces would prepare to meet the conventional assault. If an attack came across the DMZ, three divisions would cover an initial withdrawal to the Danang area to permit the balance of the regular forces to come up and help stabilize the situation and await support from SEATO (Southeast Asia Treaty Organization). Once SEATO forces were in place, including, initially, an assumed two to four American divisions, a counterattack would be undertaken, which would include an amphibious landing north of the DMZ, in the vicinity of Vinh, in order to cut the enemy in two. This landing would be effected by two ARVN field divisions and a light division, with sealift provided by the U.S. Navy, and support from the USMC (U.S. Marine Corps).

It was on this plan that the ARVN was created, not without some objections from South Vietnamese military leaders. Their protests were derived not from any doctrinal disputes but rather because the organization of higher formations required concentrating the scattered small elements of the army, thereby lowering the political independence of company and battalion commanders, not to mention reducing the opportunities for graft. As a result, it was not until 1955 that the new army organization began to be implemented.

Supplementing the ARVN's conventional, territorial, and regional forces would be the RVN National Police, the Civil Guard, a paramilitary rural constabulary that also served as a counterweight to possible political adventurism by military commanders. By the late 1950s, it was planned to have about 50,000–55,000 men armed as light infantry.

Of course the new organization was not precisely what the ARVN required, given the war that happened, as opposed to the war that was expected. In hindsight, O'Daniel, Williams, and others who favored the conventional model for the ARVN can be faulted for misjudging the threat of a widespread guerrilla war. At the time things were not so clear. Anticipating the Geneva Accord mandated elections, the VC were laying low militarily in 1955–56, so it looked like the back of the insurgency had been broken. When the Diem regime canceled the elections, it took the VC time to regroup, particularly as Diem's political offensive was making inroads on their infrastructure into the late 1950s. One reason the Communists in the South resumed military operations in 1958 was to strengthen their political hold over rural areas, by convincing villagers to support them, eliminating government officials, and generally trying to gain headlines. These operations remained essentially limited and were by no means universally successful. So the O'Daniel model did look sound. But the VC learned quickly, and grew markedly better. As they became better, they adopted a more aggressive policy, so that in 1959–60 they were usually getting the best of the ARVN.

REPUBLIC OF VIETNAM MARINE CORPS

The RVN Marine Corps had its origins in two battalions of Vietnamese replacements formed by the French shortly before the 1954 partition of Indochina. These were designated the Marine Infantry Corps of the Vietnamese Navy, which became the Vietnamese Marine Corps in 1956. Adopting as its motto *"Dahn-Du-To-Quoc,"* Honor and Country, by 1962, the Marine Corps had four infantry battalions. Within two years there were six battalions of infantry and three of artillery, and the corps was shortly organized as a small division. Three additional battalions were raised by 1968, making the Marine Corps a full-sized division of three brigades. Brigades took their numbers from the component battalions. For much of the war these were the 147th Brigade, which included the 1st, 4th, and 7th Battalions; the 258th Brigade, composed of the 2nd, 5th, and 8th Battalions; and the 369th Brigade, the 3rd, 6th, and 9th Battalions. There were also some combat service and combat support elements. From 1970, an attempt was made to raise additional battalions, but only three of the proposed ten new ones were actually organized.

Although on paper a subordinate command of the RVN Navy, in practice the Marine Corps served directly under the Vietnamese Joint Chiefs of Staff, as a "fire brigade." Headquartered in Saigon, its units fought in all parts of the country, depending upon circumstances.

Although raised entirely from volunteers, initially the Republic of Vietnam Marine Corps suffered from many of the same problems that plagued other Vietnamese military units, and in a fight at Binh Hoa in 1964, one battalion was virtually annihilated. But the corps improved, not least because of careful attention by its USMC advisers and sponsors, and in 1965, the 2nd Battalion earned a U.S. Presidential Unit Citation for its performance in combat, while the 5th Battalion was similarly cited in 1969. In September 1972, the RVN Marines captured Quang Tri from the enemy, who had seized it nearly five months earlier and beaten off repeated ARVN attempts to recapture the city. Perhaps the most notable action of the RVN Marines occurred in early 1973, when the headquarters of the Vietnamese Marine Division, as well as the 2nd, 4th, and 9th Marine Battalions, elements of the 2nd and 3rd Marine Artillery Battalions, and several attached ARVN units were all awarded the U.S. Valorous Unit Award for their performance as part of Task Force Tango, 26–31 January 1973. After the United States pulled out, the RVN marine and

Principal Units of the Vietnamese Marine Corps

Battalion	Emblem
1st Infantry	Wild Bird
2nd Infantry	Crazy Buffalo
3rd Infantry	Sea Wolf
4th Infantry	Killer Shark
5th Infantry	Black Dragon
6th Infantry	Sacred Bird
7th Infantry	Black Tiger
8th Infantry	Sea Eagle
9th Infantry	Mighty Tiger
1st Artillery	Lightning Fire
2nd Artillery	Sacred Arrow
3rd Artillery	Sacred Bow

Key: It was common for battalions to be nicknamed after their emblem. For example, the 1st Marine Battalion was often referred to as "the Wild Birds."

airborne divisions assumed an even greater role as fire brigades than had already been the case.

In the final months of the Vietnam War, the RVN Marine Corps, under BG Bui The Lan, put up a stout rear guard defense at Danang, and later clung tenaciously to Vung Tau until after the fall of Saigon.

THE ARVN RANGERS

The South Vietnamese Army began organizing Rangers in 1960, with training assistance from American Special Forces personnel. The first company was activated in 1961, but battalions were not organized until 1963. These were subsequently grouped into "task forces" in 1967, which were redesignated "groups" the following year.

Nicknamed "the Black Tigers," the Rangers were recruited from volunteers and tended to be bigger than the average Vietnamese. Like the marines and airborne troops, the Rangers spent most of their time as a "fire brigade," being sent in to take care of particularly critical problems or difficult situations. The Rangers also supported the Civilian Irregular Defense Corps, which later were reorganized and redesignated as Ranger Border Guard battalions; and by 1972, there were fifty-five battalions; twenty of them line units and thirty-five border ones. In that year the Rangers were reorganized into fifteen groups, totaling forty-five battalions.

The Rangers were among the most reliable troops South Vietnam had. Nevertheless, like the other elite elements of the RVN armed forces, they occasionally proved brittle in combat. Many of them were recruited from ethnic minorities or Hoi Chanh, who were particularly effective against their erstwhile comrades. Between 1960 and 1972, the Rangers are estimated to have killed about 40,000 of the enemy and to have captured 7,000, along with 12,000 weapons.

Ranger battalions were of some 660–750 men, usually organized into a small headquarters and four companies. The battalion HQ controlled the heaviest weapons, two 106mm recoilless rifles. A Ranger group (regiment) comprised a small headquarters, three Ranger battalions, and reconnaissance, transportation, and engineer companies.

THE POPULAR FORCES

The Popular Forces were essentially a rural standing militia, intended to provide some security for local villages. They were a neglected asset. Neither ARVN nor MACV thought much of them, failing to see that the Popular Forces did a lot of fighting, incurred a lot of casualties, and killed a lot of the enemy. In fact, arguably Popular Forces carried the brunt of the war for South Vietnam, and their casualties appear to have almost always exceeded those of the regular forces.

Lightly armed and supported by only about 20 percent of the South Vietnamese defense budget, the PF took about 50 percent of South Vietnamese casualties, while causing perhaps a quarter or a third of those suffered by VC/NVA

With one exception, between 1967 and 1971, the only years for which figures seem to be available, Popular Forces deaths in action were always a majority of total South Vietnamese combat deaths. The sole exception, 1968, is explainable by Tet, which caused very high casualties among the RVN regular forces; and even then, the Popular Forces suffered in proportion to their percentage of overall ARVN strength.

Popular Forces and ARVN, 1967–71

Popular Forces Within RVN Forces

Year	Strength	KIAs
1967	47%	52%
1968	48%	47%
1969	49%	54%
1970	51%	59%
1971	51%	60%

Key: Strength gives the PF as a percentage of total Republic of Vietnam military personnel, KIAs their proportion of RVN combat deaths.

MARINE COMBINED ACTION PLATOONS

The Marine Corps had spent most of the period between the two world wars in counterinsurgency operations in the Caribbean. Their experience was embodied in the *Small Wars Manual* of 1940. Unfortunately, World War II, and the general lack of any small war–type actions, led to the neglect of this publication. For many years the manual was largely ignored as the corps concentrated on amphibious operations against the Japanese, then conventional operations in Korea, and finally to adjusting to the demands of a potential nuclear battlefield in the 1950s. Some attention was paid to counterinsurgency, but when the corps came to publish a new manual for guerrilla operations in 1962, most of the lessons of the *Small Wars Manual* were ignored. Fleet Marine Force Manual 8-2, *Operations Against Guerrilla Forces*, was an ill-organized collection of borrowings from the *Small Wars Manual*, combined with some alleged lessons of more recent guerrilla wars and some theoretical musings on the subject. But some people in the corps remembered. One of the recommendations of the *Small Wars Manual* was the combination of marine personnel with local personnel in operational formations. Almost as soon as they arrived in Vietnam, the marines began organizing what became known as combined action platoons (CAP). A combined action platoon integrated a marine squad into a Vietnamese local defense platoon. Typically, a CAP included fourteen marines (a squad leader, grenadier/assistant squad leader, and three fire teams of four men each), plus three navy medical corpsmen, with a Vietnamese local defense platoon of thirty-eight men (a platoon leader, four staff personnel, and three squads of eleven men each).

CAP personnel lived with the local people, working closely with Vietnamese military and political leaders. Although primarily intended to strengthen and train local defense forces, they were also responsible for many rural development projects, such as running medical clinics, building schools, delivering supplies, and so forth.

Personnel assigned to combined action platoons were routinely drawn from the general pool of available marines. Since living conditions in the typical Vietnamese rural hamlet were pretty primitive, most marines were in for some serious culture shock when they joined their assigned platoons.

Marine CAPs, 1967–70

Year	Platoons	Personnel	
		U.S.	ARVN
1967	57	c. 970	c. 2,165
1968	80	c. 1,360	c. 3,040
1969	102	c. 1,735	c. 3,875
1970	114	c. 1,940	c. 4,330

Key: Data are as of 1 January. No data are available for 1 January 1966. Manpower figures are approximate only, as actual platoon strength varied.

Interestingly, black marines from the rural South had the fewest problems adjusting to life in the Vietnamese bush, followed by poor white country boys from the same region. This made sense, since much of the rural American South still lacked indoor plumbing and other amenities in the 1960s, and hardly anyone had air-conditioning.

The CAP program was responsible for securing many villages in the Marine Corps areas of North Vietnam. Convinced of the effectiveness of the program, the marines wanted to expand it (only a small proportion, c. 10 percent, of ARVN's local defense forces was ever involved in the program). However, this proved very difficult. Not only was the ARVN reluctant to supply troops, but senior U.S. army commanders in Vietnam saw it as a "waste" of fine infantry. In fact, at its peak in 1969, the program only involved about 2,000 marines, about two battalions' worth of manpower at a time when the United States had well over a hundred combat battalions in country. With the introduction of Vietnamization in 1970, the program was abandoned.

GENERAL MONSOON

The climate shaped the activities of both sides. Vietnam is a tropical country that still has seasons. The most influential "season" is the annual monsoon. In the north of South Vietnam, the rainy season is from September to January. In the south, especially in the Mekong Delta and the Cambodian and Laotian infiltration routes, the rains come between May and September. This period of heavy rains makes military operations difficult. It is time consuming and dangerous to make your way through the bush when in a monsoon rain. Visibility is low, the ground is muddy or slippery, and it's cold, at least compared to the normally tropical heat. While the low visibility favored Communist sapper attacks, the sapper preparations were much hindered by the bad weather. This discouraged the sappers, who depended on meticulous preparations for their assaults to succeed. The Communists had a hard time moving supplies down the Ho Chi Minh Trail during the monsoon, and this restricted the supplies available to them.

American operations were curtailed largely because helicopters were much less effective in the bad weather. More accidents, slower flying, and greater maintenance loads took away the major American military asset, thus even U.S. troops saw a marked reduction in combat during the rainy season.

So the rainy season was a time to rest and get ready for the dry season and another round of fighting.

GROUND RADAR

One of many high-tech items that got their first real workout in Vietnam was ground radar. While radar had been detecting aircraft since the 1930s, there was much "clutter" (too many things to see) on the ground and it wasn't until the 1960s that radar technology got to the point where a radar for ground targets became practical. There were large, sparsely populated areas on South Vietnam's borders where you wanted to keep an eye on things without endangering a lot of your own troops. Such an area was the Cambodian border with South Vietnam. Typically, a five-man team operated the TPS-25 ground radar, keeping a watch out for enemy troops coming over after having traveled down the Ho Chi Minh Trail. Since there were not enough radars to cover the entire border, the available radars were moved around. Thus the enemy was never sure which area would find itself under radar observation. So every three or four weeks, the radar team moved about to a different fire support base (FSB) or base camp.

The TPS-25 radar had a maximum range of fifteen miles. It used the doppler technology, which meant that there was an audio return. An experienced operator could often quickly identify a target according to the characteristic sound. Range was usually limited by tree lines or other obstacles, but this was overcome somewhat by mounting the radar dome on an eighty-four-foot tower. Even so, most targets were detected no more than eight miles out, and some as close as four hundred yards. Although the primary mission of the radar was to detect infiltration, it was not unusual for the radar to detect enemy troops moving into position to attack the camp the radar was in. This often saved the lives of the radar operators and many troops in the camp, for that warning could be the difference between holding the camp, or losing it.

The radar team usually operated the radar during the night. In tropical South Vietnam, this meant from 1800 hours to 0600. Each member of the team pulled two shifts on the radar each night. Only one man was needed to operate the radar, unless he was training a new man. When a possible target was detected, the operator would contact TOC (Tactical Operations Center). This was done using a two-way scrambled (automatically coded/decoded) radio. The operator would give the coordinates, description, and direction of movement for the target. TOC would order a fire mission, almost always artillery, once they were sure the target was not friendly troops or civilians out at night. Much of the land in these border areas had been declared a free-fire zone, meaning that if you were there and not identified, you were considered hostile and were shot at. The border areas were large, and there was not a lot of traffic, friendly or hostile. Thus only about a third of the targets spotted by the radar were fired upon. When such an artillery attack did take place, the TOC would tell the radar crew when the shells were on the way. Thus the artillery observers could see the impact and call adjustments for the next volley. It was usually necessary to go through the adjustment process.

As with any new technology, there were a lot of little improvements that made the system more capable and reliable. The eighty-four-foot tower was a way of getting the radar to look over the tall trees and at distant open spaces where infiltrators could be spotted. Another problem discovered and solved was power supply. Originally, juice came from a one-kilowatt generator. But this was barely adequate and not very reliable. The problem was solved by using a 3-kw generator.

PLASTIC ON FIRE

How did American soldiers get a fire going to cook their food in a monsoon-drenched jungle? Simple, they ignited a block of plastic explosive. One of the more common explosives used in Vietnam was C-4, or "plastique." In other words, plastic explosive. Having the consistency of silly putty (or modeling clay), it was very safe to handle. You needed a blasting cap to set it off, and you could even put a bullet into a block of C-4 without getting an explosion. The perfect explosive for troops, who have always been prone to accidents with their vast array of lethal tools.

Using C-4 as a fuel for cooking food or keeping warm during cool winter nights in the Central Highlands was not what the army had in mind when they distributed tons of C-4 to the troops. But how could you stop them? The C-4 was handed out liberally, for it was an excellent tool for blowing up enemy bunkers or taking down large trees so helicopters could come in. Most soldiers went out into the field with a pound or two of C-4 and some blasting caps to ignite it. But many soldiers didn't bother with the blasting caps; they just wanted the C-4 so they could heat up their C rations. Tear off a bit of C-4 from the block you were carrying, mold it into a small ball, and light it with your Zippo cigarette lighter and you have a nice little fire to heat up your morning coffee or C-rat stew.

When a block of C-4 wasn't available, troops would pry open claymore mines and take out some of the C-4 explosive for heating purposes. Some U.S., and many South Vietnamese, troops went overboard and took so much C-4 out of their claymores that when they tried to use them in combat, they just let off a mild-mannered "pop" and scared the enemy without injuring them too much. In those cases, the heat turned out to be very expensive. This was only one of several drawbacks to using C-4 as fuel.

C-4 is not particularly healthy if ingested, and there were a number of cases of "C-4 poisoning." These occurred because C-4 residue would cling to a knife or one's hands, and soldiers were often careless about using such implements to eat with without first cleaning them. Breathing C-4 fumes could also be harmful, and some troops using C-4 for fuel in enclosed quarters, such as a hut or the passenger compartment of an M-113, were overcome by the gas. And, by the way, never stamp out a fire made with C-4, as the compression and heat could cause the stuff to explode.

ROAD WARRIORS

Next to the infantry, the guys who saw the most combat were the long-haul truck drivers. Major bases were placed on the coast, because it was easier and safer to keep them supplied. Most stuff came from the United States via ship, and several heavily guarded ports in Vietnam handled this incoming material. But many of the smaller bases were away from the coast and helicopters, and aircraft could only be used for a small fraction of the men and material coming in and out of these bases. The rest, that is most of it, had to come in by truck.

When U.S. combat units arrived in 1965, one of the first things they started working on was clearing the major roads of enemy troops. No easy task, and a lot of the Agent Orange used was applied along the sides of roads, so ambushers would have no place to hide. But there were thousands of miles of roads and not all could be patrolled and cleared of sinister vegetation. The transportation people distributed color-coded road maps. Green roads meant they were generally safe (at least in daylight), amber ones were dangerous. Red lines indicated roads that needed a substantial armed escort and the expectation of a fight if you wanted to get through.

The convoys had to get through and the "combat convoys" were organized for trouble. The refrigerated trucks were put near the front, so their refrigeration equipment would not get jammed with dust from a lot of vehicles. In the rear were the trucks carrying flammable and explosive cargo, so that these were less likely to get hit, and if they did, they would not block the convoy route. Everything else went in the middle. The trucks themselves were sometimes armored, using sheets of steel that would stop shell fragments and some bullets. Sandbags were also used to limit damage from mines and stop some more bullets. The driver and his assistant had M-16s, and some trucks had a machine gun mounted on the cab. On dangerous routes, as many as one truck in ten was a "combat truck" that was more heavily armored and mounted several machine guns. Each "serial" (one to three dozen trucks traveling together) on dangerous routes had one or two armored cars manned by Military Police. Sometimes a helicopter was sent along to look for ambushes, but more often a gunship and several other helicopters were on alert, on the ground and ready for action should the convoy get hit. For really heavy duty action, tracked armored vehicles (M-113 APCs) would be sent along.

The Viet Cong never let up trying to close the roads. Often the ambushers were ambushed, especially when a lot of helicopters showed up or the convoy was more heavily armed than expected. The truck companies lost about a quarter of their carrying capacity to these security measures, plus thousands of trucks damaged and destroyed by the attacks.

These fighting truck drivers were recognized as such by being allowed to wear a special "long haul" patch that indicated someone who was a real life Road Warrior. And one of them earned a Medal of Honor in the process.

SOME USEFUL FIELD EXPEDIENTS

Although the armed forces usually invest a lot of time, manpower, and money in developing weapons and equipment for use in combat, it's not possible to take every possible development into account. Often, the troops in the field run across problems that no one ever thought about before. So they improvise. Sometimes the improvisations can be as simple as they are effective.

Body Bag Bedding. It can get pretty chilly in the central highlands (40–50 degrees Farenheit), which sometimes presented a problem for specialist troops, such as explosives disposal experts, who found themselves accidentally spending a few days at remote outposts without their normal gear. Some of the more hardened types would often improvise a sleeping bag out of a "Pouch, Human Remains," better known as a "body bag." While this sometimes gave even seasoned veterans pause, those who made use of the expedient reported the bags reasonably cozy, particularly if you rolled up your flak jacket for a pillow, which proved quite comfortable.

Enemy Equipment. As good as much U.S. military equipment was, it was often discovered that some enemy gear was superior. Some U.S. troops preferred the AK-47 assault rifle, especially before the bugs were worked out in the generally superior U.S. M-16. North Vietnamese rucksacks were often seen as superior to U.S. ones, and could easily be obtained from dead Communist troops (although a little patching might be required). LRRPs on patrol sometimes preferred the lightweight "black pajamas" that many Vietnamese wore (for work or war). Of course, there were occasional drawbacks to using enemy equipment: The AK-47, for example, has a unique "popping" sound when fired, which might make other U.S. troops think you were the enemy if you were using one. Of course, the distinctive sound of an AK-47 fired by an American soldier was often used to confuse the enemy when you were caught in an ambush or pursued by enemy troops. To prevent problems with enemy clothing, LRRPs would usually start their patrols in American uniforms and only switch to their black pajamas when in "bandit country."

Muzzle Seals. Dirt in one's rifle barrel can have ruinous consequences, and not just to the weapon. So keeping dirt out of the barrel is of some importance. There were several ways of sealing the muzzle while still leaving the weapon ready for instant use. Some troops used condoms, but these were not as secure as duct tape, which was easier to affix to the muzzle. A close examination of pictures of troops on patrol will often reveal that each muzzle is neatly sealed with some duct tape.

Piggy-Back Clipping. The army never issued many of the thirty-round clips for the M-16 rifle, apparently fearing that in the heat of combat the troops would fire off too much ammunition. This, of course, was precisely what the troops wanted to do. They soon found that they could tape two clips together in such a way that when the first one was empty they could remove it, flip it over, and insert the second much faster than they could reach for a fresh clip carried in their ammo pouches.

Street Fighting. During the Battle of the Hue in 1968, marines found themselves unprepared for fighting in a city. Normally, the marines were out in the bush, a form of combat they had been well trained for. But the Tet Offensive saw the city of Hue occupied by many Communist forces and the marines were the only troops available to root them out. Many of the marines, faced with the unfamiliar situation, fell back on the only examples of street fighting they had seen recently, a popular TV show called *Combat*. This program, fortunately, was uncharacteristically realistic in how it portrayed U.S. Army soldiers fighting in European towns and cities during World War II, since a lot of veterans were involved in making the series. The marines used the combat drills they had seen on TV with great success and went on to clear out Hue.

Tape. One of the secret weapons of the Vietnam War was tape (masking tape, duct tape, or other types used to temporarily repair equipment.) It had a seemingly infinite number of uses. As already noted, the troops used it to make piggyback clips and muzzle seals. But they also used it to tape their dog tags (lest "you sound like a cow") and other equipment likely to make noise, to secure grenade pins that had been deliberately loosened, to bind together C-4 charges, and whatever else they could think of.

Vermin Control. Rats were a big problem in firebases and base camps, where the troops lived in bunkers. It was discovered that adding a minute bit of C-4 (plastic explosive) to some peanut butter (which rats loved) caused the vermin to die from the toxic effects of the explosive. After a while, the rats would catch on, but not before a large dent was made in the local vermin population.

Weapons Modifications. Troops very often modified their equipment to make it work better. For example, machine gunners often improvised a feeder guide out of ration cans and welded it onto the slot into which one fed the ammo belt for their M-60s, which greatly facilitated loading at night. Men sometimes straightened the pins on grenades to make them easier to pull, a practice not without hazard. A loosened pin might be drawn accidentally if it caught on a branch or some piece of equipment, so they then added a bit of duct tape to make the pin a bit more secure. M-113 APC crewmen would often scrounge stray M-60 machine guns to affix to their vehicles, and sailors and coastguardsmen on coastal and riverine duty would frequently do the same to their patrol boats.

TIGERS, ELEPHANTS, POISONOUS REPTILES, AND DETERMINED VERMIN

Vietnam's central highlands were part of the major jungle wilderness area in Asia. That meant lots of exotic wild life, including some species not discovered until the 1990s and no doubt others still living in obscurity. But as violent as the fighting was in that area, humans were not the only lethal species in residence. There were also several hundred Asian tigers. Adults weighed in at seven hundred to eight hundred pounds, and their heads were as big as the rucksacks many soldiers carried on their backs. There were even more elephants, which weighed four or five times as much as the tigers, but were usually of much more docile demeanor. More numerous still were the poisonous snakes, including some truly impressive cobras. And then there were the rats, most of whom seemed to work for the Communists.

GIs in the central highlands often came across tiger tracks around their camps. This delighted the animal lovers in the ranks. But most troops found the presence of big cats made everyone a bit nervous. The tigers were apparently willing to wander around American base camps at night. Somehow they always missed the mines and booby traps.

Tigers love to stalk, often doing it just for entertainment. With thousands of soldiers marching down the Ho Chi Minh Trail and stalking each other in the bush, there were many documented (with a dead tiger, or tiger's meal, to show for it) and semidocumented (several witnesses to a close encounter) accounts of tigers at work. The Communists had the most problem with tigers, for the North Vietnamese and Viet Cong lived in the bush most of the time. The Communists also lacked aircraft with which to track the tigers from the air. Many a tiger met its end when a helicopter machine gunner opened up while the cat was caught unawares in the open. These airborne hunts were often at the behest of a local Montagnard chief, who was anxious to eliminate an older tiger that had taken to easier game like farm animals and children. In at least one case, the soldiers were able to locate a GI with taxidermy skills who saved the pelt. In most cases, there was brisk action near the furry corpse, as pictures were taken of GIs and Montagnards standing, rifle in hand, next to the tiger. These dead tigers created a large number of hunting stories, accompanied by the picture of the mighty hunter and his prey. The Montagnards loved it, for the tiger was hard to take in the bush, even after the Montagnards received a large number of American weapons. The dead tigers often had the tables further turned by being served up for dinner. It's been reported that the meat was tough and not all that tasty.

Out in the bush, often at night, the tiger was in its element, and this is where some of the more nerve-wracking encounters took place. Patrols were particularly at risk, as these small (rarely more than a dozen men) groups were spread out, walking slowly and quietly through the bush. This was just the sort of target tigers love to stalk, and eat if they were hungry. Many times, grisly evidence was found of tigers catching up with troops in the bush. Sometimes the evidence was closer to home.

Out in tiger country, most of the enemy troops were North Vietnamese from urban and farming areas where tigers were unknown. It was customary for small groups (two or three) of North Vietnamese soldiers to sneak around at night to mine roads. On several occasions, U.S. troops found an odd scene on these country roads. There was usually a partially dug hole in the road. Next to the hole was a mine, ready to go into the hole. One or more AK-47s were lying about, as well as some bits of bloody clothing and North Vietnamese–type backpacks. A bloody trail led off into the bush. When U.S. soldiers followed the bloody trail, they would find chewed up bodies hidden in the bush. It didn't take long to figure out what had happened. The local civilians also knew what was going on. A tiger had stalked the North Vietnamese as they moved through the bush toward the spot in the road they wanted to mine. While the men were busy digging the hole in the road, the tiger would leap out of the bush and quickly kill some, or all, of the North Vietnamese before they could grab their rifles. When one or more North Vietnamese got away, they would make it straight back to their camp, without trying to go after the tiger in the dark. The soldiers knew that the gunfire might bring nearby American or South Vietnamese patrols. Sometimes the North Vietnamese would get a few shots off. Rarely did much good. In truth, American troops would tend to ignore the sound of an AK-47 going off at night. They would check it out after daylight, and sometimes they would find a tiger's handiwork.

Communist soldiers who survived their encounters began spreading the word that there were worse things to fear at night than enemy ambushes. Getting shot was one thing, being torn up and eaten by a tiger was far worse. Still, the North Vietnamese were philosophical about it, often commenting when a patrol failed to return, "The tigers must have got them." Somehow, this seemed a preferable fate, for their professional pride, than thinking the Americans got the drop on them.

But the tigers were impartial and would stalk any two-legged critter they came across at night, or even during the day. U.S. LRRPs (long-range recon patrols) often had encounters with stalking tigers. Usually this was when the patrol (usually five or six troops) stopped by day (to watch a trail) or by night (to watch and get some rest). It was customary for these patrols to place claymore mines ten or more meters from their position, facing likely approaches the enemy might take. In thick bush, the troops would sit back to back when manning an ambush or observation post. Most would face the area under observation, while at least one would face the other direction. In one instance, the lone fellow "watching the back" began to notice some bushes moving off in the distance. Not wanting to embarrass himself in front of his more experienced comrades, he did not give the alarm immediately. But those bushes were definitely moving. Then he saw it, and was frozen in terror. A tiger had been sniffing around the claymore mine (hidden in the bush) and was now following the detonation wire right back to the troops. The soldier clicked off his safety and nudged the soldier behind him, who turned around, took one look, and then brought his rifle around, clicking off the safety as he did. The tiger, less than twenty yards away, heard that click, lifted up his head, stared at the two soldiers pointing rifles at him, decided this meal wasn't worth it, turned, and disappeared silently into the bush. The troops waited for a few minutes then decided to move elsewhere and let the local North Vietnamese soldiers deal with this hungry tiger.

The North Vietnamese had had to deal with tigers long before the Americans did. Ever since they began coming down the Ho Chi Minh Trail in 1959, they had had encounters with tigers. Most of these were the seriously sick trekkers, who'd had to be left behind beside the trail, lying in their hammocks waiting to die, recover, or get eaten by a passing tiger.

There were fewer encounters with elephants, an animal that rarely stalked prey (they are vegetarian) and generally avoided people. Unless, of course, they were domesticated elephants, which were widely used in Laos and Cambodia for heavy lifting. But there were two situations where troops would come into violent contact with elephants. The more common (but still rare) situation was when U.S. helicopters came across North Vietnamese troops using elephants to haul supplies or artillery. This was fairly common in Cambodia and Laos, and when discovered, the poor pachyderms were instantly reclassified as enemy vehicles and were attacked, usually with machine guns. This was rough on the elephants, and several LRRPs had reason to believe that the knowledge of such shooting spread among the elephant community. On several occasions, LRRPs, moving quietly through the bush in Laos or Cambodia, found that they were being followed (stalked might be too strong a word) by one or more elephants. In most cases, the elephants were just curious. But in at least one documented case, the elephant was out for blood. After following a patrol for three days, the elephant attacked. The troops scattered and fled, with one soldier getting stepped on (though not fatally). The elephant was driven off and the patrol leader then had to explain over the radio why they needed a medevac when there was no enemy activity.

Tigers and elephants were rare. Most troopers in the bush would never see one of either, although they might run into some soldiers who had (really, not just urban myth stories, some troops brought back photos from their encounters). Snakes, however, were quite common. And many of them were poisonous.

The most common snakes were usually encountered by the point man of a patrol or larger unit, where the reptile is startled by the slow and cautious approach of some guy with a gun. If the snake is one of several species of constrictors (many species over ten feet long), the encounter is usually non-fatal, as the snake just slinks away into the bush. But there are also several species of cobra, including the large king cobra, in Vietnam. All cobras bite, usually fatally, and some can spit blinding venom into your eyes from five to six feet away. Soldiers customarily greeted cobras with a long burst of gunfire, a loud yell, a rapid retreat, or all three actions simultaneously. Cobras don't just wait for people to come to them; they like to visit places where people live, the better to hunt rats. If you disturb a cobra while it is looking for rats, the cobra will often bite you. Soldiers also believed that cobras traveled in pairs, mated for life, and sought revenge if you killed its mate. For that reason, killing a snake in a bunker or hut did not bring relief but anxiety over where the vengeful mate was. There rarely was another snake, but that just shows you how great the fear of snakes was.

You could encounter snakes anywhere while in the open or inside. The Anilidae was common to rice paddies and basically harmless, but being two or three feet long and prone to coil its tail up would make an unwary soldier think he was a bite away from oblivion. In fields, you might encounter the krait. There are several species of these in Vietnam, with the largest one (five feet), the banded krait, so docile that few bites have ever been recorded. But the smaller kraits are keen on biting, and half their victims die, even if they obtain antivenom treatment. However, the most common cause of poisonous snakebites was the Russell's viper, about four feet long and found most often in open country. It was well camouflaged with a black, red/orange, and white pattern, and thus easily stepped on. In the jungles and along riverbanks, troops would often encounter several species of pythons, some over twenty feet long. While not poisonous, their size and ability to kill by constriction (a fourteen-year-old boy was killed and eaten by a large reticulated python in Malaysia) made soldiers nervous. Troops learned to just let the pythons slink away and felt safe in the knowledge that the largest snakes were not poisonous.

The most common critters encountered (aside from the insects) were rats.

Rats love to live among people because that's where the food is. And Americans had a lot more food, which attracted a lot of rats. The troops that saw the most rats were the ones that were housed in underground bunkers. This kind of living arrangement was common in smaller base camps deep in enemy territory. Special Forces camps, for example, or any number of smaller camps were used just to keep an eye on the area and give the larger camps some security from surprise attacks. Living underground, these troops were safe from most enemy firepower. But all that dirt attracted rats, for the rodents loved to dig, and they loved to eat. A bunkerful of U.S. troops was rat heaven. Lots of food and lots of dirt. And lots of pissed off GIs who did not appreciate what a fine time the rats were having.

Another thing that attracted rats was bodies. Normally bodies weren't left lying around very long, for both sides made some effort to dispose of them. But in some situations, such as the siege of Khe Sahn, this wasn't possible. One of the most common recollections among veterans of Khe Sahn is the enormous number of rats feasting on dead soldiers.

While Americans took a dim view of all these rats, the Montagnards considered it a symbiotic relationship, for the Yards liked to catch and cook rats. Some Special Forces troopers played along with that by going after rats with shotgun shells filled with rice. This killed the rat, but didn't tear him up or leave the body full of bird shot. The Yards appreciated that, although they could never figure out why the Americans wouldn't join them when they feasted on roasted rat. The Montagnards never could understand why their Special Forces friends didn't enjoy chowing down on a nice fresh rat. Indeed, some of the Yards would tease their Special Forces buddies about this strange aversion. A few Special Forces troopers came over to the Montagnard way of thinking, but had to keep this to themselves when they got home.

The rats mostly came out at night, when using a shotgun was frowned upon. Some soldiers got pellet guns for quieter, nighttime rat plinking, but found that most of these tough bush rats were immune to pellets. You'd hit them and the pellet would bounce off, the rat would turn around, give you a withering glance, and then scamper off. Air rifles were more effective, but for some of the larger rats you simply needed a more powerful weapon.

More conventional remedies were used, with mixed success. The local rats were a sturdy crew and quickly adapted to poisons. You couldn't really clear a bunker of rats, for the critters only used the bunker itself as their dining room. The rats lived in a system of tunnels connected to the bunker via several openings. Keeping a nonpoisonous snake in the bunker was the only way to keep the rats out, and a few troops found out which snakes could be kept under the bed and which couldn't, obtained one of the serpents, and generally kept their mouths shut about it.

Footnote: Friendly Animals in the War. The U.S. armed forces employed a lot of dogs in Vietnam. Although dogs were sometimes used to detect mines, track enemy patrols, clear tunnels, and sniff out drugs, most served as sentries at base camps and airfields or as scouts with troops in the bush. Dogs recruited for military service had to meet rigid standards (most of the more aggressive or ferocious breeds are unsuitable for military service). They underwent six months of basic training, usually at Fort Benning, before being sent to Vietnam.

There do not seem to be any official figures on the number of dogs that served in Vietnam, nor on the number that were killed. At the end of the war most of the dogs were left behind, as they had by then acquired numerous local parasites that made it impossible for them to be returned to the United States. This was very traumatic for the dog handlers, some of whom had served with the same animal for very long periods.

That dogs served in Vietnam is generally known. Much less well-known is that the navy used specially trained marine mammals in Vietnamese waters during the war. Although the program—which continues—is still shrouded in secrecy, it is known that before the Vietnam War the navy had begun to train seals and dolphins for a variety of underwater military missions, including sentry duty, searching for enemy divers, sniffing out mines, and carrying demolition charges. The number of marine mammals deployed to Vietnam is not known, nor is there any information as to their effectiveness. Nevertheless, it would seem that the navy was quite pleased with the results, as it has continued to use seals and dolphins for such missions, most recently during the Gulf War, and has even experimented with small whales.

TUNNELS AND TUNNELING

The most important piece of equipment Communist troops had was the shovel. With this tool, American firepower was rendered much less lethal. Communist soldiers not only dug the usual trenches and foxholes, but also underground bunkers and tunnel systems. Thus one of the more unique developments of the Vietnam War was the widespread use of underground installations. While this was not new in warfare—the Japanese had made extensive use of tunnels during the Pacific war—the extent to which the Viet Cong and North Vietnamese used them was staggering. Not only were tunnels used to link defensive positions, but they were also used for literally every variety of military and many civilian activities. Whatever could be done above ground could be done underground, except growing food.

The Viet Minh had resorted to tunneling in the late 1940s as a way to avoid detection, and attack, by French aircraft. Tunnels were also useful for concealing men and equipment in the vicinity of urban areas heavily patrolled by French troops. Many of the tunnel systems in the South remained secret even after the partition of Vietnam in 1954. With the resumption of large-scale guerrilla warfare by the Viet Cong in the late 1950s, the tunnel systems became increasingly more elaborate, a trend that accelerated after massive American airpower entered the picture in 1965.

Some of the tunnel systems were literally scores of miles in length, such as that near Chu Chi, about 25 miles northeast of Saigon. Begun in the late 1940s, by the fall of Saigon in 1975, there were some 125 miles of tunnels. The connecting passages were usually about a meter high and wide. These linked rooms, which were often on four different levels. There were many false passages, to foil easy exploration by South Vietnamese or American troops, and numerous hidden exits. Facilities included hospitals, barracks, ammunition dumps and arsenals, supply depots, kitchens, offices and conference rooms, communications centers, classrooms, even workshops and factories. Electric lighting was provided, from underground generators. There were also underground wells and sewage disposal systems. This was unusual, but the area was under VC domination for many years. A similar complex existed in the so-called Iron Triangle region, farther to the northwest, for similar reasons. Some enemy tunnel complexes were literally under South Vietnamese and American installations. By some accounts there was a Viet Cong medical facility under a part of the American base at Danang.

Once B-52 bomber attacks became common in the mid-1960s, the Communists found it prudent to put as much underground as possible. The B-52s flew so high that they could not be seen or heard until the bombs hit. Then it was too late to take cover unless you were already underground. Thus the spread of tunnel systems.

Life for the denizens of a VC tunnel was relatively comfortable, albeit the lack of sunlight may have been irksome, not to mention the presence of rats, scorpions, noxious insects, and occasional poisonous snakes. But there were enough B-52 attacks to make tunnel life seem like a positive thing.

Not all areas were suited to tunneling. The high-water table in the Mekong Delta region, for example, made their construction difficult. Tunnels were most readily constructed in dry clays. They were normally dug by the troops themselves or by forced labor gangs drafted from local villagers. Communist troops actually spent much less time in combat operations than their American counterparts, thus there was ample opportunity to expand and improve their tunnel complexes.

Coping with VC and NVA tunnels was difficult. The best "cure" for a tunnel complex was a B-52 strike, which would leave craters as much as thirty feet deep and send debilitating, and sometimes fatal, shock waves along tunnels that were not immediately collapsed. But some tunnel systems were so deep that even a B-52 strike did not completely destroy them. Over half the Communist troops in tunnels would survive a B-52 attack, hardly any would survive outside tunnels.

Moreover, to call in such a strike one had to first locate the tunnel system. The surface entrances (and ventilation holes) for tunnel systems were camouflaged and often guarded. Dogs were quite useful in locating tunnel entrances, but often the discovery of a tunnel was purely accidental. Often a B-52 strike was not available to destroy a tunnel complex, so it would be trashed the old-fashioned way (with explosives). But first, it was important to check out the tunnel system for enemy documents and other items that might be useful. Someone had to go down there and do this. A distinct breed of soldier emerged from the necessity of scouting enemy tunnel systems, "the Tunnel Rat." The typical Tunnel Rat was a smallish man, a role for which many Americans of Hispanic heritage found themselves well suited. Tunnel Rats were lightly equipped, usually with a pistol, flashlight, and little else. When a tunnel entrance was discovered, it was common to drop concussion or white phosphorous grenades in, or douse it with a flamethrower or tear gas. This cleared out any enemy troops who might be down there. With a rope around his waist, the Tunnel Rat would then begin exploring the passages. It was dirty, dangerous work, performed in the dark. Tunnel Rats often succumbed to booby traps; some died from scorpion, insect, or snake bite; and several died from oxygen starvation, having entered a tunnel too soon after it had been given a Willy Pete or Ronson (white phosphorous or flamethrower) treatment, not to mention enemy action. Once the Tunnel Rat(s) had finished with scouting the complex, engineers (often with the help of Tunnel Rats) would use explosives to destroy the complex. This was important, for the Communists had many more tunnel complexes than they occupied. These "spare" systems would be occupied when others were destroyed or were in areas getting too much attention from American troops. Destroying tunnel systems forced the Communists to build another one, which kept the Communist troops busy, too busy to go out and look for a fight.

Several tunnels in Vietnam are today preserved as war memorials.

CHAPTER 4

Slicks, Puffs, and Fast Movers
(War in the Air)

From helicopters to heavy bombers, just about every combat aircraft American had was used in Vietnam. Vietnam was the greatest demonstration of American airpower in history, exceeding even World War II.

THE LARGEST BOMBING CAMPAIGN IN HISTORY

World War II saw the introduction of the heavy strategic bomber. Four-engine aircraft like the B-17, B-24, and B-29 came into use and over 40,000 of these aircraft were built. In addition, more than 100,000 smaller fighters and light bombers also dropped bombs. The Korean War saw a much more modest bombing program, using leftover World War II aircraft. During World War II, bombers dropped 68,000 tons of bombs per month (averaged over six years), about half of it from U.S. aircraft. During Korea, using a few World War II–type aircraft, only 12,777 tons per month (over three years) were dropped. During the Vietnam War, 73,000 tons per month (over seven years) were used. In the 1991 Gulf War, 40,416 tons per month were dropped over a much shorter period (two months).

The increase in bomber technology after World War II was enormous. The most common heavy bombers of World War II carried about four tons of bombs, the fighter bombers of that period carried one or two tons. By the early 1960s, you had B-52s carrying twenty to thirty tons and fighter bombers carrying four tons or more. The 1960s aircraft could also fly more often and more reliably. But most important, there was a tremendous desire to spare the U.S. infantry the casualties normally taken fighting it out with the enemy using infantry weapons. It was noted during World War II and Korea that the lavish use of bombs and artillery could kill the enemy infantry without U.S. troops getting shot up. Well, up to a point. Unlike previous wars, the Communists quickly realized the effect of the U.S. firepower advantage and adjusted their tactics to minimize its effect. From the American perspective, the Communists often just refused to fight. But the Viet Cong and North Vietnamese knew that as long as they could keep troops active in South Vietnam, even if they weren't fighting much, the Communist cause would eventually prevail. Everyone knew that time was on the side of the Communists. So a lot of the bombs went off in free-fire zones (enemy-controlled areas in South Vietnam where any civilians were warned to leave or risk getting bombed) while American ground troops swept the area looking for enemy troops and their base camps. After some sharp battles with U.S. troops in 1965, the Communists went right back to their policy of avoiding slugging it out with an army who measured ammunition in the millions of tons. Even during the 1968 Tet Offensive, when Communist troops thought they would be safe if they took over parts of South Vietnamese cities and towns, they found that American troops always used their firepower when American lives were at risk. The Viet Cong–controlled neighborhoods were pounded into rubble.

Although the Vietnam bombing was concentrated on a smaller area than in World War II, not nearly as much of it was concentrated against civilians. Whereas World War II bombing killed some two million civilians, the Vietnam bombing slaughtered 360,000 from the air. Some of these were also killed by artillery, but these weapons were used with considerably more accuracy and a bit more discretion than bombs. The big difference between World War II bombing and the Vietnam type was that during World War II a major part of the bombing was directed specifically at the civilian population. Not so in Vietnam, although the attacks in North Vietnam aimed at economic and military targets often hit adjacent populated areas. The Communists knew that bombs falling on civilians made good propaganda and that U.S. pilots were under orders to avoid such targets. So the Communists regularly put military targets among civilian structures. Antiaircraft guns were placed on schools and hospitals or among civilian housing. Troops and military supplies were also placed in the midst of civilian housing. This was also done by the Viet Cong in South Vietnam. The Viet Cong knew that American bombs falling on local civilians increased support for the Communists and made it easier to recruit fighters.

Many Americans, both troops and senior leaders, knew that the morale, and loyalty, of South Vietnamese civilians suffered when they were hit by American firepower. Although there was a lot of anxiety over bombs or shells landing on civilians, there was an even greater aversion to losing U.S. troops for want of some life-saving firepower. As long as the war was being fought with civilians in the area, there were going to be civilian casualties.

U.S. COMBAT AIRCRAFT LOSSES IN SOUTHEAST ASIA

Vietnam was a major air war, in fact the biggest air war since World War II, the 1991 Gulf War notwithstanding. Helicopters aside, fixed-wing aircraft did an enormous amount of work.

In over three million sorties, 3,338 U.S. fixed-wing aircraft were lost from all causes. Counting only airplanes lost while in flight, the loss rate was about

U.S. Fixed-Wing Sorties in Southeast Asia, 1962–73

	Southern Areas	North Vietnam	Total
Air Force	1,766,000	275,000	2,041,000
Marines	510,000	27,000	537,000
Navy	320,000	226,000	546,000
	2,596,000	528,000	3,124,000

Key: A sortie is one mission by one airplane. Figures have been rounded. Southern Areas include South Vietnam, Laos, and Cambodia. North Vietnam is limited to sorties over the DRV.

one airplane in every 986 sorties. This was much lower than in World War II (during which 21,000 airplanes were lost, including losses to accidents in the continental United States and other areas not in combat zones), but not much of a comfort to those who had to do the flying.

Although more than a quarter of all airplane losses in the Vietnam War were operational losses, this was actually a considerable improvement on previous experience. Despite the greatly increased complexity and capability of the aircraft, operational losses due to faulty maintenance or pilot error were much lower during the Vietnam War than during World War II. For example, in 1943 alone, five thousand people died in military-related aviation accidents in the continental United States. Plus, in Vietnam, there was superior training and equipment that, for all its complexity, was actually often less difficult to repair than that of prior generations. Of course the critical issue is the loss of aircraft in combat.

U.S. Airplane Losses in Southeast Asia

	Combat Losses			Operational Losses			
	Air	Ground	Total	Air	Ground	Total	Overall
Air Force	1,606	95	1,701	461	27	488	2,189
Marine Corps	173	18	191	75	5	80	271
Navy	538	0	538	315	25	340	878
Total	2,317	113	2,430	851	57	908	3,338

Key: Figures exclude losses to aircraft owned and operated by nonmilitary agencies, such as the CIA's Air America. Combat Losses are those that resulted from contact with the enemy, those on the ground having been caused by enemy rocket attacks or commando raids, which is why the navy suffered no such losses, as its aircraft operated from carriers. Operational Losses are those resulting from accidents, mechanical failure, weather, or human error in noncombat situations. This figure would be higher if Vietnam-related operational losses in the United States and elsewhere (e.g., training accidents) were counted.

The pattern of loss in combat that developed during the Vietnam War was different than what had been thought would happen. Going into the war, much was expected of radar and guided missiles—both air-to-air and surface-to-air—while much less importance was placed on the role of gunfire, whether in air combat or in an antiaircraft role. In fact, it turned out that neither the radar nor the missiles were as good as expected.

HELICOPTERS EVERYWHERE

Vietnam was the first war in which helicopters played a major role. Helicopters had first seen action during the closing days of World War II, ironically in Burma, another part of Southeast Asia.

Helicopters were the "army mules" of the Vietnam War. They performed all sorts of missions, seemed capable of going everywhere, and often took incredible amounts of punishment and just kept on flying. An important consequence of the Vietnam War was that it hastened the widespread use of helicopters by the armed forces, a trend that was already in evidence.

The busiest helicopters were the famous UH-1s, "Hueys." Army Hueys alone accumulated 7,531,955 flight hours in Vietnam between October 1966 and the end of the war in 1975. Second to the Hueys were the AH-1Gs, or "Hueycobras," the combat version of the Huey, which flew 1,038,969 flight hours during the war. In addition, medevac helicopters—which came in several varieties—flew nearly 500,000 missions, airlifting over 900,000 patients. Not all of these were battlefield evacuations of American casualties. Many of these trips were to transfer casualties from one facility to another, as well as movement of civilian and ARVN patients.

The army officially reported 4,643 helicopters lost in action in Southeast Asia, with a further 6,000 so severely damaged as to require extensive rebuilding. There were about 36 million helicopter sorties (by mid-1969, there was a daily average of c. 2,500 helicopter sorties), so about 3 out of 10,000 flights resulted in serious damage. Lesser damage occurred more frequently. However, casualties were relatively light; the 10,000 damaged helicopters resulted in only 3,000 deaths and 2,300 injured. This amounted to less than one injury for each chopper lost or damaged. When you consider that the war lasted ten years and that there were always hundreds—and at times over a thousand—helicopters assigned to army aviation units, losing a dozen or so a week was not a catastrophe. Nevertheless, flying or riding in helicopters during Vietnam was still risky, or at least nerve-wracking. Sundry bullet holes in the choppers did more damage to peace of mind than they did to the helicopters and were rarely counted as "damage." Indeed, helicopter units lost a smaller proportion of their pilots, fewer than ground units lost infantry. Still, it was, after the infantry, the highest risk job in Vietnam.

Principal Helicopters of the Vietnam War

Model	Length	Crew	Seats	Load	Speed	Endurance	Notes
Light Observation							
OH-58A Kiowa	32.4	2	2	1,700	100	130	A
OH-6A Cayuse	23.5	2	2	1,237	100	150	B
OH-13H Sioux	31.4	1	2	600	70	90	C
Utility							
UH-1B Huey	42.7	4	6	4,600	90	90	D
UH-1C Huey	42.6	4	6	4,800	110	115	E
UH-1D Huey	42.0	4	11	4,900	110	110	F
UH-1H Huey	42.0	4	11	4,900	110	115	G
Cargo and Transport							
CH-21 Shawnee	86.0	3	23	5,000	110	150	H
CH-34C Choctaw	46.8	2	18	7,800	100	140	I
CH-47A Chinook	51.0	3	33	16,000	120	60	J
CH-47B Chinook	51.0	3	33	19,000	120	60	K
CH-47C Chinook	51.0	3	33	19,700	120	120	L
CH-53A	67.1	3	38	13,000	150	100	M
CH-54A Tarhe	70.3	3	45	20,600	95	110	N
CH-54B Tarhe	70.3	3	45	21,000	80	100	O
Attack							
AH-1G Hueycobra	44.5	2	0	6,400	120	110	P

Key: A number of other helicopters saw some service in Vietnam. *Model*, type code and common name; *Length*, over all, in feet. *Crew*, the number of men needed to operate the bird. *Seats*, the number of combat-equipped troops that could be carried. *Load*, amount of cargo that could be carried, in pounds. *Speed*, in miles per hour. *Endurance*, how many minutes the helicopter can stay in the air. Normally, twenty to thirty minutes of this was not used; it was a safety reserve. The remaining minutes, cut in half, gives the max time the helicopter could fly out. *Notes* refers to the lettered comments below.

A. About two thousand Bell OH-58As served with the army, from 1969 to 1980. It could carry three passengers. A modification kit permitted it to be fitted with a 7.62 mm machine gun.

B. The OH-6A Cayuse was a military version of the Hughes Model 500 commercial helicopter. The army acquired some fourteen hundred between 1964 and 1970, many of which saw service in Vietnam. It continued in use into the 1980s. One version could carry up to seven passengers, and some versions were rather heavily armed (e.g., fourteen 2.75-in. rockets, plus a minigun or grenade launcher, or maybe some TOWs). It was nicknamed "the Loach," from LOH for light observation helicopter. Design work began in 1961 and it first flew in 1963.

C. The Sioux, which first flew in late 1945, was the oldest helicopter design in use in Vietnam. Its distinctive bubble canopy made it an excellent scout chopper. It was soon surpassed by later designs with higher speed and longer range.

D. The first of the second generation of military helicopters, the Bell UH-1 Iroquois was originally designated the HU-1 Helicopter, Utility, Model 1), from which came its common nickname, "Huey," much as the World War II "jeep" had acquired its name from GP, for "general purpose." There were numerous versions, including trainers, and many were armed, either as built (sixteen 2.75-in. rockets plus two 7.62 mm machine guns) or with the addition of a weapons packet. It could carry up to seven passengers. It was used by all the services. Over 10,000 UH-1s were produced, making the Huey the most widely produced combat aircraft since World War II. Based on an early 1950s design, the first one flew in 1956 and deliveries began in 1959. Only two hundred of the A model were built, while 1,100 of the 1960 B model were delivered before production switched to the C and D models in 1963. The B model was the first used in Vietnam on a wide scale, from 1965.

E. UH-1C. Basically the same as the B model, but enhanced in 1965 for use as a gunship. Not many were built, as the AH-1 Cobra became available in 1967 and replaced it.

F. UH-1D. This was a major upgrade in the UH-1 design and, along with the H model, the most widely produced. Entered production in 1963. Nearly two thousand built. There were many variants for the navy, air force, and marines. The army also built some eighty "night fighter" variants (UH-1M) that were used from 1969 on. These had night-vision devices and a multibarrel machinegun. The UH-D, like the other UH-1 series machines, had two notable characteristics. Most important, they used a gas turbine engine (in effect, a jet engine) to turn the rotor. This type of engine needed a lot of fuel. The UH-ID's engine used eight pounds of fuel a minute. But the benefits of a gas turbine engine were many. You could get more power more quickly, and pound for pound, it was the most powerful engine you could put in any aircraft. This made the UH-1 choppers faster and more capable than all previous helicopters. The second major asset of the UH-1 design was that it was a lot easier to maintain than earlier helicopter designs. It required about six man-hours of maintenance per hour spent in the air, and that could be skimped on in an emergency without major risks.

G. UH-IH. In 1967, this upgrade of the UH-1D design appeared and remained in production for nearly twenty years. Over five thousand built.

H. The Boeing Vertol CH-21 first flew in 1952 and remained in service until 1971. It was the first U.S. helicopter sent to Vietnam, with thirty-two arriving in 1961.

I. The Sikorsky CH-34 was originally a navy design (the S-56) and came into service a year before the UH-1. It first flew in 1953. The army bought 434 of them and many were used in Vietnam, largely by the South Vietnamese. Nicknamed "the Kingbee," it was basically a cargo helicopter and was not as maneuverable or as easy to maintain as the UH-1. It was a sturdy beast, though, and popular with pilots because they sat over the reciprocating engine, which protected them from ground fire. Unlike the more delicate gas turbine engine in the UH-1, the older type engine in the CH-34 could take a lot more punishment and keep on going. But the CH-34 required sixteen man-hours of maintenance per flight hour. Because the State Department had enough clout to keep most American aircraft out of "neutral" Laos, South Vietnamese helicopters had to be used to rescue trapped American-led patrols in the mid-1960s. South Vietnam didn't have the new UH-1 choppers, but the older CH-34. The South Vietnamese pilots who flew the Kingbee were a flamboyant lot. They would fly anywhere, under any conditions, to get the job done. The CH-34 lacked the lifting power and range of the UH-1, but it was reliable and maneuverable enough for these clandestine missions over Laos.

J. The Boeing Vertol Chinook was the army's "battlefield mobility" helicopter.

Although it was of the same generation of technology as the UH-1, it was much larger. A "heavy lifter" (of cargo and weapons like artillery), it first flew in 1961 and entered service in 1963. Eventually, over a thousand (all models) were built. Some versions were provided with light armament.

K. The CH-47B version of the Chinook was a more powerful model that appeared in 1967. With its greater lifting power, it could more easily recover damaged aircraft and helicopters, picking up over ten thousand of them during the war.

L. The CH-47C, an even more powerful and efficient model of the Chinook, appeared in 1968 and mounted defensive armament.

M. The Sikorsky CH-53 was designed for the marines. The heaviest carrier-capable helicopter, it first flew in 1964, entered service in 1967, and remains in use to the present.

N. Better known as "the Sky Crane," "Flying Crane," or "Jolly Green Giant," the enormous (c. 38,000 pounds) Sikorsky CH-54 was designed to be fitted with a variety of special pods to permit it to serve as a cargo transport, maritime mine layer, or troop transport (eighty-seven armed men or twenty-four stretcher cases), or it could be used to lift heavy objects, such as other helicopters. The CH-54A first flew in 1962 and entered service in 1965.

O. The CH-54B, which entered service in 1969, was a more powerful version of the A model. It broke many records for lifting loads by helicopter.

P. The Bell Hueycobra was designed in 1966–67 based on the highly successful UH-1. There were several versions, but the AH-1G was the most common, with more than a thousand entering service with the army by the end of the Vietnam War, as well as some in the navy and marines. The AH-1G initially carried a chin turret with 6 × 7.62 mm machine guns; later versions added a 40 mm grenade launcher and four external pods, each with nineteen 2.75-in. rockets. For the previous five years, more and more weapons had been fitted to the UH-1s more or less as a field expedient, turning them into formidable gunships. But the AH-1 went even further, restricting the crew to two (a pilot and weapons operator) and using the weight saved to carry more ammunition. Some 1,100 were eventually produced.

HELICOPTER OPERATIONS AND LOSSES

Although U.S. helicopters suffered thirteen crashes per 100,000 sorties, there were more combat casualties from situations where the helicopter under attack did not crash. The Hueys spent most of their time flying low enough to get shot at by anything the enemy had. Although everyone on board wore a flak jacket, and the pilots sat in armored seats, the helicopter was basically aluminum and thus not capable of stopping bullets. The crew did that from time to time. The crashes did not result in as many deaths as one would expect. For every hundred helicopters lost in combat, 145 crew and passengers were killed. For every hundred choppers lost for noncombat reasons, 89 people died. There was good news and bad news to all this. The good part was that helicopters did not crash with as much finality as fixed-wing aircraft. Operating close to the ground and capable of slowing down its impact even with the engine shut down ("autorotation" of the rotor), helicopter crashes were not nearly as fatal as they looked. There were a lot of injuries, though, especially broken bones and burns from all that fuel catching fire. Oh, and one final difference between helicopter crashes and the

Helicopter Loss Rates

Year	Sorties (x1,000)	Combat	Noncombat	Loss Rate
				per 100,000 sorties
1966	2,993	124	197	14
1967	5,516	264	400	12
1968	7,418	497	511	14
1969	8,441	459	589	12
1970	7,564	393	419	11
1971	4,213	230	284	12
Totals	36,145	2,076	2,566	13

fixed-wing kind. It was quite common for the largely intact helicopter wreckage to be recovered (using a much larger helicopter) and the busted chopper either be restored to flying status or used for spare parts.

Some sorties were more dangerous than others, even those categorized as "combat." There were four broad categories of sorties:

• Attack sorties (11 percent of all sorties) consisted of heavily armed helicopters attacking ground targets with various types of machine guns and rockets.

• Assault sorties (21 percent) were passenger helicopters carrying troops into a combat zone. There was not always enemy fire while the troops were landing, but often there was.

• Cargo sorties (10 percent) were the flying truck trips. In many parts of Vietnam, flying stuff in was the only practical, or safe, way to get it in. They were often under fire, as cargo had to be flown into bases under siege (a common situation out in the bush).

• Other sorties (58 percent) covers a lot of ground. Most of these were "taxi" sorties, where a few passengers are being taken somewhere. Some are reconnaissance (intentional or accidental), and others C^2 (command and control) missions, where a unit commander was directing his ground troops from the air. Some of the "taxi" sorties were the most dangerous. Normally, picking up troops was a safe sortie. But getting patrols out of the bush after enemy contact often turned out to be the most dangerous missions of all. These long-range patrols were often deep in enemy territory and the bad guys were usually numerous, heavily armed, and mad. And you were likely one of only a handful of helicopters to shoot at. Another often dangerous type of mission was the "sniffer" run, where a chopper would haul around a device that could sniff out the presence of humans down in the jungle. Accompanied by some gunships, sniffer runs often ran into some heavy firepower. But at least it was close to home. Most dangerous of all were the

"Bright Light" missions to recover downed pilots in enemy territory. The enemy was thick on the ground and hot to get both the pilot on the ground and his rescuers in the air. Late in the war another form of "sniffer" came into use. To better destroy North Vietnamese trucks on the Ho Chi Minh Trail, even when those trucks were hiding under triple canopy jungle or trees pulled together across sunken roads, Black Crow was developed. Black Crow operated on such a simple principle that it was very important to keep it secret; it picked up the electronic impulses given off by the engine ignition systems of the North Vietnamese trucks. Thus identified, the helicopters would then hose the area with machine gun and rocket fire. The secondary explosions indicated that something had been hit.

HELICOPTER SORTIES ARE DIFFERENT

Ever since the first combat aircraft took off into harm's way, that operation, from takeoff to landing (either in one piece or as a crash) was called a *sortie*. Same for helicopters. But in Vietnam it was soon discovered that since the helicopter could land just about anywhere, was a sortie still a sortie? Well, sort of. The army ended up being flexible about how to define a sortie. What it came down to was that it was a sortie for a helicopter when the pilot fired up the engine, went out and flew around, maybe landing and taking off again several times, and then landed someplace and shut the engine off. That was a sortie. From engine on to engine off. The UH-1 only carried fuel for about eighty to ninety minutes of flying, but as any kind of pilot will tell you, it's the landings and takeoffs that provide most of the excitement and that's what helicopters did a whole lot of.

But even level flight in a helicopter is a lot more exciting than in a fixed-wing aircraft. Choppers move around at much lower altitudes and deliberately hide behind hills, and even forests, to protect themselves from enemy observation and fire. At low altitudes, whoever can see you can hit you with whatever weapons they have. But there's a good side to that. In the thickly forested mountains and flatlands of Vietnam, you can hear a low-flying helicopter some miles off, but can't really tell exactly where it is until it's practically on top of you. At that point, you still have the trees and underbrush to worry about. This is why chopper crews are so nervous about approaching a "Hot LZ" (a landing zone, or open area, under fire from enemy troops). A helicopter coming down on a Hot LZ gives enemy troops a perfect target.

The North Vietnamese quickly learned that to set up ambushes for helicopters, all they had to do was look at geography the way helicopters did. This meant putting heavier machine guns (.50 cal./12.5 mm and larger) on the sides of hills with the underbrush cleared away so the gun crew could get a clear view of approaches to local LZs or valleys choppers regularly flew down. By the late 1960s, helicopter crews had to worry about these ambushes, especially if they were flying into areas the Communists had occupied for weeks or months. It didn't take long to set up these ambushes, and as the Ho Chi Minh Trail became a truck route, thousands of these heavy machine guns were sent south.

THOSE DARING YOUNG MEN IN THEIR FLYING MACHINES

Vietnam saw a unique generation of young combat aviators that no one expected. These were the warrant officer pilots the army used for its thousands of helicopters. They were young, much younger than the other professional pilots in the air force and navy. They flew under much more dangerous and difficult conditions than their air force and navy colleagues, and flew a lot more often. They got shot down more often and were more likely to get killed and injured than the jet pilots in the other services. No one seemed to notice how exceptional this lot were. But they were, by far, the hardest working and most daring pilots in the air during the Vietnam War.

Perhaps a little historical background will explain how this all came to be. The first combat pilots were the young men who took to the air in fragile aircraft in 1914. No one had any experience in combat flying back then, and the senior officers were rather dubious of how useful it would be. As a result, just about anyone with nerve enough, and a minimum degree of flying skill, could volunteer and be accepted. Even enlisted men were allowed to become combat pilots in most air forces. It wasn't until flying became widely recognized as glamorous, and useful, that pilot slots were restricted to officers. World War II saw the last of the enlisted pilots, and after 1945, combat flying became more "professional" and a lot less receptive to daring young men with a taste for daredevil flying.

Then along came Vietnam and the U.S. Army's recognition that their new UH-series helicopters were really, really useful. Unfortunately, it was easier to build more helicopters than it was to find qualified people to fly them. The army's solution was to go back about fifty years and reinvent the World War I technique of letting just about anyone fly. Rather than have enlisted pilots again, the army chose a middle course. They revived the "Warrant" rank. The U.S. armed forces had long used the rank of warrant officer for technical jobs that required more skill and authority than a noncommissioned officer (sergeant or navy petty officer) had. Using warrant officers (often just called "warrants") also solved a problem with Congress, which, technically "commissioned" officers and set the number of such officers each service could have at any one time. Okay, that solved the rank problem, but where to get the pilots? Helicopters were not as common in the civilian world as they are today and there were a lot fewer people who knew how to fly them. Moreover, flying a helicopter was quite different from flying a fixed-wing airplane. The situation was very similar to that faced by the military in 1914, and the solution was pretty much the same. The word was put out that anyone in the army who wanted to try out to be a helicopter pilot could. And that meant just about anyone. There were certain physical (good physical shape and eyesight) and mental (above average, but only enough to grasp the technical aspects) requirements, but that only excluded about half the soldiers. There were other requirements that were a bit more difficult to quantify. So the recruiting teams went around, with a helicopter, to each army battalion that generated some potential pilots and took the lads up for a pretty wild ride. This eliminated all of those who got airsick or otherwise demonstrated an aversion to the tumult of a combat helicopter doing what it often did up there. The surviving recruits were further tested to make sure they had the smarts and other characteristics needed for helicopter school. Then off they went. Many were teenagers.

Flight school washed out a lot more, although the number flunked tended to fluctuate depending on how desperate the army was to get more pilots. The army got pretty desperate during the late 1960s.

When these young warrant officers hit Vietnam, things began to get interesting, in ways the army had not anticipated. These guys were gutsy and did things with their Hueys that no one thought possible (or prudent). The young pilots turned out to be a lot more fearless than the older (and much less numerous) breed of army helicopter pilots. This fearlessness came with age and ignorance. Guys that young have not yet developed a strong sense of their mortality. They also don't know much about life in general and army life in particular. Like their World War I predecessors, they just jumped into their flying machines and did some pretty crazy things. Not knowing, or caring, about their limitations, the warrant officer pilots did things with their choppers that the brass thought impossible (or, at the very least, implausible). They were also rather popular with the troops, who appreciated the risks these warrants took to rescue the wounded, bringing in reinforcements, and doing odd jobs, such as arranging to supply an isolated firebase with cold beer and hot pizzas.

There was also another major distinction between the young warrants and the career officers who commanded them. Most of the warrants had an enlisted man's attitude toward their army service. In other words, they were doing a few years of this and then getting out. This made it much more difficult for their commanders to control them. The usual threat was to "put something in your file that will hurt your career." To these warrants, the only thing that could "hurt their career" was getting killed in action. These men basically had the same mentality as the earlier sergeant pilots, right down to creative additions to uniforms, casual attitudes toward authority, and a general demeanor of wild and crazy guys. As with the World War I crew, a lot of this was to make it easier to handle the stress of combat.

AIR COMBAT

American pilots went into Vietnam thinking they were the best. They were very good. But not as good as they believed. In fact, initially American losses to enemy fighter aircraft were shockingly high. From mid-1964 through 1969, about 10 percent of U.S. aircraft losses were caused by enemy aircraft. This was a "kill ratio" (the number of enemy aircraft shot down by your own aircraft compared to your own aircraft losses in air-to-air combat) of only about 2:1, which was a lot worse than in either World War II or Korea. And that was only because many of the enemy fighters encountered were older models, MiG-17s and MiG-19s. Encounters between MiG-21s and navy fighters were resulting in 1:1 kill ratios, bad enough, were it not for the fact that those between MiG-21s and air force fighters were even worse, running 1:3 in favor of the MiGs. Clearly there was a problem

Creating the Problem. There were several reasons for the relatively poor performance of American fighter pilots early in the Vietnam War.

1. Poor Pilot Training. Both navy and air force pilot training pitted American pilots in American airplanes using American tactics against American pilots in American airplanes using American tactics. So American pilots were very good at mock air combat with each other. But they had no practice against other types of airplanes and other types of tactics. Also, since training accidents made bad publicity, training tended to be held when the weather was good. The air force had another problem. The USAF tried to have all its fighter pilots trained for both air-to-air combat and close air support (CAS) missions. Although the army would probably have been surprised to hear it, prior to Vietnam air force fighter pilots were put through a dozen air-to-air combat drills a year, and about two hundred air-to-ground attack drills. This was not because the air force relished the mission of supporting the ground pounders, but because CAS training costs a lot less than air combat training.

2. Rotation Policies. The USAF made a number of very serious mistakes in terms of personnel management. Vietnam did not have much work for bomber pilots. Most B-52 pilots were waiting around for nuclear Armageddon rather than conducting bombing missions in Southeast Asia, while a major portion of the USAF's transport aircrew were similarly on standby to move massive numbers of reinforcements to Europe in the event of World War III. As a result there were too many heavy bomber and transport pilots, and not enough fighter pilots. So the USAF began reassigning bomber jocks and transport drivers to fighter squadrons, with minimal retraining. Up until early 1967, nearly 65 percent of USAF fighter pilots were from the Tactical Air Command; thereafter they increasingly came from other commands, notably bomber and transport, rising to about 50 percent of the total, while the MiG kill ratio fell from 3-to-1 to less than 1-to-1. Making matters worse, the USAF adopted an individual rotation system. A pilot went home after one hundred missions, which didn't do much for unit cohesion and morale (imagine going up for your one hundredth mission with a wing man who was on his first). The navy did things differently, and at least initially did not have as much of a problem with pilot quality. Taking advantage of its carriers, the navy rotated entire squadrons. This meant that navy pilots saw less time in combat on any one tour of duty, but they ended up having more combat time overall, since a carrier usually returned to the South China Sea two or three times in two years. This eventually led to a decline in the morale of navy pilots, who saw an endless series of deployments in their future.

3. Missilemania. From the end of World War II to the eve of the Vietnam War, a lot of money was spent on air-to-air missile research. So enamored was the USAF with its missiles, that it stopped work on aircraft gun systems in 1957. By the early 1960s, both the navy and air force fighters were almost exclusively armed with missiles. Unfortunately, the missiles didn't always work.

Basic Characteristics of Air-to-Air Missiles

Missile	Aspect	Range	Weight	Accuracy	Notes
AIM-4 Falcon	Rear	11	145	10%	A
AIM-7D Sparrow	All	50	450	9%	B
AIM-9B Sidewinder	Rear	3	155	14%	C
AIM-9D Sidewinder	Rear	11	170	18%	C
AA-2 ATOLL (USSR)	Rear	3	155	4%	D

Key: Missile, name of missile. Aspect, direction from which the missile-firing aircraft must approach the target. Range, distance the missile can go from launching aircraft to target, in kilometers. Weight, launch weight of the missile, in pounds. Accuracy, percentage of missiles fired that hit an enemy aircraft. Notes refer to the lettered comments below.

A. AIM-4 Falcon. A USAF missile, aside from problems like infrared detector sensitivity and excessive complexity, took too long to fire, so that by the time it left the airplane the "envelope" or opportunity was usually not there any more. During Rolling Thunder only 9 percent of fifty-four AIM-4s fired scored kills. It never got much better, and although it remained in service until 1972, by 1970, it had been eclipsed by the AIM-9.

B. AIM-7D and AIM-7E Sparrow. The D model was used on both navy and air force F-4s from April 1965 until replaced by the E model in early 1966. Prewar experiments had indicated a 71-percent hit rate. In practice this was much too high. During Rolling Thunder only 27 of 330 fired AIM-7s made kills. The missile's main problem was that it was a very complex piece of equipment, which required constant and careful attention. In fact, an official air force study ultimately determined that even under the best of circumstances the missile probably would have an accuracy of no more than 30 percent. Among the problems: the fastest way to "lock on" to a target and fire the missile gave an accuracy of only 1.5 percent, while the more careful mode took five seconds. In five seconds of air combat, a lot can happen. And the pilot had to maintain his "lock" until the missile hit the target, thereby making the F-4 a sitting duck, unless the pilot chose to abandon his "lock," thereby losing his missile: moreover, the system's radar became confused by ground return—radar waves bounding off the terrain below 8,000 feet; and so forth.

C. AIM-9B Sidewinder. Developed in the early 1950s, an advanced version of the Sidewinder is still in use as of this writing. It was a very popular missile in Vietnam because it was easy to use and very reliable. But that was only on a comparative basis. During Rolling Thunder, 187 AIM-9Bs were fired, but only twenty-nine aircraft were shot down, the other 85 percent of the missiles either malfunctioned or were fired at too great a range or otherwise missed. Its principal problem was that in order to fire a missile the attacking airplane had to approach from the rear, and it was very difficult to use against an airplane that was turning at high speed. It also had some problems with its infrared guidance system, which sometimes had trouble differentiating between heat exhaust and other sources of infrared radiation, such as clouds, the ground, or the sun; and it did not work well if the target entered a cloud due to the high moisture content. And it worked best against slow moving targets, which enemy MiGs rarely were. Prewar experiments had indicated a 65-percent hit rate. It was widely used by the USAF, and by the navy until 1966–67, when it was replaced by the AIM-9D. The AIM-9D was a bit better because it had a different coolant system, giving it an accuracy of about 18 percent, but it could not be fired from the same rails used by the B model and vice versa. One thing though, the AIM-9 was very deadly at close range: If fired within three hundred meters, the Sidewinder had a hit rate of about 90 percent, and a kill rate of about 86 percent.

D. The Atoll was a Soviet copy of the AIM-9B, and a rather shabby one at that, used widely by North Vietnamese pilots. Lower overall performance than the Sidewinder, under the best of conditions, and generally unreliable as well. Many Atolls fired managed to have their guidance system or fuze fail, much to the relief of American pilots who were their ostensible targets.

Aside from their individual problems, some of the missiles had a *minimum* range. Unfortunately, some fighter pilots often pressed their attacks so relentlessly that they were too close to the target, and the missile failed to lock on or the warhead to arm, so a kill was lost if no machine guns or cannon were being carried. This was the case with many U.S. Air Force planes early in the war.

Solving the Problem. As the relatively unfavorable kill ratio became apparent, attempts were made to redress the problem.

1. Improved Training. Interestingly, it was the navy that first took steps to enhance the skills of its fighter pilots, although they were already achieving a better kill ratio than their air force counterparts.

In 1969, the navy created its "Top Gun" air combat school. Here pilots

Overall U.S. Fighter Aircraft Kill Ratios, 1964–72

Model	Air Force	Navy/Marine	Combined
F-4	3:1	5.4:1	**
F-8	*	6:1	6:1
F-102	0:1	*	0:1
F-105	1.4:1	*	1.4:1
Overall	2.4:1	5.6:1	2.6:1

*Not used by this service.
**No figure is available.

Enemy Aircraft Lost in Air Combat

Type	Air Force	Navy/Marines	Total
MiG-17	61	39	100
MiG-19	8	2	10
MiG-21	68	18	86
	137	59	196

Key: In addition, navy fighters downed two An-2 light transport aircraft, and army UH-1s got two as well, bringing the total U.S. score in air-to-air combat to two hundred aircraft. The air force MiG-21 figure includes two shot down by B-52s.

practiced air combat against pilots trained to fly and fight using Soviet doctrine and tactics, using aircraft whose performance characteristics most closely matched those of Russian equipment, rather than against pilots using the same tactics and aircraft that they themselves were flying. A marked improvement in the performance of navy and marine pilots was quickly noticed. This inspired the air force to develop its "Red Flag" program, which added a lot of electronics to improve the simulated air-combat experience. Aircraft losses in air-to-air combat plummeted, so that the overall rate for the entire war was about 5 percent.

2. *Bringing Back the Guns.* A number of older pilots—veterans of Korea and even a handful from World War II—noticed that they were losing kills (because of problems with missiles) that they could easily have made if they were armed with cannon, and started agitating for the more "primitive" weapon system. Eventually the brass caught on. Fortunately, before the services had abandoned gun development for fighters in 1957, an excellent system had been developed, the M-61A1 Vulcan 20 mm automatic cannon.

The M-61A1 is actually an electrically operated six-barreled Gatling gun. Based on the famous nineteenth century design of Richard J. Gatling, it is

U.S. Fighter Losses to Enemy Aircraft

Type	Air Force	Navy/Marines	Total
A-1 Skyraider	1	0	1
A-4 Skyhawk	0	1	1
A-6 Intruder	0	2	2
F-4 Phantom	35	7	42
F-8 Crusader	0	3	3
F-102 Delta Dart	1	0	1
F-105 Thunderchief	21	0	21
Other	1	3	4
	59	16	76

Air Force Air Combat Victories by Weapon System

Weapon	Victories
AIM-4 Falcon	5.0
AIM-7 Sparrow	50.0
AIM-9 Sidewinder	33.0
B-52 Tail Guns	2.0
M-61 Vulcan	41.5
Other	9.5
Total	140.0

Air Force Air Combat Victories by Type and Platform

Aircraft	MiG-17s	MiG-19s	MiG-21s	Total
F-4	33.5	8.0	67.0	108.5
F-105	27.5	0.0	0.0	27.5
B-52	0.0	0.0	2.0	2.0
Totals	61.0	8.0	69.0	138.0

Key: The table omits two An-2 transports downed by F-4s.

technically not a machine gun at all, since it does not use the recoil or gases generated by the firing of one round to load and fire the next. There is a cluster of six barrels, which revolve using an electrically controlled hydraulic mechanism. Each barrel fires just one round before rotating out of the firing position to reload. It can fire at up to 7,200 rounds per minute, but operationally is used at one of two rates, either the "low" rate of 4,000 rounds per minute or the "high" rate of 6,000 rounds per minute. It can be used in both an air-to-air or air-to-ground role, and in Vietnam was mounted on fighters, ground attack aircraft, Puffs (gunships), and helicopters. It was light, only about 280 pounds, and could spit a stream of shells at nearly a kilometer a second, and was lethal up to about half a mile. Vulcan pods were soon being "retrofitted" to fighters. It proved more effective and much cheaper than missiles. Even without using a computerized aiming system that came with the weapon (i.e., when the pilot aimed manually), fighters could get a kill about once every ten firings, which was better than they could do with Falcon or Sparrow missiles. And if the computer system was used, the kill rate climbed to about 25 percent, much better than any of the air-to-air missiles. Interestingly, Soviet-built fighters scored most of the air-to-air victories using cannon. MiG-21s shot down only three American aircraft using the AA-2 Atoll missile, which had performance characteristics more or less like those of the AIM-9B, although the Russian missile was much less reliable.

Footnote: Navy Guys Do It Better. Throughout the war, navy and marine pilots put in a better performance than air force pilots. This was true even in the early years, when a lot of mistakes were being made. At that point the sea services' 1-to-1 exchange rate with MiG-21s compared well with the air force's much worse 1-to-3 rate. The navy/marine overall performance was a remarkable 5.6-to-1, as opposed to the air force's 2.4-to-1. It came down to training. Navy and marine pilots had more of it, if only because they had to spend months learning how to land on carrier decks before they shipped out to the war zone. Since combat is about the only thing in aviation more difficult than carrier landings, this extra training gave the seagoing pilots an edge. However, the overall quality of naval pilots did tend to decline during the war. The sea services had trouble keeping up a steady supply of fresh pilots (all that carrier training takes time), and the experienced hands tended to be sent back to Southeast Asia again and again, with a consequent lowering of morale.

ANTIAIRCRAFT DEFENSE

The air war to a great extent pitted American airplanes against NVA and VC antiaircraft defenses. As the air war intensified, the NVA and VC increased their antiaircraft defenses. By the end of the war the antiaircraft defenses of North Vietnam were the most elaborate in history, amounting to more than 8,000 antiaircraft guns, 25 surface-to-air missile battalions, and 250 fighter aircraft, plus over 200 radar sites and extensive communications installations. At the same time, Communist troops in the South had acquired considerable numbers of antiaircraft artillery pieces, automatic weapons, and even missiles.

The Vietnam War was the first in which antiaircraft missiles were used on a large scale. The results were somewhat surprising. During the war, 2,317 U.S. airplanes became combat losses while in the air. The following table is limited to airplanes known to have been lost to the enemy (i.e., it omits the rather large number that succumbed to unknown causes or to misadventure).

Air Losses in Combat by Service and Cause

Cause	Air Force	Marines	Navy	Total
AA Artillery	418 (31%)	24 (21%)	199 (51%)	641 (35%)
AA Automatic Weapons	755 (56%)	87 (76%)	97 (25%)	939 (51%)
Air Combat	64 (5%)	1 (<1%)	11 (3%)	76 (4%)
Surface-to-Air Missiles	112 (8%)	3 (3%)	81 (21%)	196 (11%)
Total	1,349	115	388	1,852

Key: Percentages have been rounded, and thus do not tally. *Total Lost* is the number of airplanes (i.e., omitting helicopters) lost by each service. *AA Artillery* and *AA Automatic Weapons* indicate losses from cannon fire and machine guns (which could fire anything from rifle bullets up to 57 mm, roughly a 2-in. shell), respectively. *Aerial Combat* losses were inflicted by enemy aircraft.

Only 10.6 percent of American aircraft lost in combat during the war were done in by enemy surface-to-air missiles, while old-fashioned cannon and automatic weapons fire accounted for nearly 90 percent of the loss. In fact, the statistics for surface-to-air missiles were abysmal. The Soviet SA-2 SAM was used extensively by the North Vietnamese, with some 10,000 of them launched during the war. In the eighteen months from July of 1965 to February of 1967, just thirty-one American aircraft were shot down by SAMs over North Vietnam, at an expenditure of about 1,500 missiles, roughly 50 per airplane, whereas 450 were downed by antiaircraft fire from ground units. Moreover, the effectiveness of SAMs did not improve, as the air force and navy took extensive measures to counter them. Among these were:

1. Electronic Warfare/Electronic Countermeasures. "Wild Weasel" was a device that could tell a pilot that his airplane had been detected by ground radar and sometimes even if a missile had been fired at him. Other EW measures included antimissile flares that were added to aircraft, which could be fired by the pilot if a missile was on his tail. As these burned hotter than aircraft engine exhaust, the missiles, which were heat-seeking, usually tried to pursue the flare, allowing the pilot to make his escape.

Eventually the notion of having "Wild Weasel"—electronic warfare—aircraft was developed. These virtually unarmed aircraft were equipped not only with more sophisticated detection devices that could not be installed on more heavily armed airplanes but also with a variety of jamming systems to spoof enemy radar and communications.

2. Improved Training and Tactics. Since SAMs required the target to be at some altitude in order to work, aircraft could reduce the danger to themselves by coming in low. This, of course, made them more vulnerable to conventional antiaircraft fire, but that was a different problem.

Early in the war pilots generally tried to outrun an incoming missile, usually with disastrous results. If a missile was on one's tail, the best tactic was "the split S maneuver." This required the pilot to fly directly at the missile, breaking away sharply at the last moment. Since the speed of approach between the airplane and the missile was almost always over a thousand miles an hour, the missile was usually unable to maneuver quickly enough to stay on target.

A result of these innovations was a marked decrease in lost aircraft. Whereas in 1965–66 it had taken about fifty SA-2 SAMs to down one airplane, the average for 1967 was about fifty-nine missiles fired for every U.S. airplane destroyed, and by 1968, more than one hundred were needed, a figure that seems to have remained relatively stable for the balance of the air war. As the supply of missiles to North Vietnam could not be increased sufficiently to compensate for their reduced effectiveness, the U.S. aircraft loss rate per thousand sorties declined from about 3 in 1966 to about 1.5 in 1968.

So most aircraft lost in Vietnam were not lost to missile fire but to machine gun and artillery fire from the ground. From mid-1964 through late-1969, about 83 percent of aircraft lost over North Vietnam were shot down by ground-based antiaircraft fire, a figure that increased as the threat of SAMs caused the aircraft to resort to lower altitudes.

In South Vietnam, the U.S. and South Vietnamese forces had little to worry about from enemy aircraft, as the North Vietnamese air force stayed carefully north of the DMZ most of the time. As a result, Allied antiaircraft skills were not particularly tested during the war, except at sea. The first-line air defense of the fleet was the responsibility of naval aircraft, and these kept most enemy aircraft away from the fleet most of the time. There were, however, several occasions when North Vietnamese aircraft managed to engage naval units. As a result, during the war the navy brought down seven enemy aircraft using surface-to-air missiles and, apparently, one enemy antiship missile as well. The first aircraft downed by a ship-launched surface-to-air missile under actual combat conditions was a North Vietnamese MiG, brought down by the missile cruiser USS *Long Beach* at a range of sixty-five nautical miles on 23 May 1968. This was nearly a decade after ship-borne SAMs were introduced into service, and three years into the Vietnam War.

An interesting footnote to the war is the fact that throughout the fighting, passenger airplanes belonging to British, Japanese, and other airlines regularly traversed the South China Sea, often coming dangerously close to U.S. carriers. These "intrusions" regularly caused carrier aircraft to scramble and intercept, and on at least one occasion an American missile cruiser almost opened fire before an intruder was identified as an airliner.

LIGHT AIRPLANES IN VIETNAM

Speak of aircraft in Vietnam and B-52s, fighter bombers, and Hueycobras come most readily to mind. However, there were a lot of unheralded lighter aircraft also in Vietnam. Light airplanes never received much respect, though during the war the *New York Times* did do a piece about them. But they did a great deal of work, from carrying out difficult and often dangerous reconnaissance missions to ferrying spare parts and critical supplies, and from hauling troops from place to place to hauling VIPs on tours.

Fixed-Wing Gunships

Type	Gunship I	Gunship II	Gunship III	Gunship III
Designation	AC-47	AC-130	AC119G	AC199K
Nickname	Spooky	Spectre	Shadow	Stinger
Armor	none	5,000	2,000	2,000
Armament				
7.62mm	3	4	4	4
20mm	–	4	–	2
Ammo				
7.62mm	21,000	15,000	31,500	31,500
20mm	–	8,000	–	4,500
Targeting	visual	electronic	electronic	electronic
FCS	none	computer	computer	computer
Illumination				
Flares	24–56	24	24	24
SL	–	1.5mcp	1.5mcp	1.5mcp
Airspeed	130kts	200kts	180kts	180kts
Alt	3,000	3,500	3,500	3,500
Duration	7 hrs	6.5 hrs	6.5 hrs	5 hrs
Turnaround	30 min	90 min	30 min	30 min
Crew	7	10–14	8	10

Key: Type, the version of gunship (though there were four versions, they were only numbered I-III); *Designation,* type code for the airplane (A, for attack, combined with C, for cargo); *Nickname,* the common way the airplanes were referred to; *Armor,* the weight of special protection installed on the airplane, in pounds; *Armament,* the normal number of guns and cannon carried, though this could vary, and there were many modifications (the 7.62 mm minigun could fire up to six thousand rounds a minute, though its preferred rate of fire was about three thousand, while the 20 mm cannon could get off two thousand rounds per minute): *Ammo,* the number of rounds carried for each type of weapon; *Targeting,* equipment used to acquire the target ("electronic" includes night observation sights, infrared, and side-looking radar); *FCS,* fire control system; *Illumination,* artificial illuminating equipment available (on the AC-47 the flares were tossed out by hand; on the other aircraft there was a special dispenser); *SL,* searchlight, *mcp,* million candle power); *Airspeed,* in knots; *Alt,* optimal operational altitude, in feet; *Duration,* the number of hours the airplane could stay in the air; *Turnaround,* the time necessary to rearm and refuel the airplane; *Crew,* the normal complement, including pilot, copilot, navigator, weapons officers, and weapons specialists.

Most of the light airplanes used—and some of them were *very* light—belonged to the army. The air force, the navy, and the marines used them as well; and at one point they became the focus of an unpleasant interservice dustup as to who had the right to use them.

"PUFF THE MAGIC DRAGON"

One of the most unique weapons to emerge from the Vietnam War was the aerial gunship, a cargo plane loaded with automatic weapons. Gunships delivered devastating fire against targets using a pintel turn, an aerobatic maneuver in which the airplane flies on its wing ends circling the target, which keeps its guns sighted for accurate fire. First proposed in the 1920s, the idea was revived from time to time, but never went anywhere until Vietnam. As early as 1962, some people were thinking about it again for use in suppressing ground fire to protect helicopters landing troops. New technology made the idea workable. By 1964, design work and testing was underway, and the first AC-47s entered service for combat testing late that year. They proved enormously effective, greatly facilitating the landing of assault troops by helicopter, and they became instantly popular with the troops. By 1967, there were thirty-two AC-47s in service, with "production" ending in 1969 at fifty-three, by which time AC-130 and AC-119 (Flying Boxcar) gunships were becoming available.

The gunships soon outgrew their original role, suppressing ground fire to support air-ground operations. Before long they were being used, not only to help heliborne troops land safely, but also to support troops-in-contact and to attack enemy lines of communication, troop concentrations, and base camps. Gunships also conducted reconnaissance by fire (you shoot at an area and see if anyone shoots back), and supported the defense of beleaguered Allied outposts. Affectionately nicknamed "Puffs"—after the dragon of the Peter, Paul, and Mary song, because when they're in action at night they look like a dragon spewing flame—gunships have since become a standard part of the military inventory.

THE B-52 AND ARC LIGHT MISSIONS

Officially known as "the Stratofortress," the B-52 is more affectionately referred to as "the Buff" ("Big ugly flying fucker"). B-52s were actually intercontinental strategic bombers, intended to drop nuclear weapons on distant targets. However, from June of 1965, B-52s began undertaking a variety of missions—tactical support, interdiction, strategic, and so forth—using conventional bombs (of which there was a shortage, forcing the air force to buy back at exorbitant prices old bombs it had recently sold for a song to scrap dealers). The aircraft had to be modified to perform these missions. When all modifications were completed—a process that was incremental—a B-52 could carry up to eighty-four 500-lb bombs internally and twenty-four 750

PRINCIPAL COMBAT AIRPLANES OF THE VIETNAM WAR

Name	Crew	Weight	Eng	Power	Speed	Range	Arm	Ordnance	Notes
U.S. and Allies									
A-1 Skyraider	1	12.50	1	2,700 p	321	915	2×20mm	2.0	A
A-4 Skyhawk	1	12.25	1	11,220	670	340	2×20mm	4.6	B
A-6 Intruder	2	30.20	2	18,600	644	1,010	*	9.0	C
A-7 Corsair II	1	21.00	1	14,250	693	490	1×20	5.0	D
A-37 Dragonfly	1	7.00	2	5,700 p	507	460	1×7.62mini	1.4	E
AT-28D Trojan	2	4.25	1	1,425 p	346	1,060	*	1.0	F
B-26 Invader	2	15.80	2	4,000 p	324	550	12×12.7mm	2.0	G
B-52 Stratofortress	10	244.00	8	136,000	650	12,500	1×Vulc	27.0	H
B-57 Canberra	2	27.48	2	14,800	541	805	8×.50	2.5	I
F8F-1B Bearcat	1	6.5	1	2,100 p	421	1,105	4×.50	1.0	J
F-4 Phantom II	2	28.00	1	17,660	1,415	600	4×6 msl	8.0	K
F-8 Crusader	1	17.00	1	18,000	1,133	1,425	4×20mm	2.5	L
F-100 Super Sabre	1	17.42	1	17,000	864	1,500	4×20mm	3.8	M
F-104 Starfighter	1	15.50	1	17,900	1,500	775	1×Vulc	2.0	N
F-105 Thunderchief	1	26.42	1	26,500	1,385	2,070	1×Vulc	3.0	O
North Vietnam									
MiG-17 Fresco	1	6.69	1	7,450	711	870	1×37mm & 2×20mm	0.5	P
MiG-19 Farmer	1	14.64	2	14,350	902	425	3×30mm	0.5	Q
MiG-21 Fishbed	1	10.36	1	14,550	1,400	683	2×23mm	0.5	R

Key: Name is the official designation and official nickname. *Crew,* the normal complement. *Weight* is maximum gross takeoff weight, in tons. *Eng,* the number of engines. *Power,* is in combined pounds of thrust, except for propeller planes (p), when horsepower is given. *Speed* in statute miles per hour. *Range,* maximum normal operational limit, in miles (most of these aircraft could go considerably farther when not on a combat mission). *Arm,* is armament, expressed as "1×20mm," meaning one 20 mm cannon; an asterisk (*) indicates that various weapons packages could be carried, up to the weight limit in the Ordnance column. *Ordnance,* indicates weight, in tons, of weaponry that could be carried, usually bombs, but sometimes combinations of bombs, weapons pods, or rockets. *Notes* indicate the lettered comments below.

A. The A-1 Skyraider was designed during WWII as a carrier bomber. It saw extensive service in Korea and Vietnam. A very versatile airplane, and very agile: several were landed in open fields or even rice paddies to rescue downed pilots. Data is for the A-1H. Unofficial nickname, by crew and ground troops alike, was "Spad."

B. The A-4 Skyhawk was designed in 1950–52 as a carrier bomber. About two thousand were bought in 1957–68, and it was in service with the navy into the 1980s; several served with considerable success in the Kuwaiti Air Force during the 1991 Gulf War. There were a number of models, and this data is for the A-4M.

C. One of the most successful carrier bombers ever designed, the A-6 began entering the fleet in the late 1950s and is still in service nearing the end of the 1990s. There were many models, and many upgrades. The data is for A-6E, which served in Vietnam.

D. The A-7 was designed in the early 1960s, and served with both the navy and the air force from 1967 into the 1990s. Data is for the A-7E.

E. The A-37B light bomber entered service in 1963. It served in Vietnam and elsewhere, and was still being used by some air forces into the 1980s.

F. Based on the T-28 trainer, used by the navy and air force from the early 1950s, the AT-28D was an adaptation for light attack purposes. It saw considerable service.

G. Redesignation of the World War II A-26 attack bomber. The fastest American bomber of the day, in Vietnam it was used for special warfare missions, including CIA covert operations.

H. Designed in the late 1940s as an intercontinental strategic bomber, the B-52 remains in service as both a strategic bomber and a tactical support bomber, in which later role it served in Vietnam and the Gulf War. Two shot down enemy aircraft. Nicknamed "the Buff," data given is for the B-52B.

I. The B-57 was a British-designed aircraft dating from the late 1940s. It was used as a tactical bomber by the Australians in Vietnam. There was also an American version, made by Martin, which was used by the USAF and the RVN AF. Two Australian B-57s were lost in Vietnam, one to a SAM and another to an unknown cause. Several USAF B-57s were destroyed on the ground by enemy sapper attacks.

J. Originally a carrier fighter designed in the waning days of World War II, numbers of Bearcats were supplied to the French for their war in Indochina in the late 1940s, and then passed on to the South Vietnamese air force, which wore them out through heavy use by 1960.

K. The F-4 was *the* airplane of the Vietnam War. Designed by the navy as a carrier fighter and bomber, it proved so versatile that the air force acquired it as well. Costing about $1.5 million apiece, the F-4 served from 1962 into the 1980s. Data shown is for the F-4J.

L. The F-8 was designed in 1952–53 as an air superiority fighter that could double as a tactical bomber. In service from 1957 through 1982, it could carry missiles, rockets, and bombs in various combinations. Data is for the F-8E.

M. An interceptor introduced in the mid-1950s, the F-100 remained in service (as an interceptor defending North America) until 1980 with the USAF, and even later in other air forces. Data is for the F-100D.

N. Designed in the early 1950s as an interceptor, the F-104 saw limited service in Vietnam. Data is for the F-104S.

O. Designed in the early 1950s, and entering service later that decade, the F-105 was a supersonic fighter bomber that did most of its work at subsonic speeds. It tangled often with MiGs and was usually successful. Not withdrawn from service until the 1980s, it could carry a mix of cannon, missiles, bombs, or rockets. Although intended as a fighter bomber, it proved a formidable fighter in its own right, accounting for 45 percent of the sixty-one MiG-17s downed by the air force. It was nicknamed "the Thud," from which came "Thud Ridge," for a prominent terrain feature northwest of Hanoi, which helped cover the planes from North Vietnamese radar during approaches to the city. Data is for the F-105D.

P. Introduced in 1953, the MiG-17 was approaching obsolescence by the outbreak of the Vietnam War. But it was a light, and lively fighter, with an effective cannon armament, and could be a deadly foe. Data is for the MiG-17PF.

Q. Entering service in the mid-1950s, the MiG-19 (and its Chinese counterpart, the F-6) was an effective, maneuverable fighter. Data is for the MiG-19SF.

R. First flown in 1955 and by the 1960s was the principal Communist bloc interceptor. Particularly good at high altitudes, it was agile and fast, but unforgiving for inexperienced pilots.

Principal Light Airplanes of the Vietnam War

Designation	Crew	Eng	HP	Weight	Speed	Range	Used	Notes
Observation and Reconnaissance								
O-1E Bird Dog	1	1	213	2,430	115/100	592	1951–74	A
OV-1A Mohawk	2	1	2,200	12,675	325/207	774	1960–80s	B
YO-3A Q-Star	2	1	100	1,000	130/96	200	1967–70s	C
Transport								
CV-2 Caribou	2	2	2,900	28,500	216/170	1,400	1955–	D
Utility								
U-6 Beaver	1	1	450	5,100	156/125	690	1951–80	E
U-8 Seminole	1	2	680	7,300	212/181	127	1952–80s	F
U-9 Aero Commander	1	2	1,100	7,500	225/198	1,150	1953–81	G
U-10A Super Courier	1	1	295	7,480	167/120	660	1958–90s	H
U-1A Otter	2	1	600	8,000	153/120	580	1953–81	I

Key: Only the more commonly found light airplanes have been listed. There were actually a great many more types in service, even enough Dorniers and Fokkers to make veterans of the world wars nostalgic. *Designation,* type code and common name; *Crew,* normal complement; *Eng,* number of engines; *HP,* horsepower, the maximum in cases where aircraft were later fitted with better engines; *Weight,* gross weight in pounds; *Speed,* in knots, with maximum given before cruising; *Range,* in statute miles; *Used,* the period in service; *Notes* refers to the lettered comments below.

A. About 4,400 Bird Dogs were built in several versions between 1950 and 1963.

Until 1962, they were designated the L-19. They served with the army and the Marine Corps

B. Some Mohawks were provided with fittings to permit them to be armed with a .50-cal. machine gun, plus bombs or rockets to serve as improvised CAS (close air support) aircraft, but most served as observation planes, with some modified for electronic reconnaissance and surveillance.

C. Developed specifically to meet the need for a quiet reconnaissance airplane, in 1967, two prototype Q-Stars were used experimentally in Vietnam, proving so successful that the army immediately bought more of them.

D. A STOL (short takeoff and landing) airplane from de Havilland Canada (which called it the DHC-4), the CV-2 Caribou was an "all weather tactical transport" that could carry twenty-four passengers. The army bought 159 of them and found them immensely useful in the early years in Vietnam. However, the air force took a look at the Caribou's passenger-carrying capacity and its 1,400-mile range and concluded it wasn't a "tactical transport" at all, and promptly laid claim to it. Under the terms of the "Treaty of Key West," signed among the services after the creation of the air force, the USAF was responsible for all but tactical air transport services. The Caribou was transferred to the USAF, though not without acrimony.

E. A STOL airplane, originally designated the L-20 in U.S. service, the U-6 Beaver, built by de Havilland Canada (DHC-2), could carry up to five passengers. About a thousand were acquired by the USAF.

F. Formerly the L-23, the U-8 Seminole could carry up to five passengers.

G. The U-9 Aero Commander, which could carry up to four passengers, was originally designated the L-26.

H. A STOL aircraft, about one hundred of the U-10A Helio Super Couriers (originally the L-28) were built for the USAF, which used them as courier aircraft, since they could carry up to five passengers or freight long distances.

I. The U-1A Otter, built by de Havilland Canada (as the DHC-3), was a STOL airplane that could carry up to nine passengers. The army used many of them in Vietnam, while the navy found it useful in Antarctica.

pounders on their wing racks. Although most missions were from Guam, some two thousand miles from Vietnam, some were staged out of Okinawa and Thailand.

The B-52 effort, which numbered over two hundred aircraft at its peak, ultimately delivered 3.5 million tons of bombs in 124,532 sorties. That's about 98 percent of the B-52s that took off; the others had to abort for various technical problems before dropping their loads.

Between June of 1965 and January of 1973, B-52s dropped some 3.5 million tons of bombs, about 27 percent of the 13 million tons dropped by all U.S. aircraft. A B-52 strike usually comprised two formations of three aircraft each. Each mission delivered between 150 and 160 tons of bombs, dropped from 30,000 feet. Targeting was by radar. There were two techniques. Initially helicopters would drop radar reflectors into the target area, but later ground-based "Skyspot" radar was employed to guide the aircraft to their targets. The latter made a considerable degree of precision possible, and there were instances in which bombs were dropped within 3,000 feet of engaged friendly

B-52 Sorties in Southeast Asia

Month	Sorties
Jul 65	300
Nov 66	600
Feb 67	800
Feb 68	1,200
Apr 68	1,800
Jul 69	1,600
Oct 69	1,400
Jun 71	1,000
Feb 72	1,200
Mar 72	1,500
Apr 72	1,800
Jun 72	3,150

Geographical Distribution of B-52 Missions

Area	Percentage
Cambodia	12
Laos	27
North Vietnam	6
South Vietnam	45

Key: The B-52 missions over North Vietnam in 1972, which convinced the Communists to conclude the Paris Peace Accords, were known as Linebacker (March–October) and Linebacker II (18–29 December).

troops. Arc Light strikes were enormously devastating. They usually came without warning, and would virtually obliterate an area of about a half mile wide by six miles long, roughly the width of New York's Central Park, and twice the length. Put another way, it was equal to the area between the Library of Congress and the Potomac, including the museums on both sides of the Mall.

There were never more than 200 B-52s involved, for only 740 were ever built and many of these still stood "alert," loaded with nuclear bombs. A total of 31 were lost, all to antiaircraft fire, 18 of them over North Vietnam. The approximately 13 million tons of bombs dropped by U.S. aircraft during the war was about six times the total dropped by American aircraft during World War II. The explosive force was sufficient to displace 3.4 billion tons of earth—ten times that evacuated for both the Suez and Panama Canals—that caused an estimated 26 million craters and flattened 20,000 square kilometers of forest.

Active Duty Personnel and Aircraft RVN Air Force, 1964–75

Year	Manpower	Aircraft
1964	10,600	250
1965	13,000	400
1966	14,500	360
1967	16,100	380
1968	16,200	360
1969	17,000	400
1970	29,000	750
1971	35,000	900
1972	47,000	1,400
1973	62,000	2,100
1974	63,000	1,750
1975	62,000	1,675

Key: Figures, which have been rounded, are for the end of each year, except for 1975, when 1 March is used, and omit personnel in training.

RVN AIR FORCE

Although created in 1955, the Air Force of the Republic of Vietnam was largely neglected for more than a decade. The neglect was so great that in 1960 its one combat squadron, equipped with the World War II–era F8F Bearcat fighter, had to be grounded because the aircraft were literally falling apart from overuse. Despite the fact that from 1965, Air Vice Marshal Nguyen Cao Ky held various prominent government posts (premier and finally vice president), the RVN Air Force grew slowly. By 1969, with Vietnamization already under way, it numbered only about 17,000 active personnel and about 425–450 aircraft, about a quarter of them helicopters. With a further 12,000 men in training, it found itself severely overstretched. Although the RVN AF did well enough under the circumstances, it was never large enough for all its missions.

The RVN Air Force performed a variety of missions, not all of them well. In the late-1950s and early-1960s, it was frequently employed to transport saboteurs and espionage agents into North Vietnam. As the fighting became more intense, the air force became adept at various tactical missions, mostly inside South Vietnam, and developed some skill at close air support and in helicopter assault operations.

A neglected asset, the RVN Air Force might have been a more effective force if more attention had been paid to it. For example, it was never treated as an equal service. Air units were so strongly subordinated to local ground units, that air commanders never developed much initiative, and sometimes passed up targets of opportunity because they had no orders. And the air force never amounted to more than about 5 percent of the RVN armed forces, which eventually reached about a million men.

Principal Combat Airplanes of the RVN Air Force, 1955–1975

Designation	Type	Used
A-37 Dragonfly	Light Bomber	1966–75
AD-6 Skyraider	Fighter Bomber	1960–75
AT-28D Trojan	Light Attack Bomber	1962–75
B-57 Canberra	Medium Bomber	1965–66
F-5 Freedom Fighter	Fighter Bomber	1967–75
F8F-1B Bearcat	Fighter Bomber	1955–62

ACES OF THE VIETNAM WAR

An *ace* is a pilot who has shot down five or more enemy aircraft. This may not sound like much, but is in fact a considerable feat. During World War II only about 5 percent of all pilots became aces. So an ace was usually a pretty sharp aviator, as well as being pretty lucky. Although there seemed to have been a lot of air combat during the Vietnam War, in fact, compared with either World War or even Korea, it wasn't all that much. Fewer than three hundred aircraft were shot down in aerial combat during the war—a figure occasionally attained in a single day during World War II. As a result, there weren't a lot of aces either.

American Aces of the Vietnam War

Name	Service	Aircraft	Score	Role	Notes
LT Randy Cunningham	USN	F-4	5	Pilot	A
CPT Charles B. DeBellvue	USAF	F-4	6	WSO	B
LT, j.g., William Driscoll	USN	F-4	5	WSO	A
CPT Jeffrey S. Feinstein	USAF	F-4	6	WSO	C
CPT Richard S. Ritchie	USAF	F-4	5	Pilot	B
CPT Jeffrey S. Troy	USAF	F-4	5	WSO	D

Key: While most of the categories are self-explanatory, *Role* seems to need some elaboration. A *WSO*—"Wizzo"—is the weapons officer who serves aboard some combat aircraft. So DeBellvue, Driscoll, Feinstein, and Troy were not actually flying the airplane, they were "merely" operating its electronics and weapons. As this is a pretty important duty, they are credited as aces. The *pilot* actually drives the airplane (called an "aviator" in the sea services, because pilots are the people who guide ships into and out of ports and tight channels).

A. LT Cunningham and LT, j.g., Driscoll were teamed together for all five of their kills, which included three MiG-17s shot down in the same day.

B. CPT DeBellvue was the WSO for all five of CPT Ritchie's kills.

C. CPT Feinstein's kills were achieved with three different pilots, one of whom got three MiGs in one day.

D. CPT Troy's victories were with several different pilots.

During the war, and for some time after it, it was widely believed that there were several North Vietnamese aces, the most notable of whom was a "Colonel Tomb." It has since been determined that there was no Colonel Tomb, nor any other North Vietnamese ace. The Colonel Tomb story seems to have arisen because the North Vietnamese Air Force did not use exclusive call signs. This led American traffic analysts (the guys who peruse enemy radio messages, trying to extract useful information) to mistakenly identify a single pilot as the one responsible for a half-dozen air victories.

ASSAULT HELICOPTER UNITS

Assault helicopter battalions were used to carry troops into battle and then keep them supplied. There were five such units in Vietnam. Typically, these battalions contained three "lift" companies (with thirty-one UH-1s) and one "attack" company. Combat helicopter units in Vietnam were comprised of young men, of an average age of twenty-two. These chopper units kept their aircraft in the air for 11 million hours, while conducting 30 million sorties. While most of these missions were short hops to move troops or supplies, armed helicopters killed tens of thousands of the enemy and destroyed thousands of pieces of enemy equipment. In their "flying truck" mode, the choppers carried hundreds of thousands of troops and 4.5 million tons of cargo.

NAPALM

Napalm is an incendiary chemical that burns at about 2,000 degrees Fahrenheit. It is made from gasoline and detergent, which form a jelly. Not only can it cause death by burning, but it also "deoxygenates" the air, which can cause asphyxiation, and often generates enormous quantities of carbon monoxide gas, which is poisonous.

First used in World War II, napalm is of particular value in close air support operations and close-in infantry fighting. Although it was used in flamethrowers (nicknamed "zippos" or "ronsons") after the famous cigarette lighters, the most common method of dispensing napalm by U.S. forces in Vietnam was by aircraft bombs, Dropped in front of heavily beset troops, it creates an impenetrable wall of fire. It was also used against enemy underground bunker complexes (it tends to seep into such places, or draw out the oxygen in them) and as a defoliant. As it has an enormous tendency to splatter, pilots dropping napalm bombs had to be particularly well trained. This was not always the case as the war went on, and there were instances when civilians were injured by erroneously laid napalm bombs, or because they were caught in the middle of a firefight.

During the Vietnam War, napalm became a cause célèbre as an "inhumane" weapon. Pictures of badly burned civilians were used to generate

Estimated Herbicide Usage in Southeast Asia, 1962–71

	Gallons Dispersed as Estimate by	
Year	SIPRI	Simpson
1962	17,171	49,240
1963	74,760	–
1964	281,607	218.510
1965	664,657	–
1966	2,535,788	c. 2,600,000
1967	5,123,353	4,879,000
1968	5,089,010	4,639,900
1969	4,558,817	4,265,800
1970	758,966	854,600
1971	10,039	1,900
Total	19,114,168	17,508,950

Key: SIPRI stands for the Stockholm International Peace Research Institute, a pacifist think tank in Sweden. Despite often elaborate footnoting, the estimate is largely based on secondary sources, some tainted by anti-American sentiments: The extraordinary precision—19,114,168 gallons—hardly seems appropriate for an estimate). Simpson stands for the Albert F. Simpson Research Center, part of the Air University, at Maxwell Air Force Base in Alabama. Its estimate is based on surviving reports and diaries of the units that took part in Operation RANCH HAND. Despite the obvious political differences between the two agencies, it is interesting to note that the overall conclusions are not seriously different, particularly given the fact that the Simpson Research Center was unable to find sufficient documentation to make estimates for 1963 and 1965.

considerable hostility toward its use (apparently its use against the Germans and Japanese in World War II was humane). There were demonstrations against its use and against the Dow Chemical Company, and even some physical attacks on Dow installations and personnel. Despite this pressure, the armed forces never abandoned the use of napalm.

Napalm was also used by the VC and NVA. Their preferred method of dispensing it was by flamethrower, but they also occasionally used it in incendiary devices. There were never any protests against the use of napalm by the North Vietnamese Army.

AGENT ORANGE AND "OPERATION RANCH HAND"

One of the more unusual aspects of the Vietnam War was the widespread use of herbicides for tactical and strategic purposes. There was a lot of jungle in Southeast Asia. The enemy used jungle for concealment on a massive scale. Cutting back the brush from roads and outposts to deny an enemy concealment is an ancient military practice. In the past this had been done mechanically, by men going out and chopping back the brush. The introduction of chemical defoliants was a logical evolution of this ancient practice. The USAF had long experience in spraying insecticides during unusual infestations of insects or insect-borne disease outbreaks in the United States and elsewhere. They had experimented with herbicide use to control runaway growth of certain plants in the late 1950s, at a time when the British were already using chemical defoliants with some success in Malaya. Chemical defoliants were used experimentally in Vietnam in 1960, and by 1962, the air force was conducting regular defoliation missions over Southeast Asia, in what was designated "Operation RANCH HAND."

Another ancient military custom is to deny the enemy food. In past times this was done by burning his crops or imposing a blockade. Almost as soon as chemical defoliants began being used to deny the enemy the protection of the jungle, it was suggested that they could also be used to ruin his crops.

A number of different herbicides were used in Southeast Asia. They were all denoted by a color, so that there was an "Agent Orange," an "Agent Green," and so forth. Only three were used in considerable amounts.

- **Agent Orange** contains about 1.98 part per million of dioxin, a known carcinogen. It was the most widely used herbicide. About 90 percent of it was used for defoliation, about 8 percent for crop destruction, and about 2 percent to clear base perimeters, roads, and so forth.
- **Agent White,** or triisopropaanoliamine salts, has no dioxin. About 99 percent of it was used for defoliation, and only 1 percent for all other purposes.
- **Agent Blue** is a cacodylic acid. It has no dioxin, but does have some arsenic compounds. About 49 percent of it was used for crop destruction, the balance for all other purposes.

The United States appears to have used about 90,000 tons of herbicide in Vietnam to clear away the undergrowth alongside roads and around base camps, so the enemy would not be able to get in close for attacks or ambushes. The use of herbicides in Vietnam undoubtedly saved American lives. Of course, the long-term deleterious effects of such chemicals on the environment and on the people exposed to them were not understood at the time. After the war these consequences became more apparent.

Operation RANCH HAND normally employed about 1,500 personnel, including air and ground crews, all of whom were volunteers (though they were not always fully aware of what they were volunteering for). Many of these men were exposed to massive amounts of Agent Orange or other herbicides. Numerous Vietnamese civilians were also exposed to these chemicals. Some of these people—Vietnamese civilians and American military personnel alike—may have died from the long-term effects of toxic chemicals, and it is believed that there may be some genetic damage to the offspring of those exposed. However, the scientific jury is still out. Nevertheless, as the issue has become heavily burdened by political considerations, Dow Chemical and the other manufacturers established a $180 million fund to compensate those believed to have suffered from the aftereffects of Agent Orange and the other defoliants used.

Estimated Acreage Treated with Herbicides

Year As Estimated by

	NAS	ACC	SIPRI	USN	Simpson	Average
1962	–	5,681	5,724	–	13,614	8,340
1963	–	24,947	24,920	–	21,568	23,812
1964	–	93,842	93,869	–	78,894	88,868
1965	75,501	221,559	221,552	72,327	229,920	164,172
1966	608,106	842,764	845,263	847,469	742,857	777,292
1967	1,570,114	1,707,738	1,707,784	1,599,903	1,375,241	1,592,156
1968	1,365,479	1,330,836	1,696,337	802,380	1,325,685	1,304,143
1969	1,365,754	–	1,519,606	–	1,218,800	1,368,053
1970	294,925	–	252,989	–	244,171	264,028
1971	1,259	–	3,346	–	633	1,746
Total	5,281,138	4,227,367	6,371,390	3,322,079	5,251,383	–

Key: A dash indicates that no estimate was made for that particular year. NAS is the estimate made in 1978 by National Academy of Sciences. ACC (Army Chemical Corps) was made in 1969. SIPRI (Stockholm International Peace Research Institute) did its estimate in 1976. The USN (U.S. Navy) estimate is from a partial study of the subject done in 1968. Simpson stands for the Albert F. Simpson Research Center at the Air University, in a report issued in the late 1970s. Average is actually the mean of entries for each year, the sum of which is not given since it is not compatible with the mean of the total estimates by the different agencies. Once again the extreme precision of the estimates is questionable, but once again their general agreement is interesting.

THE KINGBEE

Because the State Department had enough clout to keep most American aircraft out of "neutral" Laos, South Vietnamese helicopters had to be used to rescue trapped American-led patrols in 1965. The South Vietnamese didn't have the new UH-1 choppers, but the older H-34 model. This machine used a 32-cylinder radial engine that sat right under the cockpit. Pilots appreciated this, for it gave them a large chunk of metal between themselves and whoever was shooting at them. That big old engine could also take a lot more punishment, and keep going, than the more efficient engines used in the UH-1. The South Vietnamese pilots who flew the Kingbee would fly anywhere, under any conditions, to get the job done. The H-34 lacked the lifting power and range of the UH-1, but it was reliable and maneuverable enough.

CHAPTER 5

Blue Water, Green Water, Brown Water (The Naval War)

The navy played a major role in Vietnam, serving not only on the high seas, but also along the coasts and on the rivers, an aspect of the war that often gets overlooked.

AIRCRAFT CARRIERS IN THE WAR

The aircraft carrier replaced the battleship as the premier warship during World War II. But since World War II, the United States has so completely dominated the seas that carriers have served primarily as auxiliary airfields for land operations. In this role they have rendered yeoman service, not least in the Vietnam War, during which American carriers spent nearly 17,000 days in operation. Carriers formed Task Force 77. They were usually deployed either in the Gulf of Tonkin, for operations against North Vietnam and another farther south, for operations in South Vietnam, southern Laos, and Cambodia, which stations were cleverly nicknamed "Yankee Station" and "Dixie Station," respectively.

The carriers were of varying ages and sizes. The oldest ones had taken on the Imperial Japanese Navy in World War II, and gone on to fight in Korea as well. The newest were quite literally new, and were just entering service during the war. Technically there were two kinds of carriers operating off Vietnam. Those designated CVA were classed as "attack" carriers. These were mostly newer ships, or heavily reconstructed older ones, for general purpose operations. Ships classed as CVS were officially assigned to antisubmarine operations, but in fact could conduct general purpose combat missions with almost as much efficiency as the CVAs. The N added to the designator for the USS *Enterprise* (CVAN-65) was to advertise that she was nuclear powered.

The formula '41–'43–'43 used in the ship descriptions that follow indicate the year the ship was laid down (i.e., construction began with the laying of the ship's keel or backbone), that in which she was launched (i.e., put into the water for the first time, at which point making extensive alterations

Ship	1964	1965	1966	1967	1968	1969	1970	1971	1972	1973
CVS-10										
CVS-11										
CVS-12										
CVA-14										
CVA-19										
CVS-20										
CVA-31										
CVS-33										
CVA-34										
CVS-38										
CVA-41										
CVA-42										
CVA-43										
CVA-59										
CVA-60										
CVA-61										
CVA-62										
CVA-63										
CVA-64										
CVAN-65										
CVA-66										

Key: The table shows carrier deployments by ship, using the navy's type code designator for each vessel, which are discussed more fully in the text on pages 141–147. From early 1965 until 1970, there were never less than six carriers on station off Vietnam.

Carrier Classes of the Vietnam War

Class	Displacement	Dimensions	Spd	Crew	A/C
Essex, Group 1	28,404/40,600	898×152×30	30.0	2,905	80
Essex, Group 2	30,580/43,060	895×162×31	29.1	2,545(960)	80
Midway	42,710/62,614	977×210×35	30.6	4,060	90
Forrestal	61,163/78,509	1039×250×34	33.0	4,676(1,912)	90
Kitty Hawk	60,005/80,945	1072×252×36	33.5	4,685(1,379)	90
Enterprise	71,277/89,084	1123×255×37	32.0	5,287(1,891)	90

Key: Displacement is the weight of the water that would occupy the space the ship occupies: the first figure is, for the *Forrestal*'s, given in "standard" tons (that is, the displacement assuming normal peacetime loading), and for the others in "light" tons (displacement of the plain ship, with no fuel, crew, stores, ammunition, or even aircraft embarked), while the second figure is "full load" displacement (including maximum wartime complement, fuel, ammunition, and stores). *Dimensions* are (in feet rounded to the nearest foot) length overall (waterline length in most cases is fifty to eighty feet less), maximum beam (waterline beam for most carriers is usually a little more than half maximum), and draught, the depth of the ship below the waterline. *Spd,* speed is in knots (note that *Enterprise* is regularly rumored to be able to do much better than thirty-two knots). *Crew* is the total number necessary for the ship to undertake wartime operations, the occasional entry in parentheses indicating the number of crewmen who form the air group. *A/C* is the approximate number of aircraft carried, a figure that can vary greatly depending upon type (e.g., *Enterprise* could probably carry about 120 Skyraiders).

to her basic design becomes very difficult), and that in which she was commissioned.

Essex Class. The largest and most successful class of carriers ever built, twenty-six Essex Class ships were completed of an order of thirty-two. Sixteen saw service in World War II. Initially all were quite similar. But many differences emerged as they went through repeated modifications and reconstruction to permit them to operate ever more modern aircraft (e.g., the fitting of angled decks and steam catapults). Or to improve sea-keeping qualities (e.g., installation of a "hurricane" bow), or to perform specialized missions (i.e., as antisubmarine, helicopter, or training carriers). They formed the backbone of the U.S. carrier fleet into the 1960s, and some continued in service as training carriers into the 1980s. Due to numerous modifications, there were essentially two groups by the Vietnam War.

Group 1. Ships in this group had been subject to the SCB-27A modernization, which left them with a straight deck, which was usually replaced by an angled deck in a second rebuilding during the 1960s, when they more or less came to resemble Group 2 ships.

CVS-10 *Yorktown* ('41–'43–'43) was originally to have been named *Bon*

Homme Richard, but was renamed before launching to commemorate the famous carrier sunk at Midway. She operated throughout the Pacific, being damaged only once, and that lightly. Her aircraft helped sink the battleship *Yamato*. She later served in Korea, was rebuilt in 1953, was redesignated a CVS in 1960, and rebuilt again in 1966. She did three tours off Vietnam for a total of 396 days. Discarded in 1970, *Yorktown* is today preserved as a war memorial at Charleston, South Carolina.

CVS-12 *Hornet* ('42–'43–'43) was to have been named *Kearsarge*, but was renamed while still on the way to commemorate the famous carrier from which Doolittle's raid on Tokyo was launched. Given only a two-week shakedown cruise, the new *Hornet* was rushed off to war in early 1944. Although under attack on forty-two separate days, she was never damaged by enemy action. She later served in Korea, was rebuilt in 1953, became a CVS in 1958, and was rebuilt again in 1965. *Hornet* served three tours off Vietnam, totaling 517 days. Decommissioned in 1970, she was slated for scrapping in 1996, but a last-minute stay of execution was granted to permit a group interested in preserving her as a war memorial time to raise the funds.

CVS-20 *Bennington* ('42–'44–'44) arrived in the Pacific in early 1945. She helped sink the superbattleship *Yamato* and took part in the final operations against Japan, but in more than six months of war service was never injured by enemy action. She later served in Korea. Rebuilt in 1954, she spent several years in reserve, to be hauled out for the Vietnam War, during which she did three tours, for a total of 386 days. She was scrapped in the 1980s.

CVS-33 *Kearsage* ('44–'45–'46) was completed to a modified Essex Class design. She was rebuilt in 1952 and became a CVS in 1958. *Kearsage*, which had the same rude nickname that has plagued all ships that have ever borne the name, "Queer Barge," did four deployments to Southeast Asia, for a total 587 days, and was decommissioned in 1976.

CVA-34 *Oriskany* ('44–'45–'50), last of the Essex Class carriers to be completed, to a very modified design. She served in Korea and did seven tours off Vietnam for 1,413 days. She was taken out of service in 1976, placed in reserve in 1980, and scrapped several years later. One of her anchors is preserved in Oriskany, New York.

Group 2. These vessels were modernized according to the more elaborate SCB-27C plan, which, among other things, gave them an angled flight deck. Most Group 1 ships were eventually brought up to this standard during the Vietnam War.

CVS-11 *Intrepid* ('41–'43–'43) earned the nickname "the Evil Eye" during World War II because of the number of times she was damaged by enemy action, taking one torpedo and four kamikazes, as well as being near missed by a fifth suicide plane. She served in Korea, was rebuilt in 1954, designated as CVS in 1962, and rebuilt again in 1965. She did three tours in Vietnam for a total of 559 days. Decommissioned in 1974, *Intrepid* is preserved as a war memorial and Sea-Air-Space museum on the Hudson River in New York City.

CVA-14 *Ticonderoga* ('43–'44–'44) took two kamikazes in January 1945, which caused dangerous fires, requiring extensive flooding, but was back in action in April, taking part in the final operations against Japan. "Tico" served in Korea, was rebuilt in 1954, and designated in CVS in 1969. She did five tours in Vietnam, for a total of 1,027 days on station. She was scrapped in 1973.

CVA-19 *Hancock* ('43–'43–'44) entered World War II in late 1944 and served until the end of the surrender of Japan, being damaged once by a kamikaze and once by an accidental fuel explosion, with little effect either time. She served in Korea, and did eight tours to Southeast Asia, for a total of 1,660 days. She was scrapped in 1976.

CVA-31 *Bon Homme Richard* ('43–'44–'44) took part in the final assault on Japan, incurring no damage by enemy action. "The Bonnie Dick" later served in Korea and was rebuilt in 1955. She did six deployments to Vietnam, for 1,315 days, and was decommissioned in 1971.

CVS-38 *Shangri-La* ('43–'44–'44) entered combat in the Pacific in the spring of 1945. She was the last new carrier to see action in the war, during which she incurred no damage from enemy action. She later served during the Korean War, was rebuilt in 1955, and became a CVS in 1959. She only did one tour off Vietnam, a long one of 239 days. Decommissioned in 1971 and placed in reserve, she was scrapped several years later. Her name came about in a curious fashion. Asked by some journalists where the Doolittle Raiders had taken off from, President Roosevelt replied by saying "Shangri-La," the name of a fictional Asian country in the popular novel and film *Lost Horizon,* and the name was shortly given to the new carrier.

Midway Class. Completed too late to see service in World War II, the Midway Class ships were better protected than any previous U.S. carriers and had an enormous aircraft capacity for their day (over 130 planes). Designed and built with considerable speed (twenty-two to twenty-three months each), they began to enter service about the time that Japan surrendered. During the mid- and late-1950s, they were extensively modified, to add angled decks, steam catapults, hurricane bows, and so forth. What with further modifications during the 1960s, they were ultimately sister ships in name only.

CVA-41 *Midway* ('43–'45–'45), commissioned eight days after the surrender of Japan, she saw extensive service in Korea and later did three tours off Vietnam, for a total of 715 days. She later saw service during the Gulf War, and was scrapped in the early 1990s.

CVA-42 *Franklin Delano Roosevelt* ('43–'45–'45), originally to have been named *Coral Sea,* but renamed after the president's death. Commissioned

25 days after Japan surrendered, she served during the Korean War and did one tour off Vietnam, of 188 days. She was scrapped in the early 1980s.

CVA-43 *Coral Sea* ('44–'46–'47) served in the Korean War and did six tours off Vietnam, for a total of 1,343 days. She was discarded in the late 1980s and scrapped in the mid-1990s.

Forrestal Class. The first carriers designed after World War II to be completed, the Forrestals were only approved after years of brutal interservice bickering over the future of naval airpower. Briefly put, the air force wanted to monopolize the delivery of nuclear weapons by barring the navy from having nuclear-capable carrier aircraft. This led to the "Revolt of the Admirals," in which a number of high-ranking naval officers ruined their careers and the navy lost its first postwar carrier, *United States*. But the navy ultimately emerged a winner, with the Forrestals. They were big ships, much bigger than previous purpose-built carriers, built with all the most advanced features possible, including angled decks, steam catapults, and so forth.

CVA-59 *Forrestal* ('52–'54–'55), named after James Forrestal, who had been secretary of the navy from 1945–47 and later the first secretary of defense, began operations off Vietnam on 8 July 1967. A few weeks later she was preparing to launch another strike against North Vietnam when a fire broke out, which spread rapidly, engulfing numerous aircraft, and caused a devastating series of explosions, with heavy loss of life. Although repaired, the ship never returned to Southeast Asia. She was relegated to the reserve fleet in the early 1990s.

CVA-60 *Saratoga* ('52–'55–'56) served only one tour off Vietnam, and that at the end of the war in 1973, for 253 days. She later saw service in the Gulf War.

CVA-61 *Ranger* ('54–'56–'57) served seven tours of Vietnam, for a total of 1,445 days. She later served in the Gulf War.

CVA-62 *Independence* ('55–'58–'59) saw only one tour in Southeast Asia, for 169 days.

Kitty Hawk Class. Essentially a follow-on design for the Forrestal Class, the Kitty Hawks were virtually identical in many ways, differing primarily in certain technical details.

CVA-63 *Kitty Hawk* ('56–'60–'61) did six tours off Vietnam, for a total of 1,313 days. Late in the war the ship was plagued by serious racial disorders.

CVA-64 *Constellation* ('57–'60–'62) was severely damaged by a fire while under construction at the Brooklyn Navy Yard (she was the last warship built in Brooklyn), though she managed to enter service more or less on schedule. She deployed to Southeast Asia seven times, for a total of 1,436 days. A *Constellation* aviator, LT Everett Alvarez, was the first American pilot shot down in the war, on 5 August 1964. He was not released until 1973. The ship suffered from serious racial disorders late in the war, which caused the disruption of operations.

CVA-66 *America* ('61–'64–'65) served three tours off Vietnam, for a total of 694 days. She later served in the Gulf War.

Enterprise. The first nuclear-powered aircraft carrier and the largest warship ever built until then. Designed as a test bed to determine the utility of nuclear power for aircraft carriers.

CVAN-65 *Enterprise* ('58–'60–'61) served six tours in Vietnamese waters, for a total of 1,202 days. In January 1969, while on a training exercise off Hawaii between her third and fourth deployments, a rocket accidentally fired, setting off an explosion that caused extensive fires and a number of casualties, but the ship was repaired quickly, and soon returned to service.

The fleet carriers were not the only carriers to see service in Southeast Asia. Old escort carriers were used to haul aircraft to Vietnam. At the time she was sunk in the Saigon River by a VC underwater demolition team, the old USS *Card* had just completed delivery of dozens of Huey helicopters. Since the navy refused to admit the ship was actually sunk, it declared that she was merely "damaged," and spent a considerable sum to refloat and "repair" her.

Footnote: Carrier Accidents During the War. Short of outright combat, carrier operations are the most dangerous of naval activities, the proximity of weapons, aviation fuel, men, and aircraft making disaster an ever-present possibility. During the Vietnam War there were three major accidents aboard U.S. carriers.

1. USS *Oriskany*, 26 October 1966. Two sailors were storing flares just removed from aircraft returning from a mission over Vietnam when one of them dropped an armed flare. As it fell, the safety lanyard on the flare somehow pulled, activating it. A third sailor, seeing the sputtering flare, grabbed it and tossed it into a nearby locker, slamming the door after it. Unfortunately, the locker contained warheads for 2.75-in. rockets, which were detonated when the flare went off, in turn setting off a nearby tank of liquid oxygen. In the series of explosions and the ensuing fire, forty-four of the ship's company died and another 156 were injured. Four airplanes and two helicopters were damaged, and there was serious damage to portions of the ship as well.

2. USS *Forrestal*, 29 July 1967. During preparations for a mission over North Vietnam, a Zuñi rocket on one of the airplanes somehow fired. Streaking across the flight deck, the rocket hit a fueled and armed airplane. An avgas fire started. About ninety seconds later, even as damage-control personnel sprang into action to fight the fire, a bomb exploded. This killed most of the firefighters, and ruptured the steel flight deck. Burning fuel splashed

down onto the hanger deck. A series of explosions followed, as bombs, missile warheads, and fuel were detonated by the flames. The explosions and fire killed 134 men and injured 161 others, the worst single day's casualties in the navy since late in World War II. Damage to the ship was extensive, and twenty-one airplanes were destroyed.

The *Forrestal* accident was fully "documented" by flight deck safety surveillance cameras. These proved invaluable when the navy convened a special committee to study ways to improve its firefighting and safety techniques, which resulted in several important innovations. The films are still used by the navy as aids in training personnel to fight fires.

3. USS *Enterprise*, 15 January 1969. During routine deck operations, the hot exhaust from an aircraft engine starter was directed onto a cart loaded with four Zuñi rockets. The hot exhaust detonated one of the warheads. This sent metal shards into the airplane's fuel tank, setting off an avgas explosion. The explosion in turn caused a fire that detonated the other three Zuñi warheads. These explosions blew holes in the flight deck, so that burning fuel spilled onto the hangar deck, setting off more than a dozen bombs and rockets, wrecking further havoc. Casualties were heavy, with 28 dead and 344 injured. There was extensive damage to the ship, and fifteen airplanes were destroyed.

THE BATTLESHIP RETURNS

The battleship had lost its status as the principal arbiter of naval supremacy in World War II. However, it still retained considerable value for shore bombardment, antiaircraft defense of the fleet, and as a potent political message. To fulfill these roles, the navy kept several battleships in commission into the mid-1950s. However, by then progress in aviation and the advent of nuclear weapons seemed to make the battleship wholly useless. By the early 1960s, the navy had rid itself of all but four of its battleships, and those were in mothballs. Then came the Vietnam War. Soon after they went into action, the marines began clamoring for some serious firepower to support their operations, particularly along the DMZ. Observing that close air support was good, but battleship gunfire was better, they asked that an Iowa Class "battlewagon" or two be hauled out of mothballs for service.

The Iowas were impressive-looking ships. They displaced over 57,000 tons at full load, had a crew of some 1,900 officers and enlisted men, were nearly 900 feet long, over 100 feet wide, and could make over 32 knots. Heavily armored, with a belt of 12.2 inches, and as much as 17 inches covering some vital areas, they were also very graceful-looking ships. But none of that interested the marines. Not even their numerous 5-in. (127 mm) guns, suitable for both surface bombardment and antiaircraft work. What the marines wanted battleships for were their nine 16-in. (406 mm) rifles. Nearly 70 feet long, each gun could hurl a 1,900-lb high-explosive shell up to about 42,000 yards with considerable accuracy, particularly using radar-directed fire control.

In 1966, the navy decided that the marines had a point, and the project got underway. After examining the four battleships in reserve, it was concluded that the USS *New Jersey* was in the best condition and she was selected. Designed in the late 1930s, laid down in 1940, and completed in less than three years, *New Jersey* had an extensive combat record in World War II and Korea. The ship needed some modernization in her communications, some modifications to permit her to operate with a smaller crew than she had been designed for, her seaplane hangar had to be modified to permit the operation of helicopters, and so forth. In addition, she needed an overhaul. Work on a ten-month-long "austere" refit began in 1967, and she was recommissioned in the spring of 1968. After a shakedown cruise and gunnery practice, she departed for Vietnam, with a minimal crew of some 1,500.

New Jersey arrived off Vietnam in April 1968 and spent 120 days in combat. She was almost constantly in action, once continuously for 47 days. During her deployment she fired in anger 5,688 rounds of 16-in. ammunition (in her entire previous career she had fired only 7,442 rounds, but ammo was free, all of it being World War II stuff), as well as 14,891 rounds from her 5-in. secondary guns. *New Jersey* received high praise for the promptness and accuracy of her fire. She was withdrawn from Southeast Asia in mid-1968. Even as the ship was preparing for a second tour in Vietnamese waters in mid-1969, the secretary of defense quite suddenly declared that she was, instead, to be decommissioned once again. No satisfactory reason for the ship's withdrawal was ever made. At the time "military developments" were cited as the reason, but it is generally believed that she fell victim to interservice rivalry. Still later it was suggested that her presence jeopardized the peace negotiations that were just them beginning, as the North Vietnamese considered her a significant escalation. *New Jersey* was decommissioned once again at the end of 1969, but would return to active duty for a time in the 1980s and early 1990s, where her sisters rendered yeoman service during the Gulf War.

New Jersey was one of a number of warships that manned the gun line off the Vietnamese coast. The bombardment group, which normally comprised about eighteen to twenty-two ships, was designated Task Force 70.8.

THE GREEN WATER NAVY

Although carrier operations tended to obscure its other roles, the navy was also involved in the war in a variety of ways. One of these was the struggle to control coastal and inland waters. Coastal waters—"green waters"—had long been used by the Communists to move supplies and troops to South Vietnam from the North. Moving goods by sea is much more efficient—and cheaper—than moving them overland, and the Communists were well aware

Basic Characteristics of the USS New Jersey and Other Warships Used for Gunfire Support

Type	Class	Displ	Dimensions	Spd	Arm	Metal	Crew	Notes
BB	Iowa	57,500/48,100	888×108×36	32.5	9×16″/50	8.6 tons	1,500	A
CA	Newport News	17,255/20,434	717×75×26	33.0	12×5″/38 9×8″/55 12×5″/38	1.5 7.2 1.5	1,800	B
CAG	Boston	13,589/17,947	674×70×25	32.0	6×8″/55 10×5″38	3.9 1.2	1,550	C
CLG	Oklahoma City	11,066/15,152	610×66×26	32.0	6×6″/47 2×5″38	2.4 0.5	1,380	D
DD	Gearing	2,406/3,493	391×41×14	36.8	4×5″/38	1.0	310	E
DD	Forrest Sherman	2,800/4,050	418×45×20	33.0	3×5″/54	0.9	c. 300	F
DDG	Charles F. Adams	3,277/4,576	437×47×15	33.0	2×5″/54	0.7	350	G

Key: Type: BB, battleship; CA, heavy cruiser; CAG, heavy cruiser with guided missiles; CLG, light cruiser with guided missiles; DD, destroyer; DDG, destroyer with missiles. Displacement is the weight of the water that would occupy the space the ship occupies. For some ships the first figure is "standard" displacement (the displacement assuming normal peacetime loading), but is otherwise given as "light" displacement (the ship, with no fuel, crew, stores, or ammunition), while the second figure is "full load" displacement (including maximum wartime complement, fuel, ammunition, and stores). Dimensions are (in feet rounded to the nearest foot) length overall (waterline length in most cases is ten to twenty feet less), maximum beam, and draught, the depth of the ship below the waterline. Spd, speed is in knots. Arm is armament, with only weapons capable of surface bombardment being shown; all ships carried some antiaircraft armament, which could not be used against surface targets, and the destroyer types were equipped for antisubmarine duty as well. Metal is a theoretical calculation of the weight in tons of shells that the ship could fire in one minute, assuming sustainable rates of fire (i.e., on paper the 16-in. guns on New Jersey could fire twice a minute, but once is a more sustainable rate). Crew is the total number necessary for the ship to undertake wartime operations. Notes refers to the lettered comments below.

A. As noted in the previous text, New Jersey was very heavily armored.

B. Actually a unit of the Des Moines Class, the largest and arguably best heavy cruisers ever built, Newport News ('45-'47-'49) was retired in 1975. Her 8-in. guns were of a new pattern, fully automated and firing fixed ammunition (i.e., the shell and the powder were combined in one package) and she was quite heavily armored for a cruiser (6-in. belt, 8-in. turret faces, etc.).

C. *Boston* (CAG-1) and *Canberra* (CAG-2) were built as Baltimore Class heavy cruisers ('41–'42–'43) and converted to carry a double Terrier antiaircraft missile launcher aft in 1955–56. However, in Vietnam they did much more work with their guns than with their missiles. Their 8-in. guns had to be loaded manually, propellant and projectile being separate, and they carried some light armor. They were decommissioned in the 1970s and scrapped

D. A half-dozen light cruisers of the Cleveland Class (mostly '42–'44–'45) were converted to carry a Talos or Terrier antiaircraft missile launcher 1959–60. As with the Bostons, they did much more work with their guns. They were moderately armored. All were decommissioned in the mid-1970s.

E. Most of the World War II–era Gearing Class ('44–'45–'45) remained in service until the 1970s. Several were converted to "radar picket ships," designed to serve as early warning vessels for the fleet, which led to the loss of some of their antiaircraft capacity. This, many naval analysts believe, resulted in severe damage to the USS *Higbee* (DD-806), the only major warship in the fleet named for a woman, which was hit by an enemy air attack on 19 April 1972.

F. The Forrest Sherman Class, the last major surface warships in the navy to be armed solely with guns, was built 1953–59. Extensive modifications while in service had led to there being three basic variations. Some were specialized for antisubmarine warfare, and had only two 5"/54 guns, while some had been converted to a guided-missile configuration, with but one 5"/54 gun, plus a Tartar launcher, which raised full load displacement to c. 4,150 tons. Crew size varied from 292 to 204. They were all disposed of by the early 1990s.

G. The Charles Francis Adams Class, built 1958–67, were the first destroyers designed and built with missiles as their primary armament, carrying a Terrier system. Many saw action on the gun line off Vietnam, including the three that were built for Australia (HMASs *Hobart, Brisbane,* and *Perth*) that had a Tartar missile system rather than a Terrier.

of this. In July of 1959, they set up a special command, *Military Transportation Group 759* (the number derived from "July 1959"), to plan the seaborne movement of supplies to the South. *Group 759* began operations in October 1961. This was before the Ho Chi Minh Trail was much more than a jungle track. By 1965, *Group 759*—by then redesignated *Group 125*—was handling as much as 70 percent of the supplies moving South, and it was particularly important in getting materiél and manpower to the far south of South Vietnam. Before the U.S. Navy became involved in coastal interdiction, *Group 125* was moving an average of nearly 350 tons of supplies a month south, mostly using a score of junks, trawlers, and small merchant ships.

With the American role in the war increasing, in March 1965, the U.S. Navy undertook Operation Market Time, designed to interdict the seaborne movement of supplies to the South. The arm of the fleet responsible for this was Task Force 115, the Coastal Surveillance Force. Initially subordinate to the Seventh Fleet, TF 115 was later under the control of Naval Forces, Vietnam, which controlled USN operations in country.

TF 115 divided the 1,700-mile coastal zone into nine patrol sectors, each of which was patrolled by a mixture of aircraft, small vessels, and warships. The outer zone, 100 to 150 miles from the coast, was covered primarily by aerial patrols and a few larger warships; closer in were smaller warships, such as destroyer escorts and Coast Guard cutters. Right up along the coast, small, fast patrol boats ("Nastys" and "Swifts," capable of twenty-five knots and usually armed with .50-cal. machine guns and an 81 mm mortar) were used, supplemented by motorized junks of the South Vietnamese Navy. At its peak, in 1967–69, TF 115 operated about 140 to 150 vessels, roughly half of which were fast patrol boats. Beginning in 1969, Operation Market Time was Vietnamized, and by 1971, TF 115 was shut down. It had been remarkably effective.

By mid-1967, TF 115 had virtually choked off Communist efforts to supply their forces in the South by sea. So effective was the operation, that even after Vietnamization, the flow of supplies remained low. However, by the late 1960s, the completion of the Ho Chi Minh Trail more than made up for the shortfall.

THE BROWN WATER NAVY

The southernmost portion of South Vietnam is formed primarily by the vast Mekong Delta, which comprises about 40 percent of the country. The delta sprawls over some 26,000 square miles (rather more than half the size of New York State), and more than a third of it is rice paddies. Going into the 1960s, the Viet Cong were quite proficient at using the thousands of miles of canals, streams, and waterways in the delta for moving personnel and supplies, usually relying on sampans and other very small vessels.

To cope with the Communist use of the delta, the U.S. Navy established two special task forces, one to patrol the internal numerous waterways and the other to conduct offensive operations in conjunction with the army.

Task Force 116. Set up in December 1965, TF 116 was responsible for Operation Game Warden, patrolling and securing control of the delta waterways. After extensive preparations (special training was required for all crews, and special modifications had to be made to existing patrol craft), Game Warden got underway in March 1966. It operated five river patrol divisions, each comprised of twenty patrol boats and a base ship, supported by a navy helicopter squadron and a division of minesweepers, with three SEAL platoons on call.

TF 116 was extremely successful in securing control of the major waterways and in bringing timely support to villages under attack by enemy forces, notably during the Tet Offensive. It was less successful in interdicting enemy small boat traffic and in controlling the innumerable smaller canals and waterways, both of which tasks would have required a far greater investment in resources.

Task Force 117. Also known as the Riverine Assault Force, TF 117 was created in early 1967 to conduct offensive operations on the inland waterways of the delta region. It was part of the Army-Navy Mobile Riverine Force, the other elements of which were the 9th Infantry Division's 2nd Brigade (3 and 4/47th and 3/60th Infantry, plus 3/39th Artillery, with 105 mm howitzers), as well as the ARVN 7th and 21st Battalions, plus elements of the RVN Marine Corps and navy. TF 117 consisted of four river assault squadrons. Each squadron, which numbered about four hundred men, had a variety of specialized vessels, mostly converted from standard landing craft, such as heavily armored and armed monitors, armored personnel transports, command ships, and so forth. TF 117 could move five thousand troops 150 miles in twenty-four hours along the rivers and canals and send them into action immediately in an onshore assault, supported by helicopter and fixed-wing aircraft, and occasionally by heliborne troops.

A riverine task force consisted of a number of different specialized vessels. Most of these were based on existing designs for small or medium landing craft, whether converted or purpose built. All of the different types were often modified by their crews, to provide additional firepower, protection, or amenities.

- **Alpha Boats**. Fast, light, shallow draft boats—usually Swifts or Nastys—used to provide fire support to the troops actually making riverine assaults (which are essentially amphibious assaults). They were usually armed with a combination of machine guns and other weapons, such as grenade launchers or LAWs, (anti-tank rocket launchers) and some-times got in so close they beached.

- **Artillery barges**. Essentially lightly protected, powered rafts which carried 105 mm howitzers that could be used to provide fire support.
- **Command and Control Boats (CCBs)**. An armored landing craft jammed with communications equipment, so that commanders could get close in to the action, keeping control of operations and maintaining communications with artillery and air support. Usually CCBs were camouflaged as monitors.
- **Monitors**. Heavily armored landing craft, equipped with a turret-mounted cannon, several heavy machine guns, and other weapons. They provided the muscle during riverine operations.
- **Tango Boats**. These were actually armored troop carriers, essentially an armored water bus, able to transport a platoon in relative safety and deposit it directly on the riverbank. Tango boats were usually armed with a couple of .50-cal. machine guns plus about four lighter ones.
- **Zippo Boats**. Flamethrower boats, usually with one or two machine guns in addition to the "zippo."

For a small—company-sized—riverine assault, a "typical" task force would usually consist of one or two CCBs, several monitors, a half-dozen tango boats, plus some alpha boats and artillery barges, with a helicopter squadron in support, and still heavier stuff on call.

TF 117 was stood down in April 1971, when its remaining assets were transferred to the South Vietnamese Navy.

THE COAST GUARD

When the navy decided it needed small craft and training for coastal work, it went to the Coast Guard, asking for seventeen vessels. The Coast Guard was willing to assist, but insisted that some Coast Guard personnel should also be permitted to serve in Vietnam. As a result, several thousand Coast Guardsmen served in Vietnam, most notably in the Coastal Surveillance Force and on riverine operations.

Coast Guardsmen brought unique skills to the war. Expert in small boat operation, they were much more effective in this role than any retrained navy personnel would have been. They also brought some unique equipment, perhaps the most notable of which was the piggyback mounting of an 81 mm mortar beneath a .50-cal. machine gun, developed in 1964–65 as a means of saving space and weight aboard small vessels. The mortar was originally intended to project illuminating rounds in the furtherance of the Coast Guard's search and rescue mission, but it soon proved a potent weapon as well. Unlike "normal" mortars, the Coast Guard version was fired manually and could be used as a direct fire weapon. It was so effective that at least one was procured by Special Forces personnel, who mounted it on a flatbed truck to help support some of their operations.

Other Coast Guard innovations, most of them informally developed and often used without reference to higher authority, were a modified version of the .50-mg/81 mm mount that substituted a 40mm cannon for the machine gun, and the addition of a 2.75-in. rocket pod to the mount.

For the first two years of Operation Market Time, the Coast Guard did most of the work. Over the course of the war, Coast Guardsmen boarded some 250,000 vessels and conducted over 6,000 fire-support missions. They also provided port security personnel and helped train the South Vietnamese Navy.

The Coast Guard suffered sixty-one casualties in Vietnam, seven killed in action, fifty-three wounded, and one missing in action.

CHAPTER 6

Base Camp Follies

Most U.S. troops in Vietnam never saw combat, and spent most of their time comfortably ensconced in well-guarded "base camps." The biggest base camps were the major cities, where you had a bit more action from the local terrorists, but it was still a lot safer than being out in the bush.

UNCLE SAM'S WAY OF WAR

The Vietnam War was different for American soldiers in many ways. One important difference was the day-to-day life of the troops. Much of this lifestyle is, and was, largely unknown to people in the West. American combat troops led a lifestyle quite different from what U.S. troops had experienced in previous wars. Because American commanders followed an attrition strategy, they pushed the troops to kill or capture as many Communist troops as possible. The North Vietnamese knew this, and did their utmost to avoid contact. The U.S. infantry spent most of their time in the field. Basically it was constant patrolling. Having complete control of the air, plus aggressive use of long-range recon (LRRPs), there was always a stream of information coming in about where the Communist troops might be. The "search and destroy" missions were actually large-scale patrols. This tempo of operations wore U.S. troops down more than they did the enemy. Communist units could always retreat into Laos, Cambodia, or North Vietnam to rest and rebuild (although they often had to remain hidden to avoid bombers). As the war went on, LRRPs were sent into all these sanctuary areas, a fact kept quiet until over a decade after South Vietnam fell.

American troops operated out of bases deep in the bush. Even in densely populated areas like the Mekong Delta, U.S. bases tended to be placed where civilians were thin on the ground. As the war went on, American politicians became even more sensitive to civilian casualties in South Vietnam, so American bases were put in areas where the enormous firepower used to defend them would mostly kill attacking Communist troops and not nearby civilians.

The smaller bases were firebases, where artillery or mortars were set up to provide fire support for nearby infantry. Firebases were often temporary, set up for a particular mission and then abandoned. Firebases often contained some infantry to help out with defending the places against Communist attack. There were not a lot of troops operating from firebases; the emphasis was on protecting the big guns. Firebases were often put in hard to reach places, like the tops of hills. This made them easier to defend and gave the guns an easier shot at targets below.

Base camps were generally permanent and were larger than most firebases. Some base camps, especially division headquarters, were huge, covering hundreds of acres and containing thousands of troops. Many were pretty rough affairs, but most of the combat troops were always anxious to secure a job that kept them there and not out in the bush. Base camps for combat units had about half their troops constantly going out into the bush, while the other half generally stayed at the base to provide support (clerks, supply, maintenance, cooks, etc.). The base camp troops led a pretty normal, by army standards, life, except for having to spend more time on guard duty. Boredom was a problem. Most base camps were out in the bush and you always had to assume that the bush was full of Communist troops. So you stayed within the limited confines of the base most of the time. Catching a ride back to larger bases on a helicopter was a prize worth working for, and much energy went into thinking of creative reasons why you really had to be on that next chopper out.

Most American troops in Vietnam served in the huge base complexes in and around Saigon and places like Da Nang and Cam Ranh Bay. Here, day to day life was not much different than in any other U.S. base overseas. Unlike Germany or Korea, where most overseas troops were before Vietnam came along, there was no frigid winter to worry about. Air-conditioning was becoming cheaper and a lot more common in the early 1960s, and many of the troops in places like Saigon soldiered away in air-conditioned comfort.

Moreover, everyone in Vietnam got combat pay. This was a real perk for anyone who didn't really have to deal with combat. The greatest danger for these troops was not the occasional rocket attacks on these huge areas, but on the roads between the major towns and cities. While all bases had trenches and bomb shelters handy for protection, the troops doing convoy duty were, next to the infantry, the most likely to see enemy fire up close and personal.

LET'S MAKE A DEAL

By the time large American combat units arrived in 1965, Vietnam had experienced over twenty years of military occupation, fighting, and general mayhem. Many Vietnamese were tired of it all, including many of the South Vietnamese soldiers and Viet Cong. The North Vietnamese were another matter, and as the war went on, more and more of the combat was initiated by North Vietnamese units. Meanwhile, the South Vietnamese troops and the Viet Cong (and sometimes even Americans) made little deals to leave each other alone. This is actually fairly common in wars, particularly in civil wars (including the American Civil War). These arrangements most often took the form of, "I'll stay out of your way if you'll stay out of mine." This was particularly noticeable after the 1968 Tet Offensive, when so many of "the True Believer" Viet Cong got themselves killed, captured, or were simply demoralized in the failed Communist "final offensive." Most South Vietnamese troops and government officials were open to truces, especially if it involved a bribe or some lucrative business deal. The Viet Cong were rather less prone to corruption, but could justify paying off the local South Vietnamese garrison or simply doing a tit for tat regarding combat. The Viet Cong always told themselves, often with some justification, that this was a temporary measure so that they could build up their strength and wipe out the South Vietnamese troops and officials in the area later. Once the Americans came in and showed the South Vietnamese how to go storming into an area lost to the Communists and reclaim it, the locals often lost any enthusiasm for complete Communist control. Thus evolved the drill where the South Vietnamese owned an area during daylight, and the Communists at night. Such arrangements were usually made despite Americans being in the vicinity. The Viet Cong leaders were usually local people, or had been in the area long enough to know everyone, including the local South Vietnamese government officials. There was often communication, however tenuous, between Communists and South Vietnamese officials. Both flavors of South Vietnamese were keen to do various types of business. For example, throughout the war, the United States sent much rice and other foodstuffs to South Vietnam to make up for what had been lost when crops were destroyed by combat operations or Communist terrorism. The Communists would often approach nearby South Vietnamese officials to buy some of this American food. The Communists would also offer to buy weapons and military equipment. The only fighting was verbal, over how much the Communists would pay. At times the Communists used their knack for terrorism to scare the South Vietnamese officials into lowering the asking price. At times, the assassinations of South Vietnamese officials were over commercial disagreements, not politics. As the fictional Don Vito Corleone observed when a rival was about to be bumped off, "It's business."

Truces with American units were even more informal. One side (usually the Communists) would lighten up on the sniping and shooting. If the other side reciprocated, then both sides would continue scaling back their military operations. This would never last long when an American unit was involved, because unit commanders rarely held their jobs more than six or eight months before rotating out so someone else could get a chance to be a commander. The new guy often came in looking to make his mark. Noticing the lack of action, he would step up patrolling, employ more artillery fire at "suspected Viet Cong targets," and pretty soon Charlie would be firing back.

GOOD MORNING, VIETNAM

In 1988, Robin Williams starred in the movie *Good Morning, Vietnam*. The film was based on the career of Airman Adrian Cronauer, who had actually served in Vietnam, and spotlighted a little known aspect of overseas military life for Americans. Since World War II, just about every foreign country that played host to more than a few thousand U.S. troops also got a radio (and later a TV) station manned by American soldiers to bring a little bit of home over the airwaves for homesick GIs. Cronauer worked for Armed Forces Radio in Vietnam.

The movie itself was relatively accurate, at least as movies go. As Cronauer later observed, "If I had done half of what Robin Williams did, I would have been in jail." Cronauer entered the air force in 1962 and in May of 1965 was sent to Vietnam as a radio announcer. Cronauer later observed that "I tried to make AF radio sound like a stateside radio station. In the film it showed that I was constantly being pushed around by the brass, which wasn't really the case." As in the movie, Cronauer did teach English in his off-duty time, and he did run into news censorship, which he fought as best he could. Then again, there was no music censorship. Cronauer did go out into the field for interviews, but did not, as depicted in the movie, run over a land mine. Then again, as in the movie, he was in a diner shortly before the VC blew it up. And his station manager refused to let him report that experience on the air. And Cronauer did start each morning show by shouting "Good morning, Vietnam!" He got out of the air force in 1966 and went to law school.

More than the Vietnam War, music defined the 1960s, and the music followed the troops to Vietnam. While no one has ever complied a survey of which tunes were the most popular, there were several dozen that were heard constantly while American troops were there.

"The Letter" (the Box Tops) indicated how important mail from home was. "Leaving on a Jet Plane" (Peter, Paul, and Mary) was all about the most important event in a soldier's Vietnam experience, when he got on his "Freedom Bird" to leave the place. "We've Gotta Get Out of This Place" (the Animals) expressed a widely held sentiment about life in the bush, as did "Paint It Black" (the Rolling Stones). "The Dock of the Bay" (Otis Redding) was popular because of the way it referred to San Francisco, the last part of America many soldiers saw. And "I Left My Heart in San Francisco" (Tony Bennett), an early sixties tune, was popular in smoky bars and was immediately adopted by all U.S. troops serving in the Far East. For some reason, the group Creedence Clearwater Revival produced numerous songs that were very popular with the troops. Among the most heard were "Proud Mary" and "Bad Moon Rising." Listen to them and you'll see why. Tunes with a driving beat were often favored simply because they got your mind off the place. Most popular of these types was "Wooly Bully" (Sam the Sham & the Pharoahs).

Filling out the Vietnam hit parade were: "A Whiter Shade of Pale" (Procol Harum), "All Along the Watchtower" (Jimi Hendrix), "Aquarius/Let the Sunshine In" (the Fifth Dimension), "As Tears Go By" (the Rolling Stones), "Babe, I'm Gonna Leave You" (Led Zeppelin), "Baby Love" (Diana Ross and the Supremes), "Ballad of Ira Hayes" (Johnny Cash), "Billy and Sue" (B. J. Thomas), "Black Is Black" (Los Bravos), "Black Magic Woman" (Santana), "Bobby McGee" (Bobby Gentry and Glen Campbell), "Born on the Bayou" (Creedence Clearwater Revival), "Burning Bridges" (the Mike Curb Congregation), "Coming Home Soldier" (Bobby Vinton), "Crimson and Clover" (Tommy James & the Shondells), "Darling Be Home Soon" (the Lovin' Spoonful), "Dazed and Confused" (Jake Holmes), "Different Drum" (Linda Ronstadt and the Stone Poneys), "Do You Believe In Magic" (the Lovin' Spoonful), "Don't Worry, Baby" (the Beach Boys), "Draft Dodger Rag" (Phil Ochs), "Drive On" (Johnny Cash), "Eve of Destruction" (Barry McGuire), "For What It's Worth" (Buffalo Springfield) "Fortunate Son" (Creedence Clearwater Revival) "Galveston" (Glen Campbell), "Get Off of My Cloud" (the Rolling Stones), "Good Morning Starshine" (Oliver), "Goodnight Saigon" (Billy Joel), "Hang on Sloopy" (the McCoys), "Have You Ever Seen The Rain" (Creedence Clearwater Revival), "Heartbreaker" (the Crystals), "Hey Joe" (Jimi Hendrix), "Hey Jude" (the Beatles), "House of the Rising Sun" (the Animals), "I Heard It Through the Grapevine" (Marvin Gaye), "I Wish It Would Rain" (the Temptations), "I Feel Like I'm Fixin' to Die Rag" (Country Joe [Mcdonald] & the Fish), "I'm a Believer" (the Monkees), "In the Year 2525" (Zaeger & Evans), "Is There Anybody Here" (Phil Ochs), "Judy in Disguise" (John Fred & the Playboys), "Let's Spend the Night Together" (the Rolling Stones), "Light My Fire" (the Doors), "Long As I Can See the Light" (Creedence Clearwater Revival), "Lookin' Out My Back Door" (Creedence Clearwater Revival), "Louie Louie" (the Kingsmen), "Love the One You're With" (Stephen Stills), "Me and You and a Dog Named Boo" (Lobo), "Monday, Monday" (Mamas & the Papas), "Mr. Lonely" (Bobby Vinton), "My Girl" (the Temptations), "Nowhere Man" (the Beatles), "Ode to Billy Joe" (Bobbie Gentry), "Okie from Muskogee" (Merle Haggard), "One" (Three Dog Night), "Positively 4th Street" (Bob Dylan), "Presence of the Lord" (Blind Faith), "Proud Mary" (Ike and Tina Turner), "Purple Haze" (Jimi Hendrix), "Radio V-I-E-T-N-A-M" (Bell & Shore), "Reach Out, I'll Be There" (the Four Tops), "Rescue Mission" (Kris Kristofferson), "Ruby, Don't Take Your Love to Town" (Kenny Rogers), "Run Through the Jungle" (Creedence Clearwater Revival), "(I Can't Get No) Satisfaction" (the Rolling Stones), "Sgt. Pepper's Lonely Hearts Club

Band" (the Beatles), "Sherry" (the Four Seasons), "Silver Medals and Sweet Memories" (the Statler Brothers), "Snoopy Vs. the Red Baron" (the Royal Guardsman), "Soldier Boy" (the Shirelles), "Soul Deep" (the Box Tops), "Stand By Your Man" (Tammy Wynette), "Star-Spangled Banner" (Jimi Hendrix), "Still in Saigon" (the Charlie Daniels Band), "Sugar Pie, Honey Bunch" (the Four Tops), "Susie Q" (Creedence Clearwater Revival), "These Boots Are Made for Walkin' " (Nancy Sinatra), "Tighten Up" (Archie Bell & the Drells), "Unchained Melody" (Righteous Brothers), "Up Around the Bend" (Creedence Clearwater Revival), "Veterans Day" (Tom Russell), "Vietnam Blues" (Dave Dudley), "Walk Like a Man" (the Four Seasons), "What's Going On" (Marvin Gaye), "When a Man Loves a Woman" (Percy Sledge), "Whole Lotta Love" (Led Zeppelin), "You Didn't Have to Be So Nice" (the Lovin' Spoonful).

And then there was Vietnam veteran and Special Forces NCO S. SGT Barry Sadler who had three hit songs, all of them hitting a responsive chord with the troops in the bush: "The Ballad of the Green Berets," "I'm a Lucky One," and "Trooper's Lament."

Most of the troops in Vietnam were not out in the bush, but were stationed in more sedate military camps. For them, there were a host of other tunes that reflected on less desperate matters. While the rear area troops also related to what the bush troopers liked, for there was some danger everywhere in Vietnam, in the less desperate rear area, less desperate lyrics were enjoyed.

The music was an eclectic collection of country, rock, pop, and soul. Troops would often group themselves according to what kind of music they liked, an alignment that also reflected ethnic, racial, and class lines. Some musical groups were represented far beyond their share of the civilian record market. The Creedence Clearwater Revival were the premier example of this. Then again, Creedence had a driving rhythm and mournful lyrics that spoke to what a year in the bush was all about.

It would make quite an interesting audio "book" if one could just listen to all the above tunes in one sitting. The music said much about the war, and the troops knew it.

"BLOOMIN' GOOD PAY"

Vietnam was the last war in which America's ordinary soldiers, sailors, marines, and airmen were paid what was essentially a token sum. Indeed, in terms of the cost of living, the monthly base pay of a Vietnam-era enlisted member of the service was almost exactly the same as what his father was making in 1942. In contrast, by 1996, a Vietnam veteran's son—or daughter—in the service was earning about twice as much, adjusted for inflation. On the other hand, officer salaries, which by Vietnam had also not changed in terms of purchasing power since World War II, have increased much less

Monthly Base Military Pay, 1969 and 1997

Grade	Rank (Military/Naval)	Vietnam 1969	Today 1997
E-l	Recruit	$ 115.28	$ 833.40
E-2	Private	127.80	1,010.10
E-3	Private First Class	155.10	1,049.70
E-4	Corporal	209.20	1,113.60
E-5	Sergeant	254.70	1,194.30
E-6	Staff Sergeant	294.90	1,360.80
E-7	Sergeant First Class	342.30	1,581.90
E-8	Master Sergeant	544.50	2,265.60
E-9	Sergeant Major	648.90	2,701.80
W-1	Warrant Officer 1	378.90	1,540.20
W-2	Warrant Officer 2	454.80	1,848.60
W-3	Chief Warrant Officer 3	519.30	2,110.80
W-4	Chief Warrant Officer 4	571.20	2,322.30
W-5	Chief Warrant Officer 5	—	2,963.60
O-1	Second Lieutenant/Ensign	363.40	1,725.90
O-2	First Lieutenant/Lieutenant, j.g	449.70	1,987.80
O-3	Captain/Lieutenant	561.00	2,279.40
O-4	Major/Lieutenant Commander	603.60	2,452.80
O-5	Lieutenant Colonel/Commander	715.50	2,910.30
O-6	Colonel/Captain	894.60	3,638.40
O-7	Brigadier General/Rear Admiral (Lower Half)	1,207.20	4,909.20
O-8	Major General/Rear Admiral (Upper Half)	1,453.20	5,908.20
O-9	Lieutenant General/Vice Admiral	1,604.40	6,522.90
O-10	General/Admiral	1,810.20	7,360.20

Key: Figures are for base pay only, thus excluding additional sums for longevity, hazardous duty, combat, family allowances, and so forth. *Military* ranks are used by the army, marines, and air force, *naval* ones by the navy, Coast Guard, and certain other uniformed services, such as NOAA. Warrant officer ranks are the same for all services, except the air force, which lacks such personnel. Enlisted rank names differ so markedly among the services (there are, for example, several different degrees of E-9s in the army alone) that only army ranks have been given.

since Vietnam. The base pay of second lieutenants and ensigns today is only about 28 percent more in terms of the cost of living than during Vietnam, while full generals and admirals make only about 12 percent more. Furthermore, the ratio of remuneration between officers and enlisted personnel has changed rather dramatically: In Vietnam, basic enlisted personnel made less than 13 percent of what full colonels earned, whereas today the figure is almost 23 percent.

An additional, less visible difference between the two eras is in terms of creature comforts, privileges, and fringe benefits. While officers still have more of these than do enlisted personnel, the gap has narrowed considerably.

While still in the United States, Vietnam-era enlisted personnel lived in barracks and performed numerous housekeeping tasks, while today they usually live in collegelike dorms, with most housekeeping tasks performed by civilians. Officers, while still normally better housed, have lost considerable privilege: nowadays colonels still get rather pleasant civilian-type housing, but they mow their own lawns and don't have soldier servants.

AMERICAN WOMEN AT WAR

About 260,000 women served in the armed forces during the Vietnam War, about 3 percent of the total personnel in uniform. It is not possible to determine the number of American women who served "in country" during the Vietnam War. It was certainly in the thousands, counting only military women, and probably well over ten thousand if one includes the numerous civilian women who worked for various government agencies, relief organizations, the media, and religious groups.

Not even the number of military women can be determined with any reliability.

U.S. Military Women in Vietnam

Branch	Service	Total
Air Force	Air Force Nurse Crops	c. 200
	Women in the Air Force	c. 500
Army	Army Nurse Corps	c. 6,250
	Women's Army Corps	c. 700
Marines	Women Marines	36
Navy	Navy Nurse Corps	c. 200
	WAVES	9
Total		c. 8,000

An official Department of Defense figure has it that "7,456 women served in the military in Vietnam." Unfortunately, this conflicts with other more or less official statements as to the number of women from each of the services. In fact, some estimates put the number at about 10,000. Complicating the matter is the fact that not all members of the various nurse corps were women, there being a few men among them as well. In addition, it is extremely difficult to determine how many women from the Air Force Nurse Corps and the Navy Nurse Corps actually served in the war zone. Air force nurses regularly flew in and out of Vietnam on medevac flights, while navy nurses served on the various hospital ships offshore in some numbers. Nine American military women died in Vietnam, one, 1LT Sharon Lane, an army nurse, by enemy action, and the others in accidents or from disease.

Deaths Among American Women in the Vietnam War

Category	Deaths	KIA	Accidents	Disease	Other
Military					
Army Nurse Corps	8	1	5	2	.
Air Force Nurse Corps	1	.	1	.	.
Government Service					
Agency for International Development	1	.	.	.	1
Army Special Services	2	2	.	.	.
Central Intelligence Agency	1	1	.	.	.
Other					
American Red Cross	3	.	1	1	1
Catholic Relief Services	1	1	.	.	.
Journalists	2	2	.	.	.
Missionaries	9	9*	.	.	.
"Operation Babylift"	38	.	38**	.	.
Total	64	16	45	3	2

Key: KIA (Killed in Action), includes all deaths by enemy action, including women killed in combat, murdered by terrorists, or killed while prisoners of the enemy. *Accidents* were mostly the result of airplane or helicopter crashes. *Disease* includes one death from stroke. *Other* were murdered by U.S. personnel.

*All had been captured by enemy forces. Eight were subsequently burned to death. One is officially listed as missing.

**"Operation Baby Lift" was an attempt to evacuate by air hundreds of Vietnamese orphans in the closing hours of the war, which resulted in one C-5 crashing upon takeoff, with enormous loss of life. The figure includes one infant girl whose mother was among the thirty-seven adult American women killed in the crash. Of these women, one was a civilian teacher and the other thirty-six employees of various U.S. government agencies.

If the story of American women in Vietnam is poorly known, that of Allied women is even less so. Not only were there some women in the RVN armed forces, but some Australian women served in Vietnam, one of whom died in the war.

Women veterans of the war have encountered unusual problems in securing recognition of their service and assistance for their problems, which in many ways reflected those of the men alongside whom they served. Not until considerable political pressure was brought to bear did the Veterans Administration extend to women counseling and other services routinely provided for men who served.

The peak year for the service of American military women in Vietnam was probably 1969–70, when there were perhaps 1,750–1,800 service women in country, roughly 22 percent of all uniformed women who served in Vietnam.

If the story of American military women in Vietnam is poorly reported, that of American civilian women is virtually forgotten. In fact, a very large, if indeterminate, number of American civilian women served in Vietnam during the war, in numbers certainly exceeding those of women in uniform. These included government officials and employees, teachers, relief, development, and aid workers, entertainers, journalists, and missionaries.

THE CHAPLAINCY

Chaplains exist in the armed forces to meet the religious needs of military personnel. They also serve as unofficial ombudsmen, a means by which the troops can clue-in higher-ranking personnel to problems without creating breaches of the chain-of-command. In combat chaplains also serve as medical aidmen.

Providing chaplains for the U.S. armed forces is a rather complicated process, due to the numerous denominations to be found in America. Nearly a hundred different denominations are represented, and chaplains are recruited in proportion to the numbers of each denomination in society. This means that some smaller denominations have to cooperate to supply a single chaplain who is mutually acceptable. Some denominations cull their clergy for volunteers, while others more or less hold a "draft" among recent seminary graduates. Prospective chaplains have to be willing to provide religious assistance to persons not of their faith. Among most denominations this has not proven to be a problem, due primarily to the interfaith movement, which itself was a major consequence of the enormous number of clergy of all faiths who served in the Second World War. However, there have been occasional problems with recruitment from some denominations. The respective army and navy chaplains training programs are heavy on comparative religion, to prepare chaplains to provide basic assistance to men of other faiths, even to learning appropriate prayers (e.g., so that a Protestant can help a Catholic make an Act of Contrition or a Jew say Kadish).

On the eve of the Vietnam War there were relatively few chaplains in the service, only about 1,300 in the army and about as many more again in the navy (which provides the chaplains for the Marine Corps and Coast Guard) and the air force combined. The expansion of the chaplaincy was rather greater than that of the armed forces as a whole, so that by 1968, there were about 50 percent more chaplains in uniform. In that year there were more than 300 army chaplains in Vietnam, plus 112 navy chaplains with the Marine Corps, and an undetermined number with navy and air force personnel. Nearly a dozen chaplains were killed in action and about a hundred were wounded. Three chaplains earned the Medal of Honor in Vietnam, two of them posthumously.

Chaplains Earning the Medal of Honor in Vietnam

LT., j.g., Vincent R. Capodanno, USN

Age	State	Date	Unit	Place
38	N.Y.	4 Sep 1967	3/5th Marines	Quang Tin

CPT Charles J. Litkey, USA

Age	State	Date	Unit	Place
36	D.C.	6 Dec 1967	199th Infantry Bde	Phuoc Lai, Bien Hoa

MAJ Charles J. Watters, USA

Age	State	Date	Unit	Place
40	N.J.	19 Nov 1967	173rd Abn Bde	Hill 875, Dak To, Kontum

It is interesting to note that all three of these chaplains were Roman Catholics. Only Father Litkey survived to wear his decoration.

Footnote: The ARVN Chaplaincy. The South Vietnamese created a chaplains' corps in the late 1950s. At first only Catholics seem to have been commissioned, but later there were some Buddhist and Protestant chaplains as well.

THE CLASS OF '66

In June 1966, 579 young men graduated from West Point. They were not exactly a cross section of America. Most were white. Although about two-thirds of the men were Protestants, Catholics rather disproportionately amounted to nearly another third, while only a handful were adherents of other religions. The vast majority, two-thirds, of the men came from military families (today it's only about 6.5 percent), and more than half came from families in the higher income brackets ($10,000 a year or more, at a time when the median income was about $8,000).

During—and long after—the war, some antiwar types attempted to charge that the army "protected" the newly graduated West Point officers of the wartime classes by keeping them away from Vietnam. In a sense this was true. Most of these newly minted "butter bars" (2nd lieutenants wear a single gold bar) were not immediately sent to Vietnam. There were two simple reasons for this, neither very sinister. For one thing the army did not want to repeat errors it had made in 1917–18 and 1950 upon America's entry into World War I and upon the outbreak of the Korean War. In both cases, most of the new officers were almost immediately sent to the front, with the result that within a year of graduation these classes already had some of the highest casualty rates in the history of the academy. It was not an experience the army wished to repeat, since the loss of such highly trained young men had a serious affect on the overall effectiveness of the army as a whole. In addition, upon graduation it is quite common for many new officers to be assigned to specialized advanced training (helicopter, armor, artillery, airborne, nuclear engineering, and so forth), which could keep them from the front for a year or more. So it is true that most new West Point graduates did not go immediately to Vietnam. That doesn't mean they didn't go at all.

Within three years of their graduation virtually every member of the class of '66 had served or was serving in Vietnam. Many eventually served a second tour, and some even a third before the war ended in 1973. More than a quarter (c. 27 percent) of the men of the Class of '66 became casualties in Vietnam, thirty of them dead and over a hundred wounded. There were other kinds of casualties as well.

When they entered West Point probably every one of the men who graduated in 1966 intended to make the army a career. It didn't work out that way. Their experiences in the war and back home, confronting the declining regard for the professional soldier and the veteran, weighed heavily on the members of the Class of '66. Within five years of graduation, only about half of the class was still on active duty, a "dropout" rate that was about 50 percent higher than that for the classes between 1945 and 1965.

VD AND VIETNAM

Venereal disease (VD) has long been a major cause of nonbattle-related casualties in armies. Through World War II, the problem was of significant, but declining importance. The VD rate for the allegedly restrained Victorians of the Civil War was 82 per 1,000 men per year. By World War I, the rate in the U.S. Army was about 87 cases per 1,000 men per year. Although only slightly higher than that for the Civil War, it was much higher than that in the French Army. However, by World War II, the rate had decreased markedly, due largely to an intensive educational program alerting the troops to the dangers of venereal infections. Plus there was the introduction of penicillin, and, not incidentally, the fact that many troops campaigned in areas where there were few opportunities to contract VD (e.g., New Guinea, Guadalcanal, etc.). Despite this, VD cases still accounted for over a third of all infectious and parasitical disease cases among army personnel in World War II. Still, the army thought it had the matter under control. It didn't.

The VD rate in Korea proved to be over 300 percent higher than that in World War II, and in Vietnam it more than doubled again. What had happened? A lot of things. After World War II, the army settled down to a very comfortable routine of occupation duty in Germany and Japan. There was a lot of poverty in the two countries, and even a GI's pay was more than

VD in the U.S. Army Since 1861

War	Rate	Ratio
Civil War	82	100.0%
World War I	87	106.1%
World War II	49	46.0%
Korea	146	178.0%
Vietnam	325	396.3%

Key: Rate is the number of cases per thousand troops on strength per year. Ratio uses the U.S. Army's Civil War rate as a baseline against which to compare the rates in the other four wars. For political reasons, statistics have not been published for the Gulf War, but they are believed to be much lower than any since World War II.

enough to secure an endless supply of women. So while their mothers might have grieved when their sons were drafted, most young men looked forward to a hitch in the army as a chance for some protracted debauchery. This was particularly the case in Japan, where in prewar times it had not been unusual for parents to "sell" unwanted daughters into prostitution. With the fighting over, the army tended to treat its rising VD rate casually—after all, you could give the guy a shot of penicillin and he'd be good as new in no time. So the VD rate began to rise. The problem grew worse in Korea, another country with traditions permitting the sale of women, and was further exacerbated by the first glimmerings of "the sexual revolution" in the late 1950s and early 1960s and the rise of penicillin-resistant strains of various venereal diseases. As a result, the VD rate in Vietnam—yet another country where women could be sold into prostitution—was high from the start and remained so.

PACIFIC IDYLLS

Vietnam was not the first time U.S. forces had operated in the tropical Pacific during this century. In fact, American soldiers began the twentieth-century fighting a Vietnamlike war in the Philippines. There was some low-level guerrilla action in the Philippines every few years, something that has continued to the present. When World War II came along, a far larger army of Americans fought across the Pacific. But these earlier Pacific battles were different from Vietnam in two important respects: the World War II fighting wasn't done in any one place for more than a few months and there weren't many civilians around. Heavy fighting for U.S. troops in Vietnam went on for six years, long enough for all Americans to get tired of it. The fighting in the densely populated areas of South Vietnam was a lot more nerve-wracking for the troops and dispiriting for the folks back home.

Until Vietnam came along, the attitude toward American military operations in the Pacific was generally favorable, despite the tropical horrors many veterans endured. There had been a lot of hard fighting in places like Bataan, Tarawa, New Guinea, and Guadalcanal. But there were a lot of good memories too. Vietnam changed all that. As the first televised war, too many people saw too many ugly things. The bad memories will take a long time to fade.

CHAPTER 7

War in the Shadows

The most successful operations against the Viet Cong and the North Vietnamese were by small groups of specialists in irregular warfare. These were the Army Special Forces, the Navy SEALs, CIA operatives, and several other groups.

THE SPECIAL FORCES

Nicknamed "the Green Berets," the Special Forces had been created in the early 1950s with the mission of organizing guerrilla forces behind enemy lines. As a natural corollary to their guerrilla mission, they also began to develop a counterguerrilla doctrine. In the early 1960s, they came to the notice of Pres. John F. Kennedy, who poured a lot of resources into the program (and also gave them their berets), seeing it as a solution to the increasing problem of Communist-sponsored "wars of national liberation."

Since South Vietnam was increasingly embroiled in a war of national liberation, a lot of Special Forces personnel were already serving as advisers in Southeast Asia (c. 1,100 in 1961, roughly half of all U.S. personnel in Vietnam). In 1962, a special headquarters was activated to oversee Special Forces activities in Vietnam, a task that was taken over by the 5th Special Forces Group when it arrived in October 1965. The 5th Special Forces Group consisted of five companies. Each company had a headquarters, known as a "C-Detachment," and several subordinate commands, known as "B-Detachments." Each B-Detachment oversaw the operations of several A Teams.

An A Team was the normal operational unit of the Special Forces. It consisted of a handful of highly skilled personnel, interpreters, medics, demolitions experts, and so forth. Each man was "cross trained" in several skills, and all were supposed to be able to serve as trainers and cadres for indigenous guerrilla forces. At the peak of the war, nearly one hundred A Teams were operating under the aegis of the 5th Special Forces, and some troops from the 1st and 7th Special Forces Groups had also served.

The Special Forces performed a variety of missions. They provided the main cadre for the Montagnard personnel in the Civilian Irregular Defense Forces. They performed missions for the SOG (Studies and Observation Group), trained the South Vietnamese Special Forces, and, quite often, formed important elements of the garrisons of isolated base camps, firebases, and outposts, fighting essentially as conventional troops. They also undertook one notable raid.

Acting on what was considered reliable information concerning the presence of American prisoners of war at a compound near Son Tay, about twenty miles from Hanoi, a complex special operations mission was undertaken on 21 November 1970. Technically the raid was a remarkable achievement. The raiders got in and out quickly, killing more than thirty NVA troops with minimal casualties to themselves. But no prisoners were released, all having been moved to another location some weeks earlier.

So Green Berets did a lot of fighting.

The first Medal of Honor awarded for service in Vietnam went to a Green Beret, CPT Roger H. C. Donlon of the 7th Special Forces, who earned it at Nam Doc on 5 December 1964. Altogether seventeen Green Berets were awarded the Medal of Honor in Vietnam and eighty-eight received the Distinguished Service Cross, the second highest award in the army, while the 5th Special Forces Group was awarded a Presidential Unit Citation and a Meritorious Unit Citation.

Civic Action Activities of the 5th Special Forces Group

Construction Projects

Bridges	670
Churches	130
Classrooms	>1,000
Dispensaries	400
Hospitals	110
Markets	275
Roads	>2,000 km
Wells	6,500
Transportation Projects	1,500

Rural Development Activities

Economic Development Programs	50,000
Educational Programs	35,000
Medical Projects	11,000
Welfare Programs	35,000

Although in many ways the performance of the Special Forces was exemplary, they were not viewed favorably by the rest of the army. Since the army was essentially committed to a conventional war, the Green Berets' skills in unconventional war were not considered important, and their achievements—such as forming the CIDGs (local tribal mercenaries under their own leaders with U.S. advisers)—not recognized as important to the war effort. Moreover, since a lot of Green Berets did end up fighting in conventional roles, many of the army's brass concluded that they were not worth the investment in manpower, money, and time.

THE SECRET WAR IN LAOS

America and North Vietnam fought a secret war in Laos throughout the 1960s. North Vietnam had over a hundred thousand labor troops and thirty- to fifty-thousand combat troops in Laos through most of the 1960s. Using, at its peak strength, some eight thousand Montagnard, Laotian, and Cambodian mercenaries, and about two thousand American troops, the American force proved to be the deadliest troops the North Vietnamese (by their own admission) faced. This story is largely unknown.

SOG (Studies and Observation Group) was the top-secret organization that ran this war. Before SOG was SOG, it was called the Special Operations Group, a name that was quickly changed to provide a little more cover. Other code words for this secret operation were "Shining Brass" and "Prairie Fire." SOG was run by MACV (Military Assistance Command, Vietnam), the headquarters for all U.S. forces in Vietnam.

What eventually became the SOG operation started in 1958 as a South Vietnamese version of the U.S. Special Forces. The CIA provided assistance to the South Vietnamese in this area. The SOG took over the CIA operation in 1964. The SOG reported directly to the Pentagon, via MACV, and could appeal that high if someone didn't give them what they wanted in Vietnam. SOG had its own air and naval forces, which included U.S. Army, Navy, and Air Force units. There was also a South Vietnamese helicopter unit flying CH-34s and a C-123 transport aircraft unit with Nationalist Chinese pilots. These two outfits were needed to fly SOG teams into areas where, by treaty, U.S. forces were not supposed to be.

SOG's mandate covered a wide area. It was an intelligence organization, able to collect information where U.S. troops could not officially do so. Squad-size SOG recon teams (RTs) were dropped by parachute or landed from helicopters in areas adjacent to South Vietnam. Each RT contained Americans and Montagnards. The Americans provided the leadership and radio operators, the Montagnards provided their lifelong knowledge of the bush.

The United States had agreed in the early 1960s, to respect the neutrality of Laos and Cambodia. But when it became clear that North Vietnam was operating in those countries, SOG was sent in to find out what was going on. In addition, there were similar operations in North Vietnam and in the more remote regions of South Vietnam.

SOG also supported anti-Communist resistance movements throughout the region. The biggest one was among the Montagnards in South Vietnam itself, and this was run largely by non-SOG Special Forces troops. But the anti-Communist groups in Laos and Cambodia were supported by SOG. In North Vietnam, the best that could be done was to get agents in there to look around and then get them out. North Vietnam was a special case because it was the most effective police state in the region and had gotten rid of most of its dissidents in 1954 when Vietnam was partitioned (nearly two million people fled south), followed by the mopping up of some tens of thousands of dissidents in the late fifties.

Most SOG combat units were squads, the recon teams of three U.S. and four to nine Montagnard soldiers. About seventy RTs were formed and all were in constant action through the late 1960s.

SOG's RTs were also some of the most effective combat units fielded by the United States. This was so because RTs did not just collect information on the enemy. When an RT spotted something while deep in enemy territory, the three U.S. members of the team knew what was a worthwhile target and what wasn't. And they team called in air or artillery strikes to do something about it.

Then there were Hatchet Forces (one or more platoons, each with four to five U.S. troops and twenty to thirty Montagnards). These were used when some more muscle was needed on the ground, for things like raids and the destruction of large enemy installations.

SLAM (search, location, and annihilation mission) companies were larger versions of the Hatchet Forces, being company-size, units with three or four platoons organized like the Hatchet Force platoons.

SOG also had call on CIDG battalions. Ultimately, SOG could call on any U.S.-controlled military unit. Because SOG reported directly to the Pentagon, and often carried out missions specifically requested by the president, the Pentagon let everyone know that when SOG asked for something, you delivered it immediately.

SOG was also the chief means of rescuing POWs (prisoners of war) and downed pilots in enemy territory, especially North Vietnam, Laos, and Cambodia. The U.S. Air Force had their SAR (search and rescue) helicopters, but they often needed some knowledgeable people on the ground, and that's where one or more SOG RTs came in. Less successful were attempts to grab POWs from the Communists. Part of this was due to the fact that the Communists didn't take many prisoners in the first place. And those who were taken were moved around regularly to different jungle camps, just like all the Communist troops did.

SOG also trained all its own non-U.S. personnel. This meant many training camps for Montagnards (who did not all speak the same language) and Cambodians. South Vietnamese were also trained, especially those sent into North Vietnam. Most of the training was combat related, including parachute training for some of the Montagnards, but some of it was technical as well.

SOG was heavily involved in many of the psychological warfare operations conducted during the war. This was especially the case with what were called "black" operations (ones that required secrecy, such as planting in Communist ammo dumps mortar shells that would explode in the mortar tube). Finally, SOG was the last resort for any really, really important job that had to be done right away and was very risky. Typical example of this was getting back sensitive documents (codebooks, lists of secret agents, etc.). Going into North Vietnam to rescue downed pilots (and fight off North Vietnamese ground troops in the process) was something else SOG did, because no one else dared to.

SOG came into existence in January 1964, at a time when the U.S. government was looking for a way to escalate the war so that more pressure could be put on the North Vietnamese to stop their invasion of South Vietnam. That summer the decision was made to send an American army to Vietnam, and SOG's role began to grow quickly. By late 1967, SOG had gotten so large that it had to be broken into subcommands. Thus was created:

CCN (Command and Control North) in Danang, with FOBs (forward operating bases) in Khe Sahn, Phu Bai, and other areas as needed. This was always the largest SOG operation, with about 40 percent of SOG's troops. CCN was so large because it covered operations in North Vietnam and areas of Laos being contested by the Meo tribal army of General Pao (a U.S. Ally). In addition to the RTs, there were four SLAM companies, several Hatchet forces, and two battalions of mercenaries from the Nung tribe, under U.S. officers.

CCC (Command and Control Center) in Kontum. Controlled operations in the area where the borders of Vietnam, Cambodia, and Laos meet. In addition to a varying number of RTs and Hatchet Forces, it had four SLAM companies.

CCS (Command and Control South) in Ban Me Thuot. This was the smallest of the Command and Control operations and controlled missions sent into Cambodia, as well as Viet Cong–controlled areas of South Vietnam. With the smallest (but always varying) number of RTs, and Hatchet forces, it also had four SLAM companies.

In the spring of 1972, all these units were handed over to the South Vietnamese, who promptly ran into problems with the Montagnards and Cambodian troops who comprised most of the manpower. Although South Vietnamese Special Forces troops had worked with SOG regularly, these were specially selected soldiers who made the effort not to anger the Montagnards (who normally loathed and feared Vietnamese). The South Vietnamese government wised up before they ticked off (and ran off) a substantial number of these excellent Montagnard troops. Some of the Montagnards did later become neutral, or helped the Communists. But for about ten years, from the early 1960s to the early 1970s, SOG's Montagnard mercenaries were some of the best and most effective troops in the region. Though never more than about ten thousand men were under arms, these soldiers were the most feared by the Communist, for the SOG troops tended to show up where you didn't expect them, and then proceeded to outfight you for the duration of your encounter. Truly unsung heroes. You don't see the likes of them very often.

SOG'S WAR AGAINST THE HO CHI MINH TRAIL

There was good reason for secret attacks on the Ho Chi Minh Trail, for by the early 1960s, it was realized that a guerrilla war could not long survive if deprived of all outside support. Guerrillas in South Vietnam would only get weapons and reinforcements from North Vietnam. When North Vietnamese were seen using Laos for these supply operations, there had to be some way of at least keeping an eye on it. Thus was born SOG operations in Laos. Actually, before there was SOG there was a similar CIA operation dating from the late 1950s. SOG took this over in the early 1960s, when the American armed forces began to outnumber the CIA in Indochina.

When the North Vietnamese set up the Ho Chi Minh Trail in 1959, they went to great lengths to keep it secret. The first North Vietnamese sent down the existing tribal trails carried no identification and used captured French weapons (as were commonly found in the wilderness areas of Indochina). The people who used the trail moved at night once they crossed over into South Vietnam. Even though it was widely known that the North Vietnamese were operating in Laos, the Communists wanted to keep their supply route secret. Part of this was normal Communist practice, but it was also part of an adroit diplomatic game the North Vietnamese played to protect the Ho Chi Minh Trail.

The North Vietnamese had been operating in Laos, either with their own troops or Laotian Communists (Pathet Lao) since the mid-1950s. By 1960, the perception in the West was that the Communists were about to take over Laos. Actually, what was going on in Laos was a political struggle between three major factions and several smaller ones. The Pathet Lao was one of the major players, and the North Vietnamese backed the Communists in Laos as part of their plan to set up Communist governments throughout southeast

Asia. This struggle became another standoff between the United States and the Soviet Union. There had already been a lot of nuclear saber rattling over Cuba since 1960 and no one wanted these diplomatic shoving matches to escalate to a nuclear war. So in 1962, the United States, Russia, and other concerned nations (including both Vietnams) agreed to withdraw their troops from Laos and consider it neutral in the Cold War. Everyone pulled out, except North Vietnam. Actually, North Vietnam went through the motions of withdrawing its troops, and went to great lengths to keep the troops it did have in Laos out of the public eye.

The CIA had been operating in Laos throughout the 1950s and their operatives there soon detected something new happening along the South Vietnam border in 1960. The CIA knew something was going on in those mountainous jungles, but it took several years before they were able to nail down what it was and develop the means to do something about it. The CIA had, between 1960 and 1962, made a deal with many of the Hmong tribes in more isolated areas of Laos to fight the Communists. These areas were, quite deliberately, right on the Vietnamese border. When these Hmong tribes first moved down into the area during the nineteenth century, the king of Laos granted them the right to settle there if they would fight any Vietnamese attempts to move into Laos. The Hmong fought, the Vietnamese stayed out (mainly because the French were taking over all of Indochina in the late nineteenth century), and there the situation stood until the late 1950s. In the fifties the Vietnamese began moving into Laos again, this time the Communist Vietnamese, as part of their support of the local Pathet Lao Communists. The North Vietnamese had already decided, in 1959, to use Laos as a route to move troops and supplies to South Vietnam. And a major reason the United States agreed to "neutralize" Laos was because South Vietnam was seen as a more likely battlefield for the struggle between communism and the West. But all these deals put the Hmong right in the middle.

The Hmong did not like the Vietnamese at all. But the North Vietnamese, and even the lowland Laotians, outnumbered and outgunned the Hmong. The CIA began to arm the Hmong so that these hill tribes could defend themselves against the Communist lowlanders and the North Vietnamese. Then the CIA found an up-and-coming Laotian army officer who happened to be a Hmong. Vang Pao was one of the few Hmong serving as an officer in the Laotian army and he was indeed an exceptional fellow. A natural leader, he didn't need much encouragement from the CIA to begin forming a Hmong army. By 1962, over 10,000 Hmong were armed and trained. The 1962 agreement to neutralize slowed, but did not end, the arming of the Hmong. Most American advisers in Laos were moved to South Vietnam.

Losing their American advisers didn't stop the Hmong from defending their villages, which was the main point in arming them. But the lack of professional American troops did make it impossible to get any accurate scouting done in the border areas with Vietnam. While the Hmong were great fighters, they were also homebodies. Few wanted to leave their villages for any length of time, and those who did were not always the best educated (or even literate) fellows you wanted out there observing the North Vietnamese and bringing back comprehensible information. So it was decided to use American-led patrols, operating out of South Vietnam.

Numerous military professionals were already working with the CIA's attempts to get information out of those Laotian mountains. These included Navy SEALs and Army Special Forces in South Vietnam, who were involved in CIA attempts to infiltrate agents into North Vietnam as well as keeping an eye on all that movement along the Laotian border. The infiltration attempts into North Vietnam were never very successful.

As U.S. military involvement in South Vietnam increased, and in the wake of the failure of the CIA-sponsored invasion of Cuba in 1963, the CIA scouting and secret agent operations were turned over to the military. In early 1964, the Special Operations Group (SOG) was set up, using mainly Special Forces troops. The name was soon changed when it was realized that a bit of secrecy was required. So SOG became Studies and Observation Group, or SOG for short.

Initially, SOG had an odd collection of people and machines. Their principal air element was a squadron of C-123 transport aircraft, piloted by Nationalist Chinese who had spent years making secret flights over Mainland China. There was also a squadron of high-speed Norwegian "Nasty" class boats, piloted by Norwegians expert in the use of that kind of boat. Until 1964, most of the effort went into landing agents (by air or sea) into North Vietnam (without much success).

Finally, in mid-1964, the Pentagon demanded that something be done to find out what was going on along the Laotian border. SOG was now in the LRRP (Long Range Reconnaissance Patrol) business. But the initial program, called "Shining Brass" called for more than just finding out what the North Vietnamese were doing in Laos; something was going to be done about it. Shining Brass consisted of three phases:

1. Form five LRRP recon teams, each composed of about nine to twelve Special Forces troopers. These teams would explore southern Laos, identify Ho Chi Minh Trail truck parks and supply depots and call in air strikes on them.

2. Company-sized units of Montagnards, under Special Forces leadership, would be trained. These Hatchet Forces would be sent in by helicopter to complete the destruction of some targets found by the LRRP teams. Some targets, like ones that were largely underground or spread over a wide area, could only be destroyed by troops on the ground. Air strikes would be too expensive to get it all. Moreover, putting troops on the ground allows you to grab documents, equipment, and prisoners for further investigation.

3. More combat units would be organized in Laos, using the anti-Vietnamese tribes to supply the manpower. These units would coordinate their attacks with the air mobile operations of the Special Forces LRRPs and Hatchet Forces.

The State Department, arguing that the Soviet Union and China might cause trouble if Laotian neutrality were compromised, got most of Shining Brass canceled. All that remained were the LRRPs. These were only allowed into Laos under severe restrictions. Each team only had three American Special Forces troops, the other half-dozen or so men were Nung mercenaries. No one was to carry any identification, which, technically, allowed any captured soldier to be executed as a spy. This didn't make any difference, as the North Vietnamese didn't take prisoners when it came to SOG teams. But the State Department insisted on doing everything possible to make it appear as if these patrols were either lost, or were some other foreigners who just happened to be wandering around the Laotian jungles carrying non-U.S. weapons and equipment. South Vietnamese aircraft had to be used to get them in, and American aircraft could only be called in to extract a team in danger of being captured. What the State Department was most worried about was an American Special Forces soldier getting captured in Laos, and the North Vietnamese proving it. Should this happen, the State Department knew they would have to deal with an embarrassing situation and a lot of unrefutable propaganda from the Communists. Despite all these precautions, the SOG troopers knew that the North Vietnamese would quickly figure out what was going on, even if they didn't capture any of the patrols. The SOG felt they were just going to carry the war to the enemy's backyard, and find out what was going on there.

But the case for letting SOG into Laos was compelling. There was clear evidence that thousands of North Vietnamese troops, and tons of supplies, were coming across the Laotian border into South Vietnam every month. America troops, entering Vietnam in force during 1965, found themselves taking mortar fire from areas near the Laotian border, and apparently from within Laos itself. But before anything could be done about it, American decision makers had to have details, and evidence. Attempts to send in patrols made of South Vietnamese or Montagnards had failed. The South Vietnamese lacked the skill, and the largely illiterate Montagnards brought back garbled reports. Trained observers would have to go, and this meant at least some Special Forces troops in each patrol. So in late 1965, the SOG patrols began going into Laos. They found more than they expected, for the North Vietnamese already had some thirty thousand troops maintaining the Ho Chi Minh Trail. For the next five years, the SOG scouted the Ho Chi Minh Trail and fought the North Vietnamese they found there. The Ho Chi Minh Trail was no longer a mystery, and ultimately became a killing ground for many of the North Vietnamese who worked there, or were just passing through.

UNDERCOVER FOR UNCLE HO

One of the greatest secrets of the Vietnam War is the number of people in the government and armed forces of the Republic of Vietnam who were actually working for the other side. By one estimate—made on who knows what basis—some thirty thousand government employees or military personnel were Communist sympathizers, as were many others prominent in civil society.

A number of former Viet Minh served openly in the ARVN, among them perhaps 10 percent of the most senior officers, including Nguyen Van Thieu himself, president of the Republic of Vietnam, who had been a Viet Minh district official in 1945–46, later going over to the French. Ostensibly these men had abandoned their Viet Minh sympathies to accept amnesty from the French. Some were certainly legitimate, like Thieu. Many Nationalists had supported the Viet Minh until it became clear that the national front was actually a cover for the Communists. These people went over to the French, to serve against their erstwhile "comrades."

But there were people who deliberately went undercover, often for years, serving as government officials, army officers, and so forth, often with considerable distinction.

A few examples must suffice to illustrate the dimensions of the problem:

• Pham Ngoc Thao (who bore the French surname Albert), member of a prominent Catholic family, a colonel and notable wheel in RVN military politics, taking a role in several coups, was the head of the Communist intelligence network in Saigon from 1949. He was eventually knocked off by some of his ARVN colleagues, not because of his VC connections—which remained unknown until after the war—but because of his role in military politics. He is buried in a cemetery reserved for heroes of the Communist revolution.

• Phan Dinh Thu joined the French colonial army in 1948, became a special warfare expert, taking part in several notable missions, rose to chief of the ARVN Special Forces, and later became deputy commander of a corps during the 1970 invasion of Cambodia. When Saigon fell, Phan, by then a major general, turned out to be a member of the city's VC Revolutionary Committee.

• Pham Xuan An, a journalist, the Saigon representative for the Reuters News Agency in the early sixties and later a reporter for *Time*, turned out to have been a colonel in the VC intelligence service.

• Le Er Tang, an ARVN sergeant, for many years an analyst and cartographer for the South Vietnamese Central Intelligence Agency, was actually a captain in the People's Liberation Army (PLA) commanding an intelligence battalion. About a week before the final Communist offensive, he deserted and was shortly guiding North Vietnamese troops through the streets of Saigon.

It is also probable that some of the more than 58,000 minor South Vietnamese officials and functionaries who disappeared or were kidnapped by the VC during the war may actually have been Communist sympathizers who needed to rejoin their comrades for various reasons.

Needless to say, the benefits to the enemy of having a man like Phan Dinh Thu or Le Er Tang on their side must have been enormous.

SOG RECON TEAMS

SOG teams were organized with three Americans and six to nine Montagnard (usually Nung) mercenaries. One of the Americans was the team leader and was referred to as the 1-0 ("one oh"). His second in command was an American and was called the 1-1 ("one one"). The third American was the radio operator and was called the 1-2 ("one two"). Sometimes a South Vietnamese Special Forces officer or NCO accompanied the team to gain some tactical experience or help with some technical matter, like translating interrogations of captured North Vietnamese or the like. The SOG teams were called RTs (for recon teams) and they were named in a similar fashion, depending on which area (CCN, CCC, or CCS) they belonged too. Each area would use names, of a similar type, such as those of tools or states.

The 1-0s had to be very, very good, for the survival of an RT depended on the 1-0's skill and leadership. Naturally, anyone who was an SOG 1-0 was considered a very superior soldier. These men were usually senior NCOs.

The Nungs in an RT were carefully selected from volunteers and trained for months before going on their first mission. Nung volunteers with combat experience were preferred.

THE MONTAGNARDS

There are several distinct ethnic and cultural groups in Indochina. In the lowland river valleys, deltas, and coastal plains, there are the more numerous Vietnamese and Khmer (Cambodians). About 90 percent of the Indochinese population lives in the lowlands. The mountainous interior, however, is inhabited by a distinctive mélange of tribes whom the French dubbed the Montagnards (Mountaineers). These were a combination of Malay tribes that had been there for centuries, with more recent arrivals of Chinese (or Han extraction) from the north, as well as some Polynesians and even some Mongols. Like mountain people everywhere, the Montagnards—affectionately dubbed "the Yards" by Special Forces soldiers who worked with them—did not get along with the flatlanders. Montagnards numbered from 750,000 to 1,000,000 people thinly spread across the central highlands of South Vietnam, plus several hundred thousand more in the mountains regions of North Vietnam, about 300,000 in Laos, and another 200,000 in Cambodia.

In South Vietnam alone there were something like thirty different Montagnard communities, numbering from a relative handful up to 100,000– 120,000 people in the case of the Rhadé. Although some of the Montagnard tribes are racially akin to the Vietnamese, and most have many cultural ties with them, the Montagnards were despised by the latter, who called them *moi,* or "savages," and tended to discriminate against them. Hostile to the Vietnamese in turn, the Montagnards led a simple existence, many engaging in slash-and-burn agriculture, but with a rich cultural life.

During the First Indochina War, the Vietnamese Communists had competed with the French for the allegiance of the mountain people. The Communists won that one, especially in North Vietnam. After the partition of Vietnam in 1954, the North Vietnamese trained some ten thousand Montagnards in medical, educational, and other technical skills and managed to eliminate some of the hatred between the two groups. Also, the Communist economic control was less strict out in the bush where the Montagnards lived, so the North Vietnam Montagnards remained loyal during the American phase of the Vietnam War. Later the enmity returned when the Communists got heavy-handed in Montagnard areas.

It was different in South Vietnam, where the traditional animosities were not reduced, and there were no offers of education and economic aid to the Montagnards. Instead, South Vietnam began settling Vietnamese in traditionally Montagnard territory and abusing the locals more frequently. Often this abuse was no more than a Vietnamese making a joke about the Montagnards often darker skin or inability to speak Vietnamese well. Thus, no matter what the official policy in North Vietnam or South Vietnam, the Montagnards were treated with contempt and disdain by the average Vietnamese. The Montagnards returned the feeling, considering the Vietnamese a bunch of pompous snobs who wouldn't last a day in the bush.

In the late 1950s, under pressure from the Diem regime, which wished to exercise more political control over them, the Montagnards had begun to develop a political movement, with the intention of securing the autonomy they had enjoyed under the French. An ill-considered attack on Pleiku in 1958 resulted in a violent reaction from the Diem regime, with ARVN forces engaging in some indiscriminate massacres, while several of the most notable Montagnard leaders were arrested and detained for many years. This caused some of the southern Montagnards—not many—to adhere to the VC.

The Montagnards first came to the attention of the United States about this same time, as missionaries, anthropologists, and aid workers began drifting into the central highlands. Some of these people had ties to the CIA, and reported some Viet Cong activity among the Montagnards, who they also said were capable fighters. In one instance, a well-armed VC company was beaten off from a Montagnard village that was equipped only with spears, bows and arrows, and clubs. In October 1961, a delegation from the CIA and the Special Forces visited the Rhadé to see if they could convince the tribe to support the Saigon government. The CIA offered money, arms, and aid to the Montagnards to prevent them from joining the Communists.

The Americans had several advantages working with the Montagnards. First of all, the Americans were obviously not Vietnamese. And the Montagnards were willing to overlook the fact that America was backing South Vietnam, if their CIA and Special Forces contacts did not make much of it. Second, the Americans had lots of goodies and were generous. This had been learned during similar situations during World War II, when many tribal peoples were encountered in the Pacific, and most were convinced to support the Allied cause, or at least remain neutral. Last, the right people were sent into the hills to bargain with the Montagnards. The CIA and Special Forces folks were the kind of adventurers and macho guys the tribal warriors could relate to. These tall, mostly pasty-faced flatlanders came with loot and were generous with it. And all they want us to do is kill Vietnamese? Hey, what a deal.

The relationship was similar to what the British established with the Gurkha, and other troops from what they called "warrior races." By providing these troops with modern equipment, weapons and training, and the services of first-rate officers, combat units of exceptional quality could be turned out. The Montagnards had significant advantages when operating out in the bush. Montagnards had grown up out there and knew how to get around in the forests, mountains, and jungles of upcountry Indochina. They were warriors by inclination, constantly feuding with their neighbors and particularly with non-Montagnards. With proper training and leadership, they could be outstanding soldiers when operating in the environment they grew up in. Being largely illiterate, you could only teach skills that could be shown by instructors and memorized by the students. This was the kind of training, and combat leadership, U.S. Special Forces were able to provide.

By the end of 1963, the Special Forces had taken over from the CIA, and some 674 Green Berets, plus, surprisingly, some ARVN Special Forces personnel, were working with the Montagnards, of whom some 40,000–60,000 were under arms. Since most Montagnards were not interested in getting involved in a major war outside their own home area, the Special Forces set up several military programs that gave Montagnard villagers a choice. For Montagnards just looking for self-defense against Viet Cong attacks, there were the Regional Forces programs. The Special Forces supplied weapons and training to villagers. While the Regional Forces were staunch in defending their villages, they were not much interested in going out looking for

Communist troops. For more warlike activities, the Civilian Irregular Defense Groups (CIDGs) were set up, which not only protected the Montagnards from Communists and Communist influence, but also prevented the passage of Ho Chi Minh Trail cargo into South Vietnam. In 1965, Special Forces began organizing "Mobile Strike Force" battalions (nicknamed "Mike Force"), using Montagnard personnel, to provide more effective reaction forces for the protection of isolated camps: The idea was that if the VC hit a camp, a Mike Force battalion would immediately be sent in pursuit. These forces proved very effective in keeping the VC in check throughout the central highlands. There were five of these Mike Forces. Each consisted of a Special Forces A Team, one or more CIDG battalions, a recon company, and a Montagnard mercenary parachute company. There was one of these Strike Forces for each of the four corps areas in South Vietnam, plus one run solely by the Special Forces. "Mike Forces" were used to provide a mobile reserve for defending the areas held by CDIG units. These were mostly Montagnards and some of the better-organized religious groups. In the central highlands and border areas, the Mike Forces got a real workout. These forces were disbanded when the Special Forces left in 1971.

Not all Montagnard groups had the same military potential. Several tribes were outstanding soldiers, however. These included the Hre (110,000 people), Renago (10,000), Rhadé (120,000), Sedang (70,000), and, arguably the best of all, the Nung (15,000, with more in North Vietnam). All were originally from southern China, except the Rhadé, who were Malay-Polynesian (Pacific Islander). Rarely did more than 10 percent of a tribe join Special Forces organized units, so the outstanding reputation of the Nung—they were the most likely to be selected for particularly difficult assignments—was formed by a virtual handful of fighting men.

Many of the Montagnards were in it for the money as much as for the adventure. Their own jungle economy made little use of money, so the Special Forces often had to pay them in gold or goods. But this was still cheap. The highest-paid Montagnard warrior made less than the lowest-ranking U.S. soldier (you could put ten Montagnards in the field for what it cost to send one American out to fight). However, the Montagnards were not comparing themselves to Americans, but to Vietnamese, and they could not but notice that Uncle Sam paid them more than what South Vietnam officers earned. In the elite "Prairie Fire"/SOG scouts the lowest-paid Nung received about $60 a month, more than what a South Vietnamese captain made. The Montagnards were paid in piasters (the South Vietnamese currency), but there were always plenty of traders bringing in goods for the Montagnards to spend their new wealth on.

The Montagnards thought this was a most accurate and fair pay scale. The South Vietnamese generally kept their mouths shut.

Many of the Montagnards were warriors in the classic sense. Like the

The Special Forces Montagnard Army, 1964–70

Year	Special Forces	CIDG	Regional Forces	Mike Force
1964	951	19,000	0	0
1965	1,828	30,400	28,800	1,800
1966	2,589	34,800	28,000	3,200
1967	2,726	34,300	18,200	5,700
1968	3,581	27,000	7,300	7,000
1969	3,741	28,100	700	9,300
1970	2,904	6,300	0	1,800

Key: Figures are year-end strength. Hmong personnel in Laos are included.

Gurkhas and similar groups, they literally laughed at death and got on very well with the warrior types attracted to U.S. Army Special Forces duty. Indeed, it was the bond of trust, mutual dependence, and fighting spirit between the Special Forces troopers and the Montagnards that produced a unique military organization. Many Special Forces soldiers voluntarily went back to Vietnam for tour after tour so as to keep close to their "Yards." Some of the Special Forces folks went native, moving in with the Montagnards, learning the language and customs and sometimes even marrying Montagnard women. The Yards reciprocated, becoming expert in the use of much U.S. military technology and creating some amazingly lethal combat units. The best Yard soldiers were young men in their late teens or early twenties. Like males their age the world over, they were fascinated by American technology and Americans in general. The Special Forces soldiers proved themselves competent fighters early on, and a reputation was made that young Montagnards were eager to partake of. The Montagnards were given U.S. field uniforms to wear and weapons to use. Seeing some of the Special Forces troops dressed up (in person or in pictures), some Montagnards would emulate this. Spending their money on having replicas of Special Forces uniforms made (the green beret and better quality fatigues, starched and pressed), they would unexpectedly present themselves, spit shined boots and all, for inspection. The Special Forces NCOs and officers would go along with this, carefully scrutinizing these well turned out jungle warriors and congratulating those who got it right. Although the Montagnards were basically mercenaries (although technically they were part of the South Vietnamese armed forces), they were irresistibly drawn to these foreign warriors who shared their desire to kill Vietnamese (at least the Communist ones) and who possessed such a powerful warrior ethic of their own. This could be seen by those aspects of American culture the Montagnards were most enthusiastic about. Aside from the military technology, the Yards loved American action movies. Westerns were particular favorites, with the Yards seeing themselves as the cowboys and soldiers and the Indians as the hated

Vietnamese. They were among the more enthusiastic fans of John Wayne's much maligned movie, *The Green Berets*. This film was generally derided even by many Special Forces, mainly for the numerous inaccuracies. But the Yards loved it. Any Western or other action movie that made it to a Montagnard base would be eagerly viewed time after time, despite the fact that most Montagnards had little or no knowledge of English.

The Yards knew the bush. They could track anything over any kind of terrain and could generally detect other troops in the forest long before Americans or Vietnamese could. The Americans brought with them a lot of useful technology. The Americans had the radios and the skills needed to call in airpower and artillery. American medical technology not only went to war, but made life a lot more secure for the Montagnard families. The Montagnards were not always ideal soldiers. There is an ancient difference between warriors and soldiers. The former are eager and possess considerable combat skills, but lack discipline. Moreover, the Montagnards often served under their own leaders, which made it more difficult to turn the warrior habits into more disciplined behavior. The Special Forces worked on changing the warrior mentality, but it was slow going. Over the years, by trial, error, and determined instruction, more and more of the Montagnard warriors became disciplined fighters. But there were never enough of the disciplined Montagnards, and many of these were promoted to elite positions like paratroopers and long-range scouts. Meanwhile, the Special Forces had to be careful how they used their Montagnard warriors. The Montagnards were stalwart in the defense, but could be difficult to control in an attack and had a hard time coordinating their actions in large-scale operations.

Despite the important role that the Montagnards played in the war, relations between the tribesmen and the South Vietnamese did not improve much, and tensions between the two communities were always shaky. A Montagnard "Nationalist" movement, the United Front for the Liberation of Oppressed Peoples (known as FULRO, from its initials in French) was established by a number of tribal leaders in mid-1964, and there were occasional clashes between Montagnard troops and ARVN personnel, including a five-day "war" later that same year. Although a semblance of peace was restored, tensions were never effectively resolved. The Montagnards also had their own internal problems. In South Vietnam, each of the many different tribes (some twenty-five to thirty of them) was further divided into clans. The largest tribe, the Jarai, had 150,000 people. The next three largest, the Rhadé, Koho, and Hre, had about 100,000 each. The others got smaller and smaller, until you reached the smallest tribe, the Strieng, with about a thousand members. Throughout the war there were occasional tribal and clan clashes. However, the Montagnards remained willing to defend their region against the Communists, and did so with considerable skill and courage.

In 1970, as the United States began to "wind down" the war, administrative control of Montagnard CID and Mike Force was transferred to South Vietnam, which converted most of them into ARVN Ranger battalions. Although desertions rose, the Montagnard units remained very effective. For example, during the NVA "Easter Offensive" in 1972, Montagnards formed the backbone of the defense of the central highlands, during which most ARVN units more or less collapsed, and Montagnards fought hard in the defense of Pleiku and Kontum in 1973 and 1974. Only late in the war did the Communists make any serious inroads into the Montagnard community. During their final 1975 offensive, the Communists made promises and payments to some key Montagnard groups and the South Vietnamese found that some of the Montagnard support they had long taken for granted was no longer there. After the war, however, the Communists engaged in payback against the Montagnards. Not exactly genocide, but if your name was on "the list" you were in big trouble. And all Vietnamese went back to dumping on the Yards. As the population of lowlanders continued to increase, more Vietnamese moved into traditional Montagnard territory, increasing friction and, ultimately, displacing the Yards.

On balance, greater efforts on the part of the government of South Vietnam at reconciliation with the Montagnards might have paid enormous dividends. But not until almost literally the final months of the war did the Saigon regime offer local autonomy to the tough mountain peoples, a classic example of "too little, too late."

THE HMONG

The Hmong are the Montagnards of Laos. Relatively numerous compared with the Montagnards of South Vietnam (c. 500,000, about 15–20 percent of the population of Laos), this distinct people lived in the rugged upland parts of Laos, areas where the indigenous Lao were already heavily infiltrated by the Communist Pathet Lao. As with the Montagnards, the Hmong were not on friendly terms with the majority ethnic group, who call them *Meo* (savages). This made them potentially important allies against the various Communist movements in Southeast Asia. U.S. contacts with the Hmong began even before massive American involvement in Vietnam, during the bungled attempt to establish a rightist regime in Laos in the early 1960s. Late in 1960, the clandestine supply of American arms to the Hmong had already begun, and small contingents of Hmong were being trained in Vietnam. By early 1961, Hmong troops comprised the bulk of Laotian Royalist forces (c. 4,300 out of 6,500) operating on the Plain of Jars, and by midyear there were an estimated 9,000 Hmong on the U.S. payroll. For the United States this seemed an inexpensive way to fight communism, since the effort required only a modest investment in arms and c. 20–25 American personnel. This was during the Laotian Crisis of 1961–62, which was shortly papered over in the UN. The UN settlement did not actually end the war in Laos, particularly as the North Vietnamese continued to operate against Laotian government forces, which continued to receive clandestine American aid. Thus began the "secret war" in Laos that continued into 1975 (though by 1970, it was not much of a secret any longer). The Hmong, under the leadership of Vang Pao, a Hmong colonel in the Royal Lao Army, played a vital role in this war.

Vang Pao, an effective and popular leader, brought Hmong military strength to about 30,000 by the mid-1960s. About a third were regular combat forces, the balance serving as local militia, supported by about a thousand Americans (c. 500 of whom ultimately were killed or went missing in action), plus some non-Hmong Allies. This force formed the backbone of Royal Lao resistance to the Pathet Lao and the North Vietnamese. The war assumed a certain rhythm. During the dry season, the Pathet Lao and the NVA would conduct some local offensives. "Guerrillas Overrun the Plain of Jars" appeared in newspapers so often the headline ended up being satirized in *Mad* magazine. The Hmong counterattacked during the rainy season, occasionally with Royal Lao Army support, regaining much of the lost territory.

Hmong losses were high. As early as mid-1962, there were already some 125,000 Hmong refugees, a quarter of the total population. The war devastated the Hmong, virtually destroying the community in Laos. Perhaps 100,000 died—no two estimates agree—and literally hundreds of thousands went into exile, about 100,000 eventually settling in the United States, while many others languished in refugee camps in Thailand or Laos itself. For the Hmong, America's "war on the cheap" was a costly ordeal.

THE CAMBODIAN CONNECTION

Cambodia, one of the original Southeast Asian kingdoms, at one time controlled an area stretching well into what is now South Vietnam, including the Mekong River Delta, and also stretched into parts of what is now Thailand. This was before the Vietnamese arrived on the scene. But as Thailand and Vietnam became stronger, they both put pressure on Cambodia. The French had had control of Cambodia, along with Laos, from the late nineteenth century. Indeed, the Cambodians invited the French in as a way of keeping the Thais and Vietnamese out. When the French lost their struggle with the Vietnamese Communists in 1953, they relinquished control of Laos and Cambodia, as well as Vietnam. While the Communists took over in North Vietnam, the old royal families returned to control in Laos and Cambodia. Neither country was able to remain neutral while the North Vietnamese fought to take over South Vietnam. The North Vietnamese simply moved into Laos to set up their Ho Chi Minh Trail.

Cambodia was another story. There were local Communists in Cambodia, the Khmer Rouge. But the Cambodian Royalists had managed to maintain the allegiance of most of the people. The North Vietnamese saw an opportunity to use the Cambodian border area with South Vietnam, Cambodian neutrality, and bribery to turn Cambodia into a logistics base for Communist forces in South Vietnam.

The Viet Cong had long used the thinly populated Cambodian border areas for bases while operating in South Vietnam. The president (formerly king, and in the 1990s king once more) of Cambodia, Norodom Sihanouk, sought to play off America, China, and both Vietnams to keep Cambodia out of the war and the Communists out of Cambodian politics. He allowed the Communists to operate in those South Vietnamese border areas as long as they did not provide support for the Cambodian Communists. This worked for a while, even as Sihanouk saw, in the early 1960s, that the North Vietnamese were likely to win their war. Sihanouk reduced his support for South Vietnam and America accordingly. But the North Vietnamese kept asking for more leeway to run their logistical operations in Cambodia. Although the North Vietnamese were not openly using the ports and roads from the sea to their jungle hideouts, they were hiring Cambodian firms to do it. By early 1969, ships from Communist countries were regularly unloading food and ammunition at the Cambodian ports. Cambodian trucking companies then drove off with their stuff, and it ended up in North Vietnamese depots in the jungle, three miles from the South Vietnamese border. The North Vietnamese were supporting 200,000 Viet Cong and North Vietnamese troops, including three divisions of troops in Cambodia itself, from these depots. In effect, all their operations in the Mekong Delta (most of southern South Vietnam). It was a rather open secret, but Sihanouk insisted these depots, and the supply arrangements, did not exist. This was done with a straight face because the Cambodians had no official arrangement with the North Vietnamese; everything was done with a nod and a wink. The North Vietnamese bribed key Cambodians (mainly members of the royal family). This provided various front companies to hire Cambodians to unload the ships and truck the military supplies (labeled as something legal) to areas in rural Cambodia, where North Vietnamese drivers would take over and move the stuff to the North Vietnamese camps near the South Vietnamese border.

The Cambodian and North Vietnamese protests that nothing illegal was going on along the border worked for quite a while. There's something about professional diplomats standing up and lying in public, and doing it often, that convinces a lot of people. But the evidence on the ground, collected by American aircraft and SOG patrols, was pretty vivid. For nearly two years, SOG patrols were reporting on the North Vietnamese buildup in Cambodia. Thousands of Allied troops were killed by North Vietnamese soldiers, who came out of Cambodia, attacked, then fled back to "neutral" Cambodia. Unwilling to expand the war to Cambodia, the U.S. government ignored the North Vietnamese bases in Cambodia and publicly proclaimed they did not exist. This set the United States up for further embarrassment when a new American president (Nixon) came into office in early 1969 and found out about the Cambodian cover-up. Nixon ordered the Cambodian bases attacked, even though the United States would take a major diplomatic and public relations hit for reversing position on the North Vietnamese bases in Cambodia that, until recently, the United States had insisted did not exist, and for bringing Cambodia into the war. At first the United States bombed secretly, trying to avoid the bad publicity. It had not yet dawned on most people in Washington that B-52 raids don't long remain secret. Moreover, since the secret attacks were no more than five miles into Cambodia (to reinforce the claim that the bombing was actually on the South Vietnamese side of the border), North Vietnamese troops withdrew deeper into Cambodia. This caused resentment among Cambodians, for there was considerable and long-standing hostility between the two groups. Sihanouk had originally allowed the North Vietnamese to use the border areas as long as they stayed away from Cambodians. But the deeper the North Vietnamese moved into Cambodia, the more Cambodians they ran into and the more ill-will was generated. But Sihanouk refused to denounce the North Vietnamese or order them to leave Cambodia. He knew that the North Vietnamese were too numerous, well-armed, and determined for him to order them out of Cambodia. Meanwhile, Cambodian popular opinion was getting more hostile toward the North Vietnamese presence in their country. Sihanouk did throw most of the Communists out of his government, and became quite close to the conservatives. Unlike the Communists, the conservatives were basically proroyalist, and many were senior military commanders. He needed these to keep the Communists under control, as well as provide muscle for any other political showdowns. But the Cambodian armed forces were not strong enough to deal with the Khmer Rouge in the North and the North Vietnamese over by the South Vietnamese border. And with the Americans bombing eastern Cambodia, Cambodians were getting hurt. Worse yet, Cambodians were being reminded that there were thousands of North Vietnamese soldiers inside Cambodia. Public opinion was turning against Sihanouk. The United States approached the conservatives and suggested that they depose Sihanouk. The idea being that U.S. and South Vietnamese forces would come in on the ground and clear out the North Vietnamese once and for all. Lon Nol, an army general and Sihanouk's prime minister, took the bait and deposed Sihanouk in March of 1970 (while Sihanouk was out of the country). Lon Nol also whipped up the long-simmering resentment against the North Vietnamese in Cambodia. Mobs, unrestrained by the police, attacked the North Vietnamese and Viet Cong embassies. Ethnic Vietnamese were attacked (something that happened periodically in the best of times and continues to this day). In April, the U.S. and South Vietnamese ground forces moved into eastern Cambodia.

Actually, it wasn't the bombing and ground operations in Cambodia that caused the most trouble, it was the U.S. support for the Cambodian conservatives. This was the smallest faction in Cambodian politics, behind the Royalists and Communists. After the U.S. invasion, the North Vietnamese simply withdrew deeper into Cambodia. This made the Cambodian people angrier. Moreover, Lon Nol's support was concentrated in the nation's capital, Phnom Penh. He discovered this the hard way when Sihanouk went off to seek Chinese Communist support. Sihanouk got it, but under the condition that he became the figurehead leader of the Khmer Rouge. Since most of the people in the countryside supported Sihanouk (they were Royalists), they now supported the Khmer Rouge. As a result, the Khmer Rouge began to grow rapidly; from 4,000 in 1969, to 80,000 in 1975, when they took over the government. The United States provided support (arms and bombing missions) until 1973, when Congress cut off the aid. The bombing did slow down the advance of the Khmer Rouge, but it also made people more willing to support the Cambodian Communists.

The attacks on Cambodia did have one desired effect: they crippled the North Vietnamese support bases in eastern Cambodia. The initial bombing in 1969 proved disruptive enough to cripple a planned 1969 Tet Offensive. The 1970 invasion put the Communists in southern South Vietnam on the defensive until they could rebuild their supply bases. The objective of the Cambodian operations was to reduce American casualties while U.S. troops were withdrawing from Vietnam. This was a major issue that got Nixon elected, saving the lives of American troops and getting the United States out of Vietnam.

The Khmer Rouge took over in 1975, immediately implementing a plan to "purify" Cambodia of non-Communist ideas. They killed about two million of Cambodia's seven million people, before the Vietnamese invaded in 1978 and ran Pol Pot and his murderous (even by Communist standards) Khmer Rouge off into the jungle. They are still there.

What would have happened if President Nixon, like President Johnson, had continued to respect Cambodian neutrality (even if the North Vietnamese would not)? More American soldiers would have been killed. It's hard to say exactly how many. At least several hundred, possibly several thousand, depending on how aggressive the North Vietnamese were when using those Cambodian bases and supply lines. Once Nixon proclaimed that he would get U.S. troops out of Vietnam, the North Vietnamese knew that their final victory was only a matter of time. But the North Vietnamese and North Vietnamese–controlled Viet Cong kept on fighting despite the 1973 peace agreement (which called for U.S. troops to leave South Vietnam, but not Communist troops).

Would Pol Pot and his murderous Khmer Rouge have taken over in Cambodia if the United States had stayed out of Cambodia? Probably not. The

North Vietnamese were determined to have only Communist nations for neighbors, and the Khmer Rouge were the largest and best-organized Communist faction in Cambodia. Moreover, the Khmer Rouge had the backing of Communist China. Now that brings up an interesting point. The Vietnamese never got along with the Chinese. This is a hostility that goes back centuries. China helped Vietnamese Communists because they were Communists, not because they were Vietnamese. When all the non-Communists had been driven out of Vietnam, relations between China and Vietnam went back to what they had always been: rancorous. By 1979, China and Vietnam were fighting one another. That war was short because the Chinese quickly discovered that all those decades of fighting had made the Vietnamese better soldiers than the Chinese (who had not fought a war in over twenty-five years.) Thus, a still neutral Cambodia in 1975, with only five thousand or so Khmer Rouge fighters in the bush, might have tempted the Vietnamese to sponsor another Communist faction, one more to their liking. This had happened before. Then again, such Vietnamese backing might have backfired, allowing the Khmer Rouge to gain power anyway.

THE NORTH VIETNAM COUNTER-RECON PROGRAM

After over a year of energetic SOG patrolling in their Laotian "sanctuary," the North Vietnamese finally decided something drastic had to be done to defend their vital Ho Chi Minh Trail. So they took their only parachute unit, the 305th Brigade, disbanded it, and used many of these elite troops to form three counter-recon battalions. These troops were volunteers and true believers in the North Vietnam cause. They were good, they were capable, they were dedicated, and now they were out to kill, especially SOG patrols.

The North Vietnamese organized their antirecon units to have offensive and defensive capabilities. For defense, they had sappers, who would set ambushes for SOG patrols. Sappers were trained to carefully observe and then sneak up on enemy troops armed only with AK-47s and grenades or explosive charges. The sappers usually did this wearing only shorts, the better to feel the wind and underbrush, the better to use all their senses to navigate silently until they were among the sleeping enemy and could attack. At least two SOG teams were taken like this at night by sappers from North Vietnamese antirecon patrols. Normally sappers did not go out in the bush along the Ho Chi Minh Trail. As the evidence built up though, it was clear that the SOG teams were no longer just dealing with run-of-the-mill North Vietnamese troops. The stalkers were now being stalked.

For offensive use against SOG teams, the antirecon units had trackers, both human (local tribesmen) and canine (not bloodhounds, but good enough to follow a scent). The North Vietnamese had assigned hundreds of troops to man "LZ observation posts" around areas that held likely landing zones (LZs). One of the great weaknesses of the SOG patrols going into Laos was that they had to go in by helicopter (it would have taken too long to walk) and the helicopter needed a place to land. The terrain along the Ho Chi Minh Trail was mostly forest and mountains. There weren't too many places where you could put down a helicopter, so the North Vietnamese sent out squads to man observation posts near likely SOG LZs. These troops didn't have radios. The North Vietnamese never could afford many radios, so the observers had to fire off their rifles to alert a radio-equipped North Vietnam unit or send off a runner. Of course, the incoming SOG team would not know they had been discovered until they ran into the counter-recon units that had been alerted earlier and were now out searching for them.

The counter-recon units also brought better leadership to the chase. In the past, the local North Vietnamese units were there primarily to maintain the Ho Chi Minh Trail and not fight, much less chase down, elite U.S. recon teams. It had been fairly easy for the SOG teams to use their superior skill to evade local North Vietnamese troops. But the counter-recon units were led by officers who had a good idea how the SOG teams were thinking, what they were looking for, and where they were likely to go. By the end of 1967, SOG teams knew that, once they were discovered, they were likely to find themselves tracked until they were caught or got picked up by helicopters.

There were only about nine counter-recon companies, and it took at least a company of counter-recon troops to have a good chance of running a six- to ten-man SOG team to ground. The three counter-recon battalions were initially deployed to cover the areas generating the most SOG activity. One was the area west of Khe Sahn (just below the DMZ) and into Laos. The second one operated south of Hue, in the Ashau valley, and went into Laos. This put the two counter-recon battalions north and south of the vital Group 559 headquarters, the outfit that ran the Ho Chi Minh Trail. The third counter-recon battalion covered the rest of the Ho Chi Minh Trail south into Cambodia.

This was a huge area, nearly ten thousand square miles. And it was rough country. If a SOG team was spotted, it could take hours for the word to get back to a base area containing a counter-recon unit. But trucks were available to quickly take the counterrecon troops out to the area where the SOG troops were seen landing. Along came tribal trackers and the dogs. The counter-recon unit commander knew what was in the area that the SOG might be looking for and went in that direction. Meanwhile, any regular North Vietnam units in the area (especially those just passing down the Ho Chi Minh Trail) were brought in to beat the bushes. Nearly half the time, the SOG team was spotted. If the counter-recon company was close enough, the chase was on. It was literally a chase. This was infantry country. The North Vietnamese had few helicopters (and rarely used them during the day), while the SOG teams had access to a wide variety of helicopters and bombers to help them out. But the SOG knew that once they brought in their airpower, they were telling every North Vietnamese unit in the area where they were. This was an all-or-nothing move, to call in for the helicopters to get them out.

By 1970, the increasing North Vietnamese counter-recon efforts were having an effect, at great cost to both sides. SOG troops had a nearly 100-percent chance of getting wounded during one year of patrolling. It had gotten to the point where any man who kept going back after twenty missions was considered just asking for it. But the North Vietnamese were taking a beating too. For every SOG casualty they caused, they suffered over a hundred of their own. When the SOG team did call in bombers and helicopters for an evacuation, all those North Vietnamese troops chasing the team were splendid targets. And even when they got spotted, the SOG teams often spotted hidden North Vietnamese bases, and these got hit too.

The North Vietnamese also put bounties on the heads of any LRRPs that could be taken alive. In 1990s' money, these were something like quarter of a million dollar bounties. This was a huge amount of money for a 1960s North Vietnamese. It provided a tremendous incentive to take down LRRP teams. But on several occasions, while tracking an LRRP team and attempting to attack it, the North Vietnamese had the tables turned and were themselves wiped out in the process. A lot of this had to do with the lessons the North Vietnamese had learned from the Russian and Chinese Communists. Especially the Communist preference for mass, or quantity over quality. Rather than have a handful of superb counter-recon teams, they had three battalions. And several times these battalions would corner an LRRP team, only to see mostly North Vietnamese killed as the LRRPs exercised their own considerable combat skills while calling in enormous amounts of artillery and bombs.

The North Vietnamese were never able to eliminate the SOG patrols, and they had to keep three divisions in Laos, plus special counter-recon units, to keep the SOG from shutting down the Ho Chi Minh Trail. But the price paid by the SOG troopers was high. Like many battles, it was hard to tell who was the winner and who was the loser.

PLAYING ON PARANOIA

The Vietnam War saw extensive use of spies and double agents, even more so than in most wars. While the proliferation of Communist spies in South Vietnam was widely known, American spymasters were able to beat the Communists at their own game more than once. The more successful U.S. operations played on the intense paranoia the Communist intelligence organizations suffered from. The Communists' attitude toward their subjects was to trust no one and to jump on the least evidence of disloyalty.

The Communists were particularly anxious about any of their people who were captured and were then either released or escaped. These poor folks were subjected to intense interrogation and examination. The Communist political police took the attitude that these Vietnamese were "contaminated" and guilty (of something) until they were satisfied the people were innocent. So the United States and South Vietnamese decided to "set up" some innocent North Vietnamese in a series of deception operations.

The first such operation was set up in 1967 and used a phony "liberated" village staffed with South Vietnamese who could pass for North Vietnamese (duplicate the regional accent). North Vietnamese fishing boats would be captured by boats of the Sacred Sword of the Patriotic League. Taken to the phony village, actually an island off the South Vietnamese coast and called "Paradise Island" by the Special Forces people running it, the fishermen would be fed good food and artful propaganda about the anti-Communist "League." Even during the war, there was a lot of resentment in North Vietnam against overbearing and increasingly corrupt Communist officials. The phony village caper did not expect to cause a rebellion in North Vietnam. But by sending "contaminated" people back to, for many of them, intense interrogation by North Vietnamese secret police, more damaging rumors would be set loose in North Vietnam among the general population as well as the inner circles of the government. The fishermen who appeared to be the most dedicated Communists had spy gear hidden in their clothing or on their boat. Unaware of these plants, the diligent North Vietnam interrogators would find it and continue to grill the perplexed "spies," many of whom were taken away, never to be seen again. This caused much ill-will among the fisherman's family and neighbors, who always knew him to be an ardent Communist.

When the late 1968 U.S. bombing halt went into effect, it included a halt on sending agents into North Vietnam. The Communists were very specific about this item, including the operations along the coast, showing how effective it was becoming. To replace the order forbidding operations in North Vietnam, new operations were thought up to take advantage of the many North Vietnamese prisoners of war being taken in South Vietnam.

By now, the Special Forces knew that the North Vietnamese were very effective in uncovering agents, especially among their own people. But it was also known that the dark side of this was an intense paranoia. The North Vietnamese were suspicious of everything. So captured North Vietnamese were recruited as spies, even though it was known that few would follow through and fewer still would be successful at it. But that was not the point of the exercise. Part of the six-week training these double agents underwent was briefing on the (nonexistent) network of agents in North Vietnam and their role in it. This was the sting, and the North Vietnamese fell for it. Several other scams were developed to enhance the effect. One was the tube of ultraviolet paste each new agent was given when released (to wander back into Communist-controlled territory and tell of their escape). The paste was to be used to mark other defectors they would recruit. Defectors so marked would be treated very well when they surrendered to an American unit. The North Vietnamese, on finding out about this gimmick, had to scramble to find black light equipment to start screening their own troops.

The most ambitious angle on this spy scam was to select some of the agents to parachute into North Vietnam with new teams of agents. The North Vietnamese was given parachute training and taken to an airfield at night, where he got on a large aircraft for the jump. On board were the other members of the team which, for security reasons (something any North Vietnamese could appreciate), he could not be introduced to earlier. On board the plane were numerous containers of supplies to be parachuted to the North Vietnamese anti-Communist agents waiting below. Once in the air, the North Vietnamese agent was told that he had done so well in his training, and because this was his first jump, he would be given the honor of being the first one to jump (the "man in the door" before the signal to begin jumping was given). The North Vietnamese spy dutifully jumped and, once on the ground, went running for the nearest North Vietnamese authorities to report his chums who had jumped right after him. But no one had jumped after him. The other "agents" quickly got out of their parachutes and opened some of the containers to reveal blocks of ice that were quickly attached to the parachutes that were promptly sent out the aircraft. Several hours later, when these parachutes were found, the ice would have melted and the North Vietnamese would have every reason to believe that the other agents had gotten away, along with the other North Vietnamese anti-Communists waiting for them, as well as all those containers of weapons, ammunition, and radio equipment. The North Vietnamese never quit looking for those spies, and their inability to find them only made them more nervous. What made the North Vietnamese security officials particularly anxious was the fact that here was clear evidence that, not only had the Americans set up agent networks in North Vietnam, but that they were successfully reinforcing and resupplying them. And all the North Vietnamese Ministry of Security was able to do was get agents the Americans had recruited from prisoners who decided to turn themselves in.

But that was not all. Perhaps the most diabolical phony agent routine involved "agents" who were released in Laos with a tiny transponder hidden in their gear. These fellows were supposed to meet up with other members of the nonexistent spy network. As expected, they would promptly seek out a North Vietnamese unit and surrender. They would then be taken to a local headquarters for interrogation. Overhead, U.S. aircraft were tracking the transponder. When it was determined that an agent was staying in one place for seventy-two hours, a B-52 raid was sent in where the transponder was squawking, thereby wiping out an enemy headquarters.

But some sincere agents were obtained from all those North Vietnamese prisoners interviewed. These were not wasted, but were instead formed into about a dozen teams of "Earth Angels." Given authentic uniforms, documents, and passwords (gathered from other intelligence operations), these agents were set down on the Ho Chi Minh Trail so that they could march up or down the trail for a few days, posing as couriers and collecting information. At a prearranged time and place, they would be taken out by helicopter. These agents proved very successful, which is understandable as these men were former North Vietnamese officers and NCOs who had soured on the Communist system and wanted a little payback.

SNIFF THIS, FIDO

The SOG patrols in Laos knew the North Vietnamese were really on their case when they found they were being tracked with dogs. It turned out that these were nothing fancy like bloodhounds, just some of the local mutts, selected for their better-than-average sense of smell, and quickly trained to pick up a specific scent and follow it. This made life much more difficult for the patrols. Hitherto the North Vietnamese had always had a hard time keeping up with the more experienced SOG troopers. The Special Forces–led patrols had a vast array of tricks for breaking contact with their Communist pursuers; and once that contact was broken, the North Vietnamese were rarely able to pick up the enemy patrol again. The use of dogs changed all that. You could fool the North Vietnamese infantry much more easily than you could fool a dog's nose.

During the first few encounters with dogs, patrols did what they could to throw the hounds off, like moving along a stream for a distance. When the dogs got real close, you could also shoot them and their handlers. But there wasn't always a stream handy, and when the dogs were close enough to get shot, they were too close. Something was needed to foil the hounds. The solution was an old one. The patrols carried some of the powder that gave tear gas its teary quality. This was much better than the pepper dust used for this purpose at times, for the tear gas stuff put the dog's noses out of action for hours. The powder was particularly useful when the patrol stopped and hid to get some sleep. Spreading a little powder on the path you followed, but some hundred or more meters away, did the trick. When the dogs hit the powder they let out a loud yelp and ceased tracking. The patrol, thus alerted, could quietly make their getaway.

THE PROBLEM OF MOLES

The top-secret nature of the SOG patrols into Laos meant that few people knew about them. Because South Vietnamese helicopters and bombers were often used to get SOG patrols out (after being discovered and chased), it was necessary to alert the South Vietnamese headquarters when a patrol was going in so that some of the South Vietnamese airpower would be available if there were an emergency. The SOG planners quickly learned to be careful what they told the South Vietnamese, for it soon became apparent that there were, not unexpectedly, Communist spies in the South Vietnam headquarters. Attempts to get information about SOG missions kept away from the office the mole apparently worked in were shot down by the need to "maintain cooperation with the South Vietnamese." So SOG began to get a little sloppy about how they passed mission data on to the South Vietnamese, and the problems in the field shrank a bit. Then came Tet, in 1968, and many Communist agents got themselves caught out in the open and eliminated. But even after that, the problem persisted. No matter what SOG did, even to the point of not telling the South Vietnamese about a mission, the North Vietnamese seemed to know. Something else was going on here.

All was revealed some twenty years later, when the Walker family of spies was caught and tried. Several of the Walkers worked with secret codes, and from about 1968, they were selling these to the Soviet Union. The Russians, now able to read our secret messages, and allowed to set up monitoring stations anywhere the North Vietnamese had a military presence, were apparently passing the SOG information back to the North Vietnamese. The Russians had a vested interest in doing this and hurting SOG. At times there were hundreds of Russian advisers in Laos, and the bombers SOG teams called in didn't discriminate between Russian or Vietnamese Communists.

FLIGHT OF THE PHOENIX

One of the more effective special operations programs undertaken by U.S. forces in Vietnam was the *Phung Huang* program, named after a bird in Vietnamese myth that is very much like the Phoenix of Greek mythology. Although the Phoenix program was officially organized in July of 1968, it was actually several years older. It had originated in a CIA program to create a "counterterrorist" force. This led to the formation of Provincial Reconnaissance Units composed of South Vietnamese personnel, both military and volunteer. What happened in 1968 was that the army took over the program.

The object of the Phoenix program was to destroy VC cadres. Although generally regarded as an assassination program, this was not its primary purpose.

The main objective of the Phoenix program—which apparently never had more than about four thousand personnel—was to destroy the political infrastructure of the VC. The preferred means of doing this was by "turning" VC operatives and leaving them behind as clandestine supporters of the Saigon government. Turncoats would continue to function, which would be far more dangerous to the enemy than killing or capturing them. Dead or captured VC leaders could be replaced. However, this never really worked

Phoenix Program Effectiveness

VC Cadres	Number
Captured	c. 28,000
Killed	c. 20,000
Turned	c. 17,000
Total	c. 65,000

very well. Although some seventeen thousand VC cadres did *Chieu Hoi,* that is agree to support the South Vietnamese regime, most of them did so openly, joining the ARVN or other arms of the Saigon government.

The Phoenix program was really the only initiative that caused genuine concern among the Communist leaders, for if a significant number of their operatives could have been turned into supporters of the Republic of Vietnam, their movement would have collapsed.

And by the way, not all of the twenty thousand VC cadres who were killed died at the hands of an assassin. Many were killed in conventional combat with Phoenix program operatives. And despite the claims of some antiwar intellectuals, Phoenix operatives did not kill children, a policy in which Communist political terrorists regularly indulged.

After the war, surviving Viet Cong commanders admitted that the Phoenix program had hurt them badly, often wiping out the Viet Cong presence in many areas.

PAPER PARATROOPERS

The tribal mercenaries, used by the Special Forces to go with them on scouting missions into Laos, were a clever and fearless bunch. Nothing better demonstrates this than an incident in the mid-1960s. The Special Forces had begun to train some of the Montagnards as paratroopers for special operations. The Montagnards noted that anyone who had a certificate showing he had passed the parachute course, got extra pay each month. So many of the Montagnards arranged to get forged parachute school certificates. This was soon noticed, and senior Special Forces staffers decided the best way to deal with this was to announce a parachute jump ("just to stay in practice") for all qualified Montagnards. None of the Montagnards backed off. Some had a real hard time getting the parachute (which they had never seen before) on. But they all got into the plane, jumped, and survived. And they all kept their monthly parachute pay.

STRATA

Early attempts to put recon teams and spies into North Vietnam were largely a failure. These projects were a secret for many years, and only in 1990 were

the full details revealed and payments of $50,000 made to the South Viet-
namese survivors or their families. All those teams had been betrayed by
North Vietnamese agents serving in the South Vietnamese armed forces. This
was finally discovered in 1968. But even before the North Vietnamese coun-
terintelligence coup had been uncovered, the Special Forces people running these operations had developed some more successful methods. One of
these was the Short Term Road Watch and Target Acquisition (STRATA)
program. In 1967 and 1968, fourteen STRATA teams were formed. South
Vietnamese volunteers, given special training and outfitted with North Vietnamese uniforms and weapons, were taken by helicopter into North Vietnam. They stayed south of the twentieth parallel and usually within ten miles
of the Laotian border. It was dangerous business, as even the North Vietnamese uniforms would not always protect you from discovery and pursuit. A
quarter of the 102 STRATA agents were killed or caught, including two entire
teams.

When President Johnson decided to call a bombing halt in late 1968 (to
encourage the North Vietnamese to negotiate a peace settlement), SOG was
ordered to get its STRATA teams out of North Vietnam.

Despite the earlier dismal CIA performance, the Special Forces showed
that you could put agents into North Vietnam. The trick was not to get
overly ambitious, and to keep cooperation with South Vietnamese armed
forces people to a minimum. North Vietnam was a tightly controlled police
state. It was exceptionally difficult to insert spies, and the Communists had
spies all over the place in South Vietnam. So the Special Forces set the
STRATA agents up as short-term recon units: in for two weeks, then get
them out. While the North Vietnamese captured the earlier CIA teams and
turned many into double agents, this was not possible with STRATA teams
because they were either gotten out in a week or two or written off as captured if they did not come out. And the STRATA personnel were kept away
from just about everyone during their training.

Thus the capability was there to run a lot more clandestine operations
into the North. The Communist police state was not as impenetrable as it
appeared. The major obstacle to running more spies and agents into North
Vietnam was political. Because the United States insisted that we were just
"assisting" South Vietnam, it was policy (sometimes gotten around) to clear
all operations through South Vietnamese headquarters, where North Vietnamese agents usually picked up on it and passed the information north.

THE LIFELINE FROM ABOVE

As effective as helicopters were in rescuing troops about to be overrun, there
was not always a place for a helicopter to land. Vietnam was full of forests,
much of it double- or triple-canopy jungle. Often the best a desperate guy
on the ground could do was to get to an area where he could at least see,

and be seen by, a helicopter. From that came a clever device that saved many a beleaguered LRRP. Called the McGuire Rig, it was invented by a Special Forces sergeant major of the same name. The device was simplicity itself: a hundred-foot length of sturdy rope with a six-foot loop at the lower end and a padded canvas seat. A Huey could carry four of these, two on each side. The crew chief let out the lines and watched for the troops on the ground to sit themselves on the seat and astride the loop. Then the crew chief signaled the pilot to lift off and fly away. As soon as a safe, open spot was found, the helicopter would set down close enough to the ground so the guys on the McGuire Rigs could get off, then board the helicopter when it landed. It was dangerous riding the rig. If the rope got snarled in a tree while lifting off, the crew chief had to cut the line. If a trooper in a rig lost his grip and fell off, it was a long, and usually fatal, fall. But overall, the rig was a lifesaver most of the time, a desperate measure for men in even more desperate situations.

THE RELIGIOUS FACTOR

There were five million militant members of various minority religious sects in South Vietnam during the war. This was over 25 percent of South Vietnam's population. The largest group, with nearly three million adherents, was the Cao Dai. This was a religion that was formed in Vietnam relatively recently. Founded in the 1920s, it combined Buddhism and Christianity into what it considered the supreme religion. Then there were one and a half million Roman Catholics, most of them refugees from North Vietnam. Finally, there was the million or so members of the well-organized and militant Hoa Hao sect of Buddhism.

The traditional religions of Vietnam were Buddhism and Confuciusm (actually more a cultural ethic than a religion). The Montagnards often practiced various forms of nature worship as well. The Communists set themselves up as the enemy of religion, while assuming many of the elements of a religion. There were several million dedicated Communists in the 1960s (not to be confused with the millions of dedicated Nationalists who served with the Communists). The Communists were the largest and most successful militant religious group in Vietnam, but the three others, the Cao Dai, the Hoa Hao, and the Catholics, were also pretty powerful. There was also a huge cultlike gangster operation, the Binh Xuyen. This gang fielded forty thousand troops in 1955. The Cao Dai, Hoa Hao, and Binh Xuyen refused to break up their private armies when South Vietnam became independent in 1954. The new government of South Vietnam was led by Catholics, so in 1955 there commenced a short war between the Catholic-led government and the united Cao Dai/Hoa Hao/Binh Xuyen forces. The Catholics won. The Cao Dai split into several different factions, some of which went over to the government, others sided with the Viet Cong, while some remained neutral. In the 1980s, the Communist government of Vietnam recognized the Cao Dai as a religion and several million people still practice their faith in Vietnam. The Hoa Hao took two years to crush, and some went over to the Viet Cong, while most moved over near the Cambodian border and kept their heads down for the rest of the war. The Binh Xuyen broke up, with several leaders leaving the country to join their money in Europe. Many of the gangsters went back to being freelance crooks, while the more altruistic ones joined the Viet Cong.

Throughout the war, the Catholics had influence in the government far greater than their numbers would indicate. This created friction with the Buddhist majority, especially when the government sought to restrict Buddhist religious ceremonies. Until 1966, when the Buddhists finally got tired of getting shot at and beaten by government troops, the Buddhists were the principal group calling for an end to military dictatorship in South Vietnam and the holding of democratic elections. But after 1966, caught between the military dictatorships of North and South Vietnam, the Buddhists withdrew from public protests.

THE ULTIMATE KILLING MACHINE

The SOG teams operating in Laos were the most lethal soldiers of the war. For every American Special Forces soldier lost in Laos, the North Vietnamese lost between 100 and 150 troops. Taking into account the Montagnards' (who comprised about two-thirds of the people on the missions) losses, as well as aircrew lost getting SOG troops in and out of Laos, the ratio was still about 30 to 1. That was about ten times the ratio of non-SOG troops (U.S. and South Vietnamese troops killed about three times their number of Viet Cong and North Vietnamese soldiers).

But there were lots of friendly losses, especially once the North Vietnamese became aware of what SOG was doing and began to organize resistance to the patrols. In 1968, the fifteen SOG teams operating out of the central highlands lost 36 Americans, half of whom were killed and the rest MIA (missing in action) and presumed dead. Another 199 were wounded in Laos. This was a lot worse than it appears, because the SOG company in that area had fewer than a hundred Americans assigned to it at any one time. Most SOG troopers were wounded more than once in the course of a year. Losses among the Nung were comparable, and the helicopter crews took somewhat less of a beating.

But it was worse on the North Vietnamese side. By early 1969, the action in Laos was getting really hot. In January and February, SOG patrols killed some 1,400 enemy soldiers (intelligence officers debriefed the team members, helicopter crews, and bomber pilots to identify the damage to the enemy). Much of the damage was done by the bombers the SOG teams called in when the troops found something worth hitting on the ground. The bomber pilots counted 455 secondary explosions from their attacks and 100 instances where whatever they hit just kept on burning. Pilots knew how to distinguish between jungle burning (and it didn't burn very well) and something man-made that had been touched off. The North Vietnamese stored a lot of ammunition and fuel in the jungle, stuff that burned quite spectacularly when bombed. But these supply depots were also surrounded by armed North Vietnamese. During that same period, fifteen Americans were killed or MIA. Another sixty to eighty were wounded, and ten helicopters were lost.

This pointed out the downside to these operations; there always is one when we're dealing with combat. The SOG troops, the Nung Montagnards who fought with them, were the best of the best. There were never more than a few hundred SOG troops in action, and about twice that many Montagnards. These guys were both fearless and extremely capable. Man-for-man, the most decorated unit in the Vietnam War was the sixty-man SOG company operating out of Kontum, in the central highlands. Five of the troops in this unit were awarded the Medal of Honor, and all other decorations in equal abundance. No other unit in this century has even come close to that record.

Because of all the secrecy that enveloped SOG operations, it's difficult to even know exactly how many SOG troops were lost in Laos. It appears that about three hundred SOG Special Forces troopers were killed in Laos, with fifty-seven MIA (missing in action), and some fifteen known to have been captured. But the Communists never admitted to having captured any SOG troops. The North Vietnamese were greatly embarrassed with the SOG operations in Laos and basically had a "shoot to kill" mentality. Some captured SOG troops were known to have been executed in particularly gruesome ways (the bodies were later found by SOG recovery teams). It's probably not a rash assumption that some of those captured SOGs were tortured and executed. It's unknown if any are still alive, thirty years later.

BRIGHT LIGHT

The U.S. Air Force called special operations to rescue downed pilots "Bright Light" missions. When the aircraft went down over friendly territory, this was a fairly routine and safe procedure and was not considered Bright Light. But when the pilot was down in enemy territory, it was quite another matter. Here Special Forces troops would often be called in to assist in getting the downed pilot out. Often there was a lot of ground fire directed at the rescue helicopters, and sometimes there was some ground fighting as well. SOG LRRP troops were sometimes used to go into Laos or North Vietnam to help recover downed pilots about to be captured. It was a hairy business at times, with additional aircraft and helicopters sometimes being lost. All this was essential for pilot morale. You fly into enemy territory with a lot more confidence and assurance if you know that extraordinary measures will be taken to rescue you.

DEAD PLANTS AND BITTER RICE

Not all military technology involved weapons. A lot of it was just chemicals. While poison gas has been against the generally accepted "Laws of Land Warfare" for most of this century, there are other military uses for chemicals that are not outlawed. The use of chemical defoliants like Agent Orange is one. There were no qualms about using Agent Orange (basically a weed killer) to clear away the underbrush around Allied camps and the roads they used, the better to protect the troops from attacks and ambushes. Later on it was found that large-scale use of such "agricultural chemicals" could, and did, have long-term ill effects on anyone exposed to the agent for any length of time. Thus, while Agent Orange saved a lot of friendly lives, it caused a lot of long-term health problems to friends and enemies alike.

There were other cases in which the use of chemicals was proposed and turned down. One such case was the proposed use of Bitrex, a chemical similar to alum, but many times more bitter. It was proposed that enemy rice caches, when discovered in the bush, have a water and Bitrex solution poured over them. The rice would still be edible, but it would be so bitter that it would be nearly impossible to swallow. A solution such as this was needed because LRRPs often came across large enemy rice stores and had no way to destroy them quickly. Rice doesn't burn all that well, and if you blow it up, the grains can still be collected by sufficiently hungry troops. Fearful that the Communists would turn the use of Bitrex into a credible accusation of "chemical warfare," the proposal was turned down. Thus were the Communist troops spared the ordeal of trying to eat bitter rice.

THE REAL RAMBO

Rambo, the fictional war hero in several Sylvester Stallone movies, was the kind of image that gave drill sergeants in basic training fits. Good infantry soldiers tend to be unassuming and able to fade into the background. That's a good survival trait on the battlefield. But some soldiers really are larger than life warriors, and several of them were in the SOG. Perhaps the most spectacular of them all was SFC Jerry "Mad Dog" Shriver. He got his nickname direct from Radio Hanoi, which granted him the ultimate accolade from an enemy; public denunciation for having killed so many of their soldiers. Although Sergeant Shriver admitted to his friends that he knew he should quit before he got killed, he confessed that he lived for the recon operations. Normally, few SOG troops survived twenty missions. Shriver had gotten through forty before he was killed in April 1969. Shriver dressed the part, carrying a sawed-off shotgun, pistol, knives, and the usual weapons and equipment. He was a big man and spent his spare time training or sneaking out on extra missions. He lived for his time in the field. Out there he was more alive than he was back at the base camp. He always slept with a loaded M-16. His most memorable exploit was when his team was surrounded by enemy troops who were closing in fast and the rescue helicopters had yet to arrive. SOG headquarters radioed to ask if he was going to be overwhelmed before help could arrive. Shriver replied, "No, no, I've got 'em right where I want 'em; surrounded from the inside." Sergeant Shriver was last seen charging into enemy fire at the head of his Montagnards.

CHAPTER 8

Leadership

As all wars are, the Vietnam War was driven by leadership. The side with the better leaders at all levels won. This chapter explores this usually overlooked angle on the war.

"FOLLOW ME!" LEADERSHIP PROBLEMS IN VIETNAM

The troops who were sent into Vietnam in 1964 were good—officers, NCOs, and common soldiers alike—possibly the best troops the United States had ever put in the field at the start of a war, at least until the 1990–91 Gulf War. The cadre, the regular officers and NCOs, was heavily seasoned with combat veterans from World War II and Korea, while the younger personnel, whether volunteers or draftees, were well educated, carefully selected, and thoroughly trained. Standards were high. But those standards could not be maintained. As the war went on several developments tended to lower the quality of the personnel.

A major problem was that the war was fought by "short timers." Soon after basic training, a man went to Vietnam for his year, and then went home. So the typical combat soldier never really became seasoned to the extent that some of the VC and NVA regulars were, with their years in the field. Worse, the troops in a unit were never all in Vietnam as a group for that year: men were rotated into units as "replacements" whenever they were needed, and rotated out precisely on the day that their year "in country" expired. This did not encourage unit cohesion, which often was poor. Some senior officers argued for an eighteen-month tour of duty or for unit rotation (sending an entire division to Vietnam for a year, then rotating it back home for rest, recuperation, and recruitment, before another tour later). But instituting such changes would have caused a political storm of enormous proportions (e.g., unit rotation would have required a larger army to permit a pool of replacement units to be maintained in the continental United States). Of course, as the war went on, a lot of men managed to avoid service by various devices, such as getting married, going to college, joining the reserves or the National Guard, or even getting arrested for some minor, but disqualifying infraction. So the pool of quality manpower grew smaller, forcing the army to lower intellectual standards.

Good leadership might have overcome the problems this created. But leadership declined as well. Obviously the loss of seasoned personnel hurt. Nor were those losses due entirely to casualties. By the second or third year of the war many seasoned officers—even West Point graduates—and NCOs began concluding that the war was ill-managed, certainly ill-considered and probably unwinnable. A surprising number of midlevel officers and NCOs left the army prematurely during the war, either retiring at twenty years, when they might have opted for thirty, or abandoning their careers with only two or three years to go until retirement. Nor was the army able to recruit more quality leaders easily, as the war became increasingly unpopular. But the army still needed leaders, or at least men it could put into leadership positions.

The shortage of NCOs was addressed by selecting recruits with "leadership potential" for advanced training as NCOs. So after eight weeks of basic training, a prospective NCO was sent to a special NCO course, to emerge twenty-one weeks later as a newly minted sergeant (E-5) or even staff sergeant (E-6), ranks attained in 29 weeks that, prior to the Vietnam War, would have been unusual for a draftee to reach within his 104-week hitch. Nicknamed "Shake 'n Bake" NCOs, these men lacked the skill, wisdom, and experience of the men they replaced. The only thing most of them didn't lack was dedication and courage, and lots of them died.

The green troops and instant NCOs were then led by equally inexperienced officers. Indeed, if anything, the officers were less prepared than the troops they led. Despite the image of West Point as the army's officer training institution, during the 1960s it only supplied about 5 percent of newly commissioned second lieutenants. Even in peacetime the army got most of its officers from ROTC programs, supplemented by OCS programs for promising college graduates and enlisted personnel. The increasing disenchantment with the Vietnam War in academe caused enrollments in ROTC to dry up, and, in fact, many campuses banned the institution altogether. In order to secure sufficient officers, the army lowered its standards. Many men became officers who would not have qualified for a commission just a few years earlier. Like William L. Calley, Jr., who had flunked out of junior college. The result was some junior officers who lacked the education, intellect, or character to lead men in combat. As a result the army ended up with some officers no better prepared than were their men. And then the army proceeded to make things worse.

Oddly, despite the shortage of officers, there were too many officers in the army for the combat slots available. For example, there were about 130 combat slots in Vietnam that required a lieutenant colonel, while the army had a pool of about 2,500 lieutenant colonels, with the qualifications to command them. To fill about 75 combat jobs for colonels in Vietnam, there was a pool of about 2,000 qualified officers (there were 6,000 colonels in the army, but many of those were not in the combat arms). For 13 combat commands in Vietnam requiring a major general (two stars), there were 200 officers. So, on the theory that it would be good for their military education, not to mention ensuring that everyone got some career-enhancing combat, the army adopted a policy of giving as many officers as possible some "combat experience." As a result, most officers in Vietnam spent six months or less with combat units. These officers arrived in Vietnam and took command of units that were already in the field, units that had presumably acquired some expertise in combat. So most officers were less well prepared than many of the men they were supposed to be leading. Moreover, since they stayed in the field only half as long as the troops, they rarely attained the expertise in combat of their more senior NCOs and men. Even during the war many lieutenants and captains criticized six-month rotations, one observing that it had taken him four months to learn the ropes, so just as he was coming into his own as a combat leader he was transferred elsewhere. As with the "Shake 'n Bake" NCOs, many of these officers tried hard, and many died. But there were many who proved inept and even harmful to the morale and efficiency of their troops, one consequence of which was the My Lai massacre.

Some good senior officers tried to do what they could to protect the troops from inept commanders. Numerous lower-level officers were sacked. From March 1966 through February of 1967, MG William E. DePuy of the 1st Infantry Division relieved thirty-one combat battalion commanders, a rate of about 300 percent. DePuy may have been a mite aggressive in this regard, but overall it appears that a battalion commander had between a 30-percent and a 50-percent chance of being sacked. The precise figure was difficult to nail down since many inept—or merely inefficient—officers were not formally relieved, but simply transferred to a "better" assignment before their normal tour of duty ended. Nor were lower-ranking officers immune. In 1969, the hapless 4th Battalion, 39th Infantry, which had suffered numerous casualties, mostly from booby traps, mines, and snipers, but who had never once actually come to grips with the enemy, received a new commander, who began a complete overhaul of the entire unit, among other things relieving fifty-nine lieutenants, eight captains, and two majors, a turnover rate of some 300 percent, greatly improving the battalion's performance.

Some division commanders should probably have been relieved as well. Certainly a couple of them did little to improve the character of the leadership in their commands, and some tried to cover up unpleasant realities. MG Samuel W. Koster, who had commanded the Americal Division at the time of the My Lai massacre, would later pay for such a cover-up with his career. However, the nature of the war was such that only one division commander—also of the Americal Division, in mid-1971—screwed up so badly that the "old boy network" was unable to cover things up in order to avoid a sacking. So most division commanders "led" their divisions for the prescribed year and then returned stateside.

Few people realized at the time how much the quality of all troops declined during the war because ill-prepared leaders were unable to adequately train their subordinates, to motivate them, or to lead them in combat. By the end of the war, the army's manpower quality had fallen so low that officers and NCOs were being attacked by their own troops ("fragged"). There were race riots in the barracks, and muggings, robberies, and even rapes were occurring in military installations, while drug abuse was widespread. It would take a decade for the army to recover.

THE MISMANAGEMENT OF ARVN

The Army of the Republic of Vietnam (ARVN) was the force that U.S. troops were supporting throughout the Vietnam War. It was the failure of the ARVN to come together as efficiently as the North Vietnamese armed forces that, more than anything else, led to the fall of South Vietnam. The Army of the Republic of Vietnam had a lot of problems. Some of them were self-inflicted and some of them were inflicted by the United States.

Like many postcolonial armies, the ARVN inherited the flaws of its colonial antecedent, the "Vietnam National Army." The gap between officers and enlisted personnel was very wide, not merely in terms of education and class (not unusual in most armies), but also of religion and regional origins (the Saigon regime favoring Catholics and northern exiles over southerners and Buddhists). Little attention was paid to the well-being of the enlisted personnel. Discipline was arbitrary and draconian by American—though not by VC—standards (e.g., relatively minor infractions might result in confinement to wire cages on bread and water for several days), pay poor (even for officers), rations slender, training limited, and political indoctrination inadequate. Little attention was paid to the plight of soldiers' families, who often suffered considerable privation as a result. These problems were exacerbated by the endemic corruption of the officer corps. As a result, desertion was a constant problem. Some ten to sixteen men per thousand on strength per month deserted the colors during the war, and by one calculation desertions exceeded casualties by 6 to 1 in the course of the war. Although throughout 1964–75, battalions averaged about 91 percent of authorized strength, they usually had only about 68 percent of their troops officially present for duty, and only about 50 percent normally available for combat, which was not conducive to quality performance under fire. To be sure, the VC and NVA shared many of these problems, but they exercised an even more draconian control over their troops, were more successful at political indoctrination, and kept the press at arm's length.

The United States made a number of mistakes as it "guided" the development of the ARVN. Aside from the fundamental errors made in the late 1950s, when the ARVN was formed (see "Creating ARVN," in chapter 3), the United States made a number of other blunders that did not help promote greater effectiveness on the part of the South Vietnamese Army. Most American advisers thought their advice was largely ignored by the Vietnamese. Some military commanders argued that the United States should have taken a greater role in overseeing the ARVN. During the Korean War, the United States had virtually taken over the ROK Army, and the South Koreans had greatly benefited from the experience. Greater American control over the ARVN would probably have improved leadership, by forcing out inept but politically connected commanders in favor of more capable leaders. It would almost certainly have improved aggressiveness, and probably curbed corruption to some extent. However, given the politics of the Vietnam War—with the enemy taking the Nationalist high ground—it probably would have been very difficult to impose greater American control over the ARVN. As it was, some ARVN officers were notably hostile to Americans, as pushy foreigners (it didn't help that some American advisers *were* arrogant know-it-alls). And it is not necessarily the case that more American control might have improved the army's performance.

Some military critics have argued that the massive inflow of U.S. advisers and forces actually hampered the development of the ARVN. Vietnamese units lacked the resources that American ones had, and U.S. advisers often overlooked that fact. There was also a tendency for Vietnamese units to become less aggressive as the U.S. buildup proceeded. Interestingly, while ARVN did not do well during the 1970 invasion of Cambodia, when "Vietnamization" had begun to limit the U.S. role in ground operations, in 1972, during the Communist "Easter Offensive," ARVN proved quite effective, supported only by U.S. airpower.

Perhaps the biggest liability America imposed on the ARVN was the U.S. concept of how wars are fought. Initially, in the late 1950s, U.S. advisers suggested a somewhat lighter version of U.S. ground forces for South Vietnam. Invasion from North Vietnam was considered the main threat; and the rugged terrain of Vietnam, plus the possibility of some guerrilla warfare in support of the invaders, made it obvious that South Vietnam needed conventional forces. Though eventually it became obvious to American commanders in Vietnam that lighter and more independent forces were required, the bulk of the South Vietnamese forces were still trained and equipped for more conventional war, though about half of all ARVN forces were assigned to pacification from mid-1966.

A very serious problem was that the United States focused too much attention on developing ARVN's combat capabilities and much less on its administrative and managerial side. In effect, U.S. assistance stressed line functions much more than staff functions. Moreover, little attention was paid to developing an ARVN "philosophy" of staff functions, one that was not overly reliant on the sort of endless resources that Uncle Sam could bring to the party. As a result, ARVN's personnel management system remained rudimentary.

Other staff functions, such as intelligence gathering, analysis, and management, relied heavily on resources not likely to be available forever (even to the use of satellite reconnaissance). Most major operations of the war were planned by U.S. officers, and what training South Vietnamese commanders received in planning presumed the continued availability of firepower on an American scale. Amazingly, for a nation so adept at logistics, American support for the ARVN logistical staff had a low priority. Although the United States supplied an enormous amount of materiél to the South Vietnamese, it failed to promote the development of a strong logistical infrastructure within ARVN, which greatly impaired its ability to function, particularly as Vietnamization progressed. Moreover, although a lot of equipment was given to the South Vietnamese, it often was neither the most modern nor the most appropriate. Although the 1954 O'Daniel plan had envisioned forming 105 mm howitzer battalions in ARVN, it was not until 1964 that the United States began issuing these, to replace the old 4.2-in. mortars that had hitherto provided most of ARVN's firepower. Not until late 1967 did ARVN begin to get the M-16 rifle, much more suitable for the smaller, more lightly built Vietnamese soldier than the M-1s that most of them were toting. Even then distribution lagged, so that by the beginning of 1968 only about two dozen battalions were equipped with the M-16, and the M-60 machine gun—most of which were airborne, marine, and ranger units. It was not until late 1969 that the M-16 or the equally light M-2 carbine became common in ARVN.

With "Vietnamization" the United States went overboard the other way, saddling the ARVN with a lot of materiél that was unsuited to its needs or beyond its ability to support. Thus, there were no ARVN ordnance personnel skilled in repairing M-48 tanks, so that in 1972–75 heavily damaged tanks had to be shipped to the United States for repair. Nor did the ARVN need the three battalions of 8-in. cannon. And at $3,000 a round, ARVN was much too poor to make effective use of the TOW missiles with which it was supplied.

Some of the problems the ARVN had were so intractable that nothing short of the imposition of a totalitarian regime (such as existed in the North) could have resolved them. Although full mobilization was not introduced until 1968, the South Vietnamese were trying to build an army in the middle of a war that was everywhere, in contrast to the NVA who could organize and train fresh units in the relative safety of North Vietnam. The ARVN grew constantly during the war and took heavy casualties, with the result that there was always a shortage of seasoned cadres, the experienced officers and NCOs who are needed to train the troops. This was further complicated by the fact that ARVN had a weak officer corps. Corruption, favoritism, and politics were much more popular among many ARVN officers than fighting, and this attitude was quickly imparted to the troops. Moreover, many senior South Vietnamese officers were more than happy to let the American troops go off in their helicopters to chase the Communists through the jungle, while ARVN troops stayed behind to keep an eye on things. American commanders noted that it was often better that way, for ARVN units often fell apart when heavily engaged. It was easier to let the U.S. troops do the hard fighting. But that reinforced South Vietnam's dependency on the United States.

Unlike North Vietnam, which used proven techniques based on the Chinese Communist experience, South Vietnam adopted the Western techniques of the enemy the Communist Vietnamese had beaten: France. While many North Vietnamese troops had served with the Communists in China, most of the experienced South Vietnamese officers and troops had served with the French. The northerners had a tradition of winning, the southerners one of losing. This losers' attitude was reinforced by several other factors. First, there were the various internal wars South Vietnam suffered before, and during, the Communist insurgency. There were religious militias and even a gangster army that had to be put down in the 1950s. In the early 1960s, there were Buddhist rebels, as well as hostile Montagnards. All of these internal wars caused friction among many communities within South Vietnam; and when members of these groups found themselves in the South Vietnamese army, they were a little unsure of how welcome they were, or whom they could trust. The Communists took advantage of this distrust to recruit agents in the South Vietnamese military, and several of these agents worked their way up to high positions. By the late 1960s, it was common for U.S. units to go out of their way to keep the South Vietnamese in the dark about American operations. For by then it was a given that any information the South Vietnamese had, the North Vietnamese would have the next day.

All of this led to another major reason for the sorry attitude within the South Vietnamese forces, and this was the disdain most American troops felt for ARVN. While there were many exceptional units in the South Vietnamese forces (rangers, marines), and these were openly respected by U.S. troops, ARVN forces in general were treated with considerable contempt. Most U.S. soldiers had far more respect for their Communist opponents than for their Vietnamese allies. On numerous occasions American officers expressed open admiration for the enemy on camera ("He could have defended the whole southern perimeter all by himself."), while expressing contempt for the South Vietnamese ("I don't want to speak about those people"). To the average ARVN soldier, this was further proof that he was on the losing team, which did little for morale or willingness to perform well.

But one should not focus exclusively on the negatives. There were a lot of things wrong with the Communist troops. And in the final analysis, you were more likely to get killed as a Viet Cong or North Vietnamese soldier than if you were an American or ARVN trooper. Sure, the Communists won the war, but that was because their superpower supporters stayed with them longer than America did with South Vietnam. Nevertheless, on the battlefield, the ARVN often came out on top. One of the great what-if's of the Vietnam War is what could have been done to produce a more effective ARVN and what impact that would have had on the outcome of the war.

THE ARVN OFFICER CORPS

The ARVN Officer Corps grew out of the old French colonial army and the Vietnamese National Army created in 1949. But that had very few Vietnamese officers, only a handful in the late forties and only eighty ranking as captains or above by 1952, though by 1954, about 65 percent of the officers were Vietnamese, albeit mostly in the lower ranks. A small academy for Vietnamese officer candidates had been established in 1940, but was dissolved when the Japanese occupied French Indochina later that year. In 1948, with the Viet Minh war raging, the French opened a new military academy for Vietnamese cadets at Hue, and later transferred it to Dalat. This eventually became the principal training institution for ARVN's regular officers. Initially the course of study was nine months, later raised to a year and, in 1956, to two years. Only in 1966, did the Dalat academy adopt a full four-year program, akin to that at West Point. Supplementing Dalat as a source of officers were a series of reserve officer training programs. These quickly turned eligible young men into junior officers (like the "90 Day Wonders" of World War II) and OCS programs for NCOs, while direct commissions to men in the ranks brought in as many officers as these two programs together. In addition, many men received commissions in the various militia organizations (Regional Forces, Popular Forces, etc.).

While there certainly were some excellent officers in the ARVN, overall the quality was not very good. Many of them tried to preserve the numerous nineteenth-century privileges that the old French officers in Vietnam had enjoyed, such as batmen (soldiers acting as personal servants), even at the lowest levels, special rations, and so forth. Pay was poor, promotions were slow (it was not uncommon for lieutenants to command companies and captains to command battalions, even in nonemergency situations). One result of this was that a good many of the officers up to the highest levels were corrupt. Taking advantage of the weak administrative infrastructure of the ARVN, a lot of officers had their hands in the till. Battalions sometimes numbering six hundred or more men on paper could often only put about half that in the field. The balance were "ghosts," whose pay was being pocketed by the officers. There was a much greater social gap between the officers and men in the ARVN than in the other armies in Vietnam, all of which

Regional Origins of Senior ARVN Officers

Region	Percent
North (Tonkin)	18.0
Center (Annam)	23.0
South (Cochin China)	44.0
Other	5.5
Unknown	9.5

were more socially egalitarian, even the NVA and the VC, in their own ways. As officer training was weak, leadership was often poor. A lot of ARVN officers led from the rear, and the performance of their men reflected that.

Analytic data on the ARVN Officer Corps is difficult to come by. A careful sifting of materials by Dr. John Prados secured useful data on just ninety-three men who had attained senior rank by 1969. About two-thirds of them had graduated from the Dalat academy. Only about 12 percent of the senior officers secured their commissions through reserve officer programs, OCS, or direct commissions, which nevertheless were the sources for the bulk of the officers. Only one of the senior officers was originally commissioned in the militia. Interestingly, about 10 percent of these men had fought with the Viet Minh prior to the Geneva Accords. Although they were presumably Nationalists rather than Communists, there is some evidence that a few of them, at least, remained covert supporters of the Communists even while serving in the ARVN.

Religious affiliation could not be determined for most of those in the sample, but only four are known to have been Buddhists, though there were

Social Origins of ARVN Senior Officers

Class	Percent
Landowning	32.0
Middle & Upper Class	12.0
Military	10.0
Minority	1.10
Officialdom	20.0
Peasantry	3.0
Professional	5.5
Unknown	16.4

Key: *Middle and Upper Class* refers to persons from mercantile or business backgrounds; *Military* to those whose fathers were in the French colonial forces. *Minority* to a member of the non-Vietnamese Nung people. *Officialdom* includes men from both the Vietnamese mandarin class and offspring of French colonial officials. *Professional* includes the sons of doctors, lawyers, and teachers.

many former Buddhists among the several dozen Roman Catholics, the latter certainly a consequence of the favoritism shown by the Diem regime towards Catholics.

THE FIRST "HOLLOW ARMY"

The Vietnam War led to a serious weakening of America's military readiness. The need to sustain the war while not overly disturbing the civilians (i.e., by not mobilizing) led to the neglect of all forces not directly involved in the war. By 1967, the active army was experiencing severe cadre problems. There were not enough trained personnel to go around. When the 101st Airborne Division deployed to Vietnam in November 1967, it had to be filled up with "legs" (nonparachute qualified personnel), because there were just not enough airborne-qualified personnel available. There were not enough experienced officers and NCOs to both train the new recruits and staff the units already in Vietnam. The situation was so bad that the 197th Light Infantry Brigade, supposed to be the demonstration unit for the Infantry School at Fort Benning, was nicknamed "the 19-Worst," because it was routinely used as a dumping ground for troops who could not be sent to Vietnam. This shortage of training cadre was one reason for the poor preparation of the troops who were sent to Vietnam and for the declining quality of their leaders.

In order to scrape up enough personnel to run the training camps and to sustain the combat units in Vietnam, the army began to draw upon the units it had elsewhere. By late 1968, the only fully combat-ready units in the army were in Vietnam, and the Marine Corps was not much better off.

By December 1968, the military resources of the United States were pathetically slender. All units not already in Vietnam were more or less understrength, short not only of men but also of equipment (for example, there were only five helicopters available in Korea for all purposes). Of units in the CONUS, only the 82nd Airborne Division (which already had a brigade in Vietnam) was rated as suitable for combat. Units in Germany and Korea were all understrength, but were rated barely combat ready, those in Korea only with a heavy infusion of KATUSA personnel (Korean Augmentation U.S. Army, Korean troops integrated into American units, a standard practice since the early 1950s, but relied on even more during the Vietnam War).

While the United States was running down its armed forces, the Soviets took advantage of America's Southeast Asian obsession, to begin a major expansion of their armed forces. Had war come in Europe—or Korea—the United States would have been hard pressed to put up a credible defense. In such circumstances, American forces would have had to resort to nuclear weapons to prevent a devastating defeat. The Soviets understood this quite clearly, which is why they didn't attempt any military adventures.

Status of the Principal U.S. Ground Combat Formations, December 1968

Location	Unit	Status
CONUS	1st Armored Division	Unsatisfactory
	2nd Armored Division (-)	Unsatisfactory
	5th Mechanized Division (-)	Unsatisfactory
	6th Infantry Division (-)	Unsatisfactory
	82nd Airborne Division (-)	Good
	2nd Marine Division	Good
	5th Marine Division (-)	Forming
	69th Infantry Brigade	Unsatisfactory
	194th Armored Brigade	Unsatisfactory
	197th Infantry Brigade	Unsatisfactory
	6th Armored Cavalry Regiment	Unsatisfactory
Alaska	171st Infantry Brigade (-)	Fair
	172nd Infantry Brigade (-)	Fair
Germany	3rd Armored Division	Satisfactory
	3rd Infantry Division	Satisfactory
	8th Infantry Division	Satisfactory
	24th Infantry Division	Satisfactory
	2nd Armored Cavalry Regiment	Satisfactory
	3rd Armored Cavalry Regiment	Satisfactory
	14th Armored Cavalry Regiment	Satisfactory
Hawaii	29th Infantry Brigade	Unsatisfactory
Korea	2nd Infantry Division	Satisfactory
	7th Infantry Division	Satisfactory
Panama	193rd Infantry Brigade	Unsatisfactory
Vietnam	1st Cavalry Division (Airmobile)	Excellent
	1st Infantry Division	Very good
	4th Infantry Division	Satisfactory
	9th Infantry Division	Good
	23rd (Americal) Infantry Division	Unsatisfactory
	25th Infantry Division	Satisfactory
	101st Airborne Division (Airmobile)	Excellent
	1st Bde, 5th Mechanized Division	Good
	3rd Bde, 82nd Airborne Division	Excellent
	173rd Airborne Brigade	Excellent
	199th Light Infantry Brigade	Good
	11th Armored Cavalry Regiment	Excellent

Key: CONUS is the continental United States, the 48-contiguous states. A (-) indicates a unit lacking an important component, such as the 5th Mech Division, which had a brigade in Vietnam. The 5th Marine Division had been activated in mid-1966, but was never actually completely formed, since two of its regiments had been sent to Vietnam, one in 1966 and the second in 1968.

"THEY ALSO SERVE WHO ONLY STAND AND WAIT"

During the Vietnam War there were frequent criticisms of the National Guard and the reserves ("the reserve components"). Organizations supposedly ready in times of national emergency, they were not mobilized for duty in Vietnam. Many charged that those unwilling to serve in Vietnam who had the right political connections could avoid that unpleasant possibility by joining the National Guard. There was some truth in this. At the height of the war, the waiting list for the National Guard reached 100,000, and in some areas one needed political pull to get in at all, as was the case of many professional athletes, not to mention former VP Dan Quayle. There were also some complicating factors.

Early in the war the Joint Chiefs of Staff had recommended the mobilization of large numbers of National Guardsmen and reservists. The secretary of defense approved their recommendation and passed it on to the president. The president turned the suggestion down. The Joint Chiefs again requested that the reserve components be activated in 1966 and in 1967, both times with the same result. Although he never clearly articulated his thoughts on the matter, a number of factors seem to have prompted President Johnson's decision.

Mobilization of the reserve components is extremely disruptive of the nation's social, political, and economic life (one need only recall the problems created in 1990–91 when just a quarter of the reserve components were called up for the Gulf War). During the Berlin Crisis of 1961, four Army National Guard divisions (c. 45,000 men) and many Air National Guard squadrons (c. 21,000 men) had been mobilized, plus many reservists. The crisis ended quickly, even before the guardsmen and reservists had been fully activated. Nevertheless, some guardsmen and reservists activated for the Berlin Crisis were not released for almost two years. In the aftermath of the mobilization there was considerable criticism as to its wisdom, and criticism was one thing Lyndon Johnson wanted to avoid at all costs. Then too, many southern guardsmen had been activated during the Civil Rights demonstrations in the early 1960s to enforce federal court decisions and to protect demonstrators, often for long periods. (Creighton Abrams commanded several such operations, and his demonstrable tact and political skill were such that President Johnson later appointed him as Westmoreland's deputy in Vietnam.) In addition, fully activating the National Guard and the reserves would require the proclamation of a national emergency. Johnson viewed the war as an unpleasant necessity and wanted to get on with his ambitious domestic programs. He didn't want to provide his political foes with grounds for scuttling some of his domestic programs in the interests of concentrating on a national emergency.

A very important issue was the nation's other commitments, most notably that to the defense of Western Europe. The reserve components were, in the

words of Robert McNamara, a "perishable asset." Once activated and committed, they would no longer exist. As early as 1965, the Vietnam War was
putting an enormous strain on America's resources. The focus on Vietnam
led to a gradual deterioration in America's forces in or committed to Europe,
despite the fact that, then as now, Europe was far more important to American security and prosperity than Vietnam. Moreover, at that time Russia
was actually building up its forces in Europe. So we had a situation in which
the United States was practicing disarmament in Europe for no better reason
than to support a war in a region of dubious importance to American national interests. Units in Europe were allowed to fall below prescribed manpower levels (it was not unusual for infantry platoons to have half their
official complement of troops), and usually had second call on new equipment (the M-14 rifle remained in service in Europe much longer than in
Vietnam). At the time few people realized the extent to which we had abandoned the defense of Europe. If war had come in Europe, the National Guard
and the reserves would have been in the thick of it virtually from the start,
as the country had only a handful of active units available as a strategic
reserve. To help cope with the shortage of active units, the National Guard
created the Selected Reserve Force (SRF), which was intended for immediate
deployment overseas upon activation. Units in the SRF had ninety-six training assemblies a year, about twice that of "ordinary" Army National Guard
formations, and spent three weeks in summer camp, rather than two. They
were provided with full complements of arms and equipment. Units not in
the SRF often found their best equipment "mobilized" for use by the active
army or the SRF.

Meanwhile, at least 340,000 National Guardsmen served on active duty in
support of the civil authority during the Vietnam War. From the end of the
first quarter of 1965 to the end of February 1971, elements of the National
Guard were called to duty on 543 occasions, either by their states or by the
federal government. Reasons for the call-ups included finding lost children,
flood relief, suppressing prison riots, the New York postal strike, pursuing
fugitives from justice, fighting forest fires, and more, including protecting
thousands of civil rights demonstrators during the Selma-Montgomery
March and coping with civil disorders, of which there were a bumper crop
during the war. Some 54 percent of all activations were prompted by actual
or potential civil disorders, many of which were *not* related to the antiwar
movement. As a result, during 1968 roughly a quarter of all National Guard
personnel saw some active duty.

What does not seem to have been considered at the time was a partial
mobilization of the training establishments of the reserve components. The
Army Reserve maintains a number of units oriented toward training, so that
in the event of a general mobilization the army's basic training facilities can
be expanded rapidly. Had the reserve components been asked to lend a hand

National Guard Mobilizations in Support of the Civil Authority, 1965–71

Year	Activations	Troops	Average Strength by Activation	Month
1965*	16 (88%)	25,051	1,566	2,783
1966	26 (54%)	19,004	731	1,584
1967	58 (48%)	42,568	734	3,547
1968	98 (71%)	110,641	1,129	9,220
1969	157 (40%)	62,633	399	5,219
1970	162 (56%)	75,620	467	6,302
1971**	26 (23%)	3,708	143	1,285

Key: Figures are for both Army and Air National Guard. They *exclude* troops called into federal service as a result of the *Pueblo* incident of 1968. Data for 1965 (*) are based on the period 1 March–31 December, those for 1971 (**) on 1 January–28 February. *Activations* is the number of occasions on which the National Guard was called, with the percent of calls prompted by a civil disorder or potential civil disorder (including riots, rock concerts, major peace demonstrations, and so forth). The overall increase in the number of activations was only partially connected to the problem of civil disorders during the Vietnam War. The winters in the late-1960s were unusually harsh, prompting an increased number of activations up to assist in snow clearance and rescues or for flood relief the following springs. *Troops* is the number of guardsmen called up (which may include some double counting, some troops having been activated more than once in the same year). The figures shown are minimal; some states' reporting procedures differed, and the actual number of troops called was probably higher. *Average Strength by Activation* is the average number of troops called divided by the number of activations (the actual number of troops called ranged from a single soldier—in instances where a technical specialist, such as a bomb disposal expert, was needed—to some 12,000 called out for the New York postal strike of 24–30 March 1970 and the 13,393 called for the riot in Watts, Los Angeles, 13–22 August 1965. *Average Strength by Month* gives some idea as to the approximate number of Guardsmen on active duty at any time during the war.

with training, these problems would have been eased considerably, and it would also have enhanced the reserve components' readiness for a European emergency.

And in fact, some national guardsmen and reservists did get into action in Vietnam, albeit in relatively small numbers. Very early in the war, individual National Guardsmen and reservists began to volunteer for duty in Vietnam. Figures for reservists are harder to come by; but as of the end of 1967, more than two thousand National Guardsmen had already served in Vietnam, among them over two hundred army aviators. At least twenty-four of the National Guardsmen had been killed or reported as missing in action, about the same death rate as among all troops in Vietnam. And National

Guardsmen had already accumulated a number of interesting distinctions in combat:

The first Air Force Medal of Honor to be awarded in Vietnam (in fact, the first ever awarded, since the separate air force version of the decoration was not instituted until the late 1950s) went to MAJ Bernard F. Fisher, an Air Guardsman and A1E Skyraider pilot, for heroism on 10 March 1966, when he landed under fire on a field in enemy territory to rescue a fellow airman.

The first living man to be awarded the Air Force Cross, second highest decoration in the air force, was LTC James R. Riser, another Air Guardsman, an F-105 pilot, for heroism while a prisoner of the enemy from 1965.

The most decorated army aviator in Vietnam was probably CPT Jerome R. Daly, of the Pennsylvania National Guard. He earned the Distinguished Service Cross, two Silver Stars, three Distinguished Flying Crosses, and two Purple Hearts, not to mention repeated awards of the Air Medal, and the distinction of being named "Army Aviator of the Year" in 1967.

Sensitive to the criticism of the National Guard as a refuge from the war, some National Guard personnel suggested the raising of a volunteer division for service in Vietnam. The proposal was ill-considered. At best such a unit would be a one-time effort—it would be raised, trained, and sent to Vietnam, and then discharged after its tour of duty. Moreover, a call for volunteers would, of necessity, strip existing units of valuable personnel and those presumably the best and most motivated. Little came of the suggestion.

The seizure of the USS *Pueblo* by North Korean forces on 23 January 1968 finally forced the president's hand with regard to the reserve components. The Joint Chiefs requested that as many as 54,000 National Guardsmen and reservists be activated. The president authorized a more limited call that eventually amounted to about 30,000 men. As Johnson had expected, the call-up proved controversial. Many critics of the Vietnam War charged that he was using the *Pueblo* crisis to further escalate the war in Southeast Asia. Several legal challenges were mounted, on the grounds that the president lacked the legislative authority to call the troops up, or that the call violated the enlistment contracts of certain individuals, which were resolved on 7 October 1968, when the Supreme Court threw the cases out.

The *Pueblo* call-up included nearly 23,000 National Guardsmen, about 9,000 of whom eventually served in Vietnam. Beginning in August of 1968, about 7,000 Army National Guardsmen called up for the *Pueblo* crisis were sent to Vietnam, including two artillery battalions, two engineer battalions, and many smaller units. All performed well, in some cases eliciting favorable comments from regular army officers, not usually prone to be kind to the National Guard.

Perhaps the most interesting of the Army National Guard units in Viet-

The National Guard in the *Pueblo* Crisis and Vietnam, 1968

Component	Strength	Activated	Vietnam
Army National Guard	389,192	12,234 (3.1%)	c.7,000 (57.2%)
Air National Guard	75,261	10,511 (13.0%)	c.2,000 (19.0%)
Totals	464,453	22,745	c.9,000 (39.6%).

Key: *Strength* is as of the end of fiscal 1968. *Activated* is the number of troops called in January of 1968, with their percent of strength. *Vietnam* is the number who were sent to Southeast Asia, with the percent of those activated, figures that exclude Air Guardsmen who made "routine" flights into the theater but were not stationed there.

nam was D Company, 151st Infantry, from Indiana. The only ground combat maneuver unit from the reserve components to serve in Vietnam, D/151st was also the only LRRP unit in the National Guard. It served nearly a year "in country," mostly in the II Field Force, during which it suffered two men killed in action and over one hundred wounded.

Of the Air National Guardsmen activated as a result of the *Pueblo* crisis, about 2,000 (eight tactical fighter squadrons plus a tactical reconnaissance squadron) were sent to Vietnam beginning in June of 1968. In Vietnam these guardsmen undertook over 24,000 combat sorties, for nearly 39,000 combat hours. Furthermore, individual Air Guardsmen serving with the active air force's 355th Tactical Fighter Squadron, undertook approximately 6,000 combat sorties, logging 11,000 combat hours, so the Air National Guard made about 30,000 combat sorties, for about 50,000 combat hours, in Vietnam. The performance of the Air National Guard was widely hailed by senior air force personnel, one of whom observed that the Air National Guard F-100 squadrons were all "rated higher than other F-100 squadrons in the same zone."

In addition, Air National Guard and Air Force Reserve personnel and aircraft, not formally on active duty, often flew into Vietnam on transport missions during their annual two-week training periods. Air reservists alone undertook nearly 1,250 such missions during the war.

Many army and air force reservists were also activated in consequence of the *Pueblo* crisis. For a variety of reasons, determining the number who served in Vietnam is more difficult than determining the number of National Guard personnel. About 10,500 army reservists were called up, in forty-two administrative, medical, logistical, engineer, and headquarters units. Of these units, thirty-five served in Vietnam, but many were partially filled with active army personnel.

THE COMMUNIST ADVANTAGE

American soldiers could not help but notice the differences between the South Vietnamese and Communist troops. No one gave it a lot of thought at the time, but the North Vietnamese obviously had superior methods for motivating and controlling their troops. These techniques say much about the eventual North Vietnamese success in their campaign to conquer the South. These methods can be summarized as follows;

• **Nationalism.** The North Vietnamese made much of the fact that they were the original rebels against foreign rule in the twentieth century. This played well among all Vietnamese. There was a centuries-old tradition of struggle against outsiders who wished to rule Vietnam. Of course, the French had gotten in during the previous century by playing "divide and conquer" during one of the frequent periods of Vietnamese civil war. The Vietnamese were always prone to factionalism. These struggles between different power blocks within the country should have demonstrated to foreigners that the Vietnamese could be stirred up to fight fiercely even if there wasn't an outside power to battle against. This factionalism was still there, as witness the division of the country in 1954. If America had not entered the fray in 1964, the war would have just been yet another Vietnamese civil war. But with the Americans involved, the North Vietnamese made much of a continuing struggle against foreign conquerors. They called this phase of the struggle "the American war," a follow-up on the earlier "French war." Many South Vietnamese who would have fought against the northerners if it had just been a Vietnamese versus Vietnamese war went over to the North Vietnamese because of the American angle. While many South Vietnamese were quite anti-Communist, the North Vietnamese shrewdly played down the Communist angle and the Viet Cong diligently sought to include all who would struggle against the foreigners (Americans). Naturally, the Communists were lying a lot in the South, but in the heat of battle, many southerners ignored the possibility of Communist rule in the South. Many South Vietnamese patriots fought to the death for a Vietnam free of foreigners.

• **Political Control.** North Vietnam was a police state, but one that did things with a light touch, especially during the war. Communist doctrine was played down and patriotism was played up. But the Communists took no chances. They had as many "cadres" (political officials) as they did military officers in the South. Every military commander had a deputy who was a Communist Party member and answerable to the party, not the military chain of command. While many officers were party members, the cadres were responsible for morale and loyalty. The cadres were the chief source of news about what was going on in the world. While the cadres spouted a lot of propaganda, they knew that some of the troops had access to South Vietnamese newspapers and radio news from trusted sources like the

BBC Vietnamese language service. So the cadres had to stick close enough to reality when trying to get the party line across.

• **Group Think.** Communist control techniques worked differently and, arguably, more effectively in Asia than Karl Marx had predicted (he thought communism would only work in the West among the urban population). In Russia, and throughout Asia, there is much collective thinking. In Russia much of the farmland was held collectively. This was actually an ancient practice, but the habit of working together as a group made a Communist-style police state easier to establish. In China, and neighboring nations, the people in villages had to work together to maintain the water systems that made high-yield rice paddy farming possible. So when the Communists came along with their use of cadres and "working together for the common good," they hit a responsive chord. The Western idea of individual initiative and land ownership were rather foreign. The Communists went a step further by efficiently transplanting the village collective mentality to military units. That had not been done before and it proved a very effective system. Ironically, this approach did not feature the iron discipline one assumes in the kind of hard fighting units the North Vietnamese produced. The most frequent punishment for poor discipline was criticism. Each day featured at least ten minutes for the platoon to come together so troops could admit to mistakes (or be told by others) and, in effect, say they were sorry and would try harder. Generally, the system worked. But when a soldier deserted, it was not an automatic death sentence (however, going over to the South Vietnamese with your weapon was). Viet Cong soldiers did sometimes tell their commander that they were sick of the war and were going home. After a great deal of "criticism" and arguing with his fellow soldiers, the reluctant warrior would either change his mind or turn in his weapon and go home. While the Viet Cong lost a lot of troops this way (over 10 percent a year), it actually improved morale, for the ones who stayed felt (with some justification) that they were indeed volunteers. And for potential recruits, it showed that it wasn't a one-way street if they volunteered. This system also kept the officers and NCOs on their toes, for if they were not effective leaders, their troops would leave. The Communist cadres that approved promotions also had to pay attention to leadership ability. If a unit performed poorly, the commander got "criticized" by his superiors, while the cadre in that unit got the same treatment from their Communist Party superiors.

• **Good Discipline.** The Communists had a lot of rules for their soldiers, and most of them were practical and popular with the troops (even the ones that involved a lot of work). In the face of American firepower, Viet Cong and North Vietnamese units moved around a lot and dug in whenever they stopped for the night. While the troops complained about all the digging, and the trenches and dugouts were not really used that often, these fortifications were appreciated by the troops. They were very uncomfortable when, at times because of special conditions, they were unable to dig in. There were also many rules for training and a busy daily schedule of things for soldiers to do. This was ancient military wisdom. If you keep the troops busy, they will not have much opportunity to get into trouble or to think too much about the dangerous situation they are in. Also reassuring to the troops were the rules against looting. It made sense for the Viet Cong, as they often operated in areas the troops came from. But even the North Vietnamese troops were under strict orders not to steal from the locals. This was in sharp contrast to the South Vietnamese troops, or even American soldiers in units with poor leadership.

• **Distance.** North Vietnamese troops had no place to go. Deserting was not a viable option, for they generally operated in wilderness areas. Moreover, they were a month's march from North Vietnam and there were a lot of hostile troops in the way. This was a handy situation for the Communists, for during the late 1960s, America was actually winning the war. The Viet Cong was a shadow of it's former self and the North Vietnamese were taking a beating that could eventually cause them to collapse. The North Vietnamese turned this around by winning the battle for American public opinion. Meanwhile, the fact that their troops could not wander back to their village if they got too much to bear helped keep their forces intact. Some North Vietnamese troops did desert, but not as many as might have if desertion had been easier.

FRAGGING

A "fragging" was an incident in which an officer or NCO was attacked by his own troops. The name derived from fragmentation grenade, which was often the weapon of choice in such incidents, as it could be casually tossed into a tent or a hootch. In all wars some officers and NCOs have run the risk of being killed by their own men. This phenomenon is usually a consequence of a massive breakdown in morale and discipline. It has always been an uncommon occurrence, particularly in the U.S. armed forces. However, beginning in 1969, fragging incidents began to rise, a matter that soon came to the attention of the media.

Fragging Incidents, 1969–72

Year	Incidents	Deaths
1969	96–126	37–39
1970	290	34
1971	333–335	12
1972	37–59	1–4
Totals	788	86

Figures on fraggings are very uncertain. Even official army figures are unclear.

Assuming the higher figures, in 1969 there were 0.3 incidents per 1,000 men, rising to 1.75 incidents per 1,000 men by 1971. The rise in number of incidents and the decline in the number of fatalities (1 for every 2.5 attempts in 1969, declining to 1 for every 8.5 attempts in 1970, and 1 in every 27.8 attempts in 1971) suggests either overreporting, lack of serious intent, or better security on the part of officers and NCOs, probably a combination of all three. One interesting aspect to the fragging phenomenon is that several officers and NCOs were the objects of repeated attempts.

Some accounts contend that as many as a thousand deaths may have been attributable to fragging incidents. This is certainly a journalistic exaggeration, probably prompted by the fact that fragging attempts over the entire war numbered nearly a thousand (well, 788 by official count). A similar journalistic exaggeration tends to convert "casualties" into killed.

Fragging was an extreme manifestation of a breakdown in discipline that afflicted the armed forces as the war went on. Desertion, drug use, and incidents of individual and collective indiscipline multiplied about tenfold during the war. By one account, 50,000 servicemen belonged to one or another antiwar organization within the armed forces, which published an estimated 245 unauthorized newspapers (all of these figures are, of course, highly conjectural and derive from left-wing sources not necessarily inclined to accuracy). Some of these problems were not unique to the armed forces, as the men and women in uniform were reflecting problems in society that had been developing even before the Vietnam War became a divisive issue. But not all. Increasing problems with discipline were also, to a considerable extent, a manifestation of the declining quality of leadership in the armed forces.

It's worth noting that fraggings seem to have been more a phenomenon of the rear echelon troops than the guys out in the bush. The grunts might dislike an officer, but if he was good at his trade they were unlikely to bump him off, while the guys in the rear had no such compunctions. Of course, the grunts do seem occasionally to have fragged an inept officer, but that's a different matter.

THE MEDAL OF HONOR AND OTHER DECORATIONS

The awarding of decorations for valor is an ancient military custom, supplemented in more recent times by decorations for achievement and for service. The United States was slow to adopt this tradition, as the Founding Fathers viewed it with a jaundiced eye. Thus, occasional special decorations and honors aside, it was not until the Civil War that the United States created its first proper decoration for valor, the Medal of Honor, often erroneously termed "the Congressional Medal of Honor." Created in 1862, the Medal of Honor was essentially the sole decoration in the nation for more than fifty years. As such, the Medal of Honor could be awarded, not only for unusual courage in the face of the enemy, but for risking one's life to save someone in an accident. This is still grounds for awarding the Medal of Honor in the naval service, though no awards have been made in such circumstances since

Vietnam Medal of Honor Awards by Assignment

Assignment	Air Force	Army	Marines	Navy	Total	Percent	Note
Advisers	0	10	1	2	13	5.5%	A
Aircrew, Fixed Wing	10	0	0	2	12	5.0%	
Aircrew, Helicopter	2	6	2	1	11	4.6%	B
Armor	0	3	0	0	3	1.3%	
Artillery	0	4	2	0	6	2.5%	C
Leaders	0	73	29	1	103	43.3%	D
Battalion	0	2	0	0	2	0.8%	
Company	0	12	8	0	20	8.4%	
Platoon	0	26	8	0	34	14.3%	
Squad	0	21	7	0	28	11.8%	
Fire Team	0	12	6	1	19	8.0%	
Medical Personnel	0	16	0	4	20	8.4%	E
Infantry	0	41	18	0	59	24.8%	F
Engineers	0	1	1	1	3	1.3%	
Other	0	1	2	3	6	2.5%	G
Total	12	155	57	14	238		

Key: The table is based not on the formal "Military Occupational Specialty" of each awardee, but rather on the tasks that they were performing at the time they earned their Medals of Honor.

A. Includes one medical adviser not listed with medical personnel.

B. Army figure includes two medevac helicopter pilots, not listed with medical personnel.

C. Includes forward observers (artillerymen who trek out into the boonies with the grunts to provide information for artillery and air units providing fire support), but omits two air force FO pilots, listed under Aircrew, Fixed Wing.

D. These omit aviation awardees, several of whom were squadron commanders. It is limited to ground combat elements, including battalion, company, and platoon commanders, as well as XOs, company first sergeants, platoon sergeants, squad leaders, and fire team leaders. Almost all of these were infantrymen. The exceptions are one artillery battalion commander and one Navy SEAL team leader. None of these men are listed under any of the other categories.

E. Includes medical aidmen, plus three chaplains (two army, one navy), who double as medics, but omits one medical adviser to the ARVN and two medevac helicopter pilots, listed in other categories.

F. Includes riflemen, grenadiers, machine gunners, LRRPs, scouts, mortarmen, radio operators in the field, and other guys working as grunts.

G. Others include: army, one truck driver, who earned his Medal of Honor in an ambush; marines, one supply sergeant and one combat photographer; navy, three boat crewmen, two of them skippers and one a machine gunner.

1945. Medals were also awarded for unusual efficiency or devotion in the performance of one's duties, which is how Dr. Mary Walker became the first and only woman to receive a Medal of Honor during the Civil War. With American participation in World War I, however, additional decorations were created, establishing a "pyramid of honor." This made the standards for the award of the Medal of Honor very high, and they became higher still as additional decorations were created. Thus, by the time of the Vietnam War, it was awarded only for the most outstanding feats of selfless courage in the face of the enemy, and posthumous awards have become increasingly common.

The Medal of Honor was awarded to 238 men who served in Vietnam (an additional one was awarded in connection with the still unexplained Israeli attack on the USS *Liberty* in June of 1967). At times during the war it was charged that the Medal of Honor was being awarded rather generously, perhaps as a means of bolstering morale. While it is true that the ratio of the number of troops killed in action to the number of awards of the Medal of Honor was relatively low in Vietnam (199 combat deaths for every award, in contrast to 664 in World War II and 257 in Korea), this was because virtually all of the fighting in Vietnam was infantry small unit combat. This put a particularly heavy burden on the grunts and their leaders, at the company, platoon, squad, and fire team level, who paid an unusually high price. In World War II, there were a lot of combat deaths in circumstances that precluded the sort of deeds for which men are awarded the Medal of Honor. For example, when entire ships' companies went down (e.g., the USS *Juneau*, which took with her over 600 crewmen, including the five Sullivan Brothers.) Or when troop transports were torpedoed, often with horrendous loss of life. Or during the strategic air campaign against Germany, for which a dozen men were awarded the Medal of Honor, but in which some 40,000 airmen died, a ratio of 333 deaths to each award.

In Vietnam a soldier or marine was more likely to earn a Medal of Honor, not because the armed forces were awarding them lavishly, but because, relatively speaking, there were a lot more small units and close combat. What with troops going out on lengthy patrols into enemy-controlled areas, securing isolated firebases, defending base areas, or accompanying ARVN or Allied formations as advisers, there was a lot of opportunity for heroic action. At the war's peak there were only 81 U.S. Army infantry battalions in Vietnam, plus about 24 battalions of marines. There were also a dozen army tank and armored recon battalions, plus six of marines. So the "front line" strength of U.S. forces in Vietnam was only about 123 battalions. And it was the infantry that took most of the punishment. The 105 infantry battalions contained less than 90,000 troops, out of a peak U.S. strength—all services— in Vietnam of 536,000 in 1968, of whom about 330,000 were army and a further 75,000 marines. This was a ratio of one combat soldier for every five support troops within the combat zone. If you include the support troops for Vietnam forces back in the United States, the ratio climbs to well over 1 to 10.

The army suffered approximately 238,000 combat casualties, including 30,000 dead, the marines about 100,000, including some 13,000 dead. The marine figures are the key here, for proportionally far more marines are infantrymen. On average, an infantryman had a better than 50-percent chance of being wounded or killed in combat during his one-year tour. Some idea of this may be gained by comparing awards of the Medal of Honor to marines in World War II and in Vietnam.

Marine Medal of Honor Awards

World War II and Vietnam

Conflict	Awards	Battle Deaths	Ratio
World War II	82	19,733	230
Vietnam	57	13,067	229

Key: Awards, includes only those to marines, omitting those to navy personnel serving in marine units; Battle Deaths includes only marines killed or mortally wounded in action, and omits navy personnel serving in marine units; Ratio is the number of marine battle deaths divided by the number of awards.

Although there were marines in administrative assignments in Vietnam, proportionally more marines were in combat than members of the other services. The difference between the World War II Medal of Honor to battle deaths ratio and that for Vietnam hardly seems worth commenting upon. It is, in fact, considerably less than the differences in the ratio between either of those wars and Korea, where it was 104, a consequence of the use of marines as a fire brigade in the early stages of the war, the long walk out of Chosin, and the desperate outpost battles late in the war.

It's the guys at the front who have the opportunity to do the deeds for which the Medal of Honor is awarded. In this regard, it's worth noting that three Rangers and seventeen Green Berets earned the Medal of Honor, all of them in the course of either long-range patrols or while defending isolated firebases.

The rank of the personnel who were awarded the Medal of Honor also tends to demonstrate the unusual intensity of combat on the small-unit level, and the strains placed on leadership in the conditions that prevailed in Vietnam.

Captains and lieutenants in the army and marines received nearly a fifth

Awards by Rank

Pay Grade (Military/Naval)	Air Force	Army	Marines	Navy	Total	Percentage
Officers						
06 (Colonel/Captain)	1	0	0	1	2	0.8%
05 (Lieutenant Colonel/ Commander)	1	2	0	0	3	1.3%
04 (Major/ Lieutenant Commander)	3	3	0	1	7	2.9%
03 (Captain/ Lieutenant)	5	7	7	3	22	9.2%
02 (First Lieutenant/ Lieutenant, j.g.)	1	20	3	2	26	10.9%
01 (Second Lieutenant/ Ensign)	0	3	2	0	5	2.1%
W (Warrant Officers)	0	2	0	0	2	0.8%
Officer Summary	11	37	12	7	67	28.2%
Enlisted Personnel						
E-7–E-9	0	10	0	0	10	4.2%
E-6	0	24	4	0	28	11.8%
E-5	0	23	5	2	30	12.6%
E-4	0	37	4	2	43	18.1%
E-3	1	21	16	2	40	16.8%
E-2	0	3	16	1	20	8.4%
E-1	0	0	0	0	0	0.0%
Enlisted Summary	1	118	45	7	171	71.8%
Service Summary	12	155	57	14	238	
Service Percentages	5.0%	65.1%	23.9%	5.9%		

Key: Rank is that held at the time the Medal of Honor was earned, not at the time the decoration was awarded, which in some cases was a matter of a good many years.

of all awards of the Medal of Honor in Vietnam. These were the men who led companies and platoons. Mid-level NCOs (E-5s and E-6s) in the army and marines received nearly a quarter of all awards, men who served as squad leaders, platoon sergeants, and company first sergeants, in some cases assuming command when their officers had been killed. Corporals and specialists 4th Class (E4s), often fire team leaders, accounted for nearly another fifth of all awards.

One measure of the seriousness of the combat can be seen in the number of awards that were made posthumously. During World War I, 26.8 percent of the awards of the Medal of Honor were posthumous, a figure that rose to 56.8 percent in World War II, and to 71.0 percent in Korea. For Vietnam, the figure is 63.9 percent, nearly two-thirds of those earning the decoration.

Posthumous Awards of the Medal of Honor

Branch	Awards	Posthumous	Percent
Air Force	12	4	33.3%
Army	155	98	63.2%
Marines	57	44	77.2%
Navy	14	6	42.9%
Total	238	152	63.9%

Another way of looking at the subject is in terms of the principal units that fought the war, the front-line divisions, brigades, and regiments, as shown in the table on page 228. The first major U.S. formation to land in Vietnam was the 173rd Airborne Brigade, which landed on 7 May 1965 and remained until 25 August 1971, 2,301 days, a figure exceeded only by the 2,416 days of the 101st Airborne Division, which arrived later but remained longer. Third place was held by the 1st Cavalry Division, 2,056 days, followed by the 1st and 3rd Marine Divisions, 1,885 and 1,721 days, respectively. These organizations all saw a lot of combat, particularly in an offensive mode. The intensity of that combat, as well as the length of their stay in Vietnam, is partially reflected by the number of awards of the Medal of Honor earned by members of each unit. Interestingly, the most heavily decorated battalion in the war appears to have been the 1st Battalion (Airborne), 8th Cavalry, of the 1st Cavalry Division, five members of which earned the Medal of Honor.

The oldest man to earn a Medal of Honor in Vietnam was Air Force COL William A. Jones, III. An A1-H Skyraider pilot, born on 31 May 1922, he earned his medal helping to rescue a downed pilot on 15 November 1969, dying of wounds as a result, at forty-seven years, five months, and fourteen days. The youngest was Marine Cpl. Larry E. Smedley, born 4 March 1949, who was killed in action conducting a single-handed counterattack against great odds, despite being himself wounded, on 21 December 1967, at the age of eighteen years, nine months, and seven days. The last Medal of Honor awarded for Vietnam went to Special Forces MSG Roy Benavidez on 24 February 1981, by Pres. Ronald Reagan. For many years after his heroism in Cambodia on 2 May 1968, several of Benavidez's former officers had been patiently collecting the necessary evidence to support a nomination for the Medal of Honor. The decoration had actually been approved by Pres. Jimmy Carter in 1980, but he was unable to award it due to the Iran hostage crisis.

It is not possible to determine with a high degree of accuracy the ethnic background of most of the men who earned the Medal of Honor in Vietnam. Twenty black men (fifteen soldiers and five marines) received the Medal of Honor (8.4 percent), the highest ranking of whom was army LTC Charles Rodgers, who earned his while commanding an artillery battalion and even-

Awards by Major Commands

Command	Awards
Army	
101st Airborne Division	17
1st Cavalry Division	25
1st Infantry Division	10
4th Infantry Division	11
9th Infantry Division	10
23rd Infantry Division	15
25th Infantry Division	21
173rd Airborne Brigade	12
1st Aviation Brigade	1
199th Light Infantry Brigade	4
11th Armored Cavalry	3
5th Special Forces Group	13
Marine Corps	
1st Marine Division	28
3rd Marine Division	29

Key: The figure for the 1st Marine Division includes three navy awards, that for the 3rd Marine Division includes one navy award. The figure for the 23rd Infantry Division includes awards to personnel of its component brigades before the division was formed.

tually rose to major general. Based on the evidence of family name or that in combination with place of birth, it appears that the Medal of Honor was also awarded to two men with Asian roots (0.8%), ten with Mexican ties (4.2 percent), three with Puerto Rican connections (1.3 percent), and probably six of Italian background (2.5 percent), as well as three men with Slavic surnames (1.3 percent), two with a Portuguese surname (0.8 percent), and one born in Hungary (0.4 percent). While the number of men with names of Irish and German provenance is considerable, these have become so Americanized as to make assumptions as to ethnicity difficult.

Other Decorations. While it can be demonstrated that the number of awards of the Medal of Honor in the Vietnam War was by no means disproportionate, the same cannot be said for some other decorations. Partially as a means of boosting morale, and partially as a manifestation of careerism run rampant, the Silver Star (the nation's third highest decoration for valor) and other decorations of lesser prestige were distributed with a lavish hand. By 1969, it was not unusual for a battalion commander to be awarded a standard "package" comprising a Silver Star, a Legion of Merit, and several Air Medals upon completion of a six-month tour of duty. In many battalions it was common to award all departing enlisted men in the grades E-7 and above a Bronze Star. GEN Colin Powell remembered a battalion commander who received three Silver Stars, "plus a clutch of other medals," for "a fairly typical performance." Many senior officers and enlisted personnel were in the habit of collecting decorations, which may have made them feel good, but did little for the prestige of the service overall. During 1969, fifty-seven generals of various grades completed their tours of duty and were awarded a total of fifty Distinguished Service Medals and twenty-six Silver Stars, Distinguished Flying Crosses, or Bronze Stars. In contrast, of about 350,000 enlisted personnel who completed their tours of duty that same year, only about 30,000 received similar honors.

Merely getting killed in action might easily earn one several honors. It was not unusual for a rear echelon–type in a supposedly secure area, who was killed by an enemy rocket attack, to be posthumously awarded a Bronze Star and a Legion of Merit. Plus the Purple Heart given to all who are injured by enemy action. At the peak of the war, the army was awarding nearly 1.4 million decorations a year, not to mention numerous service medals. The most commonly awarded was the National Defense Service Medal, which became popularly known as the "warm body award," since everyone who entered the service received one.

The worst abuses involved the Air Medal. The Air Medal had been created during World War II, when aircrews were incurring horrendous losses during the strategic bombardment of Germany. The bloodiest U.S. campaign of the war, with some 40,000 Americans killed in action during its earliest phase, it was statistically probable that a bomber crew would be lost before it completed its prescribed twenty-five missions (remember *The Memphis Belle* and *Catch-22?*). To encourage and honor airmen, the Air Medal was instituted for those who had completed twenty-five combat air missions. This seems reasonable enough, but at the time there were no helicopters. In Vietnam, helicopters logged millions of hours and most of the country was a combat zone. Chopper pilots were soon earning repeated awards of the Air Medal. And since helicopters were effectively "battlefield taxis," lots of other personnel began accumulating multiple awards of the Air Medal as well, particularly battalion commanders and higher-ranking officers, who often flitted about just overhead supervising the battle and in the process earning the Air Medal over and over again. Even chaplains accumulated multiple awards of the Air Medal, their duties often requiring them to make the rounds of various firebases in hostile areas, which counted as an air combat mission even if no fire was received. In 1971, some 800,000 Air Medals were awarded (plus another 475,000 other decorations). One young officer, commanding a scout dog platoon, was so disgusted with the system that he put his animals in for the Air Medal, on the grounds that they, being "in country" for the duration, had logged more airtime than anyone in his division.

The Vietnam War began what can only be termed a "medal mania" in the U.S. armed forces that continues to the present, particularly in the army and the air force. By the time our young soldiers and airmen have finished their first enlistments, they are sporting more medals than ever were worn by some of the most noted military heroes of the past, such as John J. Pershing.

The Navy Cross. Second only to the Medal of Honor is the Navy Cross, which is officially coequal with the army's Distinguished Service Cross and the Air Force Cross. It is awarded for heroism in combat not deemed sufficiently outstanding as to merit a Medal of Honor to members of the naval service (sailors, marines, and coastguardsmen) and other personnel serving with the naval service. During the Vietnam War most awards were made to marines or navy medics for heroism in ground combat or to navy and marine pilots.

Vietnam Awards of the Navy Cross

Service	Number
USMC	362*
U.S. Navy	119**
U.S. Army	1
RVN Navy	1***
Total	483

*Two marines earned the Navy Cross twice in Vietnam, while two others had earned a second one in Vietnam, having received their first in Korea.
**Two other awards were made to crewmen of the USS *Liberty*.
***Awarded to a Vietnamese petty officer 3rd class who was serving with a USN SEAL team.

It hardly seems necessary to suggest that there does not seem to have been any "inflation" in the award of the Navy Cross.

THE DRUG PROBLEM

By one reckoning, the Vietnam War led to some 60,000 cases of heroin addiction among the troops. Like so much about the war, this is very difficult to pin down. If true, it would mean that approximately one out of every forty-five soldiers sent to Vietnam became a heroin addict. The extent of other addictions cannot be determined.

There certainly was a lot of drug abuse in Vietnam. Perhaps as much as there was in the United States at the time, a matter often overlooked (remember Dr. Timothy Leary's advice to young Americans?). Although conspiracy theorists have charged that the CIA introduced drugs into Vietnam, in fact they were very easy to come by in the country, and had been for some time. Illegal for many years, a corrupt political system ensured that they were more or less openly available. Marijuana grew wild, opium was cultivated in the highlands, and heroin and other drugs were widely manufactured.

By far the most commonly abused drug in Vietnam was alcohol, followed by marijuana. A lot of troops also seem to have experimentally smoked heroin and opium. Injection of drugs was less common, but still happened frequently enough to be considered an epidemic. Although there was some drug abuse among the troops right from the start, it tended to be insignificant until after Tet, when morale, previously high, began to decline. While the armed forces attempted to deal with the problem, there were too many drugs available, and the Vietnamese civil police were apparently deeply involved in the trade.

It is probable that some of the approximately 2,750 military personnel who deserted while still in Vietnam were either addicts or drug dealers, the latter perhaps feeling the CID (Criminal Investigation Division) closing in on them.

The VC and NVA seem to have had some problems with drug addiction as well. But their methods of coping with addicts and dealers were rather harsher than American ones. Where U.S. policy considered addicts sick people in need of treatment, the Communists considered them criminals in need of severe punishment. This, along with a policy of executing drug dealers, seems to have kept the problem under control.

LOOTING

Stealing from the enemy is an ancient military tradition. It was visibly present during the Vietnam War. What was different here was that one side (the South Vietnamese) were much more prone to loot than the other (the Viet Cong and North Vietnamese). The reason was simple; the Communists were fighting the war politically and militarily, while the South Vietnamese concentrated on the battlefield angle. Both sides knew that their troops would be fighting among the population and for the people's loyalty. Both sides played lip service to this "serve the people" angle. But the North Vietnamese did something about it (looting was forbidden and the rule was enforced), while the South Vietnamese did not (looting was sort of forbidden and commanders usually looked the other way). This helped the Communists a lot, for in previous wars, when both sides looted, neither could expect much voluntary assistance from the population. Not that the Communists were golden when it came to the opinion polls. The people knew that the Communists tried to exploit the public relations angle of American bombs and shells falling on civilians, and the Viet Cong would open fire on Americans from a village knowing that the return fire would level the place and kill a lot of civilians.

Not all South Vietnamese units looted, but most did. Much of what South Vietnamese combat troops did was patrol the countryside looking for Viet Cong and North Vietnamese troops. The typical Vietnamese outlook was that if someone was not from their village or family, they were strangers, potential enemies, and fair game. The South Vietnamese officers did little to change this attitude and often tolerated the looting because "it was good for morale." Sometimes the "freedom to loot" was used as a tool to control the troops and the local civilians. A commander would forbid looting in villages that resisted Viet Cong infiltration, but would allow it to "punish" an un-cooperative village. But most of the time, the troops were not punished if they came back with items (including furniture) stolen from a village they had swept through.

American helicopter crews were often shocked (at least the first time) when they came down to pick up South Vietnamese troops and found their allies expecting their loot to be airlifted too. This led to yet another dispute between Americans and their South Vietnamese allies. While American units sometimes looted, they knew it was wrong. The South Vietnamese troops often felt it was a fringe benefit.

Looting enemy military forces was another matter. The Communist soldiers were allowed to grab what they could from dead, wounded, and captured enemy troops. Everyone did that, but it meant a lot more to the Communist soldiers because they had so little in the way of material goodies to begin with. Looting the enemy had long been a necessity for the Communist troops. Lacking a steady source of weapons and supplies, taking them from the enemy made sense. Nothing was wasted. A certain percentage of bombs and shells fired at the Communists did not explode. Despite the danger, these duds would be opened up and the explosives recycled for home-made mines, grenades, and similar devices. Enemy weapons, except from things like tanks or aircraft (which required too much maintenance to keep going) were used to arm new guerrilla fighters and replace lost or broken weapons. Arguably, one could better call this approach recycling rather than looting.

Not taking things from the civilians was not entirely altruistic, for the Communist guerrillas depended on the population for donations of food and other materials, as well as information and recruits.

To many, the fact that the South Vietnamese troops looted liberally and the Communist soldiers hardly ever served to show who were the good guys and who were not. There is some truth to that, but not a lot. The South Vietnamese government was corrupt, no doubt about it. But in the fullness of time, the Communists demonstrated a talent for corruption that matched, or exceeded, whatever the South Vietnamese government had achieved.

THE MY LAI MASSACRE

The worst atrocity *ever* committed by U.S. troops was perpetrated on 16 March 1968 by personnel of C Company, 1st Battalion, 20th Infantry, an element of the 11th Light Infantry Brigade of the 23rd "Americal" Division. The incident occurred in the hamlet of My Lai 4, one of several in Son My village, a part of the Son Tinh District of Quang Ngai Province, one of the largest and most populous provinces in South Vietnam and an area known for its Viet Cong sympathies. On that morning, as part of a larger "search and destroy" operation, 2nd Lt William L. Calley had led his troops into the village, which they had been informed was occupied by a VC battalion. In fact, there were no armed VC in the hamlet. In My Lai 4, Calley basically ordered his troops to undertake a systematic massacre. At least 150 and possibly as many as 400 Vietnamese civilians, mostly old men, women, children, and even infants, were killed. Many of the troops protested, refusing to take part despite threats from Calley that they would be subject to a court-martial. One soldier going so far as to shoot himself in the foot, while a helicopter pilot, WO Hugh C. Thompson, Jr., personally prevented the murder of a number of villagers by threatening to fire on the troops with his minigun.

In the after-action report on the operation, Calley indicated that his men had killed 128 enemy troops, for which a citation was issued.

From the first, the nature of the action was known to Calley's superiors, among them his company commander, CPT Ernest Medina, who was actually present in the hamlet for a time during the massacre. The battalion commander, the task force commander, and the brigade commander all apparently knew about what had occurred almost immediately afterwards, as did the division commander, MG Samuel W. Koster, and several chaplains attached to the 11th Light Infantry Brigade. None of them did anything about the matter. Attempts by soldiers to report the incident through the chain of command were quashed. Outsiders from the army staff who inquired about anomalies in the official report of the "battle" (only a handful of weapons were reported recovered, and there were virtually no American casualties, a truly remarkable circumstance), were brushed off by double-talk or bluster. Meanwhile, Communist propaganda broadcasts began circulating information about the massacre, though this was ignored, if only because the North Vietnamese were in the habit of endlessly fabricating atrocity tales.

Not until the spring of 1969 did the massacre come to the attention of the army, when Vietnam veteran Ronald Ridenhour—who had not been present at My Lai—wrote a letter to the chairman of the Armed Services Committee, reporting that he had heard from several other soldiers that a massacre had occurred. The letter was passed on to Secretary of the Army Stanley Resor, who passed it on to GEN William Westmoreland, by then Chief-of-Staff of the Army. Westmoreland immediately ordered the army's

Criminal Investigation Division to undertake an inquiry. Soon afterward Westmoreland went further, appointing LG William R. Peers to undertake a broader investigation. Peers, himself a Vietnam veteran who had command the 4th Infantry Division (January 1967–January 1968) and the I Field Force (March 1968–March 1969), undertook an extensive probe, focusing primarily on the cover-up and the causes of the massacre, rather than the actual criminal activity, which was the responsibility of the CID.

General Peers conducted a far-reaching inquiry, journeying to My Lai itself. An enormous amount of evidence was turned up, including an extraordinary collection of chilling photographs taken by army photographer SGT Ronald Hoeberle, who had accompanied the troops into My Lai.

The conclusion of the inquiry was that there had been massive command failures right up to General Koster. Among the factors cited were poor training in the Law of War and the Rules of Engagement, a virulent anti-Vietnamese institutional culture in the division, poor discipline and poor leadership at all levels, excessive fear of the enemy, poor organization, and poor communications. Unsaid was that the army's leadership training had declined so seriously that a man like William L. Calley, who had never held a permanent job and had actually flunked out of junior college, could receive a commission.

Charges were brought against twenty-five soldiers (fourteen officers and eleven enlisted men), twelve of them for war crimes (two officers and ten enlisted men) and the rest (twelve officers and one enlisted man) for military offenses arising out of the cover-up. Among those charged were the brigade, battalion, and company commander, as well as Lieutenant Calley and several staff officers, including two chaplains. In the end, however, only four cases went to trial, the others being dismissed on technicalities (some of the investigators had committed serious procedural violations, and coercion was used to get some enlisted men to testify). Of the four men tried, three were not convicted due to technicalities. Calley was sentenced to life in prison, but this was reduced first to twenty years, then to ten by the civilian authorities, and finally to two years of house arrest. So judicial penalties for the atrocity were comparatively light. However, there were other penalties, procedural ones, which the army imposed.

General Koster, who flatly lied to the investigators, was removed from his choice post-Vietnam assignment as superintendent of cadets at West Point. He was reduced to his permanent rank of brigadier general, stripped of his Distinguished Service Medal, and received a formal reprimand, effectively ending his military career. Virtually all of the other officers who had been charged—and some who had not—found their promotion prospects reduced to nil, received reprimands, had major decorations rescinded, or some combination of all three. Eight enlisted men who had been prominent in the massacre were expelled from the army.

U.S. Military Personnel Charged with War Crimes

Service	Cases	Convictions
Army	130	75 (57.7%)
Marines	90	46 (51.1%)
Total	220	121 (55.0%)

Key: Figures do not include several instances in which the men under investigation were killed in action before formal charges were filed, nor one man found unfit to stand trial by reason of mental disorder. Most convictions were sustained by higher authorities. For example, only two of twenty-seven cases in which marines were convicted of murder were overturned, with the average sentence being six years.

AMERICAN WAR CRIMES TRIALS

Although war is inherently an atrocity, for some reason the notion that wars can be fought "humanely" persist, so soldiers are supposed to refrain from all sorts of activities. In general American troops do, with a few glaring exceptions. In fact, since the nineteenth century the United States has had a record of prosecuting its own personnel in instances where atrocities may have been perpetrated. Few other countries bother. In the Vietnam War the United States continued this practice. Altogether 220 cases were brought, and 121 men were convicted on charges ranging from rape to mass murder, as well as several instances of filing false reports to cover up atrocities.

Unfortunately, the U.S. effort to bring those guilty of war crimes to justice has received little attention. Cynics often observed that it was merely tokenism in any case. Certainly the armed forces were unable to prosecute everyone guilty of atrocities. But at least they made an effort. The enemy, conveniently overlooking their own far more numerous atrocities, kept up a steady stream of propaganda that inflated the number and scale of these incidents. Misguided journalists and antiwar activists repeated the charges without investigation, and many flatly denied the possibility that the other side had ever done anything wrong.

SOME QUESTIONABLE WEAPONS OF THE VIETNAM WAR

A lot of innovative weapons first saw combat in Vietnam. Many proved enormously effective, such as the F-4, the claymore mine, the AH-1G Huey-cobra, the gunship, and even, after some teething problems, the M-16 rifle. But some did not. Several apparently sound ideas turned out to be lemons— or perhaps semi-lemons—when tested under fire. But that's nothing new. Military equipment is usually designed in peacetime to meet a perceived need. Often only combat can tell if it's really useful. During the Vietnam War, a number of items in Uncle Sam's arsenal proved wanting.

"Ontos." The M501A1 "Ontos" (Greek for "Thing") was a tracked, self-propelled light antitank weapons system equipped with six 106 mm recoilless rifles. Marine infantry battalions included several of these early in the war. It was originally developed by the army, which subsequently refused to adopt it, which should have tipped off the Marine Corps. In combat in Vietnam, the gun mounts proved fragile. Despite this, the system proved very effective, in limited situations, such as street fighting, and it proved immensely useful in Hue during Tet. But if one had to fire more than six rounds, it proved almost impossible to reload under fire. It was withdrawn after Tet and retired by 1970.

"Mechanical Mules." The M278 "Mechanical Mule" was an odd-looking four-wheel-drive vehicle (basically it looked like an long narrow table with four wheels attached and a steering column at one end). Weighing 925 pounds, it was capable of carrying over a thousand pounds at up to fifteen miles per hour over reasonably firm, more or less level ground, and could even operate with one wheel broken ("hobbled"). For a time, marine battalions were supplied with thirty of the beasts, eight of which were equipped with a 106 mm recoilless rifle. But the Mule was noisy, and rather delicate, and not very useful in combat. They disappeared after Tet.

"People Sniffers." The XM-2 Personnel Detector, nicknamed "the People Sniffer," was an electrochemical device that could be used from aircraft to detect concentrations of enemy troops by the presence of molecules of urine and related compounds in the atmosphere. It actually did work. But it was a bit oversensitive, which probably led to the deaths of several farmers and water buffalo who had the misfortune to answer the call of nature when one of the devices was in use. In any case, the VC quickly learned to "spoof" it by hanging buckets of urine in places where they wanted us to think they had troops. The "People Sniffer" was useful, but had to be used with some caution.

"Operations Research (OR)." A series of mathematical techniques for analyzing seemingly random phenomena, OR had proven of value during World War II in the rationalization of the antisubmarine campaign in the Atlantic and, after the war, in analyzing the effects of the Strategic Bombing Campaigns against Germany and Japan. When used wisely, with careful attention paid to history and experience, it was—and remains—a useful tool. Unfortunately, it fit well with the "war is a science" thinking of Robert S. McNamara and his "slide rule commandos" at the Defense Department (whose motto might well have been "Out Manage the Foe"), who believed that new technologies and techniques of warfare had rendered experience and history irrelevant. As a result, all sorts of "quantitative measurements" (like "body counts") were developed to determine whether we were winning or not. In his memoirs Colin Powell recalled that while serving as a staff officer in Vietnam one of his duties was to supply data to an officer engaged in a very secret project. After months of work the man emerged to announce that "regression analysis" had determined that the most likely time for an enemy mortar attack was on moonless nights. As Powell noted, "Weeks of statistical analysis had taught this guy what any ARVN private could have told him in five seconds." In the post-Vietnam reform of the armed forces, OR was dethroned, but its proponents are still at work.

"The McNamara Line." Sometimes known as "the Barrier Concept," this wasn't a weapon, but a plan to stem NVA infiltration across the DMZ that stretched sixty miles along the seventeenth parallel between North and South Vietnam, from the South China Sea to Laos. The idea was to create, in the words of Robert McNamara, "an interdiction zone covered by air-laid mines and bombing attacks pinpointed by air-laid acoustical sensors," which would prevent enemy movement into and across the DMZ. First thought up by Prof. Roger Fisher of Harvard Law School in 1966, the notion was heavily worked over by scientists at the Institute for Defense Analysis, vetted by a couple of senior military officers, and presented by McNamara to President Johnson in October 1966. Johnson liked the plan because, although estimated to cost $1 billion, it was nonescalating and did not involve putting U.S. troops at risk.

Construction began with some fanfare in April 1967, when marines on the DMZ cleared an 8.2-mile strip some 660 yards wide along the DMZ, wired it in, and liberally seasoned it with mines and various types of sensors (Operation Dye Marker). There were a number of obstacles to completing the barrier. These included shellings by NVA troops and opposition by most senior American military personnel to "a jungle Maginot line," which tied down large numbers of troops, who were required not merely to build the barrier but also to guard and maintain it once it was built. There were also political difficulties with Laos, since the initial plans for the barrier envisioned driving it partially across Laos. The line was quietly abandoned in 1968.

Supersonic Aircraft. One of the new technologies that caught on in a big way in the 1950s was supersonic speed for aircraft. One of the hottest new aircraft was the US F-105, a fighter bomber that could do nearly 1,400 miles an hour. A costly bit of 1950's technology (c. $3 million in money of 1997), the F-105 was the heaviest single-seat bomber in use. It became immensely popular with the troops in Vietnam. Yet its supersonic capabilities were rarely used. There were two reasons for this. First, supersonic speed depended on an elaborate system of ductwork and flaps at the engine air intake.

This gear was difficult to maintain and was only needed for supersonic flight. In Vietnam there was never enough time to keep everything else on the aircraft operational, and in any case there weren't many opportunities to use supersonic speed. So it was common to ignore the extra equipment and just forgo supersonic flight. The other reason for doing without supersonic speed was that it was not really necessary for most bombing missions. In fact, the much higher fuel consumption of supersonic flight provided pilots with less safety margin on the long-distance bombing missions the F-105s performed over North Vietnam. Clearly, supersonic speed for the F-105 was unworkable in combat for both maintenance and tactical reasons.

The F-111 Fighter Bomber. The F-111 was a product of the McNamara era. Originally intended as a carrier-based bomber for the navy, the McNamara Whiz Kids had gotten hold of it and converted it into a "general purpose" fighter to be used by both the navy and the air force. So a lot of changes had to be made. Pretty soon the navy was complaining that it was too heavy for carrier operations, and the air force was expressing reservations as well. Nevertheless, apparently under considerable prodding from the Department of Defense (which wished to vindicate the investment), the air force sent a half-dozen F-111s to Thailand for trials in March 1968. Less than three months later, the three surviving aircraft were withdrawn. An average of one aircraft had been lost in every eighteen sorties, a horrendous rate. The three aircraft that had gone down succumbed to mechanical or electronic failure. The airplane was heavily modified. It returned to service during the Linebacker missions in 1972 and performed superbly. The F-111 went on to render excellent service during the Libyan Confrontation in 1986 and Operation Desert Storm in 1991. The problem was that the airplane was rushed into service before it had been thoroughly tested.

Missiles. By the time the United States became heavily involved in the Vietnam War, guided missiles had been around for some two decades. The public was used to seeing pictures of missiles—whether air-to-air or surface-to-air—hitting drone targets, and there had been the spectacular downing of Francis Gary Powers's U-2 spy plane over Russia in 1960. So much was expected of missiles. Yet in action, both types of missile proved disappointing. North Vietnam may have fired as many as 10,000 SA-2 surface-to-air missiles during the war, but these accounted for only 196 airplanes, about 24 percent of American airplane losses. Even the best American air-to-air missile, the AIM-9D, seems to have been effective only about 18 percent of the time. What had gone wrong? A lot. All that testing had been done under, well, "test conditions." The test missiles were maintained and installed by the same highly trained technicians who developed them. Tests were conducted under ideal weather conditions, so that careful film records could be made. And the drones were flown by pilots sitting comfortably on the ground using remote control. In combat things were a little different. Maintenance and installation of the missiles was not always done perfectly, nor were the missiles necessarily up to the extremes of heat and humidity that prevailed in Southeast Asia. The weather usually didn't cooperate either. Then, too, the targets were being flown by guys who were acutely aware of their own mortality, and thus much more likely to engage in erratic maneuvers to throw the missiles "off the scent." And, of course, those who fired the missiles during tests didn't have unfriendly folk trying to kill them. The missiles did work, and, in fact, have gotten better. But they didn't work as well as had been expected. Few weapons ever do.

CHAPTER 9

Numbers and Losses

Various forms of loss, physical and psychological, both during the war and long afterward.

AMERICAN CASUALTIES

Some 350,000 Americans became combat casualties in Vietnam. Approximately one out of every ten Americans who became a combat casualty in the Vietnam War was killed in action or died of wounds. Two others were permanently disabled, another two seriously wounded but recovered, four more were so lightly wounded as not to require hospitalization, and one was a psychoneurotic casualty. In both world wars the figures for American casualties averaged one in seven killed, one permanently disabled, four others less seriously wounded, and one psychoneurotic casualty. The decline in the proportion of killed in action was partially due to the character of the war— no warships or troop transports were sunk, there were no massive amphibious invasions, and so forth—and partially to the speed and effectiveness of American medical treatment during the war. Medevac helicopters made it possible for very severely wounded men to receive treatment far sooner than would have been the case in World War II. In addition, great strides in medicine made treatment more effective. As a result, troops who by the standards of the 1940s would probably have died, pulled through. However, this also meant that the proportion of those surviving their wounds who were permanently disabled, usually by reason of amputations or other crippling consequences of their wounds, was higher than in World War II. In this regard it's worth noting that during the Civil War approximately one out of every four men injured in combat died, but only about one out of every fifteen was permanently disabled, since most severely wounded men could not be saved by the medical technology of the times.

Although noncombat deaths in Vietnam seemed to be high (nearly 20 percent of total deaths), in fact they were the lowest of any of the country's major wars.

Some 2.6–2.8 million Americans served in the combat zone during the

American Combat Casualties in Vietnam

Type	Number	Percent of All Casualties
Combat Deaths	c. 47,000	13%
Permanently Disabled	c. 75,000	21%
Seriously Wounded	c. 80,000	23%
Lightly Wounded	c. 150,000	43%

American Military Dead in Southeast Asia, 1962–75

	Army	Navy	Marines	Air Force	Total
Killed in Action	25,341	1,097	11,490	504	38,432
Died of Wounds	3,521	146	1,454	48	5,169
Presumed Dead	1,806	266	67	735	2,874
Died as POW	34	18	8	23	83
Noncombat	7,193	910	1,684	603	10,390
Missing	166	77	43	409	695
Total	37,895	2,437	14,703	1,913	56,948

Coast Guard losses were seven KIA, fifty-three wounded, one missing.

U.S. War Deaths, 1775–1991

Conflict	All Deaths	Battle Deaths
Revolutionary War	4,400+	4,400
War of 1812	2,300+	2,300
Mexican War	13.300	1,700 (13.0%)
Civil War:		
Union	360,000	110,100 (30.6%)
Confederate	198,500	74,500 (37.5%)
Combined	558,500	184,600 (33.1%)
Spanish-American War	2,500	400 (15.7%)
Philippine Insurrection	5,000	1,000 (20.0%)
World War I	116,800	53,500 (45.9%)
World War II	407,300	292,100 (71.7%)
Korean War	55,000	33,600 (61.2%)
Vietnam War	58,000	47,400 (81.7%)
Gulf War	300	150 (50.0%)

Key: All figures are rounded, as even in bureaucratized modern societies the precise numbers are actually highly imprecise. The figure in parentheses is the percentage of all dead that were battle deaths. No figures on nonbattle deaths are available for the Revolutionary War or 1812, nor can estimates be made with any hope of precision.

Cause of American Deaths in Vietnam

Cause	Number
Accidents: General	1,366
Accidents: Other	1,326
Accidents: Self-destruction	841
Accidents: Vehicular	1,184
Aircraft: Crashes at Sea	494
Aircraft: Crashes on Land	8,461
Burns	526
Combat: Artillery and Rocket Fire	4,909
Combat: Bullets	18,452
Combat: Mines and Traps	7,429
Combat: Multiple Fragmentation	8,451
Combat: Other	50
Disease: Hepatitis	22
Disease: Malaria	117
Disease: Other	481
Drowned or suffocated	1,202
Natural Causes: Heart attack	268
Natural Causes: Stroke	42
Other: Murder	943
Other: Suicide	381
Other: Unknown	737
Unknown and not reported	567

Key: Not all combat-related deaths are listed under "Combat." Many aircraft deaths were also combat deaths, as are some of those from burns, drowning, and suffocation (tunnel rats sometimes died from lack of air in VC tunnels). Most of the categories are self-explanatory, but some may require a little explication. *Accidents: General* includes things like falling off ladders, getting run over by bulldozers, and so forth. *Accidents: Self-destruction* means someone blew himself up or shot himself—all that weaponry lying around could be lethal to the careless. *Combat: Mines and Traps* includes not only explosive mines and booby traps but things like *punji* sticks (actually very ineffective) and similar nonexplosive devices. *Combat: Multiple Fragmentation Wounds* means someone was so badly mangled as to make determining the cause of death difficult. *Combat: Other* refers to those killed in hand-to-hand fighting by knives, and even an occasional death by arrows.

Vietnam War. There was a 1.8-percent chance of being killed in action (c. 47,400), a 5.6-percent chance of being seriously wounded but surviving the experience (c. 153,300), and about the same chance of being lightly wounded (an estimated 150,000 troops suffered wounds that did not require a hospital stay). Of course, combat casualties amounted to only about 60 percent of American casualties in Vietnam, with disease accounting for another 25 percent, and misadventure (accidents, suicides, murders, and drug overdoses) for another 15 percent. Casualties from all causes, both combat and noncombat, amounted to somewhat over 58,000 dead (2.1 per-

Casualties by Rank

Rank	Grade	Killed	Percentage
MG	O-8	3	*
BG	O-7	5	*
Col	O-6	25	0.1%
LtCol	O-5	126	0.3%
Maj	O-4	304	0.8%
Capt	O-3	1,034	2.7%
1st Lt	O-2	1,487	3.9%
2nd Lt	O-1	400	1.0%
CWO	WO-3/4	425	1.1%
WO	WO-1/2	823	2.1%
SMaj	E-9	60	0.2%
MSgt	E-8	197	0.5%
FSgt	E-8	77	0.2%
PSgt	E-7	140	0.4%
SFC	E-7	1,011	2.6%
SP7	E-7	2	*
SSgt	E-6	2,434	6.4%
SP6	E-6	61	0.2%
Sgt	E-5	5,324	13.9%
SP5	E-5	1,359	3.6%
Cpl	E-4	3,674	9.6%
SP4	E-4	9,408	24.6%
PFC	E-3	9,365	24.5%
Pvt	E-2	513	1.3%
Total		38,260	100%

Key: The table includes noncombat deaths among army personnel. It is arranged by descending order of rank. Grade indicates the standard military pay grades. Certain enlisted pay grades included several fine distinctions of rank. There were no privates E-1 (trainees) in Vietnam, and the only E-2s were normally men who had been "busted" (reduced in rank) for some infraction. Other unusual ranks: SP4 (specialist 4th class) was a post–World War II rank equal to corporal (CPL), with the same pay, but not the same leadership responsibility. Corporal was the lowest NCO (non-commissioned officer) rank, while SP4 was, in effect, a "senior PFC" (private first class). Many skilled troops in infantry units were made SP4s, and often took over leadership roles when the incumbents had become casualties. SP5 and SP6 were similar ranks for the same pay grades as sergeant and staff sergeant. There were nine enlisted pay grades, from E-1 (recruit, only used for trainees) to E-9 (sergeant major). Some enlisted pay grades covered two possible ranks: an E-8 could be a first sergeant (FSgt) if the senior enlisted man in a company or a master sergeant (MSgt) if not. An E-7 would be a platoon sergeant (PSgt) if in charge of a platoon, or a sergeant first class (SFC) if not. There were ten officer ranks, from 2nd lieutenant (O-1) to four-star general (O-10). There were four warrant officer ranks (WO-1 to WO-4) to officer ranks O-1 to O-4. WO 3-4 were called "chief warrant officer." Most warrant officer casualties were helicopter pilots.

*Indicates statistically too small to show.

American Deaths in Vietnam, Year by Year

Year	Combat Dead	Other Dead	Total Dead
1966	5,008	1,045	6,053
1967	9,378	1,680	11,058
1968	14,592	1,919	16,511
1969	9,414	2,113	11,527
1970	4,221	1,844	6,065
1971	1,380	968	2,348
1972	300	261	561

Casualty Comparison Between Volunteers and Draftees in the Army During the Vietnam War

	1968	1969	1970
Draftees			
Percent of Army	42	38	39
Percent Casualties	58	61	65
Volunteers			
Percent of Army	58	61	61
Percent Casualties	42	38	35

cent of those who served), and about 362,000 wounded, sick, or injured, for a total of about 418,000. Statistically this means that just about one in every six Americans in the war zone became a casualty of some sort. Since there were some troops who were injured or ill several times, the actual figure was somewhat lower.

Obviously, not everyone had the same chances of getting killed in Vietnam. It depended a lot on what you were doing. Being in the infantry was dangerous, but even there, it could get worse. For example, infantrymen going into action via helicopter had about a 10-percent chance of hitting a "Hot LZ" (landing zone under fire). This meant higher casualties. Not coincidentally, about 9 percent of all combat deaths were in helicopters. A slightly lower number were in helicopters that had noncombat-related accidents. So just about over 15 percent of all deaths in Vietnam involved helicopters. Even with all that carnage, it was still more dangerous to be on the ground as an infantryman. Helicopter crews were a distant second in that department. The pilots actually were a little safer than their passengers (door gunners, crew chief, passengers) because the pilots had armored seats. What made helicopters so dangerous was that parachutes were not carried, a point that brought fixed-wing pilots up short when they were reminded

American Vietnam Deaths by Race

	Number	Percent
American Indian	225	.38
Black	7,273	12.36
East Asian	121	.20 (Chinese, etc.)
Malayan	254	.43 (Filipino, Indonesian, etc.)
Unknown or not reported	128	.21
White	50,478	86.31

of this fact. Helicopter pilots brought their bird down in one piece or died trying. There was no "bail out" option.

Most of the people in the armed forces are enlisted personnel. Casualties more or less naturally reflected this. In fact, the rank profile of those killed in Vietnam was pretty much the same as for World War II. The chart on page 243 shows army deaths by rank.

Early in the war, volunteers and draftees took losses roughly in proportion to their numbers. But by 1968, those faced with military service realized there was a way to avoid combat without dodging the draft. All you had to do was volunteer. Very few of the jobs in the army involved combat, and volunteers were given first pick of these noncombat jobs (to encourage volunteering). With fewer recruits volunteering for combat jobs, the ranks of the infantry had to be filled with draftees. (See chart on page 244.)

The Vietnam War was the first major war since the Civil War in which a majority of combat deaths were caused by infantry small arms, though never before had mines and similar devices caused so high a proportion of deaths.

Causes of Combat Fatalities Among Army Troops

Agent	Percent
Small Arms Fire	55%
Shelling and Shell Fragments	35%
Mines and Booby Traps	7%
Other and Undetermined	3%

Key: Small Arms Fire includes deaths caused by rifle, machine gun, or pistol bullets. Shelling and Shell Fragments includes the result of artillery, mortar, rocket, or grenade explosions. Mines and Booby Traps include nonexplosive as well as explosive devices (the dread punji stakes actually caused very few deaths, though they did inflict about 2 percent of all wounds suffered by American forces)—note that recent claims of mines having caused "63 percent" of American casualties in Vietnam have been created from whole cloth for political reasons. Other and Undetermined includes things like flamethrowers, various other agents (like knives), and cases where the cause of death was unknown.

In both world wars and in Korea more than half of all combat deaths had been inflicted by artillery fire, with small arms accounting for less than a third and mines for about 3 percent.

CASUALTIES COMPARED

Casualties of the Vietnam War

	Military Casualties			*Civilian Casualties*	
	Combat Deaths	*Other Deaths*	*Injured*	*Killed*	*Injured*
The Allies					
Australia	414	60	2,940		
South Vietnam	210,000	na	500,000	350,000	950,000
United States	46,498	10,388	180,000		
Other	4,813	na	na		
NVA/VC	800,000	na	2,100,000	65,000	180,000

Key: For North Vietnamese/VC and South Vietnamese forces, *Combat Deaths* include *Other Deaths.* For all countries *Injured* includes both combat and noncombat injuries. Under *Civilian Casualties,* all deaths are included under *Killed.* Civilian losses for Australia, the United States, and the other Allied powers are very unclear. *Other* includes New Zealand, the Philippines, South Korea, and Thailand, casualty figures for which are unclear. Officially, New Zealand lost 55 men killed in action, South Korea 4,407, and Thailand 351, but there do not seem to be published figures for noncombat deaths and nonfatal injuries. No figures at all were found for Philippine troops.

The figures for Vietnamese, military or civilian, are estimates based on the high and low figures reported in various sources. Many senior North Vietnamese leaders have admitted publicly that they have no precise figure for the losses, while South Vietnamese records were not very good to begin with, and many were lost at the end of the war. The two Vietnams fought for over twenty years, although the vast majority of the heavy fighting was in the 1960s. The United States was only heavily involved from 1965 to 1970. Vietnam as a whole took a terrible beating. With an average population of 42 million during the twenty-year war, it suffered an overall death rate of 3.6 percent and an overall casualty rate of 12 percent. Because most of the combat losses were Communist troops, and most of these were North Vietnamese, the North and the South suffered about equally when it came to casualties. But most of the fear was in the South, for that's where the Communists waged an unrelenting terror campaign among the civilian population. Some estimates put civilian casualties in the South as high as 1.8 million, including 350,000–500,000 dead, plus c. 175,000 permanently disabled.

ALLIED COMBAT BATTALIONS IN VIETNAM

At the peak of the Vietnam War nearly 1.5 million troops from seven countries were in Vietnam.

Allied Combat Battalions in Vietnam, 1965–72

Year End Strength

Country	'65	'66	'67	'68	'69	'70	'71	'72
Australia	1	2	2	3	3	3	0	0
ROK	10	22	22	22	22	22	0	0
Thailand	0	0	1	3	6	6	3	0
Philippines	2	2	2	0	0	0	0	0
New Zealand	0	0	1	1	1	1	0	0
U.S.	73	152	214	239	219	147	47	0
Allied Total	86	174	242	268	251	179	50	0
RVN	152	163	203	232	247	247	255	230
Grand Total	238	337	445	500	498	426	305	230

Key: Table lists all types of infantry battalions, as well as armor and cavalry, artillery, combat engineer, and combat aviation. ARVN strength includes marines. In 1959–64 it rose from c. 95 battalions to c. 135. The apparent reduction in ARVN strength in 1971–72 was due to reorganization of the Rangers and some other forces. In 1965–66, New Zealand had a single artillery battery in Vietnam, not shown; to which were added two infantry companies, 1967–70, to make a battalion equivalent.

U.S. Combat Battalions in Vietnam

Unit Type	1965	1966	1967	1968	1969	1970	1971	1972
Armor	1	9	11	12	12	7	2	0
Artillery	20	42	59	67	59	39	6	0
Aviation	17	24	39	44	46	37	22	0
Engineer	13	23	33	35	30	23	5	0
Infantry	22	54	72	81	72	41	12	0

EYE INJURIES IN VIETNAM

Partially as a consequence of changes in weaponry, and partially as a consequence of the nature of the war, in Vietnam eye injuries were unusually high compared with earlier experience.

The eyes represent only a very small portion of the human target. In the stand-up style of combat that prevailed during much of the Civil War, they were much less likely to be injured than some other part of the anatomy. In subsequent wars, troops routinely began to "take cover," and thus the eyes become increasingly exposed to danger, largely as a result of the reduction of the total body area exposed. Technology plays a role as well, with the introduction of explosive and fragmenting ammunition, since the eyes are more sensitive than most other parts of the body. Thus they are far more

Eye Injuries as a Proportion of All Wounds, 1861–1973

War	Eye Injuries
Civil War (1861–65)	.57%
World War I (1914–18)	2.14%
World War II (1939–45)	
ETO	c. 2.0%
Pacific	4.1%
Korean War (1950–53)	8.0%
Vietnam War (1965–72)	9.0%
Six-Day War (1967)	5.6%
Yom Kippur War (1973)	6.7%

vulnerable to minor bits of metal, glass, gravel, vegetable, mud, or anything else that might fail to penetrate a uniform or even bare skin, which requires an overpressure of some seventy-five pounds per square inch. In addition, the vision slits on armored vehicles and sights on heavy weapons greatly increase the danger to the eyes. Finally, environment plays a role. Troops fighting in rocky areas or urban settings are more likely to have eye injuries than those otherwise engaged, since hard fragments are generated in greater profusion in such environments: Israeli eye injuries on the Jerusalem front in 1967 were fully 10 percent of total injuries incurred.

PSYCHONEUROTIC CASUALTIES

Psychoneurotic disorders are a relatively new category of casualty in military experience. They were first noticed during the Civil War, when soldiers sometimes were diagnosed as suffering from "nostalgia," a general lethargy brought about by being too long in combat. By World War I, the disorder—and it took awhile for some commanders to realize it was a disorder—was called "shell shock," which became "battle fatigue" in World War II. In Vietnam it became known as "post-traumatic stress" (PTS), which covered a variety of problems, from minor to quite serious indeed. The question of psychoneurotic casualties during the Vietnam War has stirred considerable controversy, particularly when linked with the notion that the veterans are all suffering from post-traumatic stress disorder (PTSD), making them "Ticking Time Bombs." In fact, while many veterans suffer from PTS, the number suffering from PTSD—the difference is important—is much less.

PTS is a more or less normal process of "winding down" from the extraordinary stresses of combat. So victims may suffer some heightened anxiety under certain circumstances and may not handle stress too well all the time, but they are not disassociated from reality and can live quite normally. In contrast, relatively few veterans suffer from PTSD. Those with PTSD are not "winding down" well, and can't handle daily life too effectively. Their war experiences have overwhelmed their lives. They're still under fire. But

Army Psychoneurotic Cases, 1860–1973

War	Rate
Civil War	3%
World War I	3
World War II	3
Korean War	37
Vietnam War	11

Key: Rate is the number of cases per thousand troops per year.

the situation is by no means as bad as depicted by some. That said, however, there definitely were more psychoneurotic cases during the Vietnam War than in previous conflicts.

As can be seen, the Vietnam War rate is nearly 400 percent higher than the World War II rate, which was considered pretty serious at the time. Particularly since the army rejected about 10 percent of all recruits on the assumption that they matched a "profile" suggesting a susceptibility to psychoneurotic problems. Note, however, that the rate was much, much higher in Korea, when lots of ill-trained troops were wrenched from very comfortable occupation duties in Japan and sent immediately into action against the North Koreans in mid-1950. What is particularly interesting about the experience of Vietnam is that the increase in such problems was found army-wide, not merely among troops in Vietnam.

Army Psychoneurotic Cases During the Vietnam War, 1965–71

Category	Rate
All Troops	11.0
Troops in the U.S.	10.4
Troops in Europe	8.1
Troops in Vietnam	14.0

The reasons for the marked difference between the number of psychoneurotic cases in World War II and that in Vietnam are difficult to assess. It is particularly interesting that even troops in the rear—back home in the safety of the United States or even in Europe—had higher rates than prevailed for all troops during World War II. The rate of psychoneurotic problems varies, depending on the period under study. Armies are pretty big, and nowadays sprawl all over the place. Even in World War II a majority of American military personnel—and a majority of the army—did not serve in combat. The character of the troops is important too. Troops seeing combat for the first time have a lot more problems than those who have been "blooded" (gone through their baptism of fire), but guys who have been in combat for more than five or six months begin developing serious problems.

The nature of a unit's recent combat experience is also important. A unit that has done well is less likely to have a high psychoneurotic caseload than one that has had a bad time. And a unit that is advancing has fewer cases than one that is engaged in static combat, which is more or less what characterized the fighting in Vietnam. Even leadership has a lot to do with it, as leaders set the tone and help sustain the morale of the troops. By way of illustration, during the Battle of the Bulge one of the most heavily hit American divisions had just come out of a severe mauling in the Hurtgen Forest. Another was a poorly led green outfit seeing combat for the first time. The rate of psychoneurotic problems in these units seems to have approached 101 cases per thousand men on strength.

So a lot of factors came together to result in a higher psychoneurotic caseload in Vietnam than in World War II. The average soldier was under fire for 240 days or so in Vietnam, much longer than his father had been during World War II. He was also more or less engaged in static warfare, patrolling the same real estate for weeks on end, never seeming to be getting anywhere. And, of course, there was little support back home.

During the first six months of 1966, the U.S. Army in Vietnam had 757 psychoneurotic cases, a rate of about three per thousand, while the Australian contingent had about 25 cases, for an annual rate of about four cases per thousand.

PRISONERS OF THE NORTH VIETNAMESE

As many as two thousand Americans became prisoners of the Viet Cong and North Vietnamese. We'll never know the exact number because so many died early in captivity from the rigors of jungle life, untended wounds, or the massive American artillery and bombing that always followed their Communist captors. In this respect, the experience was similar to that of U.S. POWs in other wars, but also different because of the unique nature of the Vietnam War.

When the Viet Cong took their first American prisoners, they kept them in South Vietnam under primitive conditions. This was the norm until the late 1960s, when the Communists realized that many of their prisoners were dying, and that live prisoners might be useful in the peace negotiations. They began moving their captives to better facilities in North Vietnam.

The number of Americans captured by the NVA or the VC is not known. Officially the figure is less than 700. The North Vietnamese released 591 prisoners early in 1973 in accordance with the Paris Peace Agreement, while a further 83 are known to have died in captivity, and a handful of others (such as Robert Garwood) are known to have been held as well.

Americans held prisoner by the enemy had a rough time. Even when their captors were not subjecting them to deliberate abuse, they were housed in harsh conditions, denied adequate food and medical care, and refused permission to communicate with their families, as prescribed by the Geneva Convention. Some men coped with imprisonment better than others. One U.S. Navy pilot captured after being shot down during an air strike on Haiphong was interrogated by the North Vietnamese, who were trying to get him to tell them what was to be the next target on his squadron's bombing schedule. They refused to accept that this was not the sort of information routinely passed on to pilots. To get them off his back he told them that, in a move calculated as a blow against their morale, the next major target was to be the principal brewery in North Vietnam. This appeared to satisfy his interrogators, who left him alone thereafter. It also seems to have spurred an increase in antiaircraft defenses around several breweries.

It had been the experience of earlier wars that older men, and more senior men, handle the stress of being a prisoner of war better than younger men. This was more or less true of those men who became prisoners in Vietnam. Older men have memories to fall back on, have their families to worry about, and have a greater commitment to their military careers.

THE GARWOOD CASE

Few of the men taken prisoner in 1965–67 survived their captivity. Those who did either learned to cope with jungle life or collaborated. One of the more notable collaborators was Marine PFC Robert Garwood, who did not return from Vietnam until 1979.

Garwood, captured in September 1965, soon became something of a trustee and was kept separate from the other prisoners. Garwood tried to smuggle his fellow prisoners food from time to time, but basically he was used to keep an eye on his fellow prisoners and report escape attempts (which Garwood did on several occasions). He served his Communist masters so well that he was eventually made a lieutenant in the VC and was permitted to tote a rifle.

Life in captivity was rough for prisoners of the Viet Cong. The Communists deliberately used people like Garwood to keep the prisoners off balance and mistrustful of each other. Even without the Garwoods, there was a lot of tension among the underfed, overworked, and often ill prisoners. In early 1973, North Vietnam released 591 American prisoners. All had stories to tell, and it quickly became obvious that many had collaborated to one degree or another. Given the grim conditions these prisoners had endured, it was decided to ignore all except the most blatant cases of collaboration. One compelling reason for this was that the definition of collaboration had changed considerably between 1964, when U.S. combat troops first entered Vietnam, and 1973, when the last prisoners were released.

The Viet Cong were not reluctant to torture their captives, and Soviet-trained brainwashing specialists were available from North Vietnam. This, plus the normal rigors of living in the bush, reduced the resistance of many captives. The result was that a number of men signed confessions for bogus "war crimes," and even taped confessions for later broadcast. Robert Garwood was one of the few who actually went over to the enemy. Indeed, Garwood's enthusiasm for his new Communist friends was so great that Garwood refused to be returned with the rest of the prisoners. When the returned prisoners were debriefed, Garwood's name and deeds came up, but there was no confirmation of what had happened and it was assumed that he died in the jungle (like so many other prisoners and their North Vietnamese captors).

From his capture in late 1965, until his departure for Hanoi in 1969, Garwood lived with other American prisoners in the South Vietnam jungle. These prisoners, several of whom survived their captivity, saw Garwood become more and more a trusted servant of the Communists. Over the years Garwood was allowed to come and go from the prisoner area as he pleased, was given a weapon, and at one point, in the summer of 1968, was sent to where American units were operating to try and entice GIs and marines to desert. This last task got him wounded in a shoot-out with American troops.

Garwood was also made a Viet Cong soldier and given at least one promotion. He eventually came back to America to face the music because even a slow learner like himself eventually caught on to the nightmare life communism eventually creates. Attempts to turn him into some sort of a hero who had been unjustly picked on by the militarists were pathetic.

TREATING THE WOUNDED

For American and Allied troops, the treatment of the wounded during the Vietnam War exceeded all previous standards of excellence. A wounded man had an excellent chance of recovery. Immediate assistance was available from an army or navy medic on the battlefield, and helicopter "dust off" missions ensured the rapid movement of the injured to elaborate facilities in the rear. Since the average time between a soldier being wounded and his being delivered to a medical facility was just about an hour, this greatly facilitated the delivery of extensive treatment of the most sophisticated standards. As a result, there was a higher recovery rate than that which prevailed in earlier wars. Wounded men who made it to an aid station had something like a 98-percent chance of survival, which increased to better then 99 percent after the first twenty-four hours of treatment.

The movement of the wounded from the battlefield did not always end at medical facilities in Vietnam. Seriously wounded troops were often given primary treatment in Vietnam and then sent on to hospitals in the Pacific Command (Hawaii or Japan) or the continental United States. During 1965

Combat Casualty Survival Rates in America's Wars

Conflict	KIA/MW	Wounded	Total	Survived
Revolutionary War	4,435	6,188	10,623	58.6%
War of 1812	2,260	4,505	6,765	66.6%
Mexican War	1,733	4,152	5,885	70.6%
Civil War:				
Union	110,070	249,458	359,528	69.9%
Confederate	75,000	125,000	200,000	62.5%
Combined	185,070	374,458	559,528	66.9%
Spanish-American	385	1,662	2,047	81.1%
World War I	53,513	204,002	257,515	79.2%
World War II	292,131	670,846	962,977	69.7%
Korean War	33,651	103,284	136,954	75.4%
Vietnam War	47,369	153,303	200,672	76.4%
Gulf War	148	467	615	75.9%

Key: Casualty figures are notoriously unreliable. Even officially issued figures often vary by hundreds and sometimes thousands, due to differing bases of calculation. For example, prisoners of war murdered by the enemy are sometimes counted as "combat deaths" and sometimes not. Or figures can vary with the passage of time. Figures compiled at the end of a war are usually lower than those compiled two generations later, which tend to include deaths resulting from the long-term effects of wartime wounds. Figures for the Confederacy are estimated, and probably are too low. In all instances many minor wounds that were treated at the front, with the soldiers immediately returning to duty, are not included (e.g., c. 150,000 in Vietnam), so the actual recovery rate was higher in all cases, though this does not seriously alter the overall statistics.

some 10,000 wounded troops were evacuated from Vietnam, a figure that by 1968 had risen to about 35,000.

The rapid evacuation of the wounded, coupled with advances in medical science, not only saved more lives, but led to shorter hospital stays.

Summary of the Fate of Evacuated Casualties, 1965–70

Of each 1,000 casualties evacuated from the front,
310 were treated and returned to duty almost immediately
690 required some hospitalization.
Of every 690 hospitalized casualties, about 97 percent would survive:
    290 were treated in Vietnam and returned to duty there,
    52 were treated and returned to duty in the Pacific Command, but not in Vietnam
    230 returned to duty in the CONUS (continental United States),
    19 were still hospitalized as of end of 1970,
    79 had been discharged or been transferred to VA facilities, and
    20 had died.

Key: Figures have been rounded.

Comparative Average Length of Hospital Stays in Three Wars

War	Days
World War II	80
Korea	75
Vietnam	63

BLOOD

An important factor in helping to save many of the wounded was the prompt delivery of blood and blood by-products. The Army Medical Corps maintained a substantial stockpile of blood in Vietnam. Over one million units of blood were shipped to Vietnam during the war, and at its peak (1968–69), the monthly average blood supply was about 30,000 units. Of course not all of this blood was actually used. Wastage was high. Aging was one problem, as whole blood has a "shelf life" of twenty-one days, and that only when properly refrigerated. At times 50 percent of the supply had to be discarded due to age, though the average discard rate for age was about 29 percent.

Blood initially came from the existing blood bank system in the United States, supplemented by frequent donations by troops and their families in noncombat areas. Asking combat troops to donate blood is bad for morale and is particularly not recommended if the troops are likely to be going into action any time soon. There was also some procurement of blood from commercial sources.

There were a number of problems with procuring particular blood types.

Type B is relatively rare among Americans, but quite common among Vietnamese. It was not possible to procure blood in Vietnam for reasons both cultural (blood donation is quite uncommon in most Buddhist countries) and medical (screening the blood supply for the numerous endemic parasitical problems common in Vietnam would have been enormously difficult). Procuring sufficient Type B blood was difficult, particularly since the group of Americans most likely to have Type B blood—persons of Asian or African descent—were not generally donors. As a result, Type O ("Universal Donor") was substituted, comprising something like 70 percent of the blood supplied.

Blood Type Frequency by Nationality

Troops	A	AB	B	O
U.S.	39%	3%	14%	44%
Vietnamese	21%	6%	31%	42%

HOSPITAL SHIPS

One of the fastest ways to deliver quality medical care to injured soldiers is via hospital ship. The U.S. Navy had been operating hospital ships almost continuously since the 1890s. Most of these vessels were conversions from merchant ships (in fact, only one USN hospital ship has ever been designed and built as such from scratch), and so they were not always ideally suited for use as floating hospitals. When the major U.S. commitment of troops to Vietnam began in mid-1965, the navy had only one operational hospital ship, left over from World War II, with three others in reserve. The reserve vessels were quickly taken out of mothballs. Refurbished and given more modern medical facilities, they were soon operating off Vietnam. Normally a hospital ship stayed on station about eighty-five days out of every ninety, the other five being taken up with repairs and resupply that could not be accomplished by helicopter, which were usually performed at Subic Bay in the Philippines.

The hospital ships of the Vietnam era were USS *Haven* (AH-12), USS *Repose* (AH-16), and USS *Sanctuary* (AH-17). They were sisters to the famous *Hope* (ex-*Constellation*, AH-15) which served for many years as a floating medical clinic and school in the Third World.

The medical facilities aboard a hospital ship were quite elaborate, with surgical operating rooms, X-ray equipment, laboratories, pharmacological facilities, and so forth. The staffs usually included about two dozen or so medical officers, doctors and pharmacists, plus several dentists, and a few medical service officers (who managed the facilities but were not themselves medically trained). These were supported by about 30 registered nurses, and some 225–250 dental technicians, medical technicians, pharmacists' mates, hospital corpsman, and the like. The apparent shortage of doctors and nurses should be viewed against the large number of medical

Hospital Ships in Vietnam

The Ships

Built	1943–45
Displacement	11,400 light/15,400 full load
Dimensions	520' × 71' 6" × 24'
Speed	18 knots
Range	10,000 nautical miles at 12 knots
Crew	250

The Hospitals

Beds	c. 560, expandable to c. 750
Staff	c. 300–325

Key: These figures should be taken as approximate. Although the hospital ships were all based on the same standard C4-S-B-2 merchant hulls and were converted at more or less the same time, they differed in many small ways.

corpsmen. A navy hospital corpsman is essentially a physician's assistant, and capable of delivering fairly elaborate care.

Hospital ships usually handled personnel who had already received some treatment by front-line medics. Their principal function was to provide more elaborate care, to stabilize the patient, and to prepare him for evacuation to permanent facilities in the Philippines, Okinawa, Hawaii, or the continental United States. So stays in hospital ships were usually relatively short. In fact, many wounded men probably never learned the name of the ship in which they were treated.

After the Vietnam War, all of the navy's hospital ships were put back into mothballs, so that by 1974 none were in commission. All the ships were eventually disposed of. Not until the mid-1980s would the navy acquire two new ones, much larger vessels (able to handle 1,000 patients), converted from former oil tankers.

CHAPTER 10

The Home Front

The United States lost the war on the home front, not in Vietnam, and here we look at this in some unconventional ways. Actually ARVN lost the war by about 1965; the U.S. then took over. We had the Communists on the run by 1968 then we gave up on the attempt. But this was not how it appeared from the United States.

GETTING IN AND GETTING READY

The Korean War had left behind a public aversion to American involvement in Asian wars. But when U.S. diplomacy got America mixed up in Vietnamese politics, it was only a matter of time before an American president would have to fish or cut bait.

President Eisenhower had refused to aid the French when they faced defeat in their Vietnam War. This was in 1953, and the highly unpopular Korean War had just ended. Eisenhower, no matter what else he thought, knew there was no way the American public would tolerate another Asian war. But Eisenhower did offer economic and military aid to the new nation of South Vietnam. From this small involvement in 1954, the number of American soldiers in Vietnam grew year by year. When North Vietnam began to support an uprising in South Vietnam in 1959, the number of American military advisers also increased more rapidly. At that point North Vietnam was dedicated to absorbing South Vietnam and America was dedicated to preventing that. The coming war was set to go, but neither government was willing to admit it.

The North Vietnamese also had a war weariness problem in 1954, but a few years of peace solved this and the political, military, and diplomatic campaign to take over South Vietnam got under way. This multifaceted campaign was not fully understood by the American populace or government for quite some time. Adopting techniques used by their Soviet and Chinese allies, the North Vietnamese went to war on the ground, in the world media, and diplomatically. Weapons and men were sent to South Vietnam to attack the local government with guns and propaganda. Meanwhile, in North Vietnam, a police state was established that controlled everything and made any attempt to do what was being done in South Vietnam impossible. The Communist system was very good at keeping the locals down and outsiders out. Using the tight control in North Vietnam and the openness in South Vietnam, the Communists skillfully played (and played and played) the theme to the world media that North Vietnam was a workers' paradise while South Vietnam was full of slaves dominated by foreign nations (France and the United States, etc.). This technique had worked before in Russia and China, and the lies it concealed via slanted media reports were not all revealed until some years later. But the political/military and media campaigns were only buildups for the diplomatic campaign. North Vietnam denied any involvement in the fighting going on in neighboring Laos and South Vietnam, and negotiated treaties to make Laos and Cambodia neutral in the growing wars centered around South Vietnam. Moreover, North Vietnam had the diplomatic heft of China and the Soviet Union to back them up. Many Third World nations and Soviet satellites fell in behind this program, making it appear to many in the United States that North Vietnam was the innocent victim, rather than the chief troublemaker.

By the early 1960s, this was the situation in Vietnam and the United States. The stage was set and the players were ready.

THE MEDIA

The media did not, as popular myth has it, serve as a lapdog of the North Vietnamese and turn the American people against the war effort. The media followed what people were thinking, and when people saw that President Johnson's assurances that the war would be over quickly with little loss of American life was untrue, the public mood turned ugly. This was nowhere more apparent than in the aftermath of the Communist 1968 Tet Offensive. The North Vietnamese launched this massive attack because they had been beaten on the battlefields out in the countryside, but thought one major attack would reverse their declining fortunes. They thought they had support in the towns and cities, and a major Communist attack would trigger a general uprising among the people. The Communists guessed wrong. Militarily, the attack was a disaster, with some 50,000 Communist dead and many more wounded. This was over ten times American and South Vietnamese losses. The population did not rise in support of the VC. At least not the South Vietnamese population. But the American people did respond. Having been told for the past year that the Communists in Vietnam were just about finished, the Tet Offensive showed that the end was not just around the corner. Feeling that they were being deceived, and not very enthusiastic about the war in the first place, American public opinion suddenly turned strongly against war. The American victory during Tet was meaningless in this context. The media responded to the public mood and began pursuing a lot of antigovernment stories that had previously been avoided. The war now became an even bigger issue, and before 1968 ended, even the government had decided that victory was no longer the issue in Vietnam, but how soon American troops could be gotten out. That said, there were a number of problems with media coverage of the Vietnam War.

The war was "overreported." There were too many journalists all trying for a hot story. Some idea of the extent of this may be gained by comparing the ratio of soldiers to journalists in several major wars.

In peacetime there are normally only a few score journalists who specialize in military affairs. Nevertheless, when a war comes along all sorts of journalists—of all political outlooks—flock to the scene in the hopes of securing a story. Most of them are ill-equipped to understand the nature of the military profession, which has its own language, just as any other profession does. So some journalists saw obfuscation in the use of technical jargon, like "close air support," calling it a "euphemism for bombing." This is like saying "surgical procedure" is a "euphemism for stabbing the patient." It's true, in a narrow sense, but not exactly accurate.

Many journalists also displayed a profound lack of understanding of the law of war. Although the Geneva Convention sets the rules for mitigating the horrors of war, the enforcement mechanism is often overlooked, resulting in swift retaliation. For example, anyone found engaging in combat in civilian dress can be shot without trial. So when, on the streets of Saigon on 1 February 1968, South Vietnamese National Police BG Nguyen Ngoc Loan shot out of hand a VC officer who had engaged in military operations (and murdered several civilians in the bargain) while wearing civilian clothes, he was acting fully in accordance with the terms of the Geneva Convention. U.S. forces in World War II did the same to Germans captured in American uniforms during the Battle of the Bulge, which certainly was not reported as an atrocity.

Reporters with the Troops

Conflict	Date	Event	Troops	Journalists	Ratio
World War I	11 Nov 1918	Armistice	2.040	38	53,684:1
World War II	6 Jun 1944	D-Day	2.600	300	8,667:1
Korea	1 Jan 1951	Stalemate	.800	300	2,667:1
Vietnam	1 Feb 1968	Tet	1.400	500	2,800:1
Gulf	1 Feb 1991	Desert Storm	.750	1300	577:1

Key: Figures are for millions of personnel involved in the indicated operation and have been rounded. Those for World War I are for U.S. troops only, those for other conflicts include Allied forces as well. Ratio is the number of troops per journalist in theater. For some more recent smaller American military operations, the ratio has tended to be even lower: Grenada (1983), 39:1 and Panama (1989), 69:1.

SOME NOTABLE BLUNDERS OF THE PEACE MOVEMENT

The peace movement was not monolithic. Its adherents ranged across the political spectrum to include a surprising number of conservatives along with a lot more liberals and radicals. Although it did have considerable support, it utterly failed to mobilize a majority of the American people. This was partially because the movement was so fragmented that it went off in so many different ways as to drive away many potential supporters. Certainly some of the most characteristic actions of some of the more outspoken people in the peace movement actually served to increase support for the war among some groups.

Elitism. For a group that purported to represent the common man against the vested interests—militarists, capitalists, and so forth—who were supposedly benefiting from the war, the peace movement had a very anticommon-man thrust. For example, in the 1970 film *Joe*, the protagonist, a working-class World War II vet who supports the war, is depicted as a homicidal, boorish, bigot, which, while it may have warmed the cockles of the hearts of many a sensitive antiwar intellectual, seems hardly likely to have presented some useful reasons why the much greater number of people who were working-class World War II veterans should join the peace movement.

Flag Burning. Many patriotic Americans had reservations about the war, but the anti-Americanism of many peace activists made the average person much less likely to listen to anything else they said. Level-headed elements in the movement saw this problem. Asked to comment on flag burning, veteran Socialist Norman Thomas decried it as a poor gesture, saying, "Washing the flag would be a better symbol." Arguably the strongly anti-American—even revolutionary—tone that much of the peace movement adopted probably drove many conservatives into being supporters of U.S. policy in Vietnam, about which many of them initially had serious reservations: The John Birch Society, for example, opposed sending troops to Vietnam.

Supporting the Enemy. "Peace activists" who posed alongside North Vietnamese antiaircraft guns, raised funds for North Vietnam, or hobnobbed with North Vietnamese officialdom seemed to have a decidedly odd definition of peace. Likewise, opposing "war" but supporting "armed struggle" or "revolutionary struggle" was hardly a way to convince someone that you believed in peace. In fact, when antiwar advocates cheered for Ho Chi Minh and said things like, "I would welcome a Viet Cong victory," they immediately turned off the largest group of people in the country who had reservations about the war, those whose sons were fighting it. By one survey conducted at the time, 85 percent of the people in this group were dissatisfied with the war.

Violence. Blowing up offices and killing scientists or draft officials was certainly no way to promote the "peace" movement.

THINGS ARE NOT ALWAYS AS THEY SEEM—NOR ARE PEOPLE

During—and after—the Vietnam War a lot of people had a lot to say about it, on all sides of the issue. Afterward—often long afterward—some of them turned out to have had some odd skeletons in their closets.

Some Antiwar Activists with Dubious Credentials. Critics of the war claimed that their opposition was a principled one, rooted in pacifism, respect for human dignity, and anti-imperialism. Many were. But not all. In fact, many of them seem to have been conscious supporters of the Communists, some were freelance agents of the Soviet Union, and some were on the KGB payroll. For example, in December 1976 a group of prominent former war protesters, including the singer Joan Baez, publicly censured the Socialist Republic of Vietnam for violations of human rights. This elicited a swift and quite vicious reaction from many of their erstwhile allies in the antiwar movement, who severely criticized them for attacking a "democratic socialist" government. Interestingly, Miss Baez's singing career never recovered.

• The Black Panthers, alleged champions of the poor and oppressed, were in fact more interested in their criminal activities, which included drug dealing. They apparently knocked off their accountant, who seems to have discovered that money being collected for their famous children's breakfast program was being siphoned off to procure arms and drugs and they seem to have set up some of their "Brothers" to be killed in order to create martyrs. Huey P. Newton, one of the founders and most prominent of the gang, was later killed in a crack deal gone bad.

• Wilfred G. Burchett, leftist Australian journalist and author (*China, Cambodia, Vietnam Triangle, Grasshoppers and Elephants: Why Vietnam Fell,* and *Ho-Chi-Minh: An Appreciation*) and ardent supporter of the Viet Cong, seems to have been on the payroll of the KGB, the Soviet counterpart of the CIA. The Russians got their money's worth in this case.

• Noam Chomsky, leftist intellectual, critic, and outspoken opponent of American participation in the Vietnam War, was also an ardent apologist for Pol Pot and his murderous regime in Cambodia.

• William Sloan Coffin, prominent clergyman, who had served as an army officer in World War II, claimed to be a pacifist. He was in the forefront of those opposed to the "American invasion of Vietnam," but has since become an important voice in promoting what some leftists term American "invasions" of Somalia, Bosnia, and other places.

• Ira Eisenberg, prominent antiwar and environmental activist (he was one of the founders of "Earth Day," which is observed on Lenin's birthday) who led numerous rallies and was one of the stars of the "New Left," had a penchant for beating up his girlfriends and eventually murdered one. Arrested for the murder in 1981, he was bailed out by a coterie of leftist intellectuals and movie stars, who apparently believed his claim that he had been framed by the FBI, despite the fact that he had stashed the body in his closet for some eighteen months. He promptly jumped bail, not to be apprehended until more than sixteen years later in France, where his good leftist credentials managed to prevent his extradition in 1998.

• Jane Fonda, actress and prominent figure of the New Left, an ardent supporter of the "Democratic Republic of Vietnam" (despite having done a stint as "Miss Army Recruiting"), turned up at the Soviet-sponsored "World Youth Festival," along with Angela Davis, rising star of the U.S. Communist Party, posed on a North Vietmanese antiaircraft piece, and was one of those highly critical of the December 1976 stand by Joan Baez and a number of other war protesters against the totalitarianism of the "Socialist Republic of Vietnam."

• Abbie Hoffman, leader of the "Youth International Party," specialized in causing riots in places like Grand Central Terminal, and was later found to have been a major cocaine dealer, though, of course, he claimed to have been framed.

• Pablo Neruda, Latin American poet and Nobelist in literature, a prominent supporter of leftist causes and close friend to Fidel Castro, was in fact also a KGB operative.

• Republic of New Afrika, a black nationalist antiwar revolutionary group (their stated political objective was the proclamation of a black republic in several southern states), was later discovered to have been subsidized by the KGB.

• Bertrand Russell, outspoken war critic and leftist philosopher and scientist, was perhaps compensating for his earlier advocacy of "preventive nuclear war," back in the days when the United States had a monopoly on "the Bomb."

• Pete Seeger, folklorist and environmentalist, as well as champion of leftist causes, whose opposition to the war may perhaps be explained by his strong advocacy of the Stalinist view of history (e.g., for example, the Nazi-Soviet Pact was not a military alliance between the century's two greatest killers).

• I. F. Stone, noted muckraker (The History of the Korean War) and champion of leftist causes, seems to have been a paid agent of the Russians for many, many years.

• Youth Against War and Fascism. A pre–World War II peace group, was, as its name suggests, a Communist front organization. The only wars they seemed to have been opposed to were those against leftists, and they had no problem supporting "revolutionary struggles."

• Veterans of the Abraham Lincoln Brigade (made up of American veterans of the Spanish Civil War who had survived the Fascist bullets and still believed the Communist lies), kept up their traditional ties to Moscow, participating in numerous antiwar demonstrations, including the famous one in which the Pentagon was allegedly levitated by the "good vibes" of those present.

• War Resistors League. A leftish antiwar group formed shortly after World War I, whose judgment on the Vietnam War may perhaps be viewed against the fact that it also didn't think fighting Hitler was such a good idea either.

Some Supporters of the War with Questionable Motives. As in the case of many in the antiwar movement, so too in the case of some in what might be called the "prowar movement." The list is shorter, perhaps because the paper trail has been better concealed.

• American Friends of Vietnam, headed by Prof. Wesely Fishel and based at Michigan State University, was formed in 1955 by a group of liberal anti-Communist academics to bolster U.S. public support for South Vietnam. It became a major source of support for the Johnson administration policy in Vietnam during 1965–66, by which time most of the liberal intellectuals had dropped out. It was later revealed to have been subsidized by the South Vietnamese government.

• Tom Dooley, medical missionary in Vietnam and writer of inspirational anti-Communist literature (*The Night They Burned the Mountain*), worked for the CIA.

• National Students' Association, originally a legitimate organization of college students, was infiltrated by federal agents, who gradually took it over, and turned it into a flack for U.S. policy in Southeast Asia.

THE CONSPIRACY OF THE MOMENT

The antiwar movement was rife with paranoia. A lot of rumors circulated, many finding their way into print. A sampler follows.

The government is planning to:

• **Close the Colleges.** This one began circulating on campuses about 1968. Also occasionally heard was that libraries were to be shut down, which prompted some ardent supporters of the left to begin memorizing whole volumes so that they could "preserve" the wisdom contained therein for posterity.

- **Tap My Phone.** Many supporters of the peace movement were convinced that their phones were being tapped by the FBI or some other even more secretive agency for nefarious purposes, often citing as evidence static, "mysterious" wrong numbers, and other oddities of telephony. The FBI was, of course, tapping some phones and engaging in even more serious illegal activities. But most people who claimed their phones were tapped were too unimportant to bother with. Interestingly, when the Freedom of Information Act was passed, many people were dismayed to discover that the government had no files on them whatsoever. Some of them immediately charged that the *real* files were being withheld illegally.

- **Control All Radios.** The assumption here was that a secret government project was developing a device that would automatically switch every radio in the country to a single frequency, so that the government could broadcast prowar propaganda. The most extreme manifestation of this bit of paranoia had it that the government would be able to switch on radios, thereby forcing you to listen.

- **Intern All War Protesters.** This one appeared in several leftist publications, some of which were embellished with lists of the camps in which the unfortunate internees were to be stashed. By a curious coincidence these were the camps in which Japanese-, Italian-, German-, and some other hyphenated Americans of allegedly dubious loyalty had been detained during World War II, all of which were in advanced states of deterioration.

Not all the paranoia was on the left. The John Birch Society, for example, was adamantly convinced that the war was a conspiracy of "the liberals" to turn Southeast Asia over to the Communists.

KENT STATE

On Monday, 4 May 1970, a detachment of the Ohio National Guard fired on a group of demonstrators on the campus of Kent State University.

The incident occurred after several days of disorder on the campus following Pres. Richard M. Nixon's 30 April announcement of the invasion of Cambodia. An antiwar demonstration on campus on Thursday, 1 May, degenerated into a riot, which continued the following day, when the campus ROTC building was burned down and several people injured. Despite this, the college president, who was traveling, did not return to campus. Although the local police believed they could handle the matter themselves, Gov. John Rhodes of Ohio ordered the National Guard to duty. His intention apparently was to hold them in reserve, but a series of miscommunications sent them onto the campus on Saturday, May 2. On Monday the Guardsmen, many of whom had had little or no sleep for two days, had actually been ordered to leave.

Meanwhile, at noon a large demonstration began to protest the Cambodian incursion and the presence of the National Guard on campus (despite the fact that the Guardsmen were under orders to leave). The Guardsmen were ordered into riot formation. Some of the demonstrators began throwing rocks. The Guardsmen were ordered to throw tear gas. Quite suddenly, a single shot was heard, reportedly a pistol shot. At that, several of the Guardsmen opened fire, most apparently shooting into the air. Officers immediately ordered a cease-fire, but by then four students had been killed and nine others wounded, one of whom was paralyzed.

Those killed were:

- Alisa Krause, one of the demonstrators
- Jeffrey Miller, an antiwar activist and student leader
- Sandra Scheuer
- William Schroeder, an ROTC cadet, who was walking to class quite a distance away

A subsequent investigation concluded that the firing was certainly not ordered. The incident resulted from serious miscommunications, combined with a confrontational attitude on the part of some of the demonstrators. In fact, the Guardsmen were poorly trained, poorly disciplined, poorly led (for example, it is clear weapons had not been inspected to ensure that they were not loaded), and quite tired.

Although no definitive reason for the firing has ever been established, the random locations of those killed and injured suggests that someone—possibly an officer, as there was a report of a pistol shot just before the rifle fire—tried to scare off the demonstrators by firing a "warning shot" over their heads. Police are trained never to fire warning shots, as they must come down somewhere.

Kent State caused an enormous public outcry. The paranoia that was already infecting political discourse on all sides increased. Peace activists and leftists argued that the Guardsmen had been ordered to fire, often claiming that the incident had been planned by President Nixon himself in order to cow the antiwar movement into passivity. Many rightists argued that the Guardsmen had reacted to imminent danger, and some went so far as to describe those killed—including ROTC cadet William Schroeder—as drug-abusing degenerate radicals. The presence of a teenage runaway who had been "crashing" on campus and was photographed moments after the shooting crying over one of the victims was used by some right wingers as "evidence" that there was a well-coordinated nation-wide leftist conspiracy to hide runaways and draft dodgers.

In fact, the tragedy was none of these.

JACKSON STATE

Ten days after the shootings at Kent State, Mississippi State Police killed two black student demonstrators at Jackson State College. For several days students had been protesting the war and racism. On Thursday, 24 May, state policemen opened fire on a crowd of demonstrators, some of whom were behaving violently. Two were killed and a dozen others wounded.

Coming in the wake of the Kent State shootings, the incident at Jackson State received less focused attention, which led many black radicals to charge that the media was employing a double standard, one in which the lives of black students were less important than those of white students. Nevertheless, since the incident at Jackson State involved a notoriously racist police agency, a federal investigation was instituted, which had not been done for Kent State.

Although the Mississippi State Police claimed to have fired in self-defense, after having been fired upon by a hidden gunman, there was no evidence to support this contention. The conclusion of the investigation was that the state police had acted with deliberate malice.

PEACE WITH HONOR

At 12:30 Paris time, Tuesday, 23 January 1973, the Agreement on Ending the War and Restoring Peace in Vietnam was initialed by Dr. Henry Kissinger, on behalf of the United States, and Special Adviser Le Duc Tho, on behalf of the Democratic Republic of Vietnam. The agreement was formally signed by the parties participating in the Paris Conference on Vietnam on 27 January 1973 at the International Conference Center in Paris. The ceasefire took effect at 2400 Greenwich Mean Time, 27 January 1973. The United States and the Democratic Republic of Vietnam expressed the hope that this agreement would ensure stable peace in Vietnam and contribute to the preservation of lasting peace in Indochina and Southeast Asia.

It didn't.

CHAPTER 11

The Other Side

The war from the enemy perspective. It was different over there.

BORN IN THE NORTH TO DIE IN THE SOUTH

With a population of 22 million, and another 4 to 8 million in South Vietnam they could recruit from, the North Vietnamese raised over 4 million troops to fight American and South Vietnamese forces. At its peak, over 40 percent of the military-aged (eighteen to thirty-four) North Vietnamese male population was in the army. Two million of those troops were killed or wounded. Because of poor medical facilities, half the casualties died. Three million of those troops came from North Vietnam, and the death rate was so high in the late 1960s that some young recruits had themselves tattooed with the phrase, "Born in the North to Die in the South."

A 40–50-percent casualty rate for an army is not unknown in military history. Union forces in the American Civil War suffered a 28-percent death rate. The Russians suffered a higher rate during World War II, but the overall rate for World War II was about 15 percent; and in World War I, despite its reputation for senseless slaughter, it was only 13 percent. But if you were an infantryman in World War II, you suffered a 25-percent casualty rate. Most of the North Vietnam combat deaths were among the infantry who marched down the Ho Chi Minh Trail and never came back. This was noticed up north. Although the North Vietnamese troops in South Vietnam spent most of their time just staying alive, there was so much American firepower being tossed around that it was easy to get blasted by a bomb or shell even if you were trying to keep a low profile. If the American bombs didn't get you, disease often would. North Vietnamese soldiers were drafted into the army until the war was over or they were killed or maimed. The troops that went south stayed there for the duration. None of the thirteen-month tour of duty stuff that prevailed in the U.S. Army.

Many North Vietnamese troops never made it down the Ho Chi Minh Trail. For the first five or six years of its existence, marching the length of the trail was an unhealthy experience. Many died on the way, or arrived in a very unhealthy state. Until the trail was much upgraded in the late 1960s, it took well-conditioned troops to even attempt the march and often required a few weeks of rest at the other end before the travelers were ready for any other duty.

After the first battles with U.S. troops in 1965, North Vietnamese commanders realized that it was a losing proposition fighting American troops in pitched battles. The Communist strategy had always been to attack only when the situation was favorable, and otherwise to hold back and outwait their opponent, using guerrilla attacks, terror, and propaganda to weaken their enemies. When the enemy was weak enough, you went over to big battles. This was where the Communists were in South Vietnam in 1964, just before (and the main reason why) American troops entered the fray. So, except for some major offensives, over 90 percent of the attacks after 1965 were in less than battalion (up to six hundred men) strength. A favorite method was attacks by a company (about a hundred men) led by a platoon of sappers (twenty to thirty troops). Often sappers went in alone, for the purpose of blowing things up and then getting out.

Realizing that the enemy no longer wanted to come out and play, U.S. commanders developed the "search and destroy" tactics. Despite the bad press this technique got back home, it made sense at the front. The Viet Cong and North Vietnam units established themselves in the countryside, where they taxed the local farmers (as a percentage of their crops, at a lower level than the South Vietnam government and landlords) and grew their own food as well. The Communists also promised the farmers land of their own (a lie, but this was not obvious until after South Vietnam was conquered in 1975). Secure in their base areas, the Communist troops could carry on raiding South Vietnamese territory and building up their troops' strength indefinitely. So the search and destroy operations were used to root the Viet Cong and North Vietnam units out of their bases and return control of the areas to South Vietnam. This often worked, for the Communist units stood and fought only when they could not slip away, and often they were trapped in these operations. But whether they fought or were able to move to other base areas, the search and destroy tactics caused casualties among the North Vietnam troops. If forced out of their base areas, losses from disease and malnutrition increased. Fleeing units often ended up in uninhabited areas, where food was hard to come by and living conditions were unhealthy.

The success of the search and destroy operations led the U.S. leadership to think they were winning the war. The Communist tactic of avoiding combat left the impression that there were fewer enemy troops out there. Such was not the case, as the early 1968 Communist Tet Offensive demonstrated. That campaign was disastrous for the Viet Cong, who wrongly believed that the South Vietnam people were fed up with their corrupt government and indiscriminate American firepower. Such was not the case. All Vietnamese were tired of the war and were not keen on sticking their collective necks out by fighting South Vietnamese troops or police. But the Tet fighting did bring American and South Vietnamese troops in from the countryside so that the Communists could be cleaned out of the urban areas. The Communists took advantage of this to move back into some of their rural base areas, and by late 1968, the search and destroy operations were again being waged on a large scale.

By 1967, over 10,000 North Vietnam troops a month were marching down the Ho Chi Minh Trail. Those who had survived the Tet Offensive found themselves caught up in another round of search and destroy battles. U.S. airpower and artillery became more widely used and more effective. As U.S. troops began to withdraw in 1969, the Communists became more aggressive against South Vietnamese troops, and in 1972, there was another major offensive to bring down the South Vietnam government. Unexpectedly fierce resistance by South Vietnamese troops and massive American airpower defeated this offensive, and many more North Vietnamese troops died. Only the final, 1975 offensive, went off as planned. But meanwhile over 400,000 young men from North Vietnam were, indeed, born in the north, only to die in the south.

A DAY IN THE LIFE OF UNCLE HO'S NEPHEWS

Allied and Communist soldiers had quite different lifestyles in the field. Put simply, Allied troops went looking for a fight, while Communist soldiers spent most of their time avoiding one. At the beginning and end of the war it was a bit different. In 1965–66, the North Vietnamese divisions tried to fight it out with the Americans. They lost and tried the "big push" only three more times for the rest of the war. Twice, in Tet (1968) and the Easter Offensive (1972), the result was a disaster for the Communists. The Final Offensive (1975) worked and brought the war to an end. But except for less than a year's worth of hard campaigning, the Communists basically preferred "warfare lite." They had good reason for this. They discovered in 1965–66 that American troops were fierce fighters and had enormous firepower on call. The Communists also knew that time was on their side. The American public would not tolerate a long war, while the Communist-controlled population was living in a police state, where enthusiasm for a long war was encouraged. So for most of the war the Communist troops concentrated on staying alive, while keeping the Americans aware that all was not safe out there in the bush. This involved:

• Few permanent camps, especially within South Vietnam itself. In Laos, North Vietnam, and Cambodia there were permanent camps, although as the war went on even these camps in "safe areas" tended to be largely underground. Within South Vietnam, each Viet Cong or North Vietnamese unit had several entrenched camps. Communist units would constantly move around, rarely staying in one place more than a few weeks, and usually never more than a few days. By moving around like this, casualties were minimized. American troops out sweeping the countryside looking for the enemy were also unnerved whenever they came across one of these unused camps. What was particularly scary was how well hidden the Communist camps were. Sometimes an American patrol didn't find one until they were in the middle of it. This did not do much for American troop morale.

• Lots of digging. Whenever a Communist unit stopped for the night, the first thing the troops did was dig some trenches and foxholes, in case there was an air raid or artillery attack. The Communist troops had a healthy respect for American firepower, and went to sometimes extreme lengths to reassure their troops that there were ways to survive all those bombs and shells. Thus it was difficult to do a lot of damage using bombs and shells unless you caught Communist troops out in the open. Even then, the enemy would promptly flee. The Communists may have been outgunned, but they were not outsmarted. They knew the value of a well-used shovel. As Carl Sandburg put it, "The shovel is brother to the gun."

• Self-sufficiency. In some areas deep in the bush North Vietnamese troops would plant crops, usually vegetable gardens, but they would not permanently camp near things like this unless they felt really secure. This was not often the case after 1966. Viet Cong units would usually be people from the area and would set up their own local government, taking a share of the crops as a "tax." Money would be collected from businesses and deals would be made with local South Vietnamese government officials.

• Routines. Even while marching around the back country, often at night, most of the troops' time was spent in some kind of makeshift camp, where there was a detailed routine of who did what. This was quite like American units when not out in the bush. There was time set aside for training, maintenance of equipment, exercise, and political meetings. There was time off for sports and hunting (to spice up the monotonous rice and vegetable diet) as well as visiting nearby Communist-controlled towns or villages (when these were available).

• Taking care of themselves. Despite the low budget and primitive nature of the Communist units, they did maintain a wide variety of services for the troops. There was medical care, including underground (and above ground) hospitals deep in Communist-controlled areas. Since the Communists didn't have helicopters and few trucks, ill or wounded troops needing care had to be carried long distances to receive specialized care. But this would be done, even though the patient often did not survive the trip. The effort was good for everyone's morale. There was mail service, although because of the American firepower along the Ho Chi Minh Trail and the need to carry the mail much of the way via courier, a lot of it never arrived, or took months to do so if it did. There were even entertainers, similar to the American USO, who traveled down the Ho Chi Minh Trail to entertain the troops with songs, dances, and plays. Personal hygiene supplies, at the very least soap, ~~was~~ *Were* almost always available and officers were strict about the troops keeping themselves clean.

• Combat operations. The Communist combat units did conduct attacks during their long "avoid the enemy" periods. But they worked really hard to make sure they only attacked when conditions were very much in their favor. It was standard Communist practice to carefully plan any attack. This meant weeks, or months, of observing the target area. If enough information on the enemy was collected, and enough troops and weapons could be brought into the area, the attack would be made. But there would be no assault most of the time, for the Communists knew they had to win most of these set piece battles or else morale would take a dive. So most planned attacks were called off because there was some uncertainty about the enemy's defenses, or not enough troops or weapons could be obtained to do the job properly. Over 90 percent of these attacks were small affairs, involving from a dozen to a few hundred Communist troops. The Allies had thousands of small, fortified bases throughout South Vietnam, providing many targets. There were always many ambush opportunities, but these could backfire if the Americans had too much artillery or too many helicopters nearby. Although American troops complained of being constantly on guard against Communist booby traps and ambushes, it was actually worse for the Communists. Allied airpower and communications were able to bring in massive firepower soon after any Communist troops were spotted. You had to live under this threat to appreciate how unnerving it was.

GROUP THINK AND MIND CONTROL

The North Vietnamese had a major advantage in the way they controlled their own population. Learning well from their Russian and Chinese mentors, the North Vietnamese created a system than enabled them to control their population and motivate millions to fight on under seemingly hopeless conditions.

The great terrors of this century were Socialist dictatorships (Nazi or Communist) that mobilized huge populations for orgies of death and destruction. One of the key tools used was a keen appreciation of how to control and use mass media. It's no coincidence that Communists and Nazis came to power at the same time that mass media entered that crucial period, early in this century, when radio extended the reach that print (mass circulation newspapers) had achieved only in the past few generations. Radio was particularly important for reaching people who could not read, which made it possible to practice the "big lie" technique in preindustrial nations. The Communists took over in Russia by the early 1920s, just before radio sets became available to the public. The Communists had to use print, even though a large chunk of the rural population was illiterate. So thousands of "agitators" went out and basically pitched the (future) advantages of communism in person. Inventing things as they went along, these Russian Communists developed techniques for controlling large populations that withstood the upheavals of World War II and, for several decades, the patent failure of the Socialist economic system. The Russians passed their techniques on to their Chinese Communist colleagues, who provided Asian examples of how this worked for Communists in other Asian countries, like Vietnam, where the lessons of molding and coercing public opinion at the same time were studied and developed intently.

Nazism and communism were both scams that involved promising more than you could deliver and encouraging "any means necessary" (including a permanent police state and, as needed, mass murder) to hasten the time when the new age of peace and plenty would arrive. It can work for a few generations, until it becomes obvious that the bad old days were not as grim as this. Unfortunately, few knew this in the early 1960s and the Communist system was working quite well in North Vietnam.

The North Vietnamese had another advantage in that the division of Vietnam in 1954 allowed the Communists to send all their dissidents south. This included a lot of anti-Communists who could be troublesome for any government. In addition to several militant religious sects, there were people who supported the French colonial government and those who, for any number of reasons, were anti-Communist. As a result, the North Vietnamese were able to depend on Vietnam nationalism more than the secret police to keep the people in a warlike mood throughout the 1960s. But at its core, the North Vietnamese Communists were using propaganda and the threat of personal harm to keep everyone in line. While still nominally a Communist country in the 1990s, the economy is increasingly market driven and the Communist Party is unable to recruit enough new members to keep itself in power.

THE OTHER SIDE'S DRAFT DODGERS

It was widely known that many young American men tried to avoid getting drafted for the Vietnam War. What is less well known is that the Communists had the same problem. Communist troops in South Vietnamese suffered a 10-percent annual desertion rate for most of the war. Of course, American psychological warfare programs encouraged this, but then so did the Communists encourage South Vietnamese soldiers to desert (and about 20 percent a year did).

In North Vietnam, it was more difficult to "dodge the draft," more so than in the United States. The North Vietnamese knew they were at war. American bombers came over often enough and most of the populated areas of North Vietnam got bombed at least once, to turn the majority of the population into supporters of the government's war effort. But still many of the young men were not enthusiastic about going south. It was noted, by 1966, that not only was no one coming back, but many young soldiers were no longer writing home. North Vietnam did not have an efficient system for notifying a dead soldier's family. There was a primitive mail system, for on many parts of the Ho Chi Minh Trail there was truck traffic and on other parts there were porters going back and forth. While much mail sent back north was lost, it was noticed when, over a period of many months, no mail came back at all from many soldiers who had gone south. The young men waiting for their draft notice surmised that going south was something of a death sentence.

Like the United States, North Vietnam had an upper class that could send their sons on to college. North Vietnam also deferred military service for these students. In addition, North Vietnam had some 25,000 students studying in foreign universities. Most of these were in Communist countries, but some were in Western Europe. No matter, these young men were not fighting in South Vietnam, nor were they being bombed in North Vietnam.

North Vietnam had a very practical attitude toward reluctant soldiers. If a soldier in the north deserted, or refused to show up for military duty, some soldiers were sent to the man's village or city neighborhood and spoke with his family. Avoiding military service was shameful, although parents were willing to look the other way if Sonny seemed to be getting away with it. But if soldiers showed up looking for their child, parents rarely resisted. The kid was taken away, sometimes forcefully, and that was that.

Like Germany during World War II, "the south" elicited the same fear as "the Russian front." Even if a soldier was drafted, not all soldiers went south. With the right connections, or by maneuvering oneself into the right job or unit, service in the south could be avoided. But if you were in uniform and you made yourself unpopular with your superiors, you would soon find yourself on a list of soldiers going south.

Naturally, many of these soldiers surrendered at the first chance, once they got into South Vietnam. It wasn't easy to surrender because the North Vietnamese soldiers spent most of their time in the bush just staying alive. And when Communist soldiers did run into Americans, it was usually just a lot of American firepower. Not easy to surrender to shells or bombs. But thousands of North Vietnamese troops did get a chance to give up, and that is how it was discovered that North Vietnam had draft dodgers too, and a lot of them.

TRAINING

North Vietnamese soldiers were trained much the same way American ones were. Two months of basic training was pretty standard, followed by one or more months of specialist training (even for infantrymen). Bright soldiers might be given a year or more of technical training for electronic equipment.

Once sent to their units, training continued. Most of the time, Viet Cong and North Vietnamese units were not involved in combat operations. During these more relaxed times, the Communist units followed a strict schedule. Up at 0500 (5:00 A.M.) two hours of preparing and eating breakfast and cleaning up the camp. Then came several hours of political lectures, training, or working on fortifications. Then came the traditional midday siesta, during the hottest part of the day. Then another five hours of work. Then another two to three hours for the evening meal and rest. Often there followed several hours of night training.

All of this training could get pretty boring, and the officers and Communist Party officials had to work hard to keep the troops at it. Viet Cong units often set up camp near civilians, so there was always the temptation to sneak away for some youthful entertainment. The North Vietnamese units were usually out in the bush, so mixing with civilians was less of a problem. But even out in the forest, the troops would wander off to relax, an ancient tradition among soldiers. Because of variations in the quality of leaders, some units were better disciplined than others.

Soldiers who showed better attitude and aptitude were given special training in more technical areas (antiaircraft guns, explosives, radios, etc.) or allowed to attend sapper school to become commandos. All the schools were set up in South Vietnam, for it was not practical, until the late 1960s, to send anyone back up the Ho Chi Minh Trail.

While American troops were in Vietnam for only a year, Communist troops were in for the duration and, if they survived all the battles and bombings, would get more and more skilled after years of training and practical experience.

BAD MEDICINE

In a repeat of the American World War II experience with jungle fighting, Vietnam saw U.S. troops getting decisively better medical care than their opponents. But the North Vietnamese were not nearly as bad off as the Japanese during World War II. The Communists suffered far more from lack of medical care then the Americans, but were able to make enough of an effort to correct the situation and avoid severe morale problems. They used several techniques to stay even in the medical game:

• **Every unit had a medic.** This was not to hard to accomplish, for in all armies the medic is little more than a soldier with additional first-aid training. But the North Vietnamese adopted ideas from the Chinese and Russian Communists, wherein the unit medic was officially given a lot more power and responsibility in medical matters. Naturally, there was not a lot of medical supplies or equipment for the medics, but just the fact that this guy was always there looking after the troops made a big difference in morale, and the troops' physical health as well.

• **Always evacuate the wounded.** Even if they got shot up some more while doing so, the Communists insisted that the troops always try and bring the wounded back with them. Again, this ancient practice was more for morale than medical reasons, for the Communists rarely had the transportation to move the wounded very far, nor the medical means to offer much treatment. But the troops in the bush knew that both sides regularly shot the enemy wounded, so injured soldiers getting dragged out of the battle by their buddies at least avoided their almost certain death at the hands of the enemy.

• **Use enemy medical facilities.** Aside from the usual black market for medical supplies (mostly from South Vietnamese troops), there was also the custom of pregnant Communist soldiers being ordered to "cross over" to the Allied side for the good of the baby and the mother. It took awhile for the Americans to catch on to this, and when they did they simply kept Mom and the kid in a POW camp for the duration.

• **Build hospitals in the bush.** American troops were amazed when they first came across tunnel complexes that contained hospitals, including X-ray machines and operating rooms. As more stuff came down the Ho Chi Minh Trail in the late 1960s, some of it was for equipping hospitals in Communist-controlled areas. While some of these were underground, most were above ground, spread out over several acres of jungle in small huts that were impossible to spot from the air (and not easy to find on the ground either). In addition to more of the ever popular and solicitous medics, the hospitals also had many expert doctors, surgeons, and medical technicians. Here is where you found most of the North Vietnamese female military personnel in the south, serving as nurses and medical technicians.

So while Communist troops continued to suffer more than twice the disease losses as their opponents, and lose over twice as many wounded for lack of medical care, the troops fought on, knowing they were still getting the best medical aid available.

THE SAPPERS

The Communists developed one type of elite soldiers who were as unique as they were effective. These were the sappers. The term *sapper* usually indicates combat engineers. These are normally troops who get out in front of the infantry and tanks to clear minefields and obstacles when assaulting a heavily fortified position. This was some of what the North Vietnamese and Viet Cong sappers did, but with a big difference. The sappers did it all themselves. There was no mass of infantry behind the sappers. Often half a dozen sappers would attack an American fortified base containing over a hundred troops. The sappers would get through all the minefields and barbed wire, blow up much of the American base, killing and wounding many of the American troops, and then get away, sometimes without taking any casualties. The main job of the sappers was to destroy things, not people. And they did so with remarkable success. Not just enemy bases, but also aircraft on the ground and ships anchored in South Vietnamese ports. At one point, naval sappers even sank a small American aircraft carrier.

How did they do this?

It was quite simple, actually. The sappers were well trained, carefully selected, troops engaging in thoroughly planned assaults. This was a winning combination much of the time.

The sapper concept was developed by the Vietnamese Communists during the war with the French (1945–54). The first Communist troops sent to fight in South Vietnam, in 1957, were sappers. By 1975, there were nearly 20,000 men (and some women) in sapper units. Throughout the entire American phase of the Vietnam War, over 50,000 served in sapper units. As careful as the sappers were, they took a lot of casualties.

Sappers were organized into 100–150-man "battalions." Each battalion had three 36-man companies, each company had two 18-man platoons, each platoon had three 6-man squads, and each squad had two 3-man cells. This last element, the 3-man cell, indicates the political origins of the sapper units. The 3-man cell was the basic element of Communist Party organization. Sappers were expected to be good Communists, but not all were. By war's end, it was enough if a sapper was simply an exceptional soldier. Each sapper battalion had a variable number of sapper and nonsapper troops attached for command (officers, radio operators, even a clerk or two) and support (medical and technical).

Many infantry battalions, especially the Viet Cong ones, had a sapper platoon. The Viet Cong, however, were not usually as well trained as the North Vietnamese units and the Viet Cong sappers were also less well trained. The sappers attached to infantry battalions were there mainly to provide expertise in handling explosives. But anyone with the title sapper felt they should be able to perform the daring attacks that sappers were famous for. Then again, the Viet Cong sappers usually had more opportunity to get combat experience. Those who survived a few sapper attacks became quite good sappers.

Not just anyone could be a sapper. In North Vietnam, volunteers were accepted, if veteran sappers approved of a candidate's potential. But often experienced sappers would examine new draftees, after their basic training, and select the more promising ones for sapper school.

Sappers recruited in North Vietnam, and that's where most of them came from, were given six to twelve months' training. The key subjects were:

- **Assault Techniques.** How to attack an enemy position most effectively. A lot of this was based on the experience of many sappers in many attacks (both successful and otherwise). This consisted of learning how to assign different sappers to hit different targets when the assault began. This way, you could shut down the enemy defenses quickly. New sappers were shown how to move when assaulting, when to take cover, and when to shoot. They also had to know how to coordinate their specific tasks with the support they would get from other sappers and nonsapper units. Assaults would often have mortars and machine guns supporting it, or even a nonsapper infantry attack to distract the defender. A lot of these assault techniques were drill, to make the right moves automatic. There was little time to think during an assault, especially for new sappers who had no experience under fire.

- **Breaching Obstacles.** Sappers were carefully trained on the best techniques for getting through barbed wire, minefields, and floodlit areas. A lot of this was just practice, practice, practice. You had to be able to do this quickly, perfectly, silently, and in the dark. Failure in any aspect of this would get you, and the rest of your sapper team, killed.

- **Camouflage.** Sappers had to remain hidden while planning and setting up their assault. This was best accomplished by knowing how to hide yourself in plain sight. Trainees learned how to use natural materials to hide themselves when setting up positions close to their objectives and how to hide themselves as they moved in to make the actual attack. Because of the ever-present American airpower, camouflage was essential all the time and success at it was a matter of life, death, and success in doing what sappers do.

- **Exfiltration.** Sappers were not suicide troops and they were expected to get away with their mayhem unscathed. Exfiltration was a lot like infiltration, but could (and often had to) be done faster. A lot of this was tricks of the trade passed on by more experienced sappers.

- **Explosives.** Sappers used explosives to blow up obstacles and to destroy enemy fortifications and equipment. A favorite target was airfields, and sappers were taught where to place what kind of explosives to do the maximum damage to various types of aircraft. Special types of explosive devices were used for getting through barbed wire and or minefields. Different explosive devices were used for knocking out bunkers or destroying other structures or equipment. Finally, sappers were told how to handle the different types of explosives themselves. Some of these materials required very special handling when being used or stored. Sappers were also given some instruction on how to build various types of explosive devices. To assist in this, sappers were taught about American explosives and munitions. Sappers often used captured material. A well-trained sapper team could use Russian or Chinese explosives, or American gear, or make their own from bits and pieces of whatever they could lay their hands on. Sappers were making fertilizer bombs long before any other terrorists had even heard of this technique.

• **Infiltration.** This was the sapper specialty that constantly surprised American and South Vietnamese defenders. Sappers were known for their ability to sneak through the most formidable obstacles. They did this by moving slowly and carefully. The reason the breaching team (the first sappers through the defenders' minefields and barbed wire) wore only shorts, or went naked, was so that they had more skin exposed that could feel things, like wire, mines, or booby traps. Again, it was a matter of repeated practice and perfecting the techniques. Sappers were trained to take as much as an hour (or more) to go through a few feet of barbed wire and mines.

• **Navigation.** Sappers had to get around in the jungle more adroitly than nonsapper troops. Sapper teams were often quite small, so every man had to be able to find his way. Nonsapper troops often traveled in large groups led by guides. Sappers had to be their own guides, and they were taught techniques of how to find their way through unfamiliar territory. Again, a lot of this was practice. Sappers spent a lot of time in the field practicing.

• **Planning.** Probably one of the least appreciated advantages of the sappers was the degree of planning they put into their operations. These planning procedures were drilled into sapper recruits and it was made clear that the difference between success and failure, not to mention life and death, was in how well the planning phase of an operation was done. The first part of the planning process was the decision of the local Viet Cong or North Vietnamese army commander to have sappers go after a particular target. If an experienced sapper officer was available to advise the commander, a target would be selected and enough sappers assigned to the task. If the commander made a mistake, it could well turn into a very high-risk operation. Once the sapper unit was assigned to a target, the real planning began. Most sapper operations were taken care of using only a sapper company (20–40 sappers) or battalion (80–150 sappers). The first task was reconnaissance. Back at the sapper base, a small-scale model (of dirt, twigs, and rocks) of the base would be built using all available information and making it obvious where information was missing. Sappers were trained on how U.S. and South Vietnamese bases were laid out and what installations were found in all of them. So more reconnaissance was done until the model of the enemy base was complete. The sapper subunits would be given their assignments and would use the model to go through who would do what and when. The sapper commander would keep drilling his troops with the model until he was sure everyone knew their tasks. Thus prepared, the assault would be carried out.

• **Reconnaissance.** Information on the enemy situation was absolutely necessary for a sapper operation to succeed. This data was obtained by some very energetic reconnaissance. Friendly units in the vicinity would be asked for all they knew about the target. If it was a base in a populated area, the local Viet Cong might even have an agent or two working inside. Once the locals had been pumped for information, the sappers would begin their own reconnaissance. This began with just examining the base from a distance. If there were no friendly agents inside the base, then a few sappers would make their way past the base defenses at night to scout the place out. This was always done anyway, mainly to test the defenses and make note of how effective they were and how they were laid out. Senior sappers would do this reconnaissance, often the commander of the sapper unit himself. Many times the defenders caught the sappers making this reconnaissance and either thought it was a full-scale attack or correctly deduced that this was just a recon and that the assault itself would follow in a few days. Sometimes the assault was called off if the recon was discovered, but sometimes it was only delayed or even went ahead on schedule. The recon had good reason to remain undetected, for sapper attacks depended on surprise for success.

• **Small Unit Tactics.** Sapper units were also considered light infantry and were taught how to operate as an infantry unit. This training was the basis of specialized sapper training anyway, and sapper units trained hard so that they could do these small unit drills better than regular infantry units. Such tactics covered how to deploy on the battlefield for various types of operations (deliberate attack, hasty attack, meeting engagement, withdrawal, hasty and deliberate defense, regular patrolling, etc.).

• **Special Equipment Training.** Naval sappers had to learn the use of underwater diving equipment. Some sapper raids were for stealing vehicles, so some sappers were taught how to drive various types of vehicles. There's no time to try and figure it out when you're in a hurry and under fire.

• **Weapons Training.** In addition to all the usual infantry weapons (assault rifles, machine guns, antitank rocket launchers, grenades), sappers also learned how to use enemy weapons. During their raids, they could expect to get their hands on unfamiliar weapons (like the U.S. grenade launcher) or similar weapons that operated a little differently (like U.S. machine guns). There were also some specialized sapper weapons, like flamethrowers, that might be used from time to time. Sappers not only had to be expert with a wide variety of weapons, but had to know how to handle them flawlessly at night.

The sappers recruited in South Vietnam did not normally get as much training as the North Vietnamese ones did. Viet Cong sapper recruits might get by with only a few weeks' training. Then again, sappers in the south were usually recruited from the ranks of veteran Viet Cong fighters. Such men (and a few women) already had a lot of sapper skills and only needed some specialist training to make them capable of sapper operations.

Sappers conducted thousands of assaults throughout the war. Most attacks by regular infantry units were led by sappers, who then performed the traditional role of leading the infantry through enemy barbed wire, minefields, and fortifications.

Sapper assaults were fast, being over in less than an hour in most cases.

Shock and surprise were their major assets, for as time went by during the assault, the defenders became less shocked and surprised. Sappers typically attacked a camp with a much larger number of troops than the sapper team. Since it was at night, most of the enemy were asleep. But the noise of the assault would wake them up, and it wouldn't take long for the enemy to organize a more lethal defense. Sappers anticipated this and planned their actions to prolong the surprise and even up the odds. One of the first things they went for was the camp power supply (usually a generator). Other sappers would attempt to hurl explosives into the barracks, while another group of sappers shot it out with the enemy night shift. Reconnaissance had pinpointed where enemy heavy weapons (machine guns and mortars) were, as well as bunkers. All of these were attacked in the order of danger they presented to the sappers.

Sapper assaults divided their forces into different elements, depending on their job. The main element was the assault force. These are the folks who went through the wire and minefields. There was usually a fire-support force that fired mortars, machine guns, and sometimes recoilless rifles at the camp just when the assault force was through and ready to do their worst inside the camp. While the fire-support weapons would wake everyone up in the camp, it would also make them think it was just a mortar attack. Thus distracted by their efforts to get into a slit trench or bunker (often not taking their rifles with them), the sappers could do their work with less interference.

Depending on the situation, there might also be a security force and an exploitation force. The security force would be used to prevent enemy reinforcements from coming to the aid of the attacked camp, or portion of the camp under attack. The security force would be small, usually not more than a dozen troops, armed with AK-47s and a machine gun or two. They would position themselves where they could ambush any reinforcements the defenders might get. Sometimes there were several camps within a mile or two of each other, and if the sappers knew the enemy had a plan to immediately send a reinforcement force to a camp under attack, the sapper security force would be there to slow the reinforcements down.

An exploitation force would be for larger camps that required more troops to do the needed destruction. If the sappers were simply leading the way for regular infantry, then several companies or even a battalion or more of troops would go through the breeches the sappers had made in the enemy defenses. For a larger attack like this, there would often be two or more assault forces, each working on a separate breech in the enemy wire and mines.

The sappers acquired a formidable reputation in Vietnam, and it was well deserved. The sappers were not supermen, but they were generally very good at what they did. The main problem for the Communists was that they never had enough sappers. Although the number of sapper battalions was increased throughout the war, as the years went by, losses exceeded the ability to train new recruits. Communist troops were in until the war was over and against American firepower it was only a (short) matter of time before even the most skilled combat soldier got killed. This was particularly true with the sappers, whose daring missions tended to result in complete success and little or no casualties, or a failure in which everyone in the assault element got killed (and many others besides).

But the reputation of the sappers proved a powerful lure to the young, eager, and able recruits. Not many sappers survived, but their reputation continued to grow.

ELECTRONICS

While America was the acknowledged leader in high tech during the Vietnam War, the North Vietnamese were not without resources in this area. In the field, an infantry battalion rarely had more than half a dozen Chinese-made radios. These had a range of some fifty kilometers and were only used for communication between companies and battalion headquarters in emergencies or as part of a deception. The Communists knew that the Americans had an enormous advantage in electronic warfare equipment. U.S. radio detection gear could fix the location of Communist radios within minutes and have artillery fire or bombs on the target within an hour or less. Communist units relied more on telephone wire laid through the jungle, troops carrying messages or other signals (rifle shots, flares, etc.) to communicate in battle.

An American infantry battalion had over a hundred radios of various types and these were used freely in the field. The Communists used this abundance of enemy radio traffic as one of their own weapons. Using captured U.S. radios manned by English-speaking operators, the Communists would monitor American radio traffic during operations and, despite code words and the like, were able to obtain a lot of information on what the enemy was up to. This provided a tremendous advantage, for the Communist units sent nearly all of their messages by foot or telephone and were thus almost impossible to intercept. Meanwhile, American and South Vietnamese units broadcast their plans for the Communists to hear. Using spies in South Vietnamese and American base camps, it was often possible to obtain code words and battle plans that made the seemingly chaotic American radio traffic provide useful information for Communist troops.

There was even more extensive electronic gear in North Vietnam, along with thousands of Russian soldiers to help maintain and operate it. Again, this Russian and Chinese gear was no match for the higher tech and better built U.S. stuff, but taking advantage of the American sense of superiority in this area, the Communists were able to keep everyone wondering how they knew so much.

THE WELL-CLAD GUERRILLA

The NVA and the Viet Cong were adequately, if plainly, uniformed. Albeit while perhaps not up to the sartorial standards of the U.S. armed forces, in fact the NVA and the VC had simple but adequate standard uniforms during the war.

For the most part, NVA uniforms were serviceable, if less than attractive. Cheaply made, in many cases hand sewn, probably by village laborers, the uniforms were sturdy, if inelegant. Most troops usually had one uniform, which they wore until it had to be replaced. The pattern was simple, and they were for the most part all made in one size, though the troops seem to have often made alterations to improve the fit. The basic outfit consisted of cotton trousers and a shirt, which could be supplemented by a sort of sweat suit for colder weather and a cheap plastic poncho for the rain. The trousers had one pocket on each side, with one in the back, a system of buttons to adjust the waist to a better fit, and a web belt with an aluminum buckle. Though occasional variations were found, the shirt was simple, with two pleated pockets, closed by a pointy flap, and a few buttons down the front.

The troops were issued an equipment belt. The standard one was initially of canvas, but later was often made from plastic webbing, occasionally webbing captured from American and South Vietnamese forces. The buckle was aluminum, in several patterns, including a unique one for officers, one of their few identifying marks, though they were sometimes issued a leather belt. Some troops were issued belts procured from the Communist Chinese, and some reportedly had French ones, captured in the earlier war.

As can be seen, NVA and VC uniforms were only generally uniform, particularly since there were some variations in color, beyond normal fading, due partially to administrative decisions and, probably, to a shortage of dye-stuffs as well.

Initially the uniform was a khaki color. This was worn by NVA personnel in all areas, main force Viet Cong units in the south, and, apparently, also by some main force Khmer Rouge and Pathet Lao forces as well, since they were largely supported by the NVA. VC militia units usually made do with standard peasant garb. The color was changed to a dark olive green beginning in 1966. Though the exact shade varied somewhat, due to quality-control problems, it was usually darker than that worn by American and South Vietnamese forces. North Vietnamese militia units often wore the same pattern uniform in several other colors, including blue, a dark purple, brown, white (apparently also issued to naval personnel), and gray, and these sometimes turned up being worn by NVA units in the south, particularly during major operations, such as Tet. Occasionally, troops were found wearing a Chinese Communist–style uniform, with its tunic bearing four pockets for officers and two for enlisted men.

The NVA for a time issued a kind of simple tennis shoe made of canvas and rubber, but these didn't do well in the field, wearing out quickly, so that many soldiers were barefoot even before they reached the south. Most troops ended up wearing sandals improvised from pieces of old tires held together by straps cut from old inner tubes. Nicknamed "Ho Chi Minh Freedom Sandals," they were durable, cheap, and practical.

The standard head covering was a sun helmet, which came in several patterns, usually of plasticized cardboard but occasionally of plastic. There was also a wide-brimmed "jungle hat" and occasionally a more formal-looking dress cap, much like a baseball cap. Occasionally troops were issued steel helmets. Some troops wore old Japanese helmets, and a few were issued the elegant—and virtually useless—French "Adrian" helmet, dating from World War I, but most were Soviet bloc patterns, sturdy enough by any standards.

The NVA had a series of dress uniforms, though most troops never received one. For the most part they seem to have been issued to senior officers and ceremonial troops. The winter dress was similar to the standard Soviet service uniform. It consisted of a tunic, shirt, tie, and trousers in olive green, with a Soviet-style service cap. The summer dress was a white cotton version of this.

When in the field the troops were supposed to have a canteen (there were two basic patterns), with pouch, a simple mess kit, several grenade pouches, ammo carrier (a sort of apron that could hold three magazines plus four boxes of spare ammunition), a simple medical kit, and a backpack, or rucksack, which had one large compartment and three smaller outside pockets; officers were sometimes issued one with a "secret compartment," to hold documents, maps, and the like.

American helmets and South Vietnamese uniforms were sometimes issued to troops as a deceptive measure. On 10 September 1967, the NVA *812th Regiment* attacked the perimeter of the 3/26th Marines wearing U.S. helmets and flak jackets. Although the marines beat off the assault, there seems to have been some initial confusion due to the enemy's use of American equipment (which is, by the way, a violation of the Geneva Convention, punishable by death without trial).

NORTH VIETNAM'S ALLIES IN THE WAR

One of the genuine "dirty little secrets" of the Vietnam War is the extent to which various Communist bloc countries contributed manpower to support the North Vietnamese. The Pathet Lao and the Khmer Rouge, of course, lent a hand, but they were to some extent adjuncts to the North Vietnamese. There were also Red Chinese and Soviet troops in Southeast Asia and small contingents from other Communist countries as well. Even now, more than twenty years after the fall of Saigon, information about these troops is sparse.

The Red Chinese seem to have maintained about 20,000 troops in northern North Vietnam through most of the war, primarily engineer and logistical personnel, helping to maintain the flow of supplies from China. Some of these troops also seem to have manned antiaircraft batteries and to have engaged U.S. aircraft from time to time. They are believed to have suffered some casualties. A figure of 10,000 dead was once cited, but this cannot be confirmed and seems rather high, since the total number of Chinese troops in North Vietnam was probably only c. 150,000 over the duration of the war.

Information on the role of Soviet troops is somewhat better, if only because the post–Soviet Russian government actually admitted there had indeed been Russian troops in Vietnam. Apparently an annual contingent of about three thousand Soviet troops served in Vietnam from about 1965 to the fall of Saigon. By some accounts, it was Soviet antiaircraft personnel who shot down the first American aircraft lost over North Vietnam in 1965, but thereafter the Russians restricted their activities to serving as technical advisers. Although Russian sources state that no Soviet personnel served in South Vietnam, on at least one occasion there was a report of a uniformed white man serving as a consultant to an NVA commander in the south. According to official Russian sources, 16 Soviet military personnel were killed during the Vietnam War.

Information on the role of military personnel from other Communist countries is even sparser than that on the Chinese and Russians. On one occasion an American LRRP killed a Polish military adviser in a skirmish in Laos. Since the U.S. troops were not supposed to be operating in that area, no public announcement was made at the time. Nevertheless, his presence, and that of a Czech officer who worked as an interrogator with Americans held as prisoners of war in North Vietnam, suggests the presence of at least some Warsaw Pact advisers in Indochina. There is also evidence that some Cubans may have served in an advisory capacity.

Castro's Cuba seems to have been an even more devoted ally of North Vietnam than either the Chinese or the Soviets. The Chinese seem to have "taken a cut" of some of the Russian supplies bound for Vietnam, and the Soviets actually reduced their support of the Hanoi regime in the early 1970s (apparently in an attempt to pressure it into making peace). The Cubans, however, actually continued to ship war materiél to North Vietnam, even drawing upon their own Soviet-supplied stocks, apparently without bothering to inform Moscow.

Apparently almost all of North Vietnam's Communist bloc Allied personnel served in an advisory or rear echelon capacity. Although at the time it was widely believed that Chinese and even Soviet pilots were at least occasionally flying North Vietnamese fighters in combat, it now seems certain that this never occurred. North Korean pilots did.

At the time the presence of Chinese and Russian troops in North Vietnam was known to U.S. military and political leaders. For political reasons it was decided not to make an issue of the matter, particularly since American personnel were often operating in areas where they were officially not supposed to be.

THE PATHET LAO

The Pathet Lao were the Communists of Laos. Although their leaders were Lao (not "Laotians"), for the most part the Pathet Lao were pretty much a wholly owned subsidiary of the Vietnamese Communist Party (which in an earlier incarnation had been the "Indochinese Communist Party"). Neither politically nor militarily were the Pathet Lao particularly well organized or effective, and they relied rather heavily on support from their Vietnamese "elder brothers."

Outline History of the Pathet Lao Movement

Period	*Activities*
1945–46	Organizational phase, limited military operations
1946–47	War against the French, with most of the work being done by the Viet Minh
1947–54	War against the Royal Laotian government
1954–59	Desultory efforts at a neutralist coalition government, with an army integrating elements of the Pathet Lao
1959–62	Renewed war with the royal government after a U.S.-sponsored coup installs a rightist regime. This led to the "Laotian Crisis of 1961–62," which was resolved by a UN-sponsored attempt at coalition government.
1962–64	"Tripartite government," a shaky neutralist coalition
1964–75	Renewed war, leading to a Pathet Lao victory, with strong support from North Vietnam

The military arm of the Pathet Lao (which means "Lao Nation") had to draw on a very small population base, since Laos had no more than about four million people, not all of them ethnic Lao (a people related to the Thai). So the fact that they were able to put 50,000–55,000 troops under arms in the early seventies is rather impressive, amounting to about 1.3 percent of the population.

Despite their rather impressive recruiting feats, the Pathet Lao were by no means a highly effective force. For most of the 1960s and 1970s there were probably more North Vietnamese troops in the country than Pathet Lao. During the seventies, NVA forces in Laos amounted to an estimated 60,000–65,000. While perhaps half of these were engaged in protecting and operating the Ho Chi Minh Trail, the balance were engaged in support of the Pathet Lao. The Pathet Lao suffered rather heavily from increased Royalist military activity in 1970–72 and from the abortive ARVN incursion of 1972.

Pathet Lao Military Forces, 1945–75

Year	Manpower	Year	Manpower
1945–52	c. 300	1964	c. 19,500
1953	c. 1,500	1965	c. 25,000
1954	c. 3,000	1966	c. 28,000
1955	c. 4,000	1967	c. 33,000
1956	c. 5,000	1968	c. 40,000
1957	c. 6,000	1969	c. 45,000
1958	c. 7,000	1970	c. 50,000
1959	c. 8,000	1971	c. 55,000
1960	c. 9,000	1972	c. 45,000
1961	c. 16,000	1973	c. 33,000
1962	c. 19,500	1974	c. 37,500
1963	c. 19,500	1975	c. 40,000

Key: Most figures estimated. Between 1945 and 1952, strength seems to have fluctuated between c. 250 and c. 350 men, occasionally more.

ENEMY ATROCITIES

Although the Communists—as well as their Western Allies and many misguided peace activists—made much of incidents like My Lai, in fact the Communists committed far more atrocities than did U.S. forces or Allied forces, including the South Vietnamese. Attacks on civilians were an inherent part of Viet Cong/North Vietnamese strategy to terrorize people into cooperating with them. Between 1957 and the end of 1972, the National Liberation Front assassinated 36,725 South Vietnamese civilians and abducted 58,499 others, most of whom simply vanished. VC death squads systematically murdered village leaders, clergy, medical personnel, social workers, teachers, small merchants, and, of course, "landowners," pretty much defined as anyone who owned as little as five hectares (c. 12 acres).

While their figures were officially compiled by the South Vietnamese government, there seems no reason to doubt their validity. In fact, the actual number of those who succumbed to VC death squads can never be known. Most of those kidnapped were probably murdered (though some may have been covert VC sympathizers in need of rescue and others may have joined the VC after "reeducation"). In addition, there were a lot of assassinations in the closing months of the war, which were never tabulated. The total is probably well above 100,000.

To put the slaughter in perspective, at the time the United States had about ten times the population of South Vietnam. So multiply the numbers on the following page by ten to see what equivalent murders and kidnappings you would have to have had in the United States. In fact, Communist political murders during this period, all by themselves, amounted to three times the murder rate in the United States, and kidnappings were incalculably higher.

Viet Cong Assassinations and Kidnappings, 1955–72

Year	Assassinations	Kidnappings
To 1960	c. 1,700	c. 2,000
1961	1,300	1,318
1962	1,118	1,118
1963	827	1,569
1964	516	1,525
1965	305	1,730
1965	1,732	3,810
1967	3,707	5,357
1968	5,399	8,759
1969	6,207	6,289
1970	5,951	6,892
1971	3,573	5,006
1972	4,405	13,119
Total	36,725	58,499

But the Communists knew that kidnapping was an excellent tool to terrorize an individual and then send him back to terrorize his family and friends with tales of Communist methods.

Nor were the targets of enemy atrocities always individuals. On 5 December 1967, Communist troops wiped out the Montagnard village of Dak Sok (Phuoc Long Province), killing hundreds of men, women, and children. And the massacre of some 3,000 to 5,000 civilians in Hue during the 1968 Tet Offensive is too well documented to deny, though it is in fact continuously denied by apologists for the Hanoi regime.

THE DECLARATION OF INDEPENDENCE OF THE DEMOCRATIC REPUBLIC OF VIETNAM

On 2 September 1945, Ho Chi Minh, recovering from a serious illness and wearing an old khaki uniform with sandals, mounted a simple dais set up in Ba Dinh Square in Hanoi to proclaim the independence of Vietnam from France. The declaration was interesting for its pointed references to the American Declaration of Independence and to the French Declaration of the Rights of Man, opening shots in a propaganda war that would continue long after Ho's death.

All men are created equal. They are endowed by their Creator with certain unalienable rights, among these are Life, Liberty, and the pursuit of Happiness.

This immortal statement was made in the Declaration of Independence of the United States of America in 1776. In a broader sense, this means: All the peoples on the earth are equal from birth, all the peoples have a right to live, to be happy and free.

The Declaration of the French Revolution made in 1791 on the Rights of Man and the Citizen also states: "All men are born free and with equal rights, and must always remain free and have equal rights." Those are undeniable truths.

Nevertheless, for more than eighty years, the French imperialists, abusing the standard of Liberty, Equality, and Fraternity, have violated our Fatherland and oppressed our fellow citizens. They have acted contrary to the ideals of humanity and justice. In the field of politics, they have deprived our people of every democratic liberty.

They have enforced inhuman laws; they have set up three distinct political regimes in the North, the Center, and the South of Vietnam in order to wreck our national unity and prevent our people from being united.

They have built more prisons than schools. They have mercilessly slain our patriots; they have drowned our uprisings in rivers of blood. They have fettered public opinion; they have practiced obscurantism against our people. To weaken our race they have forced us to use opium and alcohol.

In the fields of economics, they have fleeced us to the backbone, impoverished our people, and devastated our land.

They have robbed us of our rice fields, our mines, our forests, and our raw materials. They have monopolized the issuing of bank notes and the export trade.

They have invented numerous unjustifiable taxes and reduced our people, especially our peasantry, to a state of extreme poverty.

They have hampered the prospering of our national bourgeoisie; they have mercilessly exploited our workers.

In the autumn of 1940, when the Japanese Fascists violated Indochina's territory to establish new bases in their fight against the Allies, the French imperialists went down on their bended knees and handed over our country to them.

Thus from that date, our people were subjected to the double yoke of the French and the Japanese. Their suffering and miseries increased. The result was that from the end of last year to the beginning of this year, from Quang Tri province to the North of Vietnam, more than two million people died from starvation. On March 9, the French troops were disarmed by the Japanese. The French colonialists either fled or surrendered, showing that not only were they incapable of "protecting" us, but that, in the span of five years, they had twice sold our country to the Japanese.

On several occasions before March 9, the Vietminh league urged the French to ally themselves with it against the Japanese. Instead of agreeing to this proposal, the French colonialists so intensified their terrorist activities against the Vietminh members that before fleeing they massacred a great number of our political prisoners detained at Yen Bay and Caobang.

Notwithstanding all this, our fellow-citizens have always manifested toward the French a tolerant and humane attitude. Even after the Japanese putsch of March 1945, the Vietminh League helped many Frenchmen cross the frontier, rescued some of them from Japanese jails, and protected French lives and property.

From the autumn of 1940, our country had in fact ceased to be a French colony and had become a Japanese possession.

After the Japanese had surrendered to the Allies, our whole people rose to regain our national sovereignty and to found the Democratic Republic of Vietnam.

The truth is that we have wrested our independence from the Japanese and not from the French.

The French have fled, the Japanese have capitulated, Emperor Bao Dai has abdicated. Our people have broken the chains which for nearly a century have fettered them and have won independence for the Fatherland. Our people at the same time have overthrown the monarchic regime that has reigned supreme for dozens of centuries. In its place has been established the present Democratic Republic.

For these reasons, we, members of the Provisional Government, representing the whole Vietnamese people, declare that from now on we break off all relations of a colonial character with France; We repeal all international obligations that France has so far subscribed to on behalf of Vietnam and we abolish all the special rights the French have unlawfully acquired to our Fatherland.

The whole Vietnamese people, animated by a common purpose, are determined to fight to the bitter end against any attempt by the French colonialists to reconquer our country.

We are convinced that the Allied nations which at Tehran and San Francisco have acknowledged the principles of self determination and equality of nations, will not refuse to acknowledge the independence of Vietnam.

A people who have courageously opposed French domination for more than eighty years, a people who have fought side by side with the allies against the Fascists during these last years, such a people must be free and independent.

For these nations, we, members of the Provisional Government of the Democratic Republic of Vietnam, solemnly declare to the world that Vietnam has the right to be a free and independent country—and in fact it is so already. The entire Vietnamese people are determined in their physical and mental strength, to sacrifice their lives and property in order to safeguard their independence and liberty.

CHAPTER 12

Logistics

Amateurs study tactics, professionals study logistics. Although normally thought of as the science of supply, logistics is more than that. It's not only understanding what you need and getting it to the troops, but also determining what you might need and how your supply situation can influence operations. The North Vietnamese were better at logistics than the United States was, despite the fact that America had a lot more to work with.

CREATING THE INFRASTRUCTURE FOR WAR

An oft heard criticism of the American involvement in Vietnam is that we did not go in with enormous forces early enough, permitting the enemy to build himself up. Perhaps. But was such a course possible? In fact, aside from the problem of a shortage of immediately deployable forces, the insertion of an enormous army into Vietnam right at the start would have run into some serious logistical problems.

The American way of war relies heavily on matériel. Which means it relies heavily on getting the weapons, ammunition, supplies, spare parts, and everything else to the troops. Which, in turn, means having access to a considerable industrial infrastructure to permit the effective movement of literally mountains of matériel. And, in fact, despite more than a century of the French colonial activity in Southeast Asia, precious little had been done to develop such an infrastructure, especially in South Vietnam.

There were only two ports in South Vietnam capable of handling large ocean-going ships, Saigon and Cam Ranh. The former was a river port, with just four berths, while the latter, although blessed with one of the finest natural harbors in the world, had just one berth. Total cargo capacity was no more than about 2.4 million tons a year, even assuming that smaller vessels called at Nha Trang and Qui Nhon, the only other ports in the country of consequence. Moreover, there were few good roads, little warehousing, a poor rail net, and an inefficient communications system, all of which were important in terms of managing matériel. Even before the massive influx of U.S. forces in mid-1965, South Vietnam's logistical infrastructure was being strained: requirements for military supplies alone, virtually all of which had to be imported, were nearly 2 million tons a year. This was one reason why when the first marines arrived in Vietnam they came ashore by landing craft, rather than through a port, which would have been both cheaper and less wearing on men and equipment (another reason was so the marines could remind everyone of their amphibious capabilities). The first increment of American troops (c. 184,000 by the end of 1965) raised the annual need for military supplies to 3.4 million tons. So one of the first priorities of the American forces in Vietnam was to build the port facilities to sustain the war effort. This was not easy.

An estimate presented to GEN William Westmoreland in November 1965—by which time there were 122 ships awaiting discharge—indicated that logistical construction needs in South Vietnam amounted to 170 "battalion-months" of work. This at a time where there were only about eight battalions of army engineers in the country, perhaps 7,900 men. And, in fact, at the time the army had only one battalion of engineers trained in port construction, perhaps 850 troops. The navy was a little better off, but many of its approximately 11,000 civil engineering officers and Seebees (c. ten battalions) were not skilled in port construction. Nor was construction the only problem. Once ports were built, they had to be operated, and neither the army nor the navy had large numbers of personnel nor the numerous small vessels necessary to run ports. So rapid expansion of port construction personnel (the navy's Civil Engineering Corps grew from c. 1,700 officers to c. 10,000 during the war) and port management staffs was undertaken, and an enormous number of projects were begun.

An extraordinary amount of work was accomplished. During 1965–69, the United States spent about $1 billion on construction in South Vietnam. Not only were the existing port facilities significantly upgraded at both Saigon (to 7.2 million tons a year) and Cam Rahn (to 2.5 million tons a year, plus 200,000 barrels of petroleum products), but new deepwater port facilities were developed at Danang, Qui Nhon, Dong Ba Thin, Tuy Hoa, Nha Trang, and even at Saigon, where a whole new port area was built, cleverly dubbed "Newport." By mid-1968, South Vietnam's ports could handle about 15 million tons of cargo a year. Of course, by then there were a lot more troops in the country, and military imports alone amounted to about 13.5 million tons. Nevertheless, one of the most important military achievements of the war was the enormous logistical effort.

Note that although over 95 percent of goods shipped to Vietnam arrived by sea, some did also arrive by air, such as blood and other medicinals. As with the shortage of port facilities, there was also a shortage of good airfields when the U.S. buildup began. In 1965, there were just three airstrips in Vietnam capable of handling large transoceanic aircraft, for a cargo capacity of about 190,000 tons a year. An effort similar to that mounted to expand port facilities took place, so that by 1968, there were sixty such airstrips, with a cargo capacity of about a million tons a year.

MERCHANT SHIPPING

When the U.S. began committing large forces to Vietnam, the American merchant marine had been in decline for many years, since the end of World War II, when literally thousands of American flag ships carried a major portion of the world's commerce. There were just 965 ships of all types under American registry, including many not suited to moving military cargo, such as bulk carriers and passenger liners. There were also several thousand ships in mothballs, but only about four hundred of these—mostly Liberty ships and Victory ships left over from World War II—were in good enough condition to be returned to service. In addition, there was a shortage of merchant seamen. By the 1960s, the average American merchant mariner was middle-aged, and efforts had to be made to recruit new men. Other Western powers were having the same problem, but were providing their ships with their own officers, who commanded crews recruited from Third World nations, a policy the United States could not follow due to legal restrictions.

So in addition to a shortage of port facilities, the United States buildup in Vietnam was limited by a shortage of merchant shipping, the most efficient way of moving cargo (a ton of goods shipped by air costs about ten times what it would cost to move it by sea). Although some foreign flag merchant vessels could be hired, the bulk of the burden fell upon the American merchant marine. By 1968, by which time c. 200 of the reserve fleet ships had been brought back into service (usually with minimal modernization), nearly half of the U.S. merchant marine was engaged in carrying goods to Vietnam, and that was supplemented by military owned ships. Operations continued at about this level through the withdrawal of American troops, gradually diminishing until the fall of Saigon. In the post-Vietnam period the U.S. merchant marine declined to even lower levels. During the buildup for the 1990–91 Gulf War, many of the old World War II merchant ships were once again hauled out of reserve. These were manned by many of the same men who had served in them in previous wars, now grown gray.

REVOLUTIONARY LOGISTICS

North Vietnam fought a poor man's war. It had no choice. Without economic and military aid from Russia and China, it would not have been able to pursue its war in South Vietnam at all. North Vietnam and Viet Cong troops in South Vietnam required about 200–300 tons of food, weapons, ammunition, medical supplies, and the like per day. U.S. forces brought in about 21,000 tons of the same supplies to supply its own troops (who were about twice as numerous as their opponents). North Vietnam was able to obtain many of its supply needs locally, including about 10–20 percent of its ammunition needs, either by stealing/capturing them or buying them from corrupt South Vietnam officials, or by manufacturing them in jungle factories. Many of the booby traps and other explosive devices were made from captured America weapons and locally procured raw materials. Dud shells, mines, and the like were scavenged for explosives, despite the danger.

Most of the imports, seventy to one hundred tons a day, were weapons, munitions, and food. The weapons and munitions had to come down the Ho Chi Minh Trail from the north, but through most of the 1960s, much of the imported food was obtained locally in Cambodia and moved into South Vietnam.

The Communists had thousands of agents and sympathizers in South Vietnam, who enabled American supplies to be stolen. Sometimes bribes did it, or weapons were simply bought from South Vietnam soldiers and officials who were offering them for sale. Eventually, some unscrupulous U.S. troops, usually support troops in charge of supplies, would even sell them on the black market.

Although the Viet Cong in South Vietnam could live off the local economy, these were primarily local, part-time troops. When the Viet Cong began to form large full-time units in the early 1960s, they ran into supply problems. Each battalion of three hundred to five hundred troops required about half a ton of food each day. If you had one of these battalions marching from one area to another, or operating in a sparsely populated area, you had to have stockpiles of food (mainly rice) to feed them. Obtaining sufficient food to feed the troops was always a major chore for Viet Cong and North Vietnam commanders.

In many rural areas of South Vietnam, the Viet Cong established defacto control over the local population or shared it with the South Vietnamese government officials. The Viet Cong political line did not always gain the support of everyone in an area, but if the Viet Cong had armed men around, they could establish some kind of truce with the local officials. This, in turn, led to the possibility of commerce. For example, many areas of South Vietnam received rice and other foodstuffs from the United States. By saying they had more people than they did, or simply giving out less than they were supposed to, the South Vietnamese officials had rice they could resell to the highest bidder. Often the local Viet Cong put in the highest bid, or perhaps a lower bid plus a promise to not attack an American base in the area (which would bring in artillery, bombers, and trigger-happy GIs).

The American media and public never fully comprehended how fragile the Viet Cong, and especially the North Vietnam logistic situation, was. The Viet Cong tended to be from the area they operated in and could always disperse to their homes if their bases were hit by a search and destroy operation or bombers directed by long-range patrols. But the North Vietnamese had no home village to go back to if they were driven out of their bases.

Losing their stockpiled rice and vegetable gardens, the displaced North Vietnamese troops had to move to other North Vietnamese bases or to bases in Laos, Cambodia, or North Vietnam (depending on where the destroyed base camp was). Losing the supplies in these base camps interrupted the training of Communist troops and delayed, or canceled, attacks.

Thousands of Communist troops starved to death or died from the effects of malnutrition and disease caused by logistical problems. But hundreds of thousands of Communist troops were able to operate for years in South Vietnam using only a fraction of the supplies and logistical equipment available to the U.S. and South Vietnam forces. Few Americans fully appreciated the clever, but fragile nature of Communist logistics during the Vietnam War. The revolutionary logistics techniques developed by the Communists were, at the same time, their primary strength and their principal weakness.

THE HO CHI MINH TRAIL

Throughout the Vietnam War there were mentions of the mysterious Ho Chi Minh Trail that was supplying the Communist forces in South Vietnam. But this was more than a trail through the jungle. The Ho Chi Minh Trail was an ingenious logistics system that gave the Communists a key advantage during the war.

Most wars of this century have been decided when one side got a logistics advantage over the other. World War II saw Allied forces in Europe and the Pacific using far superior supply arrangements than their opponents. This logistics advantage proved to be a crucial advantage. The ability to move weapons, troops, and ammunition quickly made your troops more capable; but the inability to move those supplies could lose you your troops completely. Without food, the troops would literally starve. Without new weapons and more ammunition, your troops would be less able to fight. Without medical supplies, the least injury or illness could became serious or even turn fatal.

The North Vietnamese troops were even more dependent on logistics than their opponents. North Vietnam was fighting a poor man's war and had no reserves to fall back on. Many North Vietnam troops in South Vietnam, finding their rice supplies captured or destroyed by enemy troops, faced starvation. Losses due to malnutrition and attendant diseases were much higher on the Communist side. Thus there had to be a reliable means to bring forward a steady stream of supplies for the troops. This was not a problem when all the Communist troops were local guerrillas who had day jobs. It was also not a problem as long as North Vietnam was able to use fishing boats or small transports, landing men and supplies on the coast.

But in 1959, the decision was made to increase guerrilla activity in South Vietnam. The first people the Communists needed down in South Vietnam were the thousands of South Vietnamese Communists who had gone north after the 1954 partition of Vietnam (to ensure that these Communist "cadres" were not jailed or killed by the anti-Communist government in the south). It was too dangerous to try getting all of these people south via boat, because many of these boats were intercepted. Moreover, many of those going south were meant to work in areas far away from the coast. Rather than risk having these cadres caught by the South Vietnam police, it was deemed better to have them enter South Vietnam from Laos.

There was already an organization (*Group 759*) running supplies down the coast, using small boats (disguised as fishermen or transports). This had been going on throughout the late 1950s. But this could only get men and supplies to the coastal area. Until the Americans arrived in force during 1965, the North Vietnamese had no trouble crossing the DMZ (demilitarized zone) between North and South Vietnam. From there a series of trails and rest stations, a sort of "underground railroad," was moving about three hundred people a month into South Vietnam. But the South Vietnamese army and police were getting more aggressive with this route. So *Group 559* (after the date May 1959, when the group was set up) was created to organize the route through the Truong Son mountains, which formed a natural border between North Vietnam, Laos, and South Vietnam. This route was called the Truong Son Route by the North Vietnamese; Americans coined the phrase Ho Chi Minh Trail. The troops who had to walk all the way called it "the Ten Thousand Mile Route."

There was already a crude system of trails through the region, used by the local mountain peoples. Initially, all that was done was a survey of the existing trails and setting up way stations along the selected routes. The North Vietnamese *301st Division* was moved into Laos to do the work and protect the trail. It took troops or porters about a month to travel down the entire six-hundred-mile length of the trail. In a straight line, it was only three hundred miles, but jungle trails don't run in straight lines. Twenty miles a day wasn't bad speed when you consider that the trail moved over mountains and across numerous streams, ravines, and rivers. A porter could carry a fifty-five-pound load or over one hundred pounds if they used a bicycle (which was walked most of the way, at least on those portions of the trail that permitted it).

In 1961, North Vietnam and Laotian Communist troops gained control of all the border areas they needed to control the best trails. The trail began in the North Vietnam city of Vinh. It crossed the mountains, then split into three separate routes into Laos. A fourth route went right across the DMZ into South Vietnam. There was not one trail, but many parallel ones that weaved back and forth and branched into South Vietnam every dozen or so miles. When monsoon rains or U.S. air attacks closed one part of the trail, traffic could divert to a parallel route. The trail was actually ten to thirty miles wide, as well as three hundred miles long. It consisted of an interlocking

system of twelve thousand miles of trails and roads spread over some seventeen hundred square miles of hills and jungle. Several distinct routes
wound their way from just north of the DMZ to the South Vietnamese
border near Cambodia. Gradually, the trail was improved, producing "high-
speed trails" in areas that allowed it. These improved trails allowed two men
to walk abreast at a normal marching speed and had a packed earth surface.
Eventually, portions were expanded to handle trucks and tanks, which by
1973 included the entire length of the trail. Most of the trail was under jungle
canopy. Where necessary, artificial canopy was created by weaving live vegetation with rope, vines, and dead vegetation to protect the trail from air
observation.

Construction of the Ho Chi Minh Trail went on throughout the 1960s
and into the early 1970s. During the peak period, the mid-1960s, 100,000
men and women (mostly women) labored on the trail. Local Laotians and
Montagnards were often forced to work as porters and laborers.

In the early 1960s, getting down the full length of the trail was a major
undertaking that took about a month, and often took your life as well. You
had to carry most of your food with you and anything else you might need.
There were very few people living along the route, and those who did, mostly
Montagnards, had little food to spare and much hatred for any Vietnamese
they caught passing through. The North Vietnamese policy was to maintain
good relations with the locals, and that meant keeping their troops from
looting the locals. But there was little to steal. Walking the trail meant walking up and down one jungle-clad hill after another. Doing so in tropical heat
and humidity was bad enough, but there were many diseases you could catch
on the way. By the mid-1960s, the length of the trail was dotted with the
graves of those who didn't make it. If you did get a fever so bad that you
could not walk any more, you were just left in your hammock, with perhaps
some food and water and a note explaining who you were. If you were lucky,
the Vietnamese trail guides would find your body and bury you; otherwise
the jungle would reclaim you as a pile of rotting flesh and bones. There were
a lot of those along the trail too. Depending on the time of year, the rainy
season was the worst. Up to a quarter of each unit might not make it down
the trail. If you collapsed near one of the way stations where the guides lived,
you might be nursed back to health. Some lucky travelers, left behind to die,
recovered by themselves and managed to finish the trip. Anyone who made
it to South Vietnam along the trail usually required at least a few weeks, and
sometimes several months, of rest before they were capable of any strenuous
activity.

While most of the people marching down the trail were young men in
prime condition, the Communists also sent down older men, and a few
women, who were skilled in political matters. These "cadres" were important
in running the propaganda campaigns down there. But these old-timers, in

their thirties or forties, required a month or more of strenuous training before being considered fit enough to stand a chance of surviving the trip down the trail. Mainly this consisted of a lot of walking, especially up hills, with heavier and heavier packs.

Until 1964, the trail was still quite primitive, and only 6,000 people moved down it. But in 1965, U.S. and South Vietnam naval forces pretty much shut down the coastal route. So from 1965 on, the Ho Chi Minh Trail became the main supply route to the South. Trucks from China and Russia and thousands of additional troops worked at expanding the trail capacity. In 1967, the trail moved 69,000 troops into South Vietnam, along with over 10,000 tons of supplies. By 1969, the troop traffic was 100,000 men, and the supplies moved increased in equal proportion. An increasing number of troops also crossed into South Vietnamese via the DMZ. This was such a troublesome problem that most U.S. ground combat operations were in northern South Vietnam, trying to keep the North Vietnamese units there from getting any farther south. In this the U.S. Marine and Army troops were quite successful, but then there were all those North Vietnamese troops still coming down the Ho Chi Minh Trail.

The peak months for Ho Chi Minh Trail travel were November through May, the "dry season," when there was a minimum of torrential rains and mud to slow the movement of men and trucks down the trail.

By 1971, each month the Communists were (on average) sending down their system of trails and roads in Laos, Cambodia, and the border areas of South Vietnam:

- 10,000 troops
- 1,700 tons of food
- 6,600 weapons
- 800 tons of ammunition
- Several tons of other supplies

Each of those troops had to be fed and supplied with ammunition, medicine, and clothes. About forty thousand North Vietnam troops were stationed along the Laos portion of the trail. Assisting them were sixty thousand Laotian and Vietnamese porters and laborers. The porters carried matériel where bikes or trucks could not go. The laborers built and maintained the trail. The troops also staffed fifty bases where the trail staff, as well as passing troops and truck drivers, could rest along the way. In addition to the fifty bases, there were thousands of trenches and bunkers along the trail, providing refuge from U.S. bombing attacks.

By the late 1960s, it was obvious that the trail was a key North Vietnam weakness that could be exploited, if the trail could be cut. Bombing was tried, but it didn't work. The trail consisted of twelve thousand miles of roads and trails, and at any given time less than a hundred miles of it was actually occupied by enemy troops and porters. Most sensors were not capable of penetrating the vegetation covering the trail. Air-dropped acoustic sensors (microphones) had some success in identifying foot or truck convoys, but the bombers could not always get there in time. Even using artillery to hit supplies coming into South Vietnam was difficult, for the trail was well equipped with bomb shelters (bunkers or trenches). Initial attempts to interdict the trail with bombers and artillery didn't work.

Ho Chi Minh Trail traffic was also under constant observation by U.S. and Montagnard troops, organized into small patrols or "trail watcher" detachments. There was a small Hmong army (paid for and supported by the United States) that made attacks on the Ho Chi Minh Trail and its related installations, as well as reporting on North Vietnam activity. But the trail covered nearly two thousand square miles of mountains, jungle, and swamp. There were never many opportunities to hurt the movement of supplies when most were coming down on the backs of porters or carried on bicycles. At best, during this period, you could try to sniff out the depots where this matériel was collected before being sent into South Vietnam. But even these collection points did not contain a lot of matériel. Before the truck routes on the trail opened in the late 1960s, only a few hundred tons a month could be sent down the trail. The best success the United States had in slowing down trail traffic was, ironically, after the North Vietnamese had made it possible to drive trucks the full length of the trail. This made it much easier to spot traffic from the air. By 1970, the North Vietnamese were able to move matériel by truck down the full length of the Ho Chi Minh Trail. During the dry season that year, starting in November, the Communists were moving about ten thousand tons of supplies a month down the trail. But the U.S. Air Force now had a target they could relate to and deal with. That dry season, the Communists sent about sixty thousand tons of matériel down the trail. Some 80 percent of it was bombed and burned before it could reach South Vietnam. Nevertheless, the Communists were still moving about ten times more stuff down the trail than in the pretruck days.

The most effective weapon against Ho Chi Minh Trail truck traffic was the AC-130 gunship. Operating out of Thailand, these four-engine propeller-driven transport aircraft carried a wide array of machine guns, cannon, and sensors. Flying low and slow, they could detect trucks in the jungle below and shoot them up. Starting in late 1967, the AC-130s soon managed to damage or destroy nine to ten trucks per sortie. During the dry season, that added up to over a thousand trucks a month, although the year-round average was about eight hundred trucks a month. The North Vietnamese responded to this threat by filling the Ho Chi Minh Trail with antiaircraft weapons, especially those areas where it was easiest to spot trucks from the air.

The other solution was to invade Laos and cut the trail with troops. But the North Vietnamese had played their diplomatic cards right, and while denying they were even in Laos, they loudly protested anyone else violating Laotian territory. The atmosphere was so against the war that in the U.S. Congress a law was passed forbidding U.S. troops to enter Laos or Cambodia. An invasion was attempted in 1971, using South Vietnam troops, but the North Vietnamese (who officially weren't there) reacted violently and threw back the invasion force after some brutal combat. America supplied air and artillery support and lost a lot of aircraft in the process.

The bombing continued, but it only made it more expensive (in lost troops and supplies) for the North Vietnamese to get south what they needed. No matter how hard it was hammered, the trail kept operating throughout the war.

THE COST OF THE WAR

The Roman politician and philosopher Cicero once remarked, "The sinews of war are endless money." He had a point. But it has perhaps been treated with too much respect. In Vietnam, the United States had the money. In a seemingly endless supply, and we spent some. But that didn't translate into victory.

U.S. Vietnam-Related Expenditures, 1966–72

Year	Billions of Dollars	
	1966	*1998*
1966	5.8	29.0
1967	20.1	100.5
1968	26.5	132.5
1969	28.8	144.0
1970	23.1	115.5
1971	15.3	76.5
1972	13.0	65.0
Other	22.4	112.0
Total	155.0	774.7

Key: *Other* includes outlays for 1950–65 and 1973–75.

The United States spent some $155 billion dollars in Vietnam between 1950 and 1975. In money of 1998, that comes to over more than three-quarters of a trillion dollars. And these figures do not actually tell the whole story. Actually, it's sometimes very hard to decide what money was being spent for which purpose. For example, the Vietnam War engendered a major expansion of the staff at the headquarters of the Defense Department and the individual services, as well as an enormous expansion of basic-training facilities. It's not clear that the above figures—which are more or less offi-cial—reflect this. And, of course, the figures certainly do not reflect the pension burden the war left. If the pattern of previous wars holds, about three times as much will eventually be spent in pensions and veterans' ben-efits as will have been spent on the war itself, and the money may still be flowing on the hundredth anniversary of the fall of Saigon. The United States is still paying a couple of pensions to widows and disabled offspring of Civil War veterans.

CHAPTER 13

The Combat Units

No one fights alone in a war. Troops fight together in organizations called combat units. Each has a distinct character, shaped by its history and current members. Here are the combat units of the Vietnam War.

THE PRINCIPAL AMERICAN GROUND COMBAT UNITS IN VIETNAM
The largest battlefield army America raised since World War II was assembled in Vietnam. Although Americans never comprised more than 38 percent of Allied troops in Vietnam, U.S. combat units controlled most of the combat power for five years (1966–70).

Army and Marine Corps Headquarters. Militarily "corps" has several meanings. One of these is an operational headquarters overseeing several divisions. In addition to its assigned divisions, a corps normally has allocated to it a variety of smaller independent combat and combat support units, such as heavy artillery battalions, engineer battalions, and medical units. So as not to offend the South Vietnamese, who had four corps headquarters, in Vietnam U.S. corps were for the most part redesignated "field forces."

I Field Force, Vietnam. Activated in late 1965 to control American units in the ARVN II Corps area, originally merely as "Field Force, Vietnam," becoming I FFV with the activation of II FFV in March 1966. It was disbanded in April 1971.

II Field Force, Vietnam. Activated in March 1966 to oversee U.S. operations in the ARVN III Corps area. It generally commanded the largest concentrations of American troops in Vietnam, until deactivated in May 1971.

III Marine Amphibious Force (III MAF). Activated in the I Corps area in May 1965, the III MAF not only commanded all marine units in the corps area, but also oversaw operations of the army's XXIV Corps. The force pulled out of Vietnam in April 1971.

XXIV Corps. Organized in the spring of 1968 as the "Provisional Corps" in the I Corps area, from a temporary headquarters improvised from elements of MACV in February of that year, which was redesignated as the XXIV Corps in August. In an odd administrative arrangement, the corps served under the III Marine Amphibious Force, which, of course, served at least theoretically under the ARVN I Corps. The corps headquarters left Vietnam in June 1972.

U.S. Army Divisions. A division is a large (12,000–20,000) combat force of all arms (i.e., it combines infantry, armor, artillery, and various combat support and combat service elements) designed to conduct sustained combat operations. In Vietnam, the United States essentially employed three types of divisions: infantry, air mobile, and marine, which are listed separately.

1st Cavalry Division (Airmobile). Nicknamed "the First Team," the 1st Cavalry Division arrived in Vietnam in September 1965 and stayed until April 1971, for a total of 2,056 days in country. It was actually an air-assault division, rather than a cavalry division or an airmobile one. "The Cav" had lost its horses in 1943 during World War II, shortly before going to fight the Japanese in the Pacific. The division fought through to the end of the war as an infantry unit and then stayed in Japan as part of the occupation force. When the Korean War began in 1950, the division was sent there and fought until 1951, then moved back to Japan until 1957, when it went back to Korea and remained there. In the early 1960s, the army reluctantly formed the 11th Air Assault Division to test the use of helicopters in combat, naming it after an airborne division that had seen action in the Pacific during World War II. When the experiment proved a success, it was decided to send an airmobile division to Vietnam. For PR purposes, the army decided to redesignate the new unit as the 1st Cavalry Division (Airmobile). So the 1st Cavalry Division in Korea was renamed the 2nd Infantry Division, and the 11th Air Assault Division was renamed the 1st Cavalry Division (Airmobile). The hasty expansion of the 11th Air Assault Division into the 1st Cavalry Division created some problems, since the army had a shortage of helicopter pilots and of troops trained to operate with helicopters. The 1st Cavalry Division was a new kind of combat formation and was expected to be a big deal for the army, thus the decision to send the division over as the more glamorous 1st Cavalry Division.

The 1st Cav was the first full U.S. division to reach Vietnam and much was expected of it. In the fall of 1965, the division won a major battle in the Ia Drang valley. Operating in the rugged areas of central South Vietnam, it fought there until it left Vietnam in early 1971. After the division left, one brigade (the 3rd) stayed behind for a year, departing in June 1972, in turn leaving behind an infantry battalion (1/7th Cav), which itself was one of the last American units to leave Vietnam. The many departing U.S. units needed some experienced airmobile forces to cover their departure, and this elements of the 1st Cav did to the end of the American presence in Vietnam.

1st Infantry Division (the Big Red One). The first American division to go overseas in World War I, it was also one of the first divisions to go overseas in World War II, fighting in North Africa and Europe. It remained in Germany on occupation duty until 1955, when it returned to the United States Elements of the division began arriving in Vietnam in mid-1965, and it was all there by October. Division headquarters left in April 1970, 1,656 days later. In Vietnam, the division did most of its fighting in southern South Vietnam.

4th Infantry Division (the Ivy Division). Raised for service in World War I, it saw more action in World War II. It was deactivated right after World War II, but activated again in 1947, went to Germany in 1951, and returned to the United States in 1956. The division arrived in Vietnam in September 1966 and left 1,534 days later in December. Upon arrival in Vietnam, most of the division was sent to the Cambodian border, where it remained for the rest of the war. Some brigades of the division were moved around, and one brigade was swapped for a brigade of the 25th Infantry Division (the only such swap during the war). The division's nickname derived from its insignia, a sprig of ivy, a punning reference to its designation (IV). The hard-fighting troops of the 4th often referred to themselves as "Poison Ivy."

5th Mechanized Infantry Division. A veteran of both world wars, the 5th Division sent its 1st Brigade to Vietnam in July 1968 and it left in August 1971, after 1,128 days. From the early 1960s, American mechanized divisions have been almost identical to armored divisions, the main difference being about 20 percent fewer tanks and 20 percent more infantry. Only the division's 1st Brigade served in Vietnam, as there was not enough open terrain to keep a full mechanized division busy. The brigade had one tank battalion, two infantry battalions, one artillery battalion, and company-size units of engineers and recon troops, plus the usual support units. It was stationed up north on the DMZ, by the border with North Vietnam.

9th Infantry Division. The 9th Infantry Division was raised in 1940, and served in Europe from late 1942 until the end of World War II. Inactivated in 1945, it was reactivated in 1947, served until 1962, and was again deactivated. The Vietnam War caused the army to reactivate the division again in February 1966. So it was a new division, and none of the troops had served together before. It was rather hastily dispatched to Vietnam, arriving in December 1966 (properly training a new division takes about a year), and remained there for 985 days, until August 1969, though its 3rd Brigade remained in country until October 1970. The 9th Division was a unique "triphibious unit." One brigade operated afloat, on barges and boats, as a riverine force; one was traditional infantry; and the third was composed of two air assault battalions. These brigades worked with U.S. Navy riverine units to control the intricate landscape formed by the numerous canals and waterways, a task in which they were quite successful. This riverine strategy was the same one pioneered by Union forces during the American Civil War a century earlier. This unique mission led to a number of unusual problems, not least of which was the fact that 47 percent of the 9th Infantry Division's nonbattle casualties were due to "immersion foot," a serious, sometimes crippling, and occasionally fatal condition that results from having one's feet wet too much.

23rd (American) Infantry Division. The Americal Division is unique. It's the only American combat division that has never been in the United States. It's also the only division with a name, rather than a number (well, officially since the late 1940s, it only has a number, but no one ever used it, even in written orders). The division was first raised in late 1942 from some miscellaneous American units on the Pacific island of New Caledonia (hence the name *Americal*). It served in the Pacific throughout the war and was deactivated in Japan in late 1945. Redesignated as the 23rd while still in limbo (Pentagon bureaucrats apparently couldn't allow a division to have a name, even one that was inactive), it was reactivated in Panama in late 1954, but it was deactivated eighteen months later. The division was reactivated again in Vietnam in September 1967 because a division headquarters was needed to oversee the operations of several independent brigades (the 11th, 196th, and 198th) that were to operate up north where the 1st Marine Division needed some extra muscle. As the Americal had operated with the 1st Marine Division in World War II, it seemed appropriate to reactivate it. The division was deactivated in Vietnam in November 1971, having served 1,526 days. It was never actually properly organized as a division and never developed the unit spirit that characterized some of the other divisions in Vietnam. The division suffered from poor leadership and low morale. Troops from the Americal perpetrated the My Lai massacre.

25th Infantry Division (Tropic Lightning). The division was formed from elements of the old Hawaiian Division in October 1941, and took casualties during the Japanese attack on Pearl Harbor. It got even on Guadalcanal and in other parts of the Pacific, ending the war on occupation duty in Japan. When the Korean War broke out in 1950, it was among the first American units to arrive there. At the end of the Korean War, the division was stationed in Hawaii. Because its Hawaiian base had similar climate and geography to

Vietnam, the 25th provided training areas and other support for adviser troops going to Vietnam in the early 1960s, and supplied helicopter pilots and some other specialists to the advisory group in Vietnam. One brigade arrived in Vietnam in December 1965, and the rest of the division followed in March 1966. Although its 2nd Brigade remained until April 1971, the division returned to Hawaii in December 1970, after 1,716 days in Vietnam. It spent most of its time operating around Saigon and near the Cambodian border.

82nd Airborne Division (All American). The 82nd Division saw service in World War I (SGT Alvin York was its most famous soldier) and was deactivated in 1919. Reactivated on the eve of World War II, it was converted into America's first airborne division and saw extensive service in Europe. It has been on continuous active duty since. Although there were some proposals to send the division to Vietnam, by mid-1968, the army's strategic reserve (forces available for immediate deployment in emergencies) was growing pretty slender, and the 82nd was the best of the remaining units, so it was decided to retain the division stateside. However, in the aftermath of the Tet Offensive, the division's 3rd Brigade was sent to Vietnam. It took less than a week for the brigade to get from its base in North Carolina to a combat zone in Vietnam. The brigade served in Vietnam from February 1968 to December 1969, a total of 661 days, generally as a fire brigade, going where the need was greatest, and it operated from Hue, in the North, to Saigon, in the South, as well as at points in between.

101st Airborne Division (Airmobile). "The Screaming Eagles" was formed shortly before the United States entered World War II, and was immediately converted into an airborne division. During that war it served in Europe (Normandy and the defense of Bastogne), and afterward became an important element of the nation's strategic reserve. One brigade arrived in Vietnam in July 1965, and the rest of the division arrived in November 1967. The division left Vietnam in March 1972, after 1,573 days. Although it deployed as an airborne division, the number of qualified jumpers in the division was small, as the pressures of expanding the army and sustaining the airborne units already in action reduced the available pool of airborne-trained personnel. The success of the airmobile 1st Cavalry Division convinced the army that the troopers of the 101st Division would be more effective with helicopters than with parachutes. More helicopters were provided, some other changes made, and the 101st was converted to an air assault division by the summer of 1969. Using its newfound air mobility, the division operated all over South Vietnam.

Task Force Oregon. This was a temporary division-sized headquarters activated in Vietnam in April 1967 and deactivated that September. Intended to control operations in central South Vietnam, where the situation was getting out of hand, the task force was composed of a brigade borrowed from the 25th Infantry Division, plus the only brigade of the 101st Airborne Division then in Vietnam, and the independent 196th Light Infantry Brigade. By September 1967, the 25th Infantry Division wanted its brigade back, as did the 101st Airborne Division, just completing its deployment to Vietnam. The balance of the task force was grouped with two newly arrived independent brigades (the 11th and 198th) to form the American Division.

Other Major Army Combat Formations. Brigades largely replaced regiments in the U.S. Army early in the 1960s, having greater flexibility. A brigade is usually a subordinate element of a division, consisting of several battalions usually, but not always of the same arm of service (i.e., infantry, armor, or artillery). Divisional brigades are austere, lacking combat support and combat service elements, which are supplied by the division. Independent brigades are much larger, since they are usually beefed up with artillery and engineer battalions, plus various combat support and combat service elements.

1st Aviation Brigade. Much more than a brigade. The unit was formed in Vietnam in early 1966 and became the headquarters for nearly all U.S. Army aircraft not a part of combat divisions. By the late 1960s, this meant the 1st Aviation Brigade had more troops assigned than any division. But more important, it had over 4,000 aircraft assigned. About 600 of these were fixed-wing airplanes, the rest were helicopters, including about 2,200 UH-1s, 440 AH-1 attack helicopters, 300 larger CH-47s, and over 600 smaller scout choppers. The brigade had several aviation groups assigned to it, each controlling several aviation battalions. The 1st Aviation Brigade was one of the last major units to leave Vietnam, departing in March 1973.

11th Light Infantry Brigade. A rather hastily organized unit, raised to replace the 25th Infantry Division as part of the strategic reserve when the division left Hawaii for Vietnam in 1966. As the tempo of the war increased into 1967, it was decided to ship the brigade to Vietnam, and it arrived in December 1967 (a National Guard brigade originally activated for the *Pueblo* Crisis replaced it in Hawaii). For a time, part of Task Force Oregon, from September 1967 the 11th Brigade formed part of the American Division. It departed Vietnam in November 1971, after 1,425 days in country. The brigade was poorly trained and badly led when it arrived in Vietnam and was plagued by poor morale throughout the war. It was troops from the 11th Light Infantry Brigade who perpetrated the My Lai massacre.

173rd Airborne Brigade. Intended as a "fire brigade" to support U.S. interests in the Far East, the 173rd Airborne Brigade (Separate), the only independent airborne brigade in the U.S. Army since World War II, was activated in March 1963 on Okinawa. Its official nickname, *"Tien Bing*—the Sky Soldiers," was supplemented by the unofficial "the Herd." Arguably this was the best major formation in the U.S. Army on the eve of the Vietnam War. Extremely well trained, well led, it had very high morale (race relations were so good another unofficial prewar moniker for the brigade was "Two Shades of Soul").

In May 1965, the 173rd A/B Brigade became the first major U.S. Army ground combat unit to be committed to the Vietnam War, when it was deployed to the Saigon area. Joined by the Australian Task Force and the New Zealand 161st Artillery Battery, the brigade later operated in the central highlands and in the infamous "Iron Triangle" region. It was withdrawn from Vietnam in August 1971, after 2,301 days, and was disbanded the following January.

The most notable operation of the 173rd occurred on 22 February 1967, when some eight hundred men from the 2nd Battalion, 503rd Parachute Infantry (2/503rd), made a combat airdrop near Katum in War Zone C. This, the largest combat jump by American forces in the war, was part of Operation Junction City and helped to block the flight of Viet Cong fleeing a major offensive by elements of the 1st, 4th, and 25th Infantry Divisions, the 196th Infantry Brigade, and the 11th Armored Cavalry Regiment. Officially credited with having taken part in fourteen campaigns, and the recipient of four unit citations, the 173rd A/B Brigade was in a combat zone longer than any American military unit since the Revolutionary War, and the 173rd actually holds the record for the longest continuous service under fire of any American unit ever. It also lost 1,601 men killed in action, plus another 8,435 wounded. A dozen men earned the Medal of Honor.

196th Light Infantry Brigade. Organized in September 1965 for service in the Dominican Republic (where an American-led international peace-keeping force was trying to prevent a civil war), the brigade—the first "light" infantry brigade in the army—was instead sent to Vietnam in August 1966. For a time part of Task Force Oregon, it was incorporated in the Americal Division in February 1967. The brigade departed Vietnam in June 1972, having served more than 2,100 days. Like its partner in Americal Division, the 11th Light Infantry Brigade, the 196th was poorly trained and poorly led when it arrived in Vietnam, deficiencies that were never effectively remedied.

198th Light Infantry Brigade. Activated early in 1967 for the purpose of helping to man "the McNamara Line," the 198th Light Infantry Brigade was shipped to Vietnam in October 1967, months ahead of schedule, and incorporated into the Americal Division. As with the other light infantry brigades, it was poorly trained and poorly led, and like most of them suffered from low morale and a lack of discipline for the entire war. It left Vietnam in November 1971, after 1,484 days.

199th Light Infantry Brigade. Organized in June of 1966, the 199th Light Infantry Brigade was in action in Vietnam by December of that same year, when it had still not received some of its heavy equipment. The brigade initially suffered from the same handicaps that plagued the other light infantry brigades, poor training and a lack of a sound cadre. Unlike the other brigades, some good officers succeeded in turning it into a first-class combat unit, and it proved particularly effective in the defense of Long Binh and Saigon during the 1968 Tet Offensive. Nicknamed "the Redcatchers," the brigade served as a semi-independent unit in the Saigon area until withdrawn in October 1970, after some 1,400 days in country.

11th Armored Cavalry Regiment. Since the early 1960s, the only operational regiments in the U.S. Army have been armored cavalry regiments. The 11th Cavalry entered Vietnam in September 1966 and left in March 1971. With a strength of some 3,700 troops, the unit was heavily armed with fifty tanks, some three hundred APCs (armored personnel carriers), eighteen self-propelled howitzers, and forty-eight helicopters. Because of all these vehicles, the Cav troops were frequently split into smaller units to provide road convoy escorts or road-clearing forces. It operated most of the time near Saigon and participated in the 1970 invasion of Cambodia.

Major U.S. Marine Corps Units. Vietnam saw the largest concentration of marine manpower between World War II and the Gulf War. At the peak of the war, 1968–69, nearly half the corps (which expanded to four active divisions during the war, one of which was incompletely formed) was in Southeast Asia.

1st Marine Division. Tracing its origins to a brigade formed in 1913, the 1st Marine Division was activated in 1941, served throughout the Pacific War (Guadalcanal, Papua–New Guinea, New Britain, Peleliu, and Okinawa), did occupation duty in northern China after World War II, and then fought in the Korean War. Based in California, elements of the division began serving in Vietnam in 1964, but the bulk of it was only deployed in February 1966. It served in the northern part of South Vietnam until April 1971, having spent 1,877 days in Southeast Asia.

3rd Marine Division. Formed in 1942 around a cadre of personnel from the 1st and 2nd Marine Divisions, the 3rd Marine Division fought on Bougainville, Guam, and Iwo Jima during World War II. Inactivated in 1945, it was reactivated in 1952 and deployed to Okinawa. It arrived in Vietnam in May 1965 and stayed until August 1969, 1,590 days later. It operated in conjunction with the 1st Marine Division in the northern part of South Vietnam.

9th Marine Amphibious Brigade. A provisional formation organized to oversee the operations of the first elements of the 3rd Marine Division to serve in Vietnam, the 9th Marine Brigade arrived in March 1965 and was disbanded sixty-one days later in May 1965 when the bulk of 3rd Marine Division arrived. During its time in country it provided security for the Danang airbase complex.

ROK FORCES IN VIETNAM

Still recovering from the effects of the Korean War (1950–53), the Republic of Korea (ROK) was an early and enthusiastic supporter of U.S. policy in Vietnam, at least partially as a means of ensuring a continuing American commitment to Korean security, and also as a way of securing additional military aid (the United States underwrote Korean expenses in Vietnam to the tune of several scores of millions of dollars a year). The first ROK troops, a military assistance mission, arrived in South Vietnam in March of 1965. By the end of that year there were over twenty thousand ROKs in the II Corps area, which was to be the primary ROK area of operations for the entire war. ROK military strength peaked in 1968, at some fifty thousand men, and remained at slightly below that figure until 1970, when it began to drop markedly. The last ROK troops pulled out in March 1973. On a population basis, the ROK manpower commitment to the war was proportionately greater than that of any Allied country, including the United States: in 1968, about one in every five hundred Koreans was serving in Vietnam, in contrast to about one in six hundred Americans.

Highly disciplined, inured to hardship, and staunchly anti-Communist, Korean troops had a reputation for toughness and even brutality: There are tales, possibly apocryphal, of ROK patrols demolishing suspected Communist villages with their hands and feet, using tae kwon do (a kung fu–like martial art). One result of this was that the government of Vietnam placed unusually tough restrictions on ROK units. For example, they were prohibited from firing unless fired upon. Another result seems to have been that villages in ROK areas of responsibility seem to have remained "pacified" much more consistently than those in other areas.

Most ROK operations involved small units, patrolling rigidly defined sectors. These operations were normally characterized by meticulous preparations to ensure success and to minimize casualties, and what U.S. military leaders considered an excessive reliance on air support. Nevertheless, the

Koreans achieved very high kill ratios, rarely falling below 10:1 and sometimes rising to 25:1 or more.

Capital Division. Arrived in September 1965 and left in March 1973. It was the premier division of the South Korean armed forces, with hand-picked personnel; it always got the best troops, officers, and equipment. This was because the Koreans did not want to risk doing less than an excellent job in their first combat operations since the end of the Korean War in 1953. The division was based just north of Cam Ranh Bay, covering about fifty miles of the coastal area.

9th Division. The "White Horse" Division arrived in September 1966 and left in March 1973. It was not as elite as the Capital Division, but it was good enough to accomplish whatever was asked of it. It held about fifty miles of coastal area, just north of the Capital Division's area.

2nd Marine Brigade. Founded in 1949, for most of the Korean War, the ROK Marine Corps operated as a fourth regiment of the U.S. 1st Marine Division. Following the Korean War, the Marine Corps was gradually built up to division size. The 2nd Brigade (Blue Dragons), arrived in Vietnam in October 1965 and left by February 1972. It was stationed south of Danang, in an area where the two U.S. Marine Corps divisions operated. The Korean Marines were tough, just like their American counterparts and mentors, with whom they occasionally operated. Some of their more notable actions were Operation Van Buren (19 January–21 February 1966), Operation John Paul Jones (21 July–5 August 1966), Operation Daring Rebel (5–20 May 1969), and the Battle of Hoi An (7–19 September 1969).

AUSTRALIA AND NEW ZEALAND IN THE WAR

Both Australia and New Zealand needed little prompting to send assistance to South Vietnam. For several years both had been concerned about the threat of communism in Southeast Asia. Both had taken part in the Malayan Emergency, and were already involved in the "Confrontation" with Sukarno's pro-Communist Indonesia. With support of the Soviet Union, in the late 1950s, Sukarno had already wrested control of western New Guinea (hardly a part of the Indonesian ethnic or cultural sphere) from the Netherlands, using guerrilla tactics. He was believed to have ambitions with regard to the Australian-controlled half of the island (now the Republic of Papua–New Guinea), and was already supporting a guerrilla campaign to wrest Sarawak and Sabah from the newly created Malaysia. To the Australians and New Zealanders both Vietnam and Sukarno's expansionism seemed different aspects of Communist expansionism. With broad support Australia adopted conscription for overseas service on 10 November 1964.

Australian Casualties in Vietnam

	Battle	Other	Total
Deaths	414	60	474
Injured	2,026	914	2,940
Total	2,440	974	3,414

Key: A total of 40,207 Australians served. *Battle Deaths* includes three Royal Australian Air Force personnel killed in action and one RAAF missing in action. *Other Deaths* includes eight RAAF nonbattle deaths, as well as one Australian Army nurse.

The **Australian Task Force** first arrived in May 1965 and left at the end of 1971. The unit was actually a small infantry brigade (two infantry battalions, one artillery battalion, a recon company, and two companies of Special Forces troops, plus administrative personnel). New Zealand contributed one-third of the artillery battalions throughout this period, plus, in 1967, two infantry companies and a Special Forces platoon. Unlike the Americans, the Australians replaced entire infantry battalions every thirteen months, thus nine different infantry battalions saw action in Vietnam. The ATF (as it was called) operated in an area southeast of Saigon.

In addition to the ATF, there was a second, smaller Australian unit in Vietnam, the **Australian Army Training Team Vietnam,** which served in an advisory capacity from 1964 through 1970. Of the 990 Australians who served with this organization, to which a handful of New Zealanders were attached, 30 were killed in action and 122 wounded, including ten New Zealanders. Men of the AATTV earned four Victoria Crosses, plus eighty-six other decorations for valor, as well as a U.S. Meritorious Unit citation and a collective award of the Vietnamese Cross of Gallantry, making it the most highly decorated unit in the history of the Australian Army.

Australians and New Zealanders were very good troops. So good, in fact, that Westmoreland wanted more of them. He tried to get New Zealand to contribute an infantry battalion so that he could form an ANZAC (a traditional acronym for an Australian–New Zealand force, dating from World War I) brigade, but this proved politically impractical.

Australian troops had more experience at counterinsurgency than did Americans. About seven thousand Australians had served against the Communist guerrillas in Malaya, 1955–60, and about thirty-five hundred during the "Confrontation" with Indonesia, 1960–66. However, the fighting in those two wars was different than that in Vietnam. Only about one in every 250 Australian soldiers in Malaya became a combat casualty (six killed in action and twenty-two wounded), and only about one in 135 in Borneo (six killed and nine wounded). About one in every 85 Australians in Vietnam became a combat casualty.

Although they thought American troops were brave enough, and often made good "mates," the Australian troops were rather critical of American professionalism. A common observation was that American commanders were not careful enough with their troops, often attacking in circumstances when slight delays to secure more support or a better deployment might have saved lives. In addition, they contended that U.S. troops were often poor at operating in the bush, making too much noise, frequently talking while on patrol, and lighting fires at night in hostile country. The Australians also believed American troops were trigger happy, firing too often, too indiscriminately, and too much, and that American troops were not always thorough when clearing an area. On one occasion Australian troops uncovered a substantial VC camp hidden in an area that had long been patrolled by an adjacent American unit.

In addition to seeing a lot of combat, Australian troops undertook a lot of public works and rural development projects. Australia also provided a good deal of economic development money, and pledged over $30 million even after the ATF began to pull out in 1970. Unlike the Asian Allied contingents, the Australians and New Zealanders did not require an American subsidy.

There was a vocal antiwar movement in Australia and New Zealand. This more or less paralleled that in the United States. Public opinion polls in Australia showed consistent support for the war until late 1968, when it plunged below 50 percent of those polled, while those opposing a continuation of the war rose to about 30 percent, with the undecided making up the balance. Interestingly, public support for conscription remained high despite the declining support for the war; When conscription was introduced in 1964, it was supported by about 70 percent of those polled, and only fell to 55 percent in 1971, by which time the Australians were pulling out.

THAI FORCES

Bordering Cambodia and Laos, Thailand naturally had an interest in what transpired in Indochina. Staunchly anti-Communist, the Thais permitted American forces (whose numbers peaked at seventy thousand, mostly from the air force, in 1969) to operate from their soil throughout the war. And the Thais were the first Asian country to send military assistance to South Vietnam.

Thai military advisers were active in South Vietnam from 1965 training pilots and naval personnel. Initially it seems that no thought was given to using Thai ground combat forces in Vietnam. Early in the war Westmoreland was interested in requesting Thai support for a contemplated offensive into Laos, to create an area free of Communist troops that would permanently sever the Ho Chi Minh Trail. These plans were definitely shelved in 1967, and the United States then requested Thailand send ground forces to Vietnam. Rather than use existing units of their relatively small army, the Thais decide to call for volunteers. The response was impressive, over five thousand men—soldiers and civilians alike—offered themselves for service.

Royal Thai Volunteer Regiment (the Queen's Cobras). A regimental combat team (several infantry battalions plus some artillery and some combat service and support units), numbering about two thousand men, the Queen's Cobras arrived in Vietnam in September 1967 and were attached to the U.S. 9th Infantry Division, in the Delta, until the Thais left in August 1968.

Royal Thai Expeditionary Division (Black Panthers). The new Thai contingent—initially intended to number about twenty thousand men—constituted a small division that included some conscripts as well as volunteers. The whole division never actually served in Vietnam. Instead, individual brigades were rotated into Vietnam for short tours of duty, so that peak Thai strength was never more than about eleven thousand men, actually a lot for a country with an army of only about ninety thousand men. Elements of the new division began arriving in Vietnam even as the Queen's Cobras were leaving. The division left Vietnam in August 1971, to be replaced by a smaller volunteer force. The Black Panthers operated in the vicinity of Saigon.

Royal Thai Volunteer Force. This replaced the Black Panther Division in September 1971, remaining until March 1972.

Two other contingents of Thais served, one indirectly and one directly. A small Thai detachment helped bolster the defenses of the Republic of Korea during the Vietnam War. In addition, a lot of Thais were recruited for operations in Laos. By one estimate some 16,500 Thais were serving as volunteers or mercenaries with anti-Communist Laotian forces throughout the 1960s, serving mainly as trainers and support troops for the Hmong army the CIA and Special Forces created in Laos. These Thais were very effective, especially the commandos that operated with the Hmong and U.S. CIA and Special Forces.

THE PHILIPPINE CONTINGENT

Having itself defeated a Communist insurgency only a decade earlier (the Huk movement), and as a staunch ally of the U.S., the Philippines supported American efforts in Vietnam, and Filipino military advisers were at work in the country from the late 1950s. In response to President Johnson's call for America's allies to bear more of the burden of the war, in February 1966, the Philippines dispatched a "Civic Action Group." This was a composite force, consisting of small infantry and artillery battalions for self-defense (there were only about 550 combat troops), plus an engineer and medical

Filipino Civic Action Missions in Vietnam

Land Clearance	*3,000 hectares*

Construction Projects

Bridges	11
Buildings	169
Culverts	194
Refugee Centers	54
Roads	116km
Watch Towers	10

Rehabilitation Projects

Airstrips	2
Buildings	47
Outposts	12
Roads	97km
Wells	245
Training	300 persons

Health Services Delivery

Medical	c. 725,000 cases
Dental	c. 220,000 cases
Surgical	c. 35 000 cases

battalion to do the Civic Action. Based in Tay Ninh Province, Filipino engineers and medical personnel undertook a number of projects to help the Vietnamese people. They did a lot of good work.

And, by the way, Filipino troops did see some combat, since the Viet Cong recognized that such civic actions projects constituted a danger to themselves and attacked the Filipinos from time to time.

SOUTH VIETNAMESE ARMY AND MARINE UNITS

By the time U.S. forces left, the South Vietnamese armed forces had grown to over a million troops. Most of these were in the ground forces. Up north was the I Corps, with the 1st, 2nd, and 3rd Infantry Divisions. In the central highlands was the II Corps, with the 22nd and 23rd Infantry Divisions. Down south, where most of the people lived, in the sprawling Mekong River Delta, there was the III Corps, north of Saigon (with the 5th, 18th, and 25th Infantry Divisions), and the IV Corps (7th, 9th, and 21st Infantry Divisions), covering everything south of Saigon. In addition, there were some special military districts, including Saigon. As a strategic reserve, the South Vietnamese maintained the Airborne Division (with three airborne and one ranger brigade) and the Marine Division (with three brigades). In addition, each corps had a few battalions of armor and Rangers as a corps reserve.

Most of South Vietnamese army combat troops did little more than stand guard over their own bases and patrol the populated areas. The only troops that could be depended on to actually attack the enemy were the Rangers, marines, and parachutists. There were only about seventy-two battalions of these (nine each of parachute troops and marines, plus about fifty-five of Rangers), and, although organized on U.S. models, they were usually under strength. Thus there were only about forty to fifty thousand troops on whom the South Vietnamese government could really depend to any degree.

Most South Vietnamese divisions went through several redesignations during their existence. The oldest units had their origins in French mobile groups created late in the First Indochina War, which were redesignated as "infantry" divisions in 1954. In 1955, they were all redesignated as either "field divisions" or "light divisions" (see, Creating ARVN, page 85), to be renamed "infantry" divisions in 1959.

1st Infantry Division. In 1953, the French formed the 21st Mobile Group, which became the 21st Division in January 1955, and the 1st Division later that year. Throughout its twenty-two-year history, the 1st Division was one of the best South Vietnamese combat units. Based in Hue, it had four, rather than three, infantry regiments. It usually operated in Quang Tri, Thua Thien, Quang Nam, and Quang Ngai Provinces, but also took part in Lom San 719. During the final Communist offensive, the division disintegrated as the troops deserted to look after their families.

2nd Infantry Division. Organized by the French in 1953 as the 32nd Mobile Group in the Red River Delta region of North Vietnam, it was transferred after the Geneva Accords to the Danang area, where it became the 32nd Infantry Division. It was renamed the 2nd Division in 1955. Between 1955 and 1965, division headquarters shifted back and forth between Danang and Quang Ngai, before finally settling down at the latter place until 1972, when it shifted to Chu Lai. It operated mostly in Quang Nam, Quang In, and Quang Ngai provinces. Although plagued by a very high desertion rate, the 2nd Division was pretty good. It stoutly defended Tam Ky during the final Communist offensive, with its remnants withdrawing by sea to Saigon and thence to Phan Rang, where it was overwhelmed in the final days of the war.

3rd Infantry Division. Raised in October 1971 to replace American units withdrawn from the northern areas of I Corps, along the DMZ, the 3rd Division was formed from two new regiments plus one veteran outfit (the 2nd Infantry Regiment, from the 1st Division). Headquartered at Ai Tu, in Quang Tri, it had not yet completed organizing and training when it became embroiled in the Communist 1972 Easter Offensive, and quickly fell apart. This permitted the enemy to overrun Quang Tri City, which was only recovered after much effort by other forces. Reconstituted at Danang later that year, the division operated in Quang Nam and Quang Tin. It was destroyed in the defense of Danang in March 1975. It's nickname was "Yellow Star," from its insignia.

4th Infantry Division. This had a brief existence in the late 1950s. However, since four is considered an unlucky number in Vietnam (like thirteen in the West), it was redesignated, eventually becoming the 22nd. Nevertheless, it remained unlucky.

5th Infantry Division. Originally formed in 1955 as the 6th Division, which was redesignated several times before becoming the 5th Division in 1959. Originally it was almost entirely made up of Nung (tribal people of Chinese origin from the central highlands) who had served the French. Throughout the late 1950s, more ethnic Vietnamese were added, although the division always had a noticeable number of Nung in its ranks. Headquartered initially in Song Mao (Binh Thuan), it later moved to Bien Hoa. In 1963, it formed one of the main forces in the coup that overthrew the Diem regime. Transferred to Binh Duong Province in 1964, it made its headquarters at Phu Loi until 1970, when it moved to Lai Khe. It generally operated north of Saigon, but took part in the operations in Cambodia in 1970 and 1971. It successfully defended An Loc for two months, during the Communist 1972 Easter Offensive, and held the northern sector of Saigon's defenses against the final enemy offensive until the city fell on 30 April 1975. Although never considered one of the better ARVN divisions, the 5th could put up a good fight once in a while.

7th Infantry Division. Organized by the French in the early 1950s as the 7th Mobile Group, which went through several changes of designation before becoming the 7th Division in 1959, it had its roots in the Red River country of North Vietnam. Headquartered in or near My Tho from 1961, the division operated in the densely populated Mekong Delta region for the entire war, while also taking part in the operations in Cambodia in 1970 and 1971. It helped defend the Cambodian frontier during the Communist 1972 Easter Offensive, and was still holding out in Long An Province when Saigon fell in 1975. The division suffered from persistent leadership problems.

9th Infantry Division. Organized in 1962, the division was based in Binh Dinh Province until 1972, when it was transferred to Vinh Long. It operated all over the IV Corps area as a mobile strike force, took part in the Cambodian operations of 1970 and 1971, supported the 5th Division during the enemy's 1972 Easter Offensive, and held its own in the northern Mekong

Delta region during the final Communist offensive, only surrendering after the fall of Saigon. By some accounts the worst division in the ARVN, its performance was usually mediocre.

18th Infantry Division. The 18th Division began life in 1965 as the 10th Infantry Division. As both Vietnamese and GI slang used the term "Number 10" to indicate "the worst," the division was redesignated the 18th in 1967. Based at Xuan Loc (Long Khanh), the division was reputedly the worst in the ARVN ("Whether the 10th or the 18th, it's still Number 10," as the saying went), though it did help defend An Loc during the NVA 1972 Easter Offensive. The division suffered from persistent leadership problems (one early commander consulted an astrologer for military advice). Nevertheless, it put in a sterling performance in the defense of Xuan Loc during the final Communist offensive. Under BG Le Minh Dao, the division held Xuan Loc (about forty miles northeast of Saigon) from 17 March to 16 April, successively beating off three NVA divisions (the *6th* and *7th* from 17 March, reinforced by the *341st* on 9 April) before finally collapsing after one of the most intense NVA bombardments of the war and an attack by the NVA *325th Division,* one of the best in the PLA.

21st Infantry Division. In 1955, ARVN organized the 1st and 3rd Light Divisions. These took part in the fighting against the Hoa Hao movement in the Mekong Delta in 1955–56. In 1959, they were redesignated as the 11th and 13th Light Divisions. These two divisions were combined in 1959 to form the 21st Infantry Division. Although based at Sa Dec, the division's forces were for some time scattered throughout southern South Vietnam, until concentrated at Bac Lieu, in the IV Corps area. One of the units that helped bring down the Diem regime, the division served in the southern Mekong Delta region throughout the war, though large elements fought in Binh Dinh Province during the Communist 1972 Easter Offensive, during which other elements attempted to support the 5th Division at An Loc. The division was still operating effectively when Saigon fell. A good division.

22nd Infantry Division. In 1955, the 2nd and 4th Light Divisions were formed at Kontum and Ban Me Thuot, in the central highlands, the former mostly composed of men from the Mekong Delta and the latter mostly from the Montagnards. Since four is an unlucky number in Vietnam (like thirteen in the West), the 4th Light Division was shortly redesignated the 14th Light Division, and served against the Hoa Hao in the Mekong Delta in 1955–56. Back at Kontum by 1959, the 14th Light Division was redesignated the 22nd Infantry Division, into which was incorporated the personnel of the 2nd Light Division, which was disbanded. The 22nd Division was based in the five northern provinces of II Corps, with its headquarters at Ba Gi (Binh

Dinh). Its performance was mixed. During the 1972 Easter Offensive it virtually collapsed and had to be reinforced by the 23rd Infantry Division, but during the final Communist offensive in 1975, it held Binh Dinh Province until the collapse of ARVN's fortunes in the central highlands, whereupon it broke through to the coast, to be evacuated by sea, and was moved to Long An Province, southwest of Saigon, where it was still holding out when the war ended. So in the end it turned into a good division.

23rd Infantry Division. The 23rd Infantry Division was originally organized as the 5th Light Division in 1955, which, after some additional name changes, became the 23rd Infantry Division in 1959. The division helped suppress the Hoa Hao and Coa Dai sects in 1955–56 in the south, and was transferred to Ban Me Thuot, in the central highlands, in 1961. For most of its career, the division operated throughout central Vietnam, though it did take part in operations into Cambodia in 1970 and 1971. During the Communist 1972 Easter Offensive it put in a sterling performance, relieving the disintegrating 22nd Infantry Division in the defense of Kontum. During the final Communist offensive in 1975, the division attempted to retake Ban Me Thuot from the enemy but was shattered in the attempt, its remnants eventually being captured. A good division.

25th Infantry Division. Formed in Quang Ngai Province in 1962, the division operated there until 1964, when it was moved southwest of Saigon, where it remained for the remainder of the war, operating in the westernmost provinces of the III Corps area. It took part in the 1970 offensive into the Cambodian "Parrot's Beak" area, attempted to relieve the 5th Infantry Division at An Loc during the 1972 Easter Offensive, and successfully defended the western approaches to Saigon until the end of the war. Always plagued by poor leadership, the division did improve, but not enough.

Airborne Division. Nicknamed "the Rainbow Division," the South Vietnamese Airborne Division had its roots in the French *Troupes Aeroportées en Indochine,* a battalion of colonial parachute troops. This became an airborne regimental combat team in 1954, and was redesignated the Airborne Group in 1955. By 1959, the group had grown into a brigade, which became a division in 1965. As with most parachute forces, the division attracted lots of volunteers, and had the best motivated and most effective troops in the ARVN, though they, too, occasionally had a bad day. Headquartered at Tan Son Nhut airbase, the division was controlled directly by the South Vietnamese high command and used as a fire brigade. It eventually came to include nine battalions of airborne infantry and three of airborne Rangers. Among its more notable operations were the incursions into Cambodia in 1970 and 1971, Operation Lom San 719, and the 1972 Easter Offensive, during which it operated in I Corps. During the final Communist offensive in 1975, the division had to be pulled out of I Corps to bolster defenses elsewhere, which sparked the collapse of the ARVN's fortunes in the North. The division was then split up. Its 1st Brigade tried to support the 18th Division in the defense of Xuan Loc, but was badly battered and fell back into Phuoc Tuy Province, where it was regrouping when Saigon fell. The 2nd Brigade reinforced the defense of Phan Rang, during which it was badly handled, while the 3rd Brigade was destroyed in the defense of Nha Trang.

Marine Division. Although the RVN Marine Corps traced its origins to the days of French rule in Indochina (see Republic of Vietnam Marine Corps, page 88), the Marine Division was organized in 1966, initially of six infantry battalions and some artillery. Based at Saigon, the Marine Division, like the Airborne Division, was an element of the South Vietnamese strategic reserve. For the most part it served as a fire brigade, being committed in emergencies or for particularly important operations. The Marine Division took part in the incursions into Cambodia in 1970 and 1971 and then into Laos (Lom Son 719). During the 1972 Easter Offensive it recaptured Quang Tri from the enemy after several attempts by ARVN line units had failed. During the final Communist offensive, the division formed the rear guard in the defense of Danang, and then held out at Vung Tau until the end of the war.

SOUTH VIETNAMESE CORPS AREAS

For administrative purposes South Vietnam was divided into four military regions. The military regions were administrative commands, overseeing "back office" functions of the ARVN, such as recruiting, construction, and the like. In addition, each military region was coterminous with a corps. The term "corps" has several meanings. In addition to a specialized body of military personnel (e.g., the Marine Corps or the Medical Corps), it can also be an administrative territorial command, or a command echelon that groups together several divisions operating on the same front with the same objective. It was in this last sense that the term was most commonly found in Vietnam. Combat units, whether South Vietnamese or Allied, were for the most part assigned to specific corps areas and operated in those areas for most of the war. This was the primary reason why American corps headquarters were for the most part designated "field forces" in Vietnam, so as not to offend Vietnamese sensibilities.

I Corps (commonly known as "Eye Corps"). This was the northernmost of the four corps areas. The corps was responsible for the five northernmost provinces of South Vietnam: Quang Tri, Thua Thien, Quang Nam, Quang Tin, and Quang Ngai, which included part of the central highlands and the DMZ. Headquarters was in Danang.

II Corps. Oversaw operations in the dozen provinces just south of I Corps, which included most of the central highlands and the 24th Special Tactical Zone, an autonomous command that oversaw operations along part of the Laotian frontier from 1966 until 1970.

III Corps. Controlled the ten provinces just north of Saigon.

IV Corps. Supervised operations in the heavily populated sixteen southern-most provinces of South Vietnam, covering much of the Mekong Delta and about half of the populace of the country.

Capital Military District (CMD). Comprised Saigon and the adjacent province of Gia Dinh. Although loosely subordinated to the III Corps, the commander of the CMD was extremely powerful, controlling as he did the principal military forces in the capital.

NORTH VIETNAMESE AND VIET CONG COMBAT UNITS

Although they eventually became more or less interchangeable, initially there were two Communist armies operating in South Vietnam: the People's Army of Vietnam (the regular army of North Vietnam) and the People's Liberation Army (the military arm of the Viet Cong movement in South Vietnam). The two were never able to maintain more than a quarter-million fighting troops in South Vietnam. Their main problem was logistics; getting enough food, weapons, and ammunition down the Ho Chi Minh Trail to keep troops fed and armed. By the end of 1972, when American troops were leaving, North Vietnam had only 140,000 combat troops in South Vietnam. Most of these (90,000) were in North Vietnamese army units, the other 50,000 were nominally Viet Cong, although nearly half these guerrilla troops were actually conscripts from North Vietnam. The Communists had twenty-two division-size units in South Vietnam, although the average strength of these units was about 6,000 troops. The average infantry battalion (three per regiment) had two hundred to three hundred soldiers. Moreover, about half the North Vietnamese troops fighting in "the South" were not in South Vietnam, but in Laotian and Cambodian base camps. The combat units would periodically move back to these base camps to rebuild and train, then return to their operating areas in South Vietnam.

The People's Army of Vietnam (PAVN). The PAVN began life as a guerrilla force in the early 1940s. By the late 1940s, it was increasingly becoming a regular army, and it was regular troops, not guerrillas, who defeated the French at Dien Bien Phu, a fact often overlooked in superficial treatments of the war. After the 1954 partition of the country, the PAVN became even more of a regular force. As the war in the South expanded, the PAVN took an ever-increasing role. Although the North always denied that PAVN regulars were operating in the South (a position echoed by numerous antiwar types), they were already present in considerable numbers as early as 1965. In fact, enemy forces in the Ia Drang Campaign, the first major American action in the war, were primarily North Vietnamese regulars.

The People's Liberation Army (the "Viet Cong"). The PLA was the military arm of the so-called National Liberation Front. This began as a movement among the people of southern—not South—Vietnam to overthrow the "oppressive imperialistic capitalistic" government of South Vietnam, with lots of help from the North. The VC spent itself in the Tet Offensive (which apparently was considered a bad idea by Vo Nguyen Giap, who was overruled). After Tet the VC became a wholly owned subsidiary of the Democratic Republic of Vietnam (i.e., the North Vietnamese). North Vietnamese personnel began to outnumber South Vietnamese in the ranks of the VC.

In the unit descriptions that follow, only occasional distinction has been made between PAVN and PLA units, as by the late 1960s the personnel in the latter had become largely North Vietnamese. In general, most of the personnel of the *1st* through the *10th Divisions* were originally VC.

This order of battle confines itself primarily to division-sized units. There is some inexactitude with regard to division composition, as it was quite common for regiments to be shuffled around among divisions. Where known, the principal subordinate units of each division have been shown in parentheses, usually for mid-1972. For convenience, reference has sometimes been made to the South Vietnamese military regions (MR) when indicating the location of some divisions.

Note that occasional NVA and VC units are designated by a letter as well as a number, such as the *52nd-D Infantry Regiment*. This was partially a deceptive ploy on the part of the Communists, having several units with the same designation, differentiated by a letter. But it also reflected the fact that some units were clones of older ones, which were left behind in safe areas to recruit fresh troops.

1st Division (44th Sapper, 52nd-D, and 101st-D). Organized in late 1965 in the central highlands of South Vietnam from VC personnel and units that had entered the country earlier, the *1st Division* was formed from troops who had already seen combat in the region. It later served in MR 4.

2nd Division (1st PLA, 52nd, and 141st). Formed in October 1965 in Quang Nam Province from mixed VC and NVA forces that had entered the country earlier. Supposed to support guerrilla operations, the division undertook few offensive actions of its own until mid-1967. It was badly shot up later that year, and smashed in the 1968 Tet Offensive. It retreated to Laos, where it was rebuilt. It fought in Laos for a time, but was again crippled in the 1972 Easter Offensive and by a devastating B-52 raid later that year. Rebuilt, reinforced, and reorganized several times thereafter, it helped take Danang in the final 1975 offensive. A hard luck outfit, it twice had its headquarters destroyed by Allied airpower. It later fought the Cambodians.

3rd Division (2nd PLA, 12th PLA, and 21st). Organized in 1965 in Quang Nai Province, the "Gold Star" Division was unusual in having not only three infantry regiments, but also mortar, signal, engineer, and antiaircraft battalions assigned, assets usually not available to a VC division. It spent most of the war in the central highlands, and for an NVA unit was relatively lightly engaged. It later fought the Chinese.

4th Division. Formed specifically for the final 1975 offensive (unlike the ARVN, the Communists don't seem to have been superstitious about the number 4), the division later took part in the occupation of Cambodia.

5th Division (E-6th PLA, 174th, and 275th). Organized in late 1965 on the Cambodian border, the *5th Division* operated in that region for the entire war. By 1972, it was the only division that was composed largely of VC.

6th Division (24th, 207th, and 320th). Organized for the final 1975 offensive in MR 4.

7th Division (141st, 165th, and 209th). Organized in mid-1966 in the area between Saigon and the Cambodian border, the division was heavily engaged in that general region for the rest of the war, taking heavy casualties during Tet, the Allied 1970 Cambodian incursion, and the 1972 Easter Offensive, during which one regiment was virtually obliterated in a B-52 raid. Taking part in the final 1975 offensive, the *7th Division* later spent four years in Cambodia.

8th Division. Organized for the final 1975 offensive.

9th Division (95th-C, 271st, and 272nd). The *9th Division* was the first NVA division formed entirely in South Vietnam, in mid-1965, from units that had been operating there since 1961. The division spent most of its war close to Saigon, in MR 4, and was heavily engaged on numerous occasions, taking enormous losses (after Tet one battalion reportedly had suffered over 93-percent casualties). Driven into Cambodia by the Allied 1970 incursion, the division operated there against Cambodian government forces until 1972, when it returned to South Vietnam. It took part in the final 1975 offensive, and later served in Cambodia again.

10th Division (28th, 66th, and 95th-B). Organized in late-1972 from miscellaneous forces that had taken part in the Easter Offensive, the division spent most of its war in MR 2, the central highlands, taking Pleiku and Ban Me Thuot in 1974. It took part in the final drive on Saigon, capturing Tan Son Nhut Air Base. It later engaged in counterinsurgency operations against ARVN and Montagnard holdouts and took part in the Cambodian intervention.

303rd Division (201st, 205th, and 271st, plus 262nd Artillery). The division was organized in 1974 for the planned final offensive, and took part in the capture of Saigon. It later served in Cambodia and against the Chinese.

304th Division (9th, 24thB, and 66th). Organized in 1950 in North Vietnam, the division fought the French in the Red River Delta and Laos, and was at Dien Bien Phu. It entered South Vietnam in late-1966 and served in the Tay Nguyen area. It supported the Tet Offensive, taking part in the attack on Hue, and was involved in the siege of Khe Sahn. These left it badly beaten up, and it returned north in 1968 for rebuilding. It moved to Laos in 1970, helping to repulse the Lom Son 719 Offensive, and reentered South Vietnam in 1971, taking part in the 1972 Easter Offensive. During the final 1975 offensive it participated in the capture of Saigon.

304th-B Division. The division was organized in North Vietnam in 1965 to replace the *304th Division*, from which it drew some personnel. The division entered northwestern South Vietnam in 1968, and it fought at Khe Sahn.

308th Division (36th, 88th, and 102nd). This was the first division organized by the Viet Minh in North Vietnam in mid-1949. It saw extensive service against the French. In the early 1960s, it was upgraded, receiving additional artillery, engineers, signal troops, and even tanks, to become one of the most powerful units in the NVA. It began moving into South Vietnam in 1964 and was there in force for the 1968 Tet Offensive. It spent much of the war in northern South Vietnam.

312th Division (141st, 165th, and 209th). Organized in 1950, the division fought at Dien Bien Phu. Elements began moving into South Vietnam in 1963, a battalion at a time. For a long time the division was never properly concentrated, as elements were widely dispersed to support VC operations, including the 1968 Tet Offensive, in which they were badly battered. After Tet the division returned to North Vietnam to rebuild. Regrouped and reorganized, it fought in Laos from 1969–71. It reentered South Vietnam in 1972, and later took part in the final 1975 offensive.

316th Division (98th, 174th, and 176th). Organized by the Viet Minh in 1951, mostly from ethnic minorities in the North. The division began operating in South Vietnam and particularly Laos in 1967, mostly as a light infantry unit supporting the Pathet Lao. It took part in the capture of Ban Me Thuot during the final 1975 offensive, and later fought the Chinese.

320th Division (48th and 64th, plus 54th Artillery). Organized in early 1951, and known as the "Plains" or "Delta" Division from its recruiting grounds, the *320th Division* began moving into Laos in 1964 and South Vietnam in 1965. It participated in the Tet Offensive, after which it had to return to North Vietnam to be rebuilt. It returned in 1970 to operate in Laos and South Vietnam, but was so battered by 1971 that it had to once more be rebuilt in North Vietnam. Back in the South in 1972, the division later took part in the final Communist offensive in 1975.

320th-B Division (48th-B, 64th-B, and 312th). Organized in 1965 from personnel drawn from the *320th Division,* until 1970 the *320th-B Division* trained 153,000 replacements for its parent unit, sending them on a battalion at a time. It was committed as a combat unit for the 1972 Easter Offensive, to be withdrawn the following year. Elements of the division later helped fight the Chinese, and in 1979 it became the *390th Division.*

324th Division (29th, 803rd, and 812th). Organized in 1955 mainly from southerners who had fled to the North after the Geneva Accords, the *324th Division* was specialized for attacks on fortified areas. Sent south in 1966, elements took part in the assault on Hue during the 1968 Tet Offensive. It spent most of its war in northern South Vietnam.

325th Division (18th, 95th, and 101st). Organized in 1951, the *325th Division* was one of the first six Communist divisions to be raised in the southern part of Vietnam. It went north after the 1954 Geneva Accords, but entered Laos in 1961 to support the Pathet Lao and provide security for the Ho Chi Minh Trail. In 1964, elements began entering South Vietnam. Division headquarters was then redesignated as the *325th-A Division,* which remained in Laos as a training command, spawning a number of new divisions. In 1974, the *325th-D Division* was redesignated as the *325th Division.* The following year the new division played an important role in the final Communist offensive, taking Hue, Danang, and a number of smaller cities in a drive down the east coast, delivering the blow that finally crushed the ARVN 18th Infantry Division at Xuan Loc. It served in Laos in 1975–77, and later in Cambodia.

325th-B Division. Organized in 1964 from elements of the *325th-A Division*, it went south in 1966, operating in the northern part of South Vietnam for the duration.

325th-C Division. Organized in 1965 from elements of the *325th-A Division*, it went south in 1966. The division initially operated in northern South Vietnam, fighting at Khe Sahn and Hue in 1968. After Tet it was broken up, with the individual regiments moving farther south, while division headquarters returned to the North to become the *325th-D Division*.

325th-D Division. Organized in 1968 around the cadre of the former *325th-C Division*, the *325th-D Division* went south in 1969. It operated in northern South Vietnam during the 1972 Easter Offensive. By 1974, the *325th-D* was redesignated the *325th Division*.

330th Division. Organized in 1956 from South Vietnamese who had gone north, the division was essentially a replacement training command for units in South Vietnam, and it did not go south itself.

338th Division. Organized in late 1956 from southerners who had gone north after the Geneva Accords, from 1959 to 1963 the division was a major training command for troops bound south. In 1963, elements of the division were sent south and it was disbanded, to be reactivated again in the South in 1965. It was disbanded again in 1966, but reconstituted again in 1972. This was an extreme example of what affected all North Vietnam divisions operating in South Vietnam. North Vietnamese units took tremendous casualties; over 600,000 dead, based on available records. That's over three times as many troops as North Vietnam had in the South (on average) at any one time. Some units got hit worse than others, and the *338th* was definitely one of the hardest hit.

341st Division. Organized in 1962 as a light infantry division. However, the division's regiments were sent south piecemeal, and it was disbanded, to be reconstituted in the South in 1965. Disbanded again the following year, it was once more reactivated in 1972. It took part in the final drive on Saigon.

361st, 363rd, 365th, 367th, 368th, 369th, and **377th Divisions.** Antiaircraft units (some were artillery units, some missile, and some command) raised between 1966 and 1968 to defend North Vietnam from U.S.

bombing raids. China and Russia supplied thousands of antiaircraft guns, plus radars, guided missiles, and plenty of ammunition. North Vietnam provided the troops, who were trained by Soviet and Chinese instructors.

470th, 471st, 472nd, and **473rd Divisions** all belonged to *Group 559,* the organization that maintained the Ho Chi Minh Trail. They each comprised several thousand engineer and transportation troops. Each division was assigned a sector of the 1700 square-mile system of roads and trails running from North Vietnam through Laos to Cambodia, with the task of maintaining and improving it. All along the trail, there were exits into South Vietnam, where North Vietnam units received supplies and troops.

571st Transportation Division. Organized in 1973 as a a truck unit, with 2,600 vehicles and 8,500 troops, the division was attached to *Group 559* to speed the flow of supplies down the Ho Chi Minh Trail, which by then had become passable by trucks over its entire length.

711th Division (31st, 38th, and **270th).** This division had only a brief existence. Organized in Binh Dinh Province in mid-1971, it was disbanded just two years later.

B-3 Front (24th-B, 40th Artillery, and **400th Sapper).** A division-sized territorial command operating in MR 2.

B-5 Front (27th-B, 31st, 126th Naval Sapper Group, DMZ Sapper Group, 207th-B, 202nd Armor, 45th Artillery, 58th Artillery, 68th Artillery, 84th Artillery, 164th Artillery, and **166th Artillery).** A special command established in June 1966 to control forces inside South Vietnam along the DMZ.

The North Vietnamese also employed dozens of separate regiments and brigades. These were usually specialized units. There were generally a dozen or so independent infantry regiments and brigades, as well as about the same number of artillery regiments. The most prominent of the many separate units were the sapper units. By 1973, there were forty-nine battalion-sized sapper units (about fifteen thousand troops). Sappers received six months' special training in the use of explosives and infiltration. Whenever possible, sappers led assaults of fortified positions, blasting their way through barbed wire, bunkers, and even minefields.

There were also two tank brigades and an airborne brigade.

202nd Tank Brigade. Established in 1959, the brigade had about sixty World War II–era T-34 tanks, plus a few dozen self-propelled artillery pieces, and an equal number of PT-76 light tanks. Through the late 1960s, it supported the antiaircraft troops defending southern North Vietnam. In 1969, it conducted operations against the Hmong in Laos. It moved into South Vietnam for the 1972 and 1975 offensives. For the latter, it was reequipped with more modern T-59 tanks.

203rd Tank Brigade. In early 1965, elements drawn from the *202nd Tank Brigade* were used to form a new brigade, the *203rd.* It fought in the Lom Son 719 operation and took part in the final 1975 offensive.

305th Airborne Brigade. This was formed in the early 1960s, with Soviet aid, apparently as a propaganda move. As there was little chance of this unit flying anywhere, in 1967 it was disbanded. As the personnel were highly qualified, they were put to good use. About half the former paratroopers became sappers. The rest were used to staff counter-recon units in an attempt to limit the U.S. recon teams operating in Laos and Cambodia.

CHAPTER 14

The Aftermath

Wars don't just end. Their aftereffects make themselves felt for several generations. Not just in terms of war stories and popular lore, but in economic, political, and cultural changes brought about by the war. Consider how we are still experiencing the aftereffects of the American Civil War (ended 1865), World War I (ended 1918), World War II (ended 1945), and the Korean War (cease-fire, 1953, still hasn't ended). The Vietnam War had a lot of curious items swirling about in its wake, and here we cover some of them.

THE ERA OF THE "HOLLOW ARMY" AND MILITARY REFORM

The armed forces, and particularly the army, emerged from the Vietnam War with deep scars and an uncertain future. Manpower quality was declining, enlistment rates poor, morale low, and indiscipline on the rise, with murders, rapes, and muggings common on military posts. Drug use was widespread, and race relations abysmal. The NCO corps was in disarray, the officer corps undergoing a crisis of confidence, and large numbers of good men and women were leaving the service. The war had other effects as well. For over a decade budgets, thinking, and training had been focused on the conflict in Southeast Asia. As a result, by 1975 training, weapons, equipment, and doctrine were increasingly outdated. While the army, most closely identified with the war in Vietnam, suffered most seriously from these problems, the other services were affected by them as well: The situation seemed so hopeless that to many the nation had a "Hollow Army." But for all those men who left the service in despair, there were many others determined to rebuild the armed forces. Indeed, the seeds of a rebirth of the armed forces, and particularly the army, were actually planted in the waning days of the Vietnam War.

Even before the withdrawal of U.S. ground forces from Vietnam in 1972, a reassessment of the lessons of the war had begun. The prime mover in this was GEN Creighton Abrams, who had commanded in Vietnam from 1968 to 1972. Appointed chief-of-staff of the army in 1972, Abrams was instrumental in preventing the development of a "stab in the back" mood, pushing for a realistic examination of the roots of the Vietnam debacle and the problems confronting the service in its aftermath. While the perceived failure of the armed forces in Vietnam provided the impetus for their reform, it was the Arab-Israeli War of 1973 that helped point the way to the future. The speed, effectiveness, and decisiveness with which Israeli forces carried out the war proved a sobering lesson to military leaders who had spent more than a decade focused on "low-intensity" warfare. Attention returned to the "main event," a Soviet bloc offensive on the central front in Europe, one undertaken without a lengthy period of rising tension and military buildup. Right at the end of the Vietnam War, the army had created the Training and Doctrine Command (TRADOC) to study the future of war. The first commander of TRADOC was GEN William E. DePuy, a tough officer with a distinguished record in Vietnam. While commanding the 1st Infantry Division in 1966–67 he had sacked thirty-one battalion commanders. Now he launched a systematic examination of the 1973 war and of other historical conflicts, such as the Russo-German struggle during World War II. This led to the 1976 edition of the army's official "how to fight" handbook, FM 100-5. The emphasis shifted toward a "come as you are" war, one with little or no time for preparations and one fought by brigades and divisions. TRADOC began proposing fundamental changes in the organization of combat units to enable them to train more effectively in peace and fight more efficiently in war.

While TRADOC was restructuring the army's approach to war, other military leaders were pushing a revival of interest in military history. Once a mainstay of officer training, military history had been neglected by the army during the 1950s and 1960s, in the days of massive retaliation, low-intensity warfare, and the new management army, with its emphasis on management and mathematical modeling. In the aftermath of Vietnam, many military leaders, at all levels, realized that a lot of the errors made during the war might have been avoided had historical precedents been examined with greater care. One consequence of the revival of interest in military history was a revival of traditional war-gaming in the army, using historically based models. War-gaming—historical conflict simulation—had attained considerable popularity during the years when it had been neglected by the professional soldiers. As the army's interest in historical war-gaming revived, it was able to draw on the expertise of a small, but successful and experienced body of professional specialists in the field.

Meanwhile measures were undertaken to improve the quality of the army's personnel. Initially many of the people joining the army under the "All Volunteer" policy were of less than desirable physical, mental, and educational standards, enlisted primarily to meet recruiting goals. At first the army could do little if it wished to maintain force levels. However, as pay and benefits were increased, the quality of recruits began to improve. This permitted discipline to be tightened, drug abuse largely eliminated, malcontents and chronic troublemakers to be discharged, and measures taken to improve race relations. There was a lot of experimentation in personnel management during the 1970s, not all of them successful, but the ideas that worked were adopted. By the late 1970s, manpower quality in the army had risen considerably. Virtually all recruits were high school graduates, the reenlistment rate had risen, morale was high, discipline was excellent, and there had been a considerable improvement in personnel training, performance, efficiency, and readiness.

Training underwent fundamental changes, with the introduction of more realistic programs and the adoption of innovative technologies. This had actually begun during the Vietnam War. Noticing, early in the war, that its pilots were not as successful in air combat as their predecessors had been in Korea and World War II, in 1969, the navy opened its "Top Gun" school. There pilots practiced air combat against pilots trained to fly and fight using Soviet doctrine and tactics, flying aircraft whose performance characteristics most closely matched those of Russian equipment. There soon proved to be a marked improvement in the performance of navy pilots, which inspired the air force to develop its "Red Flag" program. Red Flag added a lot of electronics to simulate the performance of different weapons. Once again the combat effectiveness of pilots improved markedly. Meanwhile the navy began developing its Fleet Readiness program, which combined computer simulation with live-action exercises. By the mid-1970s, senior army trainers were increasingly aware of the effects of these programs on personnel performance. TRADOC began working on a "live" ground combat simulation of its own. In October 1980, the army opened the National Training Center (NTC), at Fort Irwin, in the Mojave Desert, employing the military integrated laser engagement system (MILES).

Put simply, MILES is an extremely sophisticated version of "laser tag." Special lasers were attached to weapons. Troops and vehicles were outfitted with sophisticated sensors that determined the effects of "hits" and inflicted casualties accordingly. Battalions were regularly rotated into the National Training Center for maneuvers, which usually involved six to ten "engagements" over a two-week period. To enhance realism, units were opposed by the "32nd Guards Motorized Rifle Regiment" (a pair of Regular Army battalions, the 6th/31st Infantry, and 1st/73rd Armor, organized and trained on Soviet lines, with equipment modified to resemble Russian stuff). Since it was constantly "fighting" simulated engagements with U.S. tank and mechanized infantry battalions, the 32nd Guards usually "won" most of its battles, earning it the sobriquet "the best Soviet motorized rifle regiment in the world." More important than winning or losing, however, was the testing of equipment, doctrine, and troops, both common soldiers and commanders, under the most realistic conditions possible. Debriefings at the end of a tour at the NTC were brutally frank, with open discussion of the errors of the troops and their commanders. This caused considerable stir, officers not usually being accustomed to having their mistakes aired before their subordinates. It was harsh, but not so harsh as the consequences of failure in combat.

Meanwhile, the NTC, which was supplemented by additional facilities and several elaborate computer simulations, began to have an effect on overall training and doctrine. As more and more units went through the program, flaws in the army's training program became more obvious and corrective measures could be taken. In addition, by the late 1980s, TRADOC had available information on literally hundreds of "engagements," which permitted appraisal of organization and tactics to a degree not possible even in wartime, leading to important adjustments in both. Results were constantly compared with the evidence of history and actual military operations that occurred during the period, such as the Anglo-Argentine War of 1982, operations in Lebanon later that same year, and the Afghanistan War (1980–89).

The net result of the decade of reform that followed the end of the Vietnam War was a great improvement in doctrine, training, and readiness, developments that went largely unnoticed by the public. A notable aspect of this military reform, the longest sustained reform in the history of the armed forces, is that it was accomplished on a relative shoestring. Public regard and support for the armed forces was low in the period, and the defense establishment had to justify every cent of expenditure. In achieving such significant improvements in training and performance, the armed forces had demonstrated an unprecedented effectiveness in managing their resources, a matter that would have an important payoff when defense budgets began to rise again in the aftermath of "the New Cold War," which began in the late 1980s, with the realization that the Soviet Union had taken advantage of the Vietnam War and the long period of American military retrenchment that followed to undertake an enormous expansion of its armed forces.

THE MIA PROBLEM

In war, some people are captured by the enemy. The Geneva Convention is supposed to govern the treatment of such personnel. The International Red Cross is supposed to be notified when a prisoner is taken and is charged with inspection of POW facilities. POWs are supposed to be fed commensurate with their normal diet, are supposed to be able to send and receive mail, including parcels, and have a number of other rights as well. Although North Vietnam claimed to adhere to the convention, in fact it flouted most of the provisions. Prisoners were ill-housed, poorly fed, and often subject to beatings.

Since Hanoi gave no formal notification of men taken prisoner by NVA/VC forces (a violation of the Geneva Convention, by the way), the number of prisoners of war soon became an important issue in the ongoing peace negotiations. Eventually the North Vietnamese admitted to holding Americans, if only for the propaganda value. With the end of active American participation in the war in early 1973, American prisoners were released by North Vietnam. But that only led to further problems.

In fact, some 2,273 Americans who were officially listed as "missing in action" in Southeast Asia were unaccounted for in 1973. This led to demands for a "full accounting" and charges that the North Vietnamese were secretly holding some Americans. A whole industry developed around the issue, selling "POW/MIA" flags and bracelets bearing the names of the missing (some of which were latter proven to have been fabricated).

This remains a controversial issue. Despite approximately $50 million a year being spent on the question, the actual fate of these men will probably never be known. In fact, only 55 of the Americans listed as "missing in action" are known to have actually been taken prisoner by the enemy. And about half of the 2,273 men listed as missing were last seen in circumstances that strongly suggest they should be classified as "presumed dead." Officially the U.S. government says only about a hundred cases are "active."

It is possible that some prisoners were deliberately detained. Soviet intelligence officials are known to have "debriefed" several POWs, but none of those who returned in 1973 reported having been interviewed by the Russians, at least publicly. So the Vietnamese Communists may have passed some POWs on to the Russians, who later quietly disposed of them.

Some POWs may well have been killed by U.S. air attacks (in World War II several thousand Americans held by the enemy perished in this fashion). In one reported instance some two dozen men captured in the South were being marched North when they were caught in a B-52 raid, with only one known survivor.

Over the last few years the Vietnamese Communist government—which has no idea as to the fate of most of its own troops who went south—has permitted what Sen. John Kerry, a highly decorated former POW, has called "the most extensive accounting in the history of human warfare." Special military forensic teams have been permitted to operate in Vietnam, and extensive excavations have been conducted on battlefields and at air crash sites (many of the MIAs are aviators). The remains of over 450 Americans have been recovered, mostly from Vietnam, and in many cases identified. Yet the controversy persists.

One of the reasons for the ongoing POW/MIA controversy is a lack of understanding of forensics. The Vietnamese climate hastens decay. Within a few years there may literally be nothing left, particularly if a plane crashed in a jungle or swamp. In such cases collateral evidence may have to be used. While it's hard to argue with an Annapolis class ring, some families have objected that merely locating wreckage at a site is not conclusive proof that their kinsman was killed, even if it is known that the man went down with his aircraft. A lot of this has to do with denial.

A comparison with other recent wars is instructive.

Americans Missing in Action, 1941–73

Conflict	Battle Deaths	MIAs
World War II	292,100	78,000 (26.7%)
Korean War	33,600	8,100 (24.1%)
Vietnam War	47,400	2,273 (4.8%)

Key: The table gives personnel officially listed as Missing in Action as a percent of battle deaths (personnel killed in action or died of wounds).

MIA SIGHTINGS

As of early 1997, there were 1,846 reported sightings of MIAs in Southeast Asia. Upon investigation, 67 percent (1,250) proved to be persons already accounted for (misidentified POWs who had already been returned, Europeans or Americans living in Vietnam, and so forth). Some 26 percent of the reports (487) have been determined to have been fabrications, concocted by Vietnamese refugees fleeing the Communist regime, in the hope of getting better treatment. Instances of alleged photographic evidence have been exposed as hoaxes, often doctored up pictures of non-Americans working in the area. The balance of the reports are either too vague to be relied upon or are still under investigation.

The issue of sightings has been further complicated by the presence of American deserters. Some went over to the Communists before the war ended. Robert Garwood is the most notorious example. Hundreds of unapprehended deserters were left behind when American military units left Vietnam. Approximately 2,750 men deserted "in country" during the war, having disappeared into the local expatriate community. Many of these fellows got involved in criminal activities (drug dealing and the black market being the most popular). Many troops deserted because they were into criminal behavior in the first place. When the Communists took over South Vietnam in 1975, they did not immediately round up all these non-Vietnamese. It was nearly a year before they got them all, or thought they had got them all. Most were eventually expelled, but not all. Some were considered criminals and were executed or imprisoned.

Between 1975 and 1991 there were thousands of Russians and Eastern Europeans wandering around Southeast Asia on official business or just wandering around. Lots of opportunity here to either make a mistaken identification or attempt a hoax for people desperate to find any American soldiers left behind.

THE AMERASIANS

An Amerasian is someone who is the offspring of an American soldier and a Vietnamese woman (or any other East Asian woman, for that matter). Almost as soon as American troops landed in South Vietnam they began to "fraternize" with Vietnamese women. So the first Amerasians came along in the normal fashion about nine months later, sometime in the 1960s. There is no way of knowing how many Amerasians there are. Estimates vary from ten thousand to two hundred thousand, though thirty thousand is most frequently cited. About two-thirds of the Amerasians are the offspring of white American troops, the balance of black soldiers.

Like all persons of mixed race, the *bu doi* (Children of Dust) were severely discriminated against in Vietnam (racism in Asia is a lot more open than in the United States), and they suffered markedly in postwar Vietnam. By the 1980s, the U.S. government began coming under increasing pressure to permit the immigration of Amerasians, as the children of American citizens. In 1982, the first of several pieces of legislation on the subject was passed, culminating in the Amerasian Homecoming Act of 1987. Essentially, anyone born in South Vietnam between 1 January 1962 and 1 January 1976, who has a noticeable admixture of white or black racial characteristics, is presumed to be an Amerasian and is eligible to enter the United States without quota restrictions. This criterion ignores certain basic facts about recent Vietnamese history: persons of Eurasian and Afrasian backgrounds were not unknown in Vietnam before American intervention, fathered by French troops of European and African descent. Moreover, there were American troops in South Vietnam before 1 January 1962, and some of them are known to have had offspring by local women. And there were some American troops of Asian descent in Vietnam during the war, but their offspring would not seem to be eligible for entry into the United States on the basis of their features alone.

Nearly twenty-five thousand Amerasians have settled in the United States, along with about sixty thousand "family members," persons presumably related to them on the Vietnamese side. Just how closely related some of these family members are has been questioned. There is some evidence of fraud, including instances of Amerasian children having been sold to families seeking to flee Vietnam.

Some of the Amerasians settled in the United States were brought over by their fathers, who in some cases had actually been looking for the youngsters. Others have been accepted by a parent who never knew they existed. But many have been rejected by their American sires or been unable to locate them. A great many have had considerable difficulties in adjusting to American life, in many cases not finding much acceptance among white or black Americans or in the Vietnamese-American community.

THE REORGANIZATION OF THE DEFENSE ESTABLISHMENT

After nearly a decade of Post-Vietnam parsimony, military budgets began to rise late in the presidency of Jimmy Carter and went up markedly in the first two years of that of Ronald Reagan. New equipment was procured and more pay and better benefits provided. But along with a sense that more money was needed was the realization that fundamental changes were needed in the structure and organization of the nation's defense establishment.

In the post-Vietnam era, public confidence in the state of the armed forces was not particularly high. It was severely shaken still further by the humiliating failure of the 24 April 1980 attempt to rescue American embassy personnel held hostage by a revolutionary regime in Tehran, a consequence of poor planning and poor interservice cooperation. The abortive hostage rescue mission provided a sobering reminder that in war things have to work right from the start. It sparked great interest in improving interservice cooperation and integration, particularly coming as it did in the wake of a series of what seemed military failures, among them Vietnam and the Mayagüez operations. As a result, the Joint Chiefs of Staff created the Special Operations Review Group (SORG) to conduct a thorough critique of the operation, authorizing it to make recommendations for improving the ability of the armed forces to conduct joint operations. Joint operations, the integration of elements from different services for the performance of a particular task, reached a high state of development during World War II, a condition arrived at due to dire necessity, and even then only after much painful experience. Following the surrender of Japan, however, the traditional tendency for each of the services to go its own way reasserted itself, made even more complicated by the creation of an independent U.S. Air Force in 1947. During the Vietnam War interservice cooperation had not been particularly good. When asked their opinion of the state of interservice cooperation during the war, 60 percent of senior army officers said it had been outstanding with the air force, but only 29 percent thought it had been so with the navy, and barely 22 percent with the marines.

The SORG worked quickly, and by 1982 some of its ideas were incorporated by TRADOC in a new edition of FM 100-5, emerging as the AirLand Battle (ALB) doctrine. ALB attempted to strike a balance between maneuver warfare and attrition warfare, reintroduced the concept of operational art, the employment of forces in large-scale campaigns, and established the idea of "over the horizon" warfare, projecting military power deep into the enemy's rear. The new doctrine stressed the use of psyops (psychological operations), deception, and special warfare; the employment of overwhelming force; and stressed "the synchronization of air, ground, and sea assets" to fight the enemy, not only at the front, but in his rear. Strengthening the case for greater integration was a speech by Chief of Staff of the Army GEN

Edward Meyer, in which he argued that, as currently organized, the armed forces were not prepared for war and urged that the chairman of the Joint Chiefs be given greater powers over strategy, operations, priorities, and organization. The speech led to much discussion in the services, in public forums, and in Congress.

In 1983, the movement toward jointness received considerable impetus with the establishment of the Army–Air Force Joint Force Development Process. Created by the chief of staff of the army GEN John A. Wickham and the chief of staff of the Air Force GEN Charles A. Gabriel (former West Point roommates), this body quickly identified over thirty programs in which army and air force efforts seemed to be duplicative or where joint doctrines could be developed. Many programs were dropped or merged, with a resulting savings in money, time, and interservice friction.

These new policies and doctrines were tested in 1983 in Lebanon when a terrorist bombing of a Marine barracks demonstrated serious failures in intelligence assessment, in the definition of objectives, and in communications, command, and control. Soon afterward came the Grenada operation, prompted by a Cuban-supported coup that installed a radical regime in that small Caribbean island nation. Mounted on less than a week's notice, with the troops receiving their orders only three days before going into action, the Grenada operation was swift and successful. Individually, American troops performed well. However, the overall conduct of the operation demonstrated that there was still much to be done. Interservice rivalries had quickly reared their heads during the planning phase, and there were failures in intelligence and communications, as well as some problems in special operations. The work of improving the armed forces continued. By 1986, a confrontation with Libya demonstrated how far the armed forces had gone in improving cooperation, as contingents from all the services took part in several well-coordinated limited operations.

The most important development of the post-Vietnam military reform was the Goldwater-Nichols Department of Defense Reorganization Act of 1986, a product of nearly four years of study, deliberation, and effort by Congress, working closely with representatives of the executive branch and the armed forces. It was a difficult piece of legislation, touching as it did on the independence of the several branches of the armed forces, and many different proposals were examined and rejected. The act established that the chairman of the Joint Chiefs of Staff is the senior military commander, under the president. Goldwater-Nichols clarified the authority of senior commanders in joint operations, regardless of service, and gave the authority and responsibility for developing joint warfare doctrine to the chairman of the Joint Chiefs. It also established specific joint commands, so that these did not have to be improvised in times of emergency. To ensure closer integration with and responsiveness to the nation's political objectives, Goldwater-Nichols improved the role of civilian agencies (including, but not necessarily limited to the president's staff and the State Department) in contingency planning.

Hard on the heels of Goldwater-Nichols came the Nunn-Warner Act of 1987, that created the U.S. Special Operations Command (SOC). All special warfare forces were subordinated to the SOC, regardless of service, in practice virtually creating a "fifth" special warfare service. The mission of SOC was to develop special warfare doctrine, tactics, and technologies to conduct joint special operations training, and to develop plans for the employment of special operations forces. By integrating the special warfare forces of all three services, the intention was to develop a virtually instantaneous response capability.

Operation Just Cause in 1989 provided the first field test of the new command structure of the armed forces. This operation was triggered when Panamanian dictator Manuel Noriega, under indictment for drug trafficking and other criminal activities in the United States, began a campaign to terrorize domestic opponents and molest American personnel and their families stationed in the country. Then Noriega declared war on the United States in December. Pres. George Bush immediately ordered SOUTHCOM, the joint services headquarters responsible for South and Central America and the Caribbean, into action. Using troops already in Panama, strengthened by additional forces—including women soldiers—brought in by air and sea, a complex series of twenty-seven objectives were secured or neutralized simultaneously, on the first day, 20 December. With most Panamanians supporting the operation, organized resistance, usually sporadic but occasionally stubborn, was broken within twenty-four hours, and the last resistance ended two days later. Casualties among American troops and Panamanians alike were low. Operation Just Cause provided an excellent demonstration of how far the armed forces had come in terms of improving training, readiness, and jointness. To be sure there were still some problems with interservice communications and turf wars, but these were subject to intensive review and corrective measures were undertaken.

It was as a result of this nearly two-decades-long period of unprecedented reform and reorganization in the American armed forces that the Gulf War of 1990–91 unfolded.

THE VIETNAM WAR DESERTERS

The formal definition of "deserter" is someone absent without leave for thirty days or more, without extenuating circumstances. However, the armed forces do not automatically class anyone so absent as a deserter. In World War II only about 40,000 men were declared deserters by the armed forces, but there were certainly many times that number who were absent for more than thirty days. In the Vietnam War, desertion assumed a certain political importance. About 550,000 troops were absent without leave or absent over leave during the Vietnam War. Of these, some 92,000 men were *declared* deserters, many of whom would probably not have been so classed in World War II (when the thirty-day rule was often overlooked if a soldier had prob-lems at home). By the mid-1970s, about 83,000 of the Vietnam-era deserters had been apprehended by the armed forces or had voluntarily surrendered themselves. Few were subject to courts-martial proceedings, which would have been required to prove intent to desert, but all were given less than honorable discharges, denying them veterans' benefits. In the mid-1970s, after the war, acting on precedents that reached back to the Civil War, pres-idents Gerald Ford and Jimmy Carter offered a general amnesty for Vietnam-era military personnel charged with desertion. This only applied to those who had no other military charges on their records (e.g., theft of government property, criminal activity, and so forth). These proposals were greeted with

Statistical Analysis of Vietnam-Era Army Deserters

Category		Deserters	Strength
Race			
White		79%	80%
Black		21%	20%
Regional Origins			
	South	37%	33%
	North Central	23%	32%
	Northeast	24%	17%
	West	16%	19%
Education			
	Less Than High School	68%	28%
	High School Graduates	27%	48%
	More Than High School	4%	25%
AFQT Mental Category			
I	93–100%-ile	2%	5%
II	65–92%-ile	12%	28%
III	31–64%-ile	44%	42%
IV	0–30%-ile	42%	24%

Key: Under *Percentages, Deserters* represents the total number of deserters applying for amnesty who belong in the indicated category, while *Strength* is the proportion of all army personnel in the same category: thus, while 20 percent of the personnel in the army during the war (1964–72) were black, blacks constituted 21 percent of deserters, at least on the basis of those men who accepted the terms of the amnesties.

some acrimony, not all of on the political right. Only about 14,000 men took advantage of the amnesties, less than a quarter of those eligible. An analysis of the statistical profiles of the men who accepted these amnesties provides some interesting insights into the backgrounds and motivations of those who deserted. (See table on the previous page.)

Although most deserters were white, blacks were about twice as likely to desert as whites overall, even more so in the air force, and much less so in the navy.

Arguably, the fact that 81 percent of those who deserted had **not** seen service in Vietnam suggests that men were deserting to avoid that unpleasant possibility. Indeed, of those deserting, 32 percent were in the combat arms (infantry, armor, artillery), men who were prime prospects for assignment to Vietnam, particularly since the combat arms comprised only about 23 percent of the army. Enlisted personnel in the three lowest grades, that is privates of various ilks, predominated among the deserters, 82 percent in all (E-1s=40 percent, E-2s=27 percent, and E-3s=15 percent), though such soldiers comprised only about a quarter of the army. Interestingly, fully 74 percent of those who deserted had not yet completed training, which correlates rather closely with the fact that half of all deserters had been in the service a year or less.

Vietnam Era Army Deserters by Age

Age	Percentage
17	2
18	7
19	13
20	26
21	20
22	11
23	7
24	5
25 plus	8

The ages of deserters were rather a close approximation of the ages of men in the ranks. Interestingly, since seventeen- and eighteen-year-olds were not being drafted, the men in question had originally volunteered to join the service.

Of those deserting, 39 percent were married, a much higher proportion of married men than was common in the army at the time. Interestingly, about 88 percent of those deserting did so within the confines of CONUS (the continental United States), while about 5 percent did so in Europe (which means they were least likely to have been sent to Vietnam), and 3 percent in Vietnam itself, though only twenty-four men actually "deserted in the face of the enemy" (i.e., deserted in a combat zone). The balance is

Deserters by Year

Year	Percent
1964–66	3%
1967	4%
1968	11%
1969	23%
1970	25%
1971	24%
1972	8%
1973–75	3%

accounted for by men who deserted elsewhere or for whom no "place" of desertion can be determined. The desertion rate ebbed and flowed, depending upon the fortunes of war.

Between 12 percent and 14 percent (there were several different surveys, and the results are not completely reconcilable) of the respondent deserters said they had done so because they objected to the war. Though they usually gave no particular reason, most deserters objected to the risk, rather than the cause. The marked increase in the proportion of respondents who deserted in 1968 is certainly a consequence of the increased sense that the war was a hopeless cause. Note that as the chances of being sent to Vietnam declined, with increased Vietnamization from 1971, the proportion of deserters fell almost as markedly as it had risen after Tet.

Interestingly, fully 89 percent of the deserters remained in the continental United States, where most of them (c. 85 percent) held jobs and lived rather openly. Nearly 7 percent went to Canada, while less than 4 percent went to other countries, which suggests that the reputations of some countries (e.g., Sweden) for protecting "fugitives from an unjust war" was itself rather unjustly earned.

About 9,000 of the deserters were never apprehended and remain technically fugitives from justice, though no one seems interested in pursuing the issue.

SOME NOTABLE AMERICANS WHO SERVED IN VIETNAM

Albert Gore, Jr., the son of Sen. Albert Gore, Sr., of Tennessee, was a leading critic of the war and active in Eugene McCarthy's 1968 bid for the presidency. However, upon graduating from Harvard in 1969, he joined the army and served in Vietnam as a military press officer and went on to become vice president in 1993.

John S. McCain III, the son of Adm. John S. McCain, Jr. (who was commander-in-chief of the Pacific theater—and thus, technically, of Vietnam—from 1968–72), was a naval aviatior aboard the USS *Forrestal* when he was shot down over Hanoi on 26 October 1967. He endured nearly six years of imprisonment. After his release he returned to active duty, retiring from the navy in 1981 to enter politics. As a U.S. senator, McCain was active in the movement to normalize relations with Vietnam.

Douglas "Pete" Peterson, the first postwar American ambassador to Vietnam, was a pilot during the war. Shot down, he spent some time in "the Hanoi Hilton."

Charles S. Robb, who married LBJ's daughter, served as a Marine platoon leader, and later entered the Senate from Virginia in 1989.

James Webb earned a Navy Cross, two Bronze Stars, and two Purple Hearts as a Marine platoon leader in Vietnam and later served as secretary of the navy under Ronald Reagan, 1987–89.

SOME NOTABLE AMERICANS WHO DIDN'T SERVE IN VIETNAM
Henry Cisneros, who served prominently as the liberal mayor of San Antonio and later as secretary of housing and urban development, had an academic deferment during the war.

William Clinton was a sometime prospective ROTC cadet turned peace activist once his deferment was assured, later becoming a Rhodes scholar and president of the United States in 1993.

James F. Dunnigan, one of the authors of this book, completed three years of active duty with the army in July 1964, and was reservist during the early years of the war.

Newt Gingrich managed an academic deferment before entering politics to become a hawkish Republican member of the House, and speaker since 1995.

Phil Graham, conservative Republican member of the senate and presidential hopeful for many years, had an academic deferment during the war.

Mark Halprin, conservative columnist for *The Wall Street Journal*, had a deferment during the Vietnam War.

Rush Limbaugh, conservative radio personality, had a medical deferment during the war.

Albert A. Nofi, one of the authors of this volume, washed out of ROTC in 1963 due to uncorrectable vision problems and was declared IV-F.

P. J. O'Rourke, the conservative columnist, had a medical deferment.

Sylvester Stallone, the actor noted for the *Rambo* series which helped perpetuate "the Troubled Vietnam Veteran" myth, was IV-F and did not serve.

THE SINO-VIETNAMESE WAR
Throughout history there never had been much love lost between Vietnam and China, and the fact that by the mid-1970s both countries were Communist didn't change that very much. Tensions between the Vietnamese

Communist leadership and that of China had been barely suppressed during the two Indochina wars in the interests of "Socialist unity." The war won, the Vietnamese Communists had to consider possible threats from their real ancient enemy, China.

Cambodia was also a country with which Vietnam had historic animosities. During the Indochina wars the Vietnamese Communists had supported the Khmer Rouge, also in the interests of "Socialist unity." But the Khmer Rouge espoused a much more radical brand of communism, genocidal for one thing, and with a strong nationalistic streak. A lot of Vietnam had formerly been part of the ancient Khmer kingdom, and they wanted it back. Even as the Khmer Rouge began the mass slaughter of their fellow countrymen in mid-1975, they also initiated a series of violations of the Vietnamese border. Although Vietnamese troops repulsed these incursions, since they were preoccupied with absorbing South Vietnam into the newly renamed Socialist Republic of Vietnam (a process not formally concluded until 2 July 1976), the Vietnamese government held off taking definitive action until late 1977.

In November 1977, after a Khmer Rouge incursion into Tau Ninh Province that caused two thousand casualties, the Vietnamese retaliated, sending strong forces to occupy several hundred square miles of "the Parrot's Beak" region of Cambodia. Backed by China, Pol Pot responded by breaking diplomatic relations. Over the next year things grew more tense. As Vietnamese government officials consulted with representatives of the Soviet Union, China curtailed aid to Vietnam and shortly recalled its ambassador. Cambodia began concentrating its army along the Vietnamese border, while a clash took place along the Sino-Vietnamese frontier. Fearing a two-front war, the Vietnamese decided to act.

In late December 1978, the Vietnamese army invaded Cambodia from Vietnam and Laos (where some forty thousand Vietnamese troops were stationed with the consent of the Communist Pathet Lao regime). Crushing at least one Cambodian division, they advanced slowly, in stages, apparently being careful to build up their logistical base. By 7 January 1979, the Vietnamese had overrun a major portion of Cambodia, brushing aside Khmer Rouge resistance to occupy six provinces and the capital, Phnom Penh. As the Khmer Rouge fled into the jungle to conduct a guerrilla war against them, the Vietnamese then installed a more moderate, pro-Vietnamese Communist regime and settled down for a long occupation.

The ouster of their protégés, the Khmer Rouge, elicited a violent reaction from the Chinese. On 17 March 1979, the Chinese sent 200,000–300,000 troops across the Vietnamese and Laotian borders on a front of nearly five hundred miles. Although in places they advanced as much as forty miles, for the most part the Chinese halted some ten to twenty miles inside Vietnam, though it is not clear whether as a result of Vietnamese resistance (compared to the battle-hardened Vietnamese, the Chinese were very poorly trained), Chinese logistical problems, or Chinese political decisions, if not a combination of all three. By 5 March, the Chinese were proclaiming a victory and began withdrawing, a process completed on 15 March. The Vietnamese never issued any casualty statements, though they did charge the Chinese with causing an enormous amount of material damage (in some categories exceeding what they claimed the United States had inflicted!). Although the Chinese claim they caused 50,000 Vietnamese casualties, at a cost of only 20,000 of their own, a high-ranking Chinese defector has stated that Chinese forces had suffered some 58,000 casualties.

The Chinese withdrawal did not entirely end the fighting, as there were occasional border incidents over the next few years, while the war in Cambodia dragged on and the Vietnamese even became embroiled with the Thais (who border both Laos and Cambodia). By the mid-1980s, tensions had eased, but were not likely to disappear entirely. The last Vietnamese troops left Cambodia in 1989.

The Sino-Vietnamese War demonstrates that some of the fundamental assumptions of American policy in Southeast Asia were seriously flawed.

A Vietnam War Glossary: Acronyms, Code Words, and Slang

Note that the word "operation" has been omitted, since there were so many.

A team. The basic Special Forces operating unit, usually of a dozen men.
alpha-alpha. Shorthand for an automatic ambush, a pattern of claymore mines linked by battery-powered electric connections that could be detonated by means of a trip wire.
Amerasian. A person of mixed American and Asian ancestry.
ao dai. Traditional Vietnamese women's garment, comprising a dress with a slit skirt over trousers, usually worn with a *non la,* a conical straw hat.
AP. Armor piercing.
APC. Armored personnel carrier.
alpha bravo. A slang expression for an ambush.
arc light. B-52 raids.
artillery ambush. Setting up a trip flare on a preregistered site in hostile country; firing every available artillery piece on the site when the flare is tripped.
ASHC. An assault support helicopter company.

B-40. American term for the Soviet RPG series antitank grenade launchers; of unknown provenance.
barrell roll. A code name for air operations against targets in Laos not associated with the Ho Chi Minh Trail.
beehive. Essentially a giant shotgun shell that artillery and tank guns could use in a direct fire (i.e., right at the enemy) during close-in fighting. The modern version of the canister used in the Civil War, though instead of containing numerous steel balls it contained numerous "flechettes," tiny steel arrows that can shred attacking troops.
berm. A built-up mound of earth that divided rice paddies or other lower areas; often overgrown with vegetation.
bird. Though a common term for any aircraft, in Vietnam it was usually used to refer to helicopters.
bouncing betty. A mine or booby trap that pops into the air two to four feet before detonating, to maximize its destructive effect.
break squelch. A means of radio communication used by troops who found themselves in situations where speaking might reveal their presence. Pressing

the "push to talk" button briefly would send a "click-hiss" to anyone on the same wavelength.

bring smoke. To pile on enormous amounts of artillery and air force firepower on an enemy position.

Bronco. An OV-10 light observation airplane.

Bushman's Scout. Australian slang for a *Hoi Chanh* (*see* Kit Carson Scout).

C & C. Command and control.

CAP. Combined action platoon, a marine squad attached to a Vietnamese local defense platoon.

CAS. Close air support, the provision of airborne firepower in direct support of troops locked in combat on the ground.

cav. Cavalry, whether mechanized or airborne; "the Cav" usually referred to the 1st Cavalry Division.

cherry. A FNG.

chicken plate. Body armor worn by helicopter crewmen.

Chieu Hoi. Vietnamese for "open arms," a program that attempted to entice VC into deserting to the RVN, which was applied by Americans to those who did so as well, who should more properly have been known as a *Hoi Chanh.*

CIDG. The South Vietnamese civilian irregular defense groups.

CONUS. The forty-eight contiguous states of the continental United States.

corpsman. Marine and navy nickname for a medic, from "Medical Corpsman."

c rations. The army's standard prepackaged rations, in use since World War II (in fact, early in the war some of the "C rats" being issued dated from World War II).

cross-check. A common practice, just prior to troops moving out, whereby the troops check each other out for things that might hamper the mission, such as loose or noisy gear.

crunchie. An infantryman, a grunt, who "crunches" through the bush.

CS. Tear gas, often used to flush the enemy out of tunnels.

DEROS. Short for "date eligible for return from overseas," the date on which one's tour in Vietnam was to end. The most important date in a soldier's life while in Vietnam. Common question troops asked each other was, "What's your DEROS?"

det cord. Detonating cord, a thin, flexible wire filled with explosive. Burning at 2,500 feet per second, it's ideal for fuzing demolition charges, claymore mines, and even felling trees, if wrapped around them several times.

deuce-and-a-half. The standard army 2.5-ton truck.

digger. An Australian term of familiarity, which occasionally created problems when addressed to black American troops.

dime-nickel. An occasional nickname for a 105 mm howitzer.

DMZ. The allegedly "demilitarized zone" separating North and South Vietnam along the seventeenth parallel.

doc. Medic.

dope. (1) Narcotic drugs or (2) marine term for adjusting the sights on one's rifle.

doughnut dolly. Female relief worker, who allegedly handed out doughnuts.
dustoff. A helicopter medevac mission.
Dye Marker. The first phase of construction of the McNamara Line.

E & E. Escape and evasion, basic skills necessary to keep out of enemy hands or
to escape from the enemy if captured.
ECM. Electronic countermeasures. Techniques and technologies such as jamming, dropping metallic strips, firing flares, and so forth to deceive or render
useless enemy radar and electronics.
ELINT. Electronic intelligence. Information gathered from traffic analysis (i.e.,
monitoring enemy radio communications, which, even if you don't understand
them due to coding, may be subject to analysis as to patterns), radar, sensors,
and so forth.
EOD. Explosive ordnance disposal. The art of getting rid of unwanted explosives,
such as duds, unexploded bombs, booby traps, and the like.

FAC. Forward air controller, an aviation-type (air force or marine) who lived
up front with the troops or flew overhead in light observation aircraft to coordinate close air support.
fast mover. A jet aircraft, particularly an F-4.
Fat Albert. Nickname for the C-5A transport aircraft, from a popular character
in a Bill Cosby routine.
fire for effect. Opening up with everything.
fire mission. Any artillery mission against a hostile target.
firecracker. An artillery round that contained numerous small bomblets; detonated over a target, the bomblets shower downward, land on the round, and
then bounce up a couple of feet for maximum destructive effect.
flak jacket. A vest, initially of fiberglass but later with ceramic plates, designed
to minimize injury from hostile fire; in Shakespeare's words, "It scalds with
safety."
Flaming Dart. Air operations above the DMZ (i.e., into North Vietnam), 1964–
65, later renamed Rolling Thunder.
flechette. A miniature steel arrow, hundreds of which were packed into Beehive
and Nail rounds (q.v.).
FNG. "Fuckin' new guy." Someone just arrived in Vietnam. Also "Cherry."
FO. Forward observer. A soldier tasked with the job of calling in artillery fire
and sometimes air support or naval gunfire as well.
frag. A grenade, particularly a fragmentation grenade.
fragging. Attack on an officer or NCO, named after fragmentation grenades,
which were commonly used in such.
free-fire zone. An area that was assumed to be wholly under enemy control,
which could be fired into at will.
freedom bird. The airplane that took one back to "the World" and the end of
one's tour of duty.
Frequent Wind. The evacuation of American and some Vietnamese personnel
from Vietnam at the end of the war.
friendly fire. The term used in Vietnam for fire from U.S. or Allied forces that

was mistakenly directed at friendly troops. Called "own fire" in World War II, "friendly fire" is one of the ultimate dirty little secrets of war, as it is far more common than generally believed.

fuze. The mechanism that detonates a bomb, artillery shell, or other explosive device.

Game Warden. Navy operations to restrict enemy river traffic.

Gomers. Slang term for North Vietnamese. From the TV show featuring a clueless peacetime marine named Gomer Pyle.

gook. Derogatory slang term for an Asian, originating in Korea.

grunt. The most common nickname for infantrymen in Vietnam; other terms were crunchy and ground pounder.

gun truck. A special "deuce-and-a-half" armed with one .50-cal. heavy machine gun, plus one or two M-60 machine guns, and occasionally other weapons, intended to provide some heavy firepower for truck convoys.

gunship. An armed helicopter or "Puff the Magic Dragon"–type airplane.

Hanoi Hilton. The Hoa Loa Prison in Hanoi, where most American prisoners-of-war were held.

harbour up. Australian slang for establishing a temporary defensive position for the night.

Hoi Chan. The proper name for one who accepted the *Cheiu Hoi* program.

horn. Slang for radio.

hose or **hose down.** A term for the massive application of automatic weapons fire.

Huey. Nickname for the UH-1 helicopter, originally designated the HU-1.

Hueycobra. The attack version of the UH-1.

hump. Move on foot, usually with a heavy load.

I&I. Informal nickname for R and R (rest and recreation), standing for "intoxication and intercourse," the two principal interests of troops on R and R.

in country. Being in Vietnam.

incoming. Receiving enemy artillery, rocket, or mortar fire.

INTEL. Intelligence.

k-bar. A Marine Corps combat knife, with a six-inch blade and hard leather handle.

Khmer Rouge. The Cambodian Communist movement; French for "Red Khmers."

KIA. Killed in action.

Kit Carson Scout. A *Hoi Chanh* serving as a scout for U.S. troops (*see* Bushman's Scout).

klick. A kilometer, sometimes shortened to K.

Linebacker. Systematic bombing raids over North Vietnam in March–October 1972 (Linebacker I) and December 1972 (Linebacker II), to force the North Vietnamese to conclude the Paris Accords.

loach. An OH-6A light observation helicopter.

LP. Short for "listening post" or "listening position." Normally a three-man detail posted outside the perimeter of a firebase for the purpose of keeping track of possible enemy activity. Although armed, and usually defended by claymore mines, the party was distinctly in harm's way.

LRRP, occasionally **LRP.** Short for Long Range Reconnaissance Patrol, pronounced "Lurp," which term also referred to the individual soldier. Also a nickname for the then-experimental ration packets now known as MREs.

LZ. A landing zone, where helicopters alit. A "Hot LZ" was one under enemy fire; an "LZ Cut" was one made by a very large bomb rolled out of the tailgate of a C-130 airplane, which would blow up above ground, leveling the vegetation and creating an instant LZ.

MACV. Abbreviation for Military Assistance Command, Vietnam (pronounced "Mack Vee"), the principal U.S. command in Vietnam.

mad minute. Full concentration of fire at the maximum rate by all weapons available.

Mama San. An older Asian woman, also refers to a madam of a brothel.

Market Time. Navy operations to restrict enemy coastal traffic.

MASH. Mobile army surgical hospital.

MAT. Mobile advisory team, usually of six U.S. personnel assigned to RF/PF units.

mech. Short for mechanized infantry.

medevac. Short for "medical evacuation," usually by helicopter; also "Dustoff."

Menu. Bombing missions over Cambodia, 1969–73.

MIA. Missing in Action.

mike. Used for "minute" in messages to avoid confusion.

Mike force. Mobile Strike Force, Montagnard personnel under Special Forces command.

mike-mike. Used for "millimeters."

mini-ponder. A miniature radio transmitter that could be used to mark locations on the ground for aircraft.

MOS. Military occupational specialty, one of thousands of jobs someone in the armed forces could be assigned to.

MPC. Military scrip ("military payment currency"), used in lieu of dollars to help control inflation and corruption in Vietnam. The design was changed periodically to prevent hoarding, which sometimes led to hysterical scenes as hoarders of illegal MPCs would try to find enough persons legally eligible to turn in MPCs.

MRF. The Mobile Riverine Force, consisting of the navy's River Assault Flotilla 1 (TF 117) and the army's 2nd Brigade, 9th Infantry Division.

nails. Flechette (q.v.) rounds for the 2.75-in. rocket launcher.

nape. Diminutive for napalm.

nav. The navigator or radar operator in an airplane.

NGFS. Short for naval gunfire support, supplied by TF 70.8.

Niagara. Air operations in support of the garrison at Khe Sahn in 1968.

Noggins. Australian derogatory term for Vietnamese.

number one. Slang for "very good."

number ten. Slang for "very bad."

number 10,000. Slang for "the worst."

nuoc mam. The Vietnamese national condiment, a fermented fish sauce probably very similar to the *garum* of which the Romans were very fond. Also a GI tag for anything Vietnamese, as "Air *Nuoc Mam*," for Air Vietnam.

NVA. Allied abbreviation for the North Vietnamese Army, actually the PAVN.

P, Ps. Piasters, South Vietnamese currency. Not worth much.

P-38. Standard army can opener, about as small as a nail clipper and carried as a souvenir by many a former soldier and marine.

Papa San. Any older Asian man.

PAVN. The People's Army of Vietnam, official name of the NVA.

PF. South Vietnam's Popular Forces, local defense groups that bore a disproportionate share of the fighting.

Phu Dung. See Prairie Fire.

PCOD. "Pussy Cut Off Date," a date several weeks before one's DEROS, when it became wise to abstain from sexual indulgence lest one catch VD, since infected persons were not permitted to leave Vietnam until cured.

point man. The guy out in front on a patrol or movement, and thus the most exposed man in the outfit.

pop. A term meaning toss or use, as in "pop a grenade," "pop a flare," or "pop smoke" (i.e., throw a smoke grenade).

POW. Prisoner of war.

Prairie Fire. *See* Shining Brass. Became Phu Dung in 1971.

PRC-25. A small radio used by the infantry, nicknamed "Prick." The PRC-77 was an improvement on this, incorporating an encryption device to code messages.

PRVN. The People's Republic of Vietnam, better known as North Vietnam.

PSP. Perforated steel plank. In World War II known as Marston Mat, it consisted of sturdy steel plates about eight-feet by three-feet, pierced full of holes to make it lighter. These could be hooked together like Lincoln Logs to create improvised airstrips, road surfaces, roofing, revetments, and so forth, very quickly, even by unskilled workers without any specialized tools.

PTS. Post-traumatic stress. Emotional and behavioral problems related to having survived highly stressful situations, such as combat. In extreme cases it manifests itself as PTSD, "post-traumatic stress disorder," a serious psychoneurotic problem affecting some veterans.

Puff and **Puff the Magic Dragon.** AC-47 or other fixed-wing gunships.

push. Instructions regarding change of radio frequency, as in "Push . . ." with the new frequency following.

PX. Post Exchange, a sort of supermarket for soldiers (called "the Base Exchange" in the air force, just to be different).

R and R. Officially, "Rest and Recreation," the one-time "out of country" leave permitted all troops each year, usually taken in Thailand, Japan, Malaya, Taiwan, Singapore, the Philippines, Australia, or, for a lucky few, Hawaii, though some troops chose to take their R and R at one of several resorts in Vietnam, including the famous "China Beach." Known by the troops as "I and I," for the two principal pastimes while on leave, intoxication and intercourse.

recon. Short for reconnaissance.

Red LZ. Alternate term for a "Hot LZ."

redleg. An artilleryman, from the red stripes they formerly sported on their trousers. Also a "Cannon Cocker" or "Gun Bunny."

REMF. Rear echelon mother fucker, anyone who works behind the front, and thus at least theoretically out of danger. Nevertheless, the guys up front can't fight unless the REMFs are passing the bullets and the beans.

RF/PF. South Vietnamese Regional Forces and Popular Forces, local defense personnel. Pronounced "Ruff Puff."

rock and roll. To cut loose with an M-16A1 or other weapon on full automatic.

ROK. The Republic of Korea and, by extension, anything Korean.

Rolling Thunder. Code name for air operations over North Vietnam from 1965.

Rome plow. A bulldozer used to cut down brush, undergrowth, and small trees.

Ronson. *See* Zippo.

Round Eye. A slang term for non-Asians, usually Europeans or Americans, as in "There's a Round Eye nurse at HQ."

RPG. Soviet antitank grenade launcher, often used by the VC/NVA for bunker busting and as an assault weapon. Two models were used in Vietnam, the RPG-2 and the RPG-7, which for some reason U.S. troops took to calling the B-40.

RPG screen. A chain-link fence strung around a position to detonate RPG rounds before they struck anything valuable.

RTO. The "radio-telephone operator," who got to carry the PRC-class radio into combat, thereby making himself a prime target.

ruck. Short for "rucksack," a backpack.

Ruff-Puffs. Shorthand for the RF/PF (q.v.).

RVN. The Republic of Vietnam, better known as South Vietnam

sappers. Special NVA and VC assault troops.

SAR. Search and rescue, especially important for finding downed pilots.

search and clear. Offensive operations intended to locate and destroy enemy forces, and to reassert RVN political control over the area or operations.

search and destroy. Offensive operations intended to locate and destroy enemy forces, with no deliberate intent to reassert RVN control over the area of operations.

SEAL. A navy special-warfare force, from "Sea-Air-Land."

Semper Fi. Short for *Semper Fidelis,* the Marine Corps motto. Latin for "Always Faithful."

Shake 'n Bake. An inexperienced draftee run through a special training course to make him an NCO; also sometimes a newly commissioned officer with no experience.

Shining Brass. Special Forces reconnaissance operations and raids into Laos from South Vietnam and Thailand, from late-1965. Became Prairie Fire in 1968.

short timer. Someone nearing the end of his "tour of duty," and hence "short."

shotgun. Door gunners and truck guards, assigned to protect helicopters or convoys, as in "riding shotgun."

sky pilot. The chaplain.

slick. A helicopter, specifically one used to lift troops or supplies, with little or no armament.

slope. A derogatory term for an Asian.

slow mover. Any propeller-driven combat airplane.

snake. Nickname for the AH-1G Cobra or Hueycobra.

SOG. Studies and Observations Group, later Special Operations Group.

sortie. An aircraft undertaking a mission.

SOS. "Shit on shingles," creamed chipped (or ground) beef on toast.

SPC. Specialist, such as SPC-4, SPC-5, and so on up to SPC-8. A soldier with higher pay due to special skills, but not normally with command authority. Midway through the war all SPC ratings were abolished, except SPC-4, the equivalent of corporal.

stand down. Rest, reorganization, and refitting, after an operation.

starlight or **starlight scope.** Infrared night-vision telescope, used by snipers and troops on perimeter defense in base camps and other fixed positions.

stay behind. An ambush technique, in which a moving force that believes itself being followed leaves a small detachment behind to jump the followers.

Steel Tiger. The code name for air operations against the Ho Chi Minh Trail in Laos, north of the seventeenth parallel.

sterilize. A common practice on LRRP and other deep-penetration missions, whereby all personnel carefully return a campsite to its original condition, not merely by removing all debris, but even to fluffing up the grass, so as not to leave any evidence.

STOL. "Short takeoff and landing." Airplanes that required very short runways, such as C-123 and C-130 transports.

sundry packs. Special parcels that included "Class 6" supplies, things normally purchased by the troops (e.g., cigarettes, writing paper, etc.), made up for distribution to men on isolated outposts with no opportunity to visit a PX.

tally-ho. Call by a pilot to indicate that he had visually "acquired" a target, whether enemy aircraft or ground objective.

Tet. New Year's festival in the Vietnamese and Chinese lunar calendar.

The World. Outside Vietnam, particularly the United States.

Thud. The F-105 Thunderchief fighter-bomber.

Thumper, sometimes **Thumpgun.** The M-79 grenade launcher.

Tiger Hound. Code name for air interdiction operations against the Ho Chi Minh Trail in Laos south of the seventeenth parallel.

TOT. Short for "time on target," coordination of multibattery artillery fire so that all shells will hit the target simultaneously.

VC. Short for "Viet Cong," which is itself short for *Viet Nam Cong Son,* or Vietnamese Communists.

Wallaby. Australian nickname for the Caribou light transport airplane.

white mice. The South Vietnamese civil police, who wore a white uniform.

WIA. Wounded in Action.

willie pete, sometimes **willie peter.** White phosphorus, which burns with very high heat and cannot be put out by water. Dispensed by grenade or mortar and artillery shells. Also used as a target marker by aircraft.

WSO. Short for weapons officer. The guy in the backseat of most two-seat fighters who navigates and runs the weapon systems. Pronouced "Wizzo."

Yards. Slang for Montagnard.

Zippo. Slang for flamethrower, from the famous lighter; more commonly Ronson (q.v.).

zone and sweep. An artillery tactic that covered a target with shells in an "X" pattern.

zap list. A crude and cruel term used by some for *The Army Times*'s weekly listing of the war dead.

zulu or **zulu report.** Casualty report, after "zulu," the last letter in the military phonetic alphabet.

RECOMMENDED READING

The literature on the Vietnam War is vast and continues to grow at a tremendous rate. Listed below are some of the books we found most useful, and thought you might also.

Alker, Joan. *Heroes Today, Homeless Tomorrow? Homelessness Among Veterans in the United States*. Washington: National Coalition for the Homeless, 1991. An interesting and revealing study.

Bass, Thomas A. *Vietnamerica: The War Comes Home*. New York: Soho, 1997. An interesting look at Amerasians.

Beede, Benjamin R. *The War of 1898 and U.S. Intervention, 1898–1934: An Encyclopedia*. New York: Garland, 1994. A gold mine of information on the U.S. experience in counterinsurgency prior to Vietnam.

Bourne, Peter G. *Men, Stress, and Vietnam*. Boston: Little, Brown, 1970. A study of psychoneurotic problems in Vietnam and among veterans.

Bowman, John S., ed. *The Vietnam War: An Alamanac*. New York: Ballentine, 1985.

Cash, John A., John N. Albright; and Allan W. Sanstrum. *Seven Firefights in Vietnam*. Washington: Center of Military History, 1989.

Cecil, Paul Frederick. *Herbicidal Warfare: The RANCH HAND Project in Vietnam*. Westport, CT: Praeger, 1986.

Clarke, Jeffrey J. *Advice and Support, the Final Years, 1965–1973. The US Army in Vietnam*. Washington: Center of Military History, 1988.

Clodfelter, Mark. *The Limits of Air Power: The American Bombing of North Vietnam*. New York: The Free Press, York, 1989. A critical look at the U.S. Air Force's continuing romance with "strategic bombardment," and how this affected the course of the Vietnam War.

Collins, James Lawton, Jr. *The Development and Training of the South Vietnamese Army, 1950–1972*. Washington: Department of the Army, 1978.

Currey, Cecil B. *Victory at Any Cost: The Genius of Vietnam's General Vo Nguyen Giap*. Washington: Brassey's, 1979. An interesting biography, with lots of background and insights.

Dong Van Khagan. *The RVNAF*. Washington: Center for Military History, 1980. An outline history of the RV armed forces.

Dunstan, Simon. *Vietnam Tracks: Armor in Battle, 1945–1975*. Novato, CA: Ospry, 1982.

Errington, Elizabet Jane, and B. J. C., McKercher, eds. *The Vietnam War as History*. Westport, Ct: Praeger, 1990. Contains several insightful essays.

Gibson, James W. *The Perfect War: Technomania in Vietnam*. Boston: Atlantic Monthly Press, 1986. Some useful insights into American technology, but rather smug and somewhat biased.

Glasser, Jeffrey D. *The Secret Vietnam War: The U.S. Air Force in Thailand, 1961–1975*. Jefferson, NC: McFarland, 1995.

Hammon, William M. *Public Affairs, the Military and the Media, 1968–1973. The US Army in Vietnam*. Washington: Center of Military History, 1996.

———. *Public Affairs: The Military and the Media, 1962–1968, The US Army in Vietnam*. Washington: Center of Military History, 1990.

Hemmingway, Albert. *Our War Was Different: Marine Combined Action Platoons in Vietnam*. Annapolis: Naval Institute, 1994.

Hersh, Seymour M. *My Lai 4: A Report on the Massacre and Its Aftermath*. New York: Random House, 1970.

———. *Cover-Up: The Army's Secret Investigation of the Massacre at My Lai 4*. New York: Random House, 1972. Both of Hersh's books are rather sensationalistic. They also display a certain lack of understanding and bias against the military.

Krepenevich, A. J. *The Army and Vietnam*. Baltimore: Johns Hopkins, 1986. Examines the thesis that the U.S. Army lost the war in Vietnam largely because it came prepared to refight World War II.

Krohn, Charles A. *The Lost Battalion: Controversy and Casualties in the Battle for Hue*. Westport, CT: Praeger, 1993. A fairly detailed look at the controversial circumstances under which the 2/12th Cavalry became "the Lost Battalion" of the Vietnam War during Tet.

Kutler, Stanley I. *Encyclopedia of the Vietnam War*. New York: Macmillan, 1996. Not bad, but some entries are rather ideologically tainted, and some rather obviously contradict others.

Lamperis, Timothy J. *From People's War to People's Rule: Insurgency, Intervention, and the Lessons of Vietnam*. Chapel Hill: University of North Carolina, 1996. It may look like a lot of metaphysics, but contained herein is a good deal of thoughtful analysis, comparing the Vietnam War with other insurgencies.

Lanning, Michael Lee. *Inside the LRRPs: Rangers in Vietnam*. New York: Ivy Books, 1988. Probably more than you will ever want to know about the LRRPs.

Lanning, Michael Lee, and Dan Cragg, *Inside the VC and the NVA: The Real Story of North Vietnam's Armed Forces* New York: Ivy Books, 1992. Excellent.

LeGro, William E. *Vietnam from Cease-Fire to Capitulation*. Washington: Center of Military History, 1984.

Lockhart, Gregory. *Nation in Army: The Origins of the People's Liberation Army of Vietnam*. London: Allen & Unwin, 1989.

McNamara, Robert S., with Brian Van De Mark. *In Retrospect: The Tragedy and Lessons of Vietnam*. New York: Random House, 1995. A lot of conclusions that would have been helpful thirty-five years ago. And not a few errors as well.

Michell, Marshall L., III. *Clashes: Air Combat over North Vietnam, 1965–1972*. Annapolis: Naval Institute, 1997. The best analysis of air combat, though it would have been nice if it included lists of the air victories.

Mikesh, Robert C. *Flying Dragons: The South Vietnamese Air Force*. London: Osprey, 1988.

O'Neal, Robert M, John P. Morris, and Raymond Madck, *No Heroes, No Villain: New Perspectives on Kent State and Jackson State*. San Francisco: Jossy-Bass, 1972. A balanced treatment of the two incidents.

Olson, James S. *Dictionary of the Vietnam War*. Westport, CT: Greenwood, 1988.

Peers, W. R. *The My Lai Inquiry*. New York: Norton, 1978. The clearest account of the events, and of the investigation.

Prados, John. *The Hidden History of the Vietnam War*. Chicago: Ivan R. Dee, 1995. Looks at a lot of unusual aspects of the war, such as the problems of creating the necessary infrastructure to support the enormous American and Allied commitment of forces to Vietnam.

Puller, Lewis B., Jr. *The Fortunate Son: The Autobiography of Lewis B. Puller, Jr*. New York: Grove Press 1991.

Schreadling, R. L. *From the Rivers to the Sea: The U.S. Navy in Vietnam*. Annapolis: Naval Institute Press, 1992.

Spector, Ronald H. *Advice and Support: The Early Years, 1941–1960. The U.S. Army in Vietnam*. Washington: Center of Military History, 1983.

Stanton, Shelby. *The Rise and Fall of an American Army: U.S. Ground Forces in Vietnam, 1965–1973*. Novato, CA: Presidio, 1985. A good history of ground operations, with a lot of background

————. *Vietnam Order of Battle*. New York: Garland, 1986.

Stevens, Paul Drew. *The Navy Cross: Vietnam*. Forest Ranch, CA: Sharp & Donnigan, 1987.

Summers, Harry G., Jr. *Historical Atlas of the Vietnam War*. Boston: Houghton Mifflin, 1995.

Uhlig, Frank, ed. *Vietnam: The Naval Story*. Annapolis: Naval Institute, 1986. Some of the essays are very useful and interesting. However, be warned, many were written in the midst of the war and have not been modified since.

Vietnam, an excellent bimonthly edited by Harry Summers, a distinguished military analyst.

Zesloff, Joseph T. *The Pathet Lao: Leadership and Organization*. Lexington, MA: D. C. Heath, 1973.

INDEX